Thinking from the Underside of History

Thinking from the Underside of History

Enrique Dussel's Philosophy of Liberation

Edited by
Linda Martín Alcoff
and
Eduardo Mendieta

ROWMAN & LITTLEFIELD PUBLISHERS, INC.
Lanham • Boulder • New York • Oxford

ROWMAN & LITTLEFIELD PUBLISHERS, INC.

Published in the United States of America
by Rowman & Littlefield Publishers, Inc.
4720 Boston Way, Lanham, Maryland 20706
http://www.rowmanlittlefield.com

12 Hid's Copse Road
Cumnor Hill, Oxford OX2 9JJ, England

British Library Cataloguing in Publication Information Available

Library of Congress Cataloging-in-Publication Data

Thinking from the underside of history : Enrique Dussel's Philosophy of liberation / edited by Linda Martín Alcoff and Eduardo Mendieta.
p. cm.
Includes bibliographical references and index.
ISBN 0-8476-9650-2 (alk. paper) — ISBN 0-8476-9651-0 (pbk. : alk. paper)
1. Dussel, Enrique D. I. Alcoff, Linda. II. Mendieta, Eduardo.

B1034.D874 T45 2000
199'.82—dc21

00-024820

Printed in the United States of America

∞™ The paper used in this publication meets the minimum requirements of American National Standard for Information Sciences—Permanence of Paper for Printed Library Materials, ANSI/NISO Z39.48–1992.

Contents

Illustrations

Acknowledgments

This book would not have been possible without the faith and support of our contributors, who trusted our ambition and cooperated unselfishly with our editorial requests and timetables. Nor would it have been possible without the encouragement, assistance, and energizing faith of Maureen MacGrogan. We owe her. We are also very grateful to our respective families for their patience, love, and support. We would like to acknowledge the support of the Faculty Development Fund at the University of San Francisco, which granted funds to pay for some of the translations. The Center for Latino Studies in the Americas (CELASA) at USF also provided logistical and research support. Eduardo would like to especially thank his assistant Martin Woessner for his dedication beyond the call of duty, eagle eye when proofreading, and cheery devotion to Heidegger and the deconstruction of Western metaphysics; also Annemarie Belda for her patience and wisdom in regard to the latest versions of word processing programs. We thank Jean-Pierre Ruíz, editor of the *Journal of Hispanic/Latino Theology,* for permission to reprint a modified version of Hans Schelkshorn's essay, and Raúl Fornet-Betancourt for granting us translation rights to Karl-Otto Apel's essay on Dussel. Most of all, we are grateful to Enrique Dussel for his hospitality, his willingness to engage with serious disagreements, and his substantive suggestions all along the way. This book is dedicated to him and to the project of overcoming Euro-centrism in philosophical thought, toward which he has made such a critical contribution.

Linda Martín Alcoff
Syracuse, New York

Eduardo Mendieta
San Francisco, California

1

Introduction

Linda Martín Alcoff and Eduardo Mendieta

Not so long ago Western societies claimed the name "modernity" for their time, their contemporaneity, assuming this to be at the forefront of the historical continuum. Modernity was a self-description that served as a self-affirmation, differentiating the West from the rest. Today, modernity has given way to globalization, or the global age, as a way to describe societies, though not merely or necessarily those of the industrialized West. Already there is a highly developed bibliography of materials seeking to explain how globalization came to pass and what its implications are for different types of societies. One thing is clear, however: globalization has made it extremely difficult to make naive universalizing claims, just as it has also made it significantly easier, if not de rigeur, to qualify one's pronouncements with a specifying prefix: European, Indian, Asian, African, Hispanic, North Atlantic, Pacific, and so on. Ronald Robertson has nicely defined this dialectic: "Its [globalization's] central *dynamic* involves the twofold process of the particularization of the universal and the universalization of the particular."[1] Such is the case with Latin American philosophy.

The project to develop a Latin American philosophy is not simply part and parcel of the construction of "imaginary communities" for the sake of nation-state consolidation. Nor is it merely the defensive and reactive posture assumed by those who feel the need to prove their humanity. Rather, the project to develop a Latin American philosophy is the project of overcoming the neocolonialism of Eurocentric thought, of provincializing European philosophy, and of bringing Latin American and, indeed, Third World realities to the center of critical thought, whether it is concerned with ethics, politics, epistemology, or religion. Western philosophy passes itself off as universal and disembodied, without cultural roots or limitations. This is its own self-deception, for which the concept of modernity provided the alibi. Philosophies born elsewhere, from the underside of modernity, are rewriting this historical self-understanding of European philosophy as well as the telos of global thought. Latin American philosophy has the potential, then, to claim universal significance, even while it has a self-avowed cultural location, through its advanced critical consciousness. It is by no means alone in this critical marginality to dominant Eurocentric thought, but what Latin American thought in particular has to contribute is its thorough knowledge of and engagement with the founding moment of Europe itself: the *encuentro,* or encounter, between two worlds, one "old," the other "new."

No one has contributed more to the development of Latin American philosophy as a critical reflection on modernity and globalization in the last half of the twentieth century than the Argentine-born philosopher Enrique Dussel. Dussel's life has included extensive studies of "pure" Western philosophy, political activism, repression and exile from a military dictatorship, a turn toward Marxism and liberation theology, and the development of the comprehensive articulation of a philosophy of liberation. Dussel has incorporated and arguably surpassed the leading critical resources of European philosophy toward this project, including the hermeneutic critique of universalism, the critique of totality in the work of Emmanuel Levinas, and the discourse ethics developed by Karl-Otto Apel and Jürgen Habermas.

Dussel insists that our primary concern must be nothing less than the ongoing global genocide. An estimated 20 million persons die each year from starvation and malnutrition perpetrated by the new world order of global capitalism. Like many African philosophers and Indian postcolonial cultural critics, Dussel is convinced that European thought is an important site at which one might interfere with the smooth reproduction of this system. In his philosophy of liberation, Dussel has sought a solution to the totalitarian thought of oppression through a recourse to what it has excluded: the perspective, and the labor, of its victims. What emerges very clearly from this approach is that liberation must be pluritopic, not mono-topic, and that it will be culturally local. Dussel calls such an approach, which revises universality by combining it with a recognition of irreducible difference, a "diversality."

In this volume, North American and European philosophers interpret, debate, and attempt to come to terms with the meaning and implications of Dussel's thought. The chapters here do not presume readers who are already acquainted with Dussel's corpus, but they provide accessible overviews of many aspects of his ideas, from ethics to politics to religion. Walter Mignolo situates Dussel vis-à-vis other critical theoretical projects such as subaltern studies, and Eduardo Mendieta explains and defends Dussel's approach to global ethics. Elina Vuola critiques the philosophy of liberation's account of feminism and of gender, and Lynda Lange explains the resources in Dussel's work for a postcolonial feminism. Roberto Goizueta defends the religious implications of Dussel's ethics, while Michael Barber considers whether Dussel has reflected enough on the inevitable tensions between making theory and recognizing alterity. Both James Marsh and Hans Schelkshorn consider Dussel's critiques of discourse ethics, each agreeing and disagreeing with aspects of his critique, and Karl-Otto Apel attempts to defend discourse ethics against Dussel's charges. Mario Sáenz criticizes Dussel's Levinasian interpretation of Marx, and Linda Martín Alcoff indicates how the use of some of Michel Foucault's work might help Dussel elude his critics. The final essay in the volume is Dussel's response to these various engagements with his work.

Our hope is that this volume will inaugurate an even broader North American engagement with the challenges Dussel brings to contemporary philosophy and to Western notions of modernity and globalization. It is in such encounters that a new era of global community might begin.

In the following sections of this introduction we summarize what the essays in this volume contribute to the understanding and debate of Dussel's philosophy; we then provide a chronological sketch of Dussel's intellectual itinerary.

I

Walter Mignolo, a foremost theorist of Occidentalism and an expert on Mesoamerican culture, opens the discussion by helpfully situating Dussel's version of liberation philosophy vis-à-vis Marxism, liberation theology, subaltern studies, and the internal critical projects within twentieth-century European philosophy, such as the work of Emmanuel Levinas. In chapter 2, "Dussel's Philosophy of Liberation: Ethics and the Geopolitics of Knowledge," Mignolo also shows how to distinguish Dussel's version of liberation philosophy from other versions: by its link to the genealogy of the modern world-system. Since the early 1970s, Dussel has been stressing the importance of the geopolitical context of various knowledges.

Dussel was transformed, by his own admission, when he first encountered the work of the French Jewish philosopher Emmanuel Levinas. By placing intersubjective domination at the center of his thought, Levinas was able to develop a powerful critique of Eurocentric totality utilizing his position of exteriority. But, as Dussel pointed out, Levinas himself does not actually view Europe from a position of exteriority vis-à-vis its colonial totality. In striving to do so himself, even while making use of Levinas's work, Mignolo explains that Dussel has opened up "the coloniality of being as a new dwelling for the liberation of philosophy." Dussel assumes, that is, "the coloniality of being as 'being in exteriority' rather than as 'the exteriority of being.'"

Dussel uses the concept of exteriority to develop a radically original interpretation of Marxism in the three-volume work published in the late 1980s and early 1990s. He criticizes the currently dominant Western interpretation of Marxism, an interpretation that is heavily Hegelian, as based in a concept of totality that is partly responsible for the problems and failures of Marxist revolutions from the October Revolution in Russia to the Sandinistas in Nicaragua. By reinterpreting Marx through the concept of exteriority, Dussel proposes the possibility of a second century of Marx's influence, but one in which Marx is in the hands of a humanity rather than a political party.

The concept of exteriority invokes a notion of living work, or labor, which exists prior to and independent of capital. On this view, land and people are not "naturally" exploitable. Capitalism is the process of transforming living labor into a commodity, thus dominating exteriority and subsuming it into the totality. Liberation, then, will occur not by making "capitalism otherwise" but through the exteriority that is "otherwise than capitalism." Mignolo finds this to be "one of the strongest arguments from the perspective of Amerindians in Latin America (e.g., the Zapatistas) and of Native Americans in the United States."

In chapter 3, "The Material Principle and the Formal Principle in Dussel's Ethics," philosopher of liberation James Marsh focuses on the arguments developed in Dussel's *Etica de la liberación en la edad de la globalización y la exclusión* (1998), which is a synthesis that draws from arguments previously introduced in earlier works. Marsh explains that the *Etica* is based in Dussel's concern with the negative effects of economic globalization on the Third World and his insistence that ethics must begin from the perspective of the poor. Marsh argues that Dussel provides a powerful and original philosophical justification for this latter claim instead of positing it simply as a bare norm or self-evident truth.

Marsh's comments concern the first section of the *Etica,* in which Dussel proposes three ethical principles: the material, the formal communicative, and the feasibility. Dussel develops and defends these principles in dialogue with the history of philosophy, ethics, and critical theory, and in ensuing chapters he applies these principles to demonstrate how global capitalism violates each of them. From this critique of the present he then develops the contours of an acceptable alternative. In his chapter, Marsh neatly summarizes the arguments concerning the first two principles and then raises critical questions, although stressing that he largely agrees with Dussel's arguments and shares his overall project.

The material principle is a claim of obligation to produce and develop the concrete human life of every subject, where concrete is not to be understood as merely physical. Dussel's justification moves from descriptive claims about what is necessary for life and about the fact that human beings clearly value life to a claim that we are then obligated to sustain life. Although he is apparently moving from an *ought* to an *is* in this justification, Dussel argues, and Marsh agrees, that this particular *ought*, at least, is contained in the *is*.

Dussel's critique of Habermas and Apel, which would also apply to John Rawls and other liberal proceduralists, is that they incorrectly give priority to the formal over the material, claiming that the formal is the means by which the material principle might be justified. This is why they consider the *right* to have priority over the *good*. Marsh questions this argument on the grounds that Dussel pays insufficient attention to the distinction Apel and Habermas make between justification and application in regard to the formal principle. That is, even if the *application* of the material principle is in fact prior to the application of the formal principle (because people must be alive to participate in a discursive process), it remains the case that the formal principle plays a necessary a role in the *justification* of the material principle. And this calls into question the singular priority Dussel accords to the latter.

The philosophical dialogue between Dussel and Apel on the comparative virtues of discourse ethics and the ethics of liberation began in Freiburg in 1989. In chapter 4, "Can 'Liberation Ethics' Be Assimilated under 'Discourse Ethics'?" Apel, who was the principal architect of discourse ethics, explains his response to Dussel's challenges. While he acknowledges the necessity of addressing the concerns voiced in the ethics of liberation, Apel believes they can be, and in fact already are, incorporated under the wider rubric of discourse ethics.

Apel understands Dussel to be making two main objections. The first is that discourse ethics does not address the problem of those who are excluded a priori from the sphere of discourse itself. To address *this* problem would require addressing the terms for an ideal community of life, not the terms for an ideal community of communication. Thus materiality is prior to discourse and yet not addressed in what is claimed to be the universal ethical theory. Second, Dussel claims that discourse ethics is not fully appreciative of the fact that no philosopher or disputant can fully escape his or her cultural situation. Apel interprets this claim to mean that "I would have to articulate myself according to Dussel within the European–North American tradition . . . whereas he supposedly articulates himself within an entirely different ethicality."

In his response Apel explains that discourse ethics, as he has developed it since his 1980 book, *Discourse and Responsibility*, actually contains two major parts, one that involves the deontological conditions for an ideal discourse, but another that involves the teleogical duty to bring about favorable conditions for the concrete application of the deontological conditions laid out in the first part. And this duty is internal to discourse ethics itself, not an ad hoc addition, because its very validity must account for not only whether there has been consent but who has been included in the process. A noninclusive consent would not provide the justificatory foundation that discourse ethics claims.

Thus Apel argues that discourse ethics does not overlook the problem of global poverty, as Dussel charges. But he believes that this also shows that discourse ethics and the ethics of liberation are complementary: both understand the necessity of addressing institutional relations and not merely interpersonal ones, and both insist on the inclusion of the poor in discursive procedures.

However, Apel retains two objections of his own against the ethics of liberation concerning aspects that he thinks are not as compatible with discourse ethics: (1) the Heideggerian thesis explained above as Dussel's second objection, which concerns the cultural situatedness of understanding, and (2) the adoption of Marxism's opposition to market economies. Apel argues that a Heideggerian approach assumes that understanding between cultures will be impossible, despite the fact that the possibility of understanding is, and must be, always already assumed, even in the "lonely thinking" of the philosopher. Moreover, Apel also rejects this view because he believes, contra Heidegger and Gadamer, that the "existential prestructure" of understanding that is given in one's form of life can be rendered conscious and thus accessible to reflection. Finally, although Apel agrees with much of Marx's critique of capitalism, he believes that Marx failed to appreciate the discursive dimensions of the relations of production and that he incorrectly believed that use values have no significance in market economies. Once these two errors are corrected, it becomes apparent that there is more room for maneuver within capitalism toward improving social justice than either Marx or Dussel envisages. And Apel holds further that it is no less implausible to think that the market can be eliminated than it is to believe that an invisible hand guides the market toward justice.

Despite their differences, the discourse ethics developed by Karl-Otto Apel and Jürgen Habermas and the ethics of liberation developed by Dussel share a very pragmatic focus and a progressive agenda. In chapter 5, "Discourse and Liberation: Toward a Critical Coordination of Discourse Ethics and Dussel's Ethics of Liberation," Hans Schelkshorn helpfully outlines both their similarities and their differences, and he persuasively argues that their differences are significantly related to their respective political and cultural genealogies. He also portrays their dialogue as a dialectic, each providing the critical missing ingredient in the other.

Discourse ethics extends from the Enlightenment project of a universal morality, whereas the ethics of liberation culminates the project of producing a genuinely Latin American thought. For Apel, the principal contemporary ethical challenges are the privatization of morality and the separation of science and value. His remedial strategy is to reveal the moral presuppositions of science, and thus the inescapability of morality from the public sphere. For Dussel, the critical problem of our time—the one that affects far more people far more adversely—is global neocolonialism. To oppose neocolonialism requires opposing, and overcoming, Euro-centrism, and he proposes that this can best, and most reliably, be done through a solidarity with the world's poor, given that they will have the most critical standpoint on the problem.

Dussel thus critiques the Enlightenment tradition of universality, and he links reason and ethics to cultural location. But he also wants to avoid relativism and thus mines Levinas's approach for ways it can help forge unconditional moral claims grounded in the concrete Other. But here is where Schelkshorn finds the weakness of the ethics of liberation. It understands itself as aimed toward a context of domination, in which conditions for equality and universality have been destroyed. Still, even in this context, the normative presuppositions revealed by discourse ethics are necessary to reformulate social identities and relations. Thus discourse ethics can show its universal relevance and even necessity despite its own nonuniversal genealogy.

However, Schelkshorn concedes Dussel's point that the norms established by discourse ethics are not *as* relevant to the most pressing global problems as the norms invoked by the ethics of liberation. This accounts, in part, for their differences over Marxism and the labor theory of value, differences that Schelkshorn nicely untangles for us. In the final analysis, although he views the ethics of liberation as having a weak theoretical base and as focused too much on appeals that are moral as opposed to practical, Schelkshorn concludes that it, unlike discourse ethics, can extend beyond the realm in which agents can assert their claims and participate in the dialogue; thus its reach can extend to the majority of those who suffer today.

In chapter 6, "Beyond Universal History: Dussel's Critique of Globalization," Eduardo Mendieta further contextualizes Dussel's work by discussing its relation to what appears to be the latest intellectual fashion of the North Atlantic marketplace of ideas. The central contention is that while globalization has the potential of becoming a critical tool in the process of decentering and dehegemonizing the West (and any imperial project for that matter), narrow economist, technological, even political-legalist readings of "globalization" (as in the discourses about the global expansion of human rights) have allowed the discourses on globalization to function once again as languages of neocolonial mastery and subalternization. Mendieta points out that globalization is not merely political and economic: it is also cultural, ecological, and even spiritual. The issue is not just what processes catalyzed globalization but also about who gets globalized and under what conditions.

Globalization is a two-way process: particular to planetary, and vice versa. In this process, the West is as much an agent of globalization as it is an object of globalization. This is how Mendieta reads Dussel's work, namely, as a critical theory or countertheory of globalization articulated from those parts of the planet whose own globalization agendas the North Atlantic nations would like to hold in abeyance. To this extent, the suggestion is that Dussel is offering a theory of globalization from below as much as from above, if one may use these terms without reading too much into them. Mendieta also commends Dussel's critical reading of globalization for its attempt at a synthesis of non-Eurocentric history and planetary macroethics. The perspective that Dussel offers in his recent work *Etica de la liberación*, argues Mendieta, brings together a historical point of view that decenters the West, incorporates history into the nonteleological development of moral perspectives, and argues for an ethical evaluation of globalization itself.

In chapter 7, "Burnt Offerings to Rationality: A Feminist Reading of the Construction of Indigenous Peoples in Dussel's Theory of Modernity," Lynda Lange considers these resources in Dussel's work for the development of a "postcolonial feminism." Dussel identifies as Eurocentric the presupposition made by many postmoderns, as well as some postcolonial theorists, that within European modernity there is an inner dynamic, or some essentially inherent or autonomous feature, that accounts for its global supremacy. But Europe, Dussel points out, is the result and not the cause of its encounter with the New World and subsequent position in the global system. In this way, Lange finds Dussel's work more helpful than postmodernism because its critique avoids a totalizing skepticism toward reason: it is not that philosophy cannot be based on reason, according to Dussel, but that it has not yet been, due to the fact that it has lacked awareness of its historical specificity. In Lange's view, feminism, which has a higher stake than postmodernism in avoiding the cynicism that skepticism engenders, should find this approach very useful.

Lange also explains, however, that, on Dussel's account, a recognition of cultural "Others" is more difficult than Western feminists might at first imagine because "the obstacles to it may include what we hold as best among our values, rather than what we more readily recognize as our cultural potential for bias." Current feminist convictions, then, may prove to be obstacles, especially when they are framed by homogeneous conceptions of gender polarity.

But some have charged Dussel's own work with producing overly homogenous constructions of the oppressed. In chapter 8, "Thinking *Other*wise: Dussel, Liberation Theology, and Feminism," Elina Vuola considers Dussel's work in relation to women. She credits Dussel as being one of the few and first liberation theologians to take up (and continue to engage) issues of gender. Vuola notes his enthusiastic support for women's liberation, which he defines as accepting of gender difference, whereas feminism, he thinks, is opposed to gender difference. Vuola argues with Dussel on this characterization, as well as on other issues, even while she defends him against some feminist charges. She also explores the problem of the Other in liberation theology in relation to their discursive construction of the poor and the oppressed. Although the Other is treated throughout liberation theology, it is Dussel's work that has most systematically developed the philosophical aspects of this topic.

Vuola points out that Dussel's characterization of feminism as antidifference is inaccurate, given the variety of positions held by feminists on the question of difference and also given that what feminists are mostly critical of are naturalistic accounts of gender rather than biological procreation as he supposes. Dussel's references include only Anglo-American and European feminisms, ignoring the long traditions of Mexican and Latin American feminisms.

Dussel believes that women will achieve liberation in or through their distinctiveness, instead of by transcending it, a position similar to the one taken by Levinas and by liberation theology generally. Against this, Vuola argues that Dussel fails to take sufficient note of the way in which the conception of women's alterity has been a male projection and that Dussel's position takes heterosexuality as both normative and determinant of gender identity. Although his positions are often in conformity with the Vatican, Vuola points out that Dussel's position on abortion is significantly better: he portrays it as a "minor evil" but he gives women the right to make the moral decision, thus according them an ability for moral judgment that the Vatican denies.

These problems are hardly unique to Dussel but beset liberation theology as a whole, in which a theoretical approval of women's equality coexists with a failure to accept it in the concrete, in terms of the actual social changes that are necessary. Vuola links this problem with the general problem of taking the poor as an undifferentiated, homogeneous group, as if poverty affected everyone in the same way despite differences of race and gender. Conflicting interests and power struggles among the impoverished of the Third World make a representation of their interests less than clear-cut. Liberation theology's support for a "theology of life," understood as opposing the forces of death perpetrated by global capitalism, is used to critique birth control policies and legalized abortion. But, as Vuola points out, although there is much reason to believe that U.S.-sponsored birth control policies, for example, are promoted as part of an ideology of blaming the poor for their poverty, it remains the case that a true "theology of life" would be concerned about the life of poor women, for whom the absence of abortion and birth control can threaten their health and their very existence.

Liberation theology needs to critique the ways in which it constructs the poor and then uses its construction as an absolute criterion of validity. It is better to acknowledge that "the people" is not so much an empirical entity as it is a social construction. However, Vuola argues that this problem also besets feminist theories that use the category of "women" or "women's experience," and thus that liberation theology and feminism actually *share* similar theoretical assumptions which many find problematic.

In chapter 9, "Locating the Absolutely Absolute Other: Toward a Transmodern Christianity," Roberto Goizueta offers an elucidation and a defense of the religious implications of Dussel's ethics, helping us to understand how Dussel explains the history of practices of Christianity in relation to the forces of globalization, starting in the period of conquest. God's transcendence transcends, and thus implicitly critiques, the status quo, which also implies that God will be found, or will be comprehensible, in "those loci that are themselves incomprehensible within our world." And this in turn implies that difference will be disclosed through God: that the very meaning of God's love must be an openness to the radically new and different.

For Dussel, however, as Goizueta explains, difference is not the empty and ahistorical difference, or Otherness, postulated in postmodern theory, a difference that, because it is empty and yet must be affirmed, effects an absolutization of particularity. An empty difference is only capable of standing as a bare particular, without relation to anything else and without entailing any *specific* obligations. Postmodernism's mistake is to accept the conceptual preconditions of modernity, especially the assumed opposition and incommensurability between affect and reason, particularity and universality. In the face of this, a critique of modernity has no choice but to affirm that which has been denigrated and to denigrate that which has been affirmed. By this logic we are left with a choice between the enforcement of one particularity as if it were universality (modernism) or the radical relativizing of all particularities and subsequent inability to perceive any universal elements within particularities (postmodernism).

Dussel's argument is that the Other is concrete and historical, existing in time and space. In our time, the Other is the poor of the Third World, the populations that have been forcibly excluded from globalization and whose exclusion, through starvation or environmental genocide, is in fact necessary for the current form of globalization to be maintained. Part of the way in which Dussel constitutes the Other in this way is to argue, following Bartolomé de Las Casas and also Marx, that socioeconomic life necessarily mediates all intersubjective relations as well as the possibilities for spiritual transcendence. Thus no concrete subjects can be conceptualized outside of their economic life, which is not to reduce them to it but to argue for its necessary relation to all other aspects of their life. In other words, in our cultural and national and other geographies of Otherness, the economic must play a necessary role as well.

The preferential option for the poor thus leads to neither irrationalism nor irreducible particularity; instead, it grants the basis for achieving universal truths and norms precisely because only an intersubjective praxis can authorize a claim of universality. Here was the error of the Enlightenment: to imagine that universality and truth could be achieved prior to dialogue across difference and that such dialogue, to the extent it was ever even allowed, would proceed with the presupposition that Europe knew what was true and what was universal. If there is any possibility for a new globalization to emerge that would not consist in domination and exclusion, and thus a globalization that would be true to its name in signifying a truly global inclusion, it must emerge out of just such dialogic encounters. A new Christianity is thus needed that can practice the *mestizaje,* the mixing of races, cultures, and religions, out of which universality alone can develop.

Liberation theology has famously found innovative ways to integrate Marxism and Christianity. According to Michael Barber in chapter 10, "Theory and Alterity: Dussel's Marx and Marion on Idolatry," Dussel has developed a very original synthesis, one that emerges from his highly original interpretation of Marx's critique of capitalism as a form of idolatry. Dussel understands Marx to be claiming that "living labor" is the creative source that exists outside of, or prior to, the system of capitalism. Capitalism does not create; it transforms and accumulates. Prior to the system is the creative source and power of human life as it manifests itself in "living labor." This then makes sense of Marx's famous analogy between capital and vampirism: capital is dead labor that feeds like a vampire on living labor. Capital is then guilty of idolatry in fetishizing commodity value as if it existed in no context of relations to living labor, and it refuses to recognize itself as the agent that has conceptually constructed commodity value in this way.

Dussel takes this to be a kind of religious critique of capitalism, not one that conflicts with or denies Marx's atheism but one that exhorts society to oppose fetishism, just as the monotheists of Judaism and Christianity exhorted their societies to cease idol worship. To the extent that Dussel is right to interpret Marx in this way, his argument produces only a negative theology, Barber admits, one that is critical rather than developmental. But it can also serve as a negative moment in a dialectic that is propadeutic to an affirmation of an alternative absolute, in this case the absolute moral prerogative of the poor. This absolute, like other monotheistic absolutes, lies in the exteriority of the current system. The fact that it provides the source of existing value in the capitalist system is obscured in the capitalist view that the "market" is the motive force. Thus, because living labor is both exterior and the true creative source, its viewpoint alone is capable of effective critical provocation.

Barber compares this analysis with Jean-Luc Marion's critique of idolatry, and both in the context of the need for theory to account for alterity. Dussel's critique of capital can be read as the claim that capital is unable and unwilling to account for alterity and that its idolatrous worship of commodity value manifests this by negating the existence of the alterity of living labor. Marion's concern is with the way in which idolatry denies the human source of theistic concepts, thus "equating God with a concept." The collapse of God to human concepts denies the alterity of God and besets any attempt to theoretically articulate God's presence. The solution can only be a repudiation of a theoretical relation to God in favor of a relation of praise.

Barber questions whether either Marion or Dussel has been sufficiently self-reflective about his own theory's (and Barber thinks Marion's arguments cannot escape theory either) relation to alterity. He suggests sources in Levinas from which such self-reflectiveness might be developed. Dussel's Marx seems to be one that can only critique *capital's* relation to alterity and does not attend to the more general problem of *theory's* relation to alterity, which calls for an awareness of its limits.

In chapter 11, "Dussel on Marx: Living Labor and the Materiality of Life," Mario Sáenz raises some similar concerns about Dussel's creative interpretation of Marx, though Sáenz is much less sanguine than Barber about the Levinasian aspects of Dussel's interpretation. Sáenz interprets Dussel's work to be fundamentally about analectical transformation, that is, a philosophy turned toward the excluded exteriority of a system of domination. Sáenz explains that Dussel pushes this analectical interpretation in reformulating three key distinctions in Marx's writings: the poiesis/praxis distinction, the living labor/labor power distinction, and the center/periphery distinction. In each case, Dussel attempts to construe one side of the distinction as the site of exteriority, or as beyond, in a Schellingian (and Levinasian) sense, the possibility of comprehension, reduction, or absorption by the other. Sáenz's main concern is that, even while Dussel critiques the Hegelian readings of Marx as overly metaphysical, Dussel's own readings reproduce a metaphysical, ahistorical construction that in fact disenables critique and transformation.

Much of this argument rests on the concept of living labor in Dussel's work, since it is this concept more than any other that allows Marxism to properly name the form that oppression takes under capitalism and the potential source from which to devise an alternative. Living labor, as Sáenz reads Dussel reading

Marx, is a kind of primordial exteriority, a pure creative force, and it is singularly independent of capital. Living labor is the creator of value in an abstract sense, not exterior to capital because it is positioned as exterior by capital in a social system of praxis but exterior to capital in an irreducibly metaphysical sense. This claim is the crux of Dussel's rejection of Georg Lukács, Herbert Marcuse, Louis Althusser, and the other "post-Hegelian" Marxists. On Dussel's account, they mistakenly ignore the importance of Friedrich Schelling and his concept of positive philosophy, which would allow them to see that Marx's concept of living labor is intended to be understood as beyond the closed totality of the Hegelian system. But Sáenz finds this argument to be an attempt to create an analectical a priori, which he finds both philosophically and politically objectionable. Though Sáenz has a partial agreement with some of Dussel's critique, he argues that human labor is exterior to capital in a metasystemic rather than a metaphysical sense; to argue otherwise is to ignore the historicity of praxis. Sáenz then attempts to show, however, that Dussel's critique of capitalism based on the claim that it exteriorizes living labor does not actually require the analectical a priori and thus that it can survive Sáenz's own critique mostly intact.

Enrique Dussel and Michel Foucault would no doubt have made an odd couple—the global ethicist and the principled localist—but both have brought power and domination center stage to any discussion of ethical norms, discursive rules, and even methods of justification. And there is an audible echo in their respective critiques of the Habermasian style of political theory for its complete inattention to the realm of the concrete, the material, and the embodied. In chapter 12, "Power/Knowledges in the Colonial Unconscious: A Dialogue between Dussel and Foucault," Linda Martín Alcoff imagines whether there might be a productive, even if occasionally volatile, dialogue between the two.

In regard to Foucault, Alcoff argues that an attentiveness to colonialism and the notion of theoretical perspective, such as Dussel employs it, would have (1) allowed him to reconcile the obvious normative undercurrents in his work with his epistemological thesis that knowledge is always connected to power and (2) expanded and deepened his analysis of the deployment of biopower and its regulatory regimes concerning populations. Foucault's own discourse replicated a colonial unconscious, and Alcoff finds this unconscious at work not only in Foucault's neglect of colonialism and refusal to consider non-European sources for European practices but also in his refusal of causal explanations.

In regard to Dussel, Alcoff takes up the main criticisms that have been lodged against his account: that it is irrational and that it is authoritarian. She then suggests how the use of Foucault's account of subjugated knowledges could help Dussel make his privileging of the perspective of the oppressed more plausible. Dussel's conception of identity has also been criticized as a form of reification, which then produces the danger of authoritarianism when absolute identities are taken to entail absolute claims. Here Alcoff suggests that some aspects, though not all, of Foucault's work on identity might help, in particular, his claim that power plays the role of not simply labeling preexisting phenomena according to its own ends but of inciting, eliciting, and shaping life in ways that connect with desire, as well as increasing its own circulations. Alcoff does not call on Dussel to surrender the appeal to identities, nor to necessarily redescribe them, but to incorporate an awareness of their complicated genealogies and effects as a guard against the dangers his critics believe to be inevitable.

In chapter 13, Dussel's epilogue to this volume, he offers appreciative but sometimes trenchant rejoinders to the criticisms of his work collected here. In some cases he emphasizes the importance of reading his work in its cultural and historical context, within the evolutionary development of the philosophy of liberation's own insights. He also emphasizes the need to differentiate his philosophical and his religious works, and to understand that these are not interchangeable discourses. These contextual limitations are especially important, he argues, in assessing what he admits to be his previously mistaken views about feminism and homosexuality.

Dussel continues to defend the primacy of the material principle over the formal because the content of practical discourse "presupposes always already a material order that responds to another logic than the merely formal one because in the end it always has a relationship with human life as a criterion of truth." He also defends his interpretation of living labor against the charge that it is metaphysical by highlighting his Levinasian interpretation of exteriority: as an internal transcendentality or a category whose intelligibility refers to the totality of capital. Though he rejects Sáenz's interpretation of his account of living labor, he does not disagree with Sáenz's insistence on the historicity of the analectical sources.

Dussel does not take issue with all of his critics, but in some cases he reiterates his agreements with their fundamental concerns, in particular, the need for theory to be self-critical, fallible, and without pretensions to mastery; the multiple identities of the oppressed; and the necessity to critique patriarchy, racism, and other forms of domination that are not sufficiently incorporated into current concepts of justice anywhere. In fact, he announces plans for a future work that will take up these concerns, thus giving evidence once again of his serious commitment to an openness in dialogue and the ongoing critically reflective evolution of his thought. Indeed, Dussel's intellectual biography reveals a philosopher much more willing than most to engage in dialogue with a variety of alternative traditions and to transform his own thinking as he learns from these encounters.

II

To offer an intellectual itinerary also means offering a chronology. A chronology is a temporal map, a distribution of significant, pivotal, cardinal events or moments over a life line that supposedly begins with birth and ends at the last or latest point on that life line. In addition, it is thought that these pivotal life events are held together by a logic, a coherence that is discernable. Offering a chronology is a way of discerning that coherence, that logic, that makes a life a unity, that person's unique human existence. Clearly, which significant, pivotal, and cardinal events or moments are picked out of countless such moments and events is the product of the intentions of the one who draws the map. The farther removed from our quotidian and historical experiences a thinker is, the more arbitrary and self-serving is our chronology, and thus the more likely it is that our chronology will be drawn according to our own standards, historical perspectives, and intellectual outlooks.

These remarks are necessary because offering even the briefest sketch of Enrique Dussel's intellectual itinerary requires that we make choices that are constrained by our audience, and the fact that this book appears in English and not in Spanish, German, or French. This chronology, furthermore, must take into account that while this volume is for the most part an engagement with Dussel's philosophical work, his oeuvre spans the fields of theology, history, and economics. If we were to be attentive to all of these other fields on which Dussel has had an impact, then our chronology would have to foreground and underscore different temporal markers.

One way in which we could temporalize Dussel's intellectual itinerary is in terms of the impact certain key Western thinkers (e.g., Maritain, Ricoeur, Heidegger, Levinas, Marx, Apel, and Habermas) have had on his intellectual development. In such narratives we might speak of a Ricoeurian, Heideggerian, Levinasian, Marxist, and so on, Dussel. In the same vein, we might speak of a Catholic Natural Law, phenomenological, ontological, hermeneutical, and philosophical anthropological Dussel. While these descriptions are possible, they would, in fact, do too much violence to Dussel's uniqueness and originality. Such chronologies would only tell us a history of the impact of European thinkers and movements on a Latin American, Third World thinker. But the way in which Enrique Dussel, a Latin American thinker, came to these movements would be lost. This is not to say that such narratives should not be offered. There is a place for them, especially as it pertains to Latin America in particular and the Americas in general, whose own philosophical traditions are related to the Old World less as cousins or adopted children and more as younger siblings. Indeed, not even a European thinker can be described solely as either a phenomenologist and hermeneuticist or a Levinasian and Heideggerian. Derrida is a phenomenologist and Heideggerian, but he is also an Algerian Jew who was formed by the experience of decolonization, the transformation of the French left, the eclipse of Marxism, and so on. Derrida is a post–World War II, French, Heideggerian phenomenologist who made the linguistic turn by way of Ferdinand de Saussure, Jacques Lacan, and Emmanuel Levinas. Similarly, Dussel's intellectual itinerary could be written as the history of phenomenology, hermeneutics, Marxism, and transcendental pragmatics, as received, appropriated, and transformed by an Argentinean philosopher who lived through one of the darkest chapters in the history of both Argentina and Latin American. As a compromise between these approaches we offer the following chronology.[2]

Student Years in Mendoza (1934–1961)

Enrique Ambrosini Dussel was born December 24, 1934, in the small town of La Paz, in the province of Mendoza, Argentina. He was the son of a doctor who had been trained at the turn of the century in the Latin American tradition of positivism and agnosticism. His paternal great-grandfather had emigrated during the 1870s from Schweinfurt, Germany, to Argentina. Enrique Dussel's mother, who was a militant Catholic, was involved in all the church activities in the town, was president of the school's parent association, and was the founder of the tennis club. From both of them, Dussel learned the importance of social service, mercy, humility, and hard work. During the 1940s, because of the war and anti-German feelings, his father was fired from his job with an English railway firm, forcing the family to move to Buenos Aires. After a few years, they moved to Mendoza, the capital of the province in which he had been born. There Dussel spent his teenage years. He was an avid *andinista* (in contrast to alpinist). He was involved in Catholic Action, and during his midteens he underwent what he has called a "profound experience of conversion to the responsibility for the Other,"[3] in the context of volunteering at the Hospital for Children with Mental Disabilities. He immersed himself in the spiritual writings of St. John of the Cross, Teresa of Avila, and St. Bernard. With his peers, he founded the Federación Universitaria de Oeste (FUO, Eastern University Federation). He was president of the Centro de Filosofía y Letras (CEFYL, Center for Philosophy and Letters). His student activism against Perón led to his arrest in 1954.

Dussel did his *bachillerato* (1946–1951) at an agricultural technical school and then attended the Escuela de Bellas Artes until 1954, having originally intended to be an artist or an architect. In 1953 he began his university studies at the National University of Cuyo and there he received what he has called "traditional" schooling. At this time in Argentina there ruled the Third Scholastic, a blend of right-wing Catholicism, Natural Law, and conservative Thomism. Dussel studied under a generation of professors who had been trained in the old Continental tradition of scholarship: rigorous knowledge of primary sources in the original languages. He was a student of, among others, Arturo Roig, Angel González Alvarez, Antonio Millán Puelles, Mauiricio Lopez (tortured to death in 1976 by the repressive regime), and Guido Soaje Ramos. Ramos made the deepest impact on the young Dussel. Soaje Ramos demanded that his students learn Greek, Latin, and German. For four years, Dussel studied ethics under Soaje Ramos, focusing on the German ethical phenomenologists Max Scheler and Dietrich von Hildebrand, as well as Aristotle and Aquinas. Ethics was his concentration during his first university years, and he graduated in 1957 with a thesis entitled "Social and Ethical Philosophy," earning a Gold Medal for his academic performance. But these were also years of intense student activism and, as a follower of Jacques Maritain, he helped found Democracia Cristiana (Christian Democracy).

Doctoral Studies in Madrid, Spain (1957–1961)

With his master's degree in hand, and financed by a scholarship, Dussel embarked on a trip to Madrid, Spain, to pursue doctoral studies in philosophy. He matriculated at the Faculty of Philosophy and Letters of the Central University of Madrid, where he was required to validate his master's by submitting a new thesis. He submitted promptly, under the direction of Antonio Millán Puelles, a new thesis entitled "Problemática del bien común en el pensar griego hasta Aristóteles" (The problem of the common good in Greek thought up to Aristotle). In March 1958 he submitted his work "El bien común en la Escuela Moderna Tomista o la Segunda Escolástica del Siglo XVI" (The common good in the modern Thomist school or the second scholastic of the XVI century) for a research contest at the Colegio Guadalupe of Madrid.[4]

Later, a revised and expanded version of the validation thesis, and his contest essay, were incorporated into a trilogy that he submitted as his doctoral dissertation. The trilogy had the general title of "El bien común: Su inconsistencia teórica" (The common good: Its theoretical inconsistency). Each volume carried its own title: volume 1 was "Introducción a la temática del bien común natural temporal (fundamentación para un comunitarismo personalista)" (Introduction to the theme of the natural temporal common good [Foundations for a personalist communitarianism]); volume 2 was "La problemática del bien común: La existencia del bien común" (The problem of the common good: The existence of the common good); and volume 3 was "Naturaleza del bien común natural temporal" (Nature of the natural temporal common good). He finished this three-volume dissertation, amounting to 944 pages, in April, and he defended it in June 1959 before a dissertation committee of five professors who unanimously voted it "outstanding."

In essence, this doctoral dissertation was an investigation into the origins, sources, and evolution of the concept of the "common good" from the pre-Socratics to Hans Kelsen. In the opinion of one of the most knowledgeable scholars of Dussel's work and life, Mariano Moreno Villa, this work is important for at least two reasons. First, in many ways it already anticipates and discloses the central preoccupation of Dussel's thought, namely, the quest after the approximation to the appropriate, although rarely attainable response to the Other. By means of this work, Dussel sought to defend Jacques Maritain against the conservative Thomist Charles de Konick. This work defended a position contrary to the one commonly accepted during those times in Spanish culture. Against a corporatist society like Spain, Dussel wanted to defend simultaneously democracy and the irreducible and uncircumventable primacy of the human person.[5] Second, it is important because the mode of work of this dissertation, learned from Werner Jaeger, whose work on Aristotle Dussel admired, anticipates the mode of production of all his other works. The careful and detailed bibliography and exegesis that marked this work would continue to characterize all of his subsequent works.[6]

In Madrid he studied with José Luis López Aranguren, Julián Marías, Xabier Zubiri, and Pedro Laín Entralgo, who were some of the remaining members of the so-called Madrid School. It was, however, Aranguren who most influenced Dussel at an existential level. Aranguren's personal commitment, his philosophical presence, and his unwillingness to disregard perfidy, which led to his expulsion from the university and exile in the United States, impressed upon Dussel the importance of philosophy's social engagement and responsibility before injustice. Philosophically, Zubiri made an impression, but Dussel only truly discovered his work much later.

Promptly after he defended his doctoral dissertation, Dussel traveled by boat to Israel to join the humble community of manual laborers lead by Paul Gauthier. Dussel spent two years in Israel, from 1960 to 1961. He made his living as a carpenter in Nazareth and as a fisherman on the Lake of Tiberias in the kibbutz Ginosar. He studied Hebrew and learned of the Jewish passion for the humble, the downtrodden, the poor, and the miserable and excluded. Gauthier, who was "obsessed with the poor," challenged Dussel to see through the eyes of the poor, from their perspective. One night, recalls Dussel, he got carried away eulogizing the merits, cunning, and bravery of Francisco Pizarro for conquering the Incas with so few men. Gauthier asked him in return: "Who were the poor in this case: Pizarro or the indians?"[7] That very night Dussel recalls writing to his friend, the historian Esteban Fontana: "One day we shall have to write the history of Latin America from the other side, from the underside, from the perspective of the oppressed, the poor!"[8] These two years crystallized into the fundamental existential experience that came to inform all of his future intellectual, epistemological, and hermeneutical turns and projects. His sojourn in the Holy Land also provided Dussel with a firsthand experience of a place in history where a different logic, a different worldview, had gathered and taken root. In Israel, Dussel confronted traces of that pivotal time in the history of humanity that Karl Jaspers had called *Achsenzeit,* the Axial Age. When he returned to Europe, therefore, he was to experience a culture shock. In his visit to Greece, now coming from the East, from the land of the deserts, the nomads, Dussel found that this supposed homeland of philosophy had become alien. He had become estranged from a worldview he had come to believe was his own. During these pivotal years Dussel realized that in order to discover, to rescue, a Latin America philosophy, he had to dismantle the myth of Greece. To discover the sources of Latin American thought, it was necessary to return to the sources, the Semitic worldview—the mytho-poetic core of Jewish culture. As he puts it: "Jerusalem spoke of the dignity of work, of the possibility of the revolution of the poor; Athens spoke of the dignity of the free noblemen, of the impossibility of the emancipation of the slaves."[9] It was from this cultural clash and these discordant moral outlooks that his first three works emerged.

The Reconstruction of European Philosophical Thinking (1961–1969)

Dussel returned to France to begin theological studies, which he concluded with a master's in theology at the Parisian Catholic Institute. There he studied with Jean Daniélou (later to become a cardinal) and Claude Tresmontat. It is during these early years of the 1960s that Dussel began to write *El humanismo helénico* (Hellenic Humanism), a work that was to be published in 1976. This work utilized much of the material from his dissertation, but here Dussel sought to make explicit the contradictions inherent in the Hellenic life world, which appeared epitomized in its ontological monism (being is one) and ontic dualism (radical distinction between body and soul), as well as in the aporias of its ethics and politics that exalted the virtue of contemplation over the *vita activa* and the life of the polis. By contrast, in his *El humanismo semita* (Semitic humanism) (finished in 1964 but only published in 1969), Dussel sought to demonstrate that the existential experience of the Semitic peoples, which departed from the beyond, the nothingness of an originating reality, allowed them to affirm the monism of anthropological carnality, that is, the unity of body and soul.[10] These two works were matched by a third, also began in the same period but finished in 1968 and only published in 1974, when Dussel had returned to Latin America: *El dualismo en la antropología de la cristiandad: Desde el origen del cristianismo hasta antes de la conquista de América* (Dualism in the anthropology of Christendom: From the origin of Christianity until before the conquest of America). The point of this work was to excavate through layers of sedimented history pressed down by the forces of *cristiandad*, Christendom, or the imperialization of Christianity. Dussel's idea was to rescue the living spirit of Christianity as a prophetic religion on the side of the poor and exploited, which had been repressed and covered over by centuries of Greek ontology and anthropological dualism. This work may be read as a philosophical prolegomena to the theological reformation that would later be known as the theology of liberation.

During his years in France, Dussel studied phenomenology and was influenced especially by Maurice Merleau-Ponty's *The Phenomenology of Perception* and Ricoeur's translations of Edmund Husserl, as well as Ricoeur's own writings, in particular *History and Truth* and *The Symbolism of Evil*. In addition, he embarked on a serious study of Martin Heidegger for the first time, who became a leading formative influence until Dussel encountered the work of Levinas in 1971. It could be said that Dussel's work during the 1960s moved from phenomenology and hermeneutics through philosophical anthropology to Heideggerian ontological hermeneutics. This trajectory is apparent in the philosophical anthropological trilogy that he undertook upon his arrival in Europe from the Middle East, as well as the essays collected in his book *América Latina: Dependencia y liberación* (Latin America: Dependency and liberation).[11]

In Paris, Dussel followed the courses of Paul Ricoeur. He worked as a librarian for two years, which gave him a unique opportunity to become aware of the extensive bibliography available to scholars in France, of which he made ample use. In 1963 he received a scholarship that allowed him to move to the Institute of European History in Magdeburg, during which time he met his wife, Johanna. It was at the institute that he developed the idea of pursuing doctoral studies in history at the Sorbonne. Under the direction of Joseph Lortz in Magdeburg and Robert Richard in Paris, he worked on another doctoral dissertation: "El episcopado latinoamericano: Institución misionera en defensa del indio (1504–1620)" (The Latin American episcopate: Missionary institution in defense of the Indian [1504–1620]). Research for this work took him to the General Archive of the Indies in Seville. Here, Dussel's ontological hermeneutics and philosophical anthropology were complemented by a rich historical understanding of Europe and of Latin America in particular. Guided by Leopoldo Zea's reflections in his *América en la historia* (1957), Dussel undertook the project of a history of Latin America from a global perspective. Thus, in a 1965 essay, Dussel challenges us to think "Iberoamérica en la historia universal" (Iberoamerica in universal history). In 1966, as a visiting professor at Resitencia (Chaco, Argentina), he delivered a lecture course entitled Hipótesis para el estudio de Latinoamérica en la historia universal" (Hypotheses for the study of Latin America in universal history). These lectures remain unpublished, although today they would be very relevant to the debates on globalization and postcoloniality. In 1968, he concluded his trilogy on the "anthropological-ethical hermeneutics" of the Greeks, Semitic peoples, and Christians with the curious but suggestive subtitle "Until before the Conquest of America."

After ten years of study abroad, Dussel returned to Argentina definitively in March 1967, carrying several boxes of unpublished materials, to accept the chair of ethics in the Philosophy Department at the National University of Cuyo. He occupied this position until 1975.

Origins of Liberation Philosophy (1969–1976)

Dussel's pedagogical orientation during the first years after his return from Europe can be characterized today as traditional, conservative, and Eurocentric. His first courses were all based on phenomenology and European thinkers: Max Scheler, Merleau-Ponty, Ricoeur, Husserl, Heidegger, and Sartre. This is quite evident from a work written during 1969, which was based on the courses he taught: "Para una de-strucción de la historia de la ética" (Toward a de-struction of the history of ethics), the first volume of a projected three-volume work (which he later abandoned for his five-volume *Toward an Ethics of Latin American Liberation*). "Toward a De-struction of the History of Ethics" begins with a discussion of Aristotle's ethics, proceeds through Aquinas and Kant, and concludes with an analysis of the contemporary axiological ethics of Max Scheler, Dietrich von Hildebrand, and Nicolai Hartmann. It is clear, however, that this is a Heideggerian work, with references to Heidegger on almost every page. Perhaps what is most interesting about this work is not what it achieves on its own but what it is meant to be a prolegomena to, namely, an "antiethics of Latin American liberation."[12]

In 1969 Dussel also wrote another important work for his later philosophical development: "La dialéctica hegeliana" (Hegelian dialectics), later to be expanded and published with the title of *Método para una filosofía de la liberación: Superación analéctica de la dialéctica hegeliana* (Method for a philosophy of liberation: Analectical superseding of the Hegelian dialectics). This work, even more than *Toward an Ethics of Latin American Liberation,* registers with clarity and precision Dussel's transition from an ontological moment to the metaphysical (in the Levinasian sense), or analectical, moment. What would be formulated in 1976 in a series of short, oracular, very dense paragraphs gathered under the title of *Filosofía de la liberación* cannot be appropriately understood without this pivotal text.

The year 1969 was particularly momentous for Argentina. This was the year of the *Cordobazo*, when the city of Cordoba was taken by students and workers, replicating in many ways what had taken place in Berkeley, Paris, Berlin, and Mexico City the year before. In a highly charged political situation, students demanded political engagement and philosophical clarity from their teachers. During these years Dussel came into contact with Latin American sociologists, economists, and political scientists talking about "underdevelopment," "the development of underdevelopment," and the "sociology of liberation." Dussel writes: "In 1969, in discussions with sociologists in Buenos Aires, I began to challenge my basic philosophical choices. From this emerged the idea: why not a philosophy of liberation? Had not Fals Borda (in Colombia) spoken of a 'sociology of liberation'? What would be the presuppositions of such a philosophy?"[13] These discussions were taking place just as two important books were published: Augusto Salazar Bondy's *¿Existe una filosofía de nuestra América?* (Is there a philosophy of our America?) (1968) and Leopoldo Zea's response to Bondy, *La filosofía americana como filosofía sin más* (American philosophy as philosophy in itself) (1969).[14] Dussel decided to enter into this debate.

Dussel's works from this period, 1969–1972, although still Heideggerian in character, are aimed at laying the foundations for a Latin American philosophy of liberation: "the terminology was Heideggerian, but the intent was Latinamerican." Ontological hermeneutics had become insufficient, even a hindrance. In 1971, following the thread of his 1969–1970 courses on Hegel's dialectics, he gave a course on the post-Hegelians: Ludwig Feuerbach, Karl Marx, and Søren Kierkegaard. At the urging of Juan Carlos Scannone, Dussel read Emmanuel Levinas's *Totality and Infinity: An Essay on Exteriority,* a book that he says awakened him from his "ontological slumber." This dramatic discovery left a very noticeable and disconcerting shift between chapters 2–3 in volume 1 of his *Toward an Ethics of Latin American Liberation*. Volume 1, which is presented as part 1 with the subheading "Presuppositions for a Philosophy of Liberation," is made up of three chapters: the first is titled "The Ontological Foundation," the second, "Ontic Possibilities," and the third, "The Meta-physical Exteriority of the Other." What became clear, as Dussel explains, was that "ontology is to think the foundation, the being of the ruling Totality. The project (Heideggerian ontological *Entwurf*) of the ruling systems justifies the oppression of the oppressed and the exclusion of the Other. Little by little there disclosed utopia (*ouk-tópos*: 'that without place' in the Totality): the project of the liberation of the Other."[15] Still, although Levinas provided the metaphysical, analectical method, he provided neither the intention nor the philosophical telos of Dussel's philosophy of liberation. A glimpse at the structure of Dussel's five-volume *Toward an Ethics of Latin American Liberation* (later reprinted as *Filosofía ética de la liberación*) bears this out. Books 1–2 are a *Grundlegung* (foundation) from which Dussel will "ascend" to levels of historical, hermeneutical, and cultural concreteness. Volumes 3–5 deal with different aspects of the Latin American subcontinent. This movement from the abstract to the concrete is mediated by a history (chapter 6, "Latin American History," made up of sections 40–41; the work is divided in chapters, and each chapter is subdivided into paragraphs): "Toward a Pre- and Proto- Latin American History" and "Toward a Latin American History." Chapter 7 deals with "Latin American Erotics"; chapter 7, "Latin American Pedagogy"; chapter 9, "Latin American Politics"; chapter 10, "Latin American Archeology."

During the early 1970s Dussel also published *Historia de la iglesia en América Latina*, as well as *Caminos de liberación latinoamericana*, in two volumes, which gathered his lecture courses on religion, church history, and theology delivered at the Latin American bishop's Pastoral Institute (Quito, Ecuador), the Theological Institute of the Catholic University of Valparaiso (Chile), and to groups of bishops in Colombia and Guatemala. Their published form, however, arose from the lecture course he delivered at Nazareth House, which was organized by the Justice and Peace Study Center in Buenos Aires. These works were particularly important for the development of liberation theology.[16] Unquestionably, these were productive and momentous years for Dussel: his work had become known throughout Latin America and Europe, Africa, and part of Asia. Moving beyond philosophy circles, he was known as a historian, theologian, and staunch supporter of all liberation movements throughout Latin America. And he became persona non grata for a government becoming progressively more violent. On October 2, 1973, Dussel's house was bombed. Although his study was destroyed, no one was hurt. During these years the right-wing Peronist forces directed repression and violence against ordinary citizens. Many of Dussel's colleagues and students were subjected to repression, torture, violence, and even murder. In March 1975, nineteen members of the faculty of the National University of Cuyo were expelled, including Dussel. Thus began his exile in Mexico.

Development of Liberation Philosophy and Mexican Exile (1976–1989)

During the first months of his stay in Mexico, having access to neither library nor archives, Dussel wrote one of his best-known books, *Philosophy of Liberation.* This book, however, belongs to the Argentinian period of the development of liberation philosophy and of Dussel's own intellectual itinerary. In it are summarized and synthesized Dussel's philosophical insights through the mid-1970s. As Dussel took up teaching in Mexico at the Universidad Autónoma Metropolitana-Iztapalapa and at the Center for Latin American Studies of the Faculty of Philosophy of the Universidad Nacional Autónoma de México (UNAM) and entered a new stage of intercontinental cooperation (as a founding member of the Ecumenical Association of Third World Theologians, or EATWOT), a new series of philosophical questions emerged for him.

First on this new philosophical agenda was the clarification of some of the failures of liberation philosophy within the Argentinean context. Some of Dussel's colleagues had become right-wing Peronist conservatives. Others had turned away from a violent reality by inmersing themselves in culturalism. Second, Dussel was interested in the role that Marx played in the architectonic of liberation philosophy. Previously, Dussel had localized Marx within the tradition of the totality or as a post-Hegelian that had hardly made the turn away from ontology. The return to Argentina after a decade of studies in Europe created a context in which Dussel had to supersede Heidegger. Now, in Mexico, he had to supersede his own liberation philosophy, to go from phenomenology and hermeneutics to politics and pragmatics.

Specifically, however, as Dussel subsequently noted, four essential facts urged him to initiate a serious archeological study of Marx. First, contrary to the promises of the "Alliance for Progress," the Latin American continent was spiraling into an abyss of poverty. Throughout the world, industrialization and so-called modernization spelled the impoverishment of greater numbers of peoples. Second, the growing poverty and the widening gap between the developed and underdeveloped worlds could only be properly confronted through a critique of capitalism: neither phenomenology nor hermeneutics was sufficient here. Third, to function as a tool of social liberation, liberation philosophy had to develop clear, firm insights into both politics and, especially, economics. And fourth, just as capitalism required criticism, so did "real socialism." A critique of "dogmatic" Marxism had to be undertaken so as to rescue Marxism for a rejuvenated, nonsectarian Latin American left.[17]

The second half of the 1970s and all of the 1980s were devoted to this project to rescue an analectical, humanist, non-Eurocentric Marx. To these years belong the following works: *Filosofía de la poiesis* (1977), later to be expanded and published as *Filosofía de la producción* (1984); *La producción teórica de Marx: Una introducción a los "Grundrisse"* (1985); *Hacia un Marx desconocido: Un comentario de los manuscritos del 61–63* (1988); *El último Marx (1863–1882) y la liberación latinoamericana: Un comentario a la tercera y cuarta redacción de "El capital"* (1990); *Las metáforas teológicas de Marx* (1994).

Although these books can be thought of as a quintet, the core is a trilogy in which Dussel undertakes, perhaps for the first time in the history of Marxist studies, a detailed study of the four redactions of Marx's *Das Kapital*. Each volume of the trilogy, namely, *The Theoretical Production of Marx: An Introduction to the "Grundrisse"*; *Toward an Unknown Marx: Commentary on the Manuscripts of 61–63*; and *The Last Marx (1863–1882) and Latin American Liberation*, is devoted to tracking down and tracing back the emergence of certain fundamental concepts in Marx's theoretical architectonic. At the same time, however, as Dussel is reconstructing the evolution of Marx's *economics,* he is deconstructing the ways in which Marx has been misreceived, misappropriated, distorted, and misunderstood by Western Marxism. In the process, the trilogy plus the complementary volumes (*The Philosophy of Production* and *The Theological Metaphors of Marx*) came to constitute a rediscovery of Marx's relevance for a postcolonial situation. Unfortunately, however, this is not very well-known in the metropolitan centers that regulate the marketplace of "philosophical" ideas. Dussel's accomplishment is not unlike that achieved by Lukács, Karl Korsch, and Antonio Gramsci in the 1930s: they discovered the historical, dialectical, philosophical Marx of the 1844 manuscripts. Dussel discovered the humanist, metaphysical, antiontological, transmodern, and proto-postcolonial Marx of a yet to be understood *Capital*.[18]

New Debates (1989–1999): Debates with Apel, Ricoeur, Rorty, Taylor, Vattimo

In 1989, two weeks after the fall of the Berlin Wall, during his stint as a visiting professor in New York and around the time he gave a lecture at the New School for Social Research about his work on Marx, Dussel traveled to Freiburg to participate in a conference organized by Raúl Fornet-Betancourt. From this encounter, a new stage of Dussel's work developed, which can be characterized primarily as a debate with Apel's transcendental pragmatics but also with Habermas's universal pragmatics, as well as the whole tradition of discourse ethics that descends from their works. To this period also belongs his internationally acclaimed book *1492: El encubrimiento del otro: Hacia el origen del mito de la modernidad* (1992), which summarizes and synthesizes Dussel's thought on the history of the "American" continent in light of the quincentennial of the "discovery" of the "new world" being celebrated in 1992. This book, in fact, is a based on the lectures that he delivered in Frankfurt that year.

The 1990s signaled a confrontation with postlinguistic philosophy in general. While the themes of language, communication, and semiosis are not foreign to Dussel's work, they appeared submerged under hermeneutics and phenomenology, generally under the subheading of symbolics. In the 1990s, the idea of a linguistification of philosophy came to the fore and becomes an explicit theme of meditation for Dussel. The question, however, was not simply, How is philosophy possible after the total linguistification of philosophical concepts? Instead, Dussel transforms this question into, How are we to express in postlinguistic language the foundations of a planetary ethics in an age of worsening exploitation and systematic exclusion from the systems and networks of communication that decide the allocation of planetary resources? Dussel juxtaposes Apel's discernment of an always already presupposed community of communication with his own discernment of the priority of the community of life. Before we are members of a community of communication, we are members of a community of life. In fact, membership in the former presupposes membership in the latter. It is not so much a question of logical priority as of ontological priority. A transcendental pragmatics (or transcendental semiotics) is empty without a transcendental economics, just as the latter is blind without the former.[19] The works that gather Dussel's confrontation with contemporary postlinguistic philosophy, that is, with the works of Apel, Rorty, Taylor, Ricoeur, and Vattimo, are *The Underside of Modernity: Apel, Ricoeur, Rorty, Taylor, and the Philosophy of Liberation* (1996) and *La ética de la liberación ante el desafio de Apel, Taylor, y Vattimo con respuesta critica inedita de K.-O. Apel* (1998). But it is his *Etica de la liberación* that exhibits Dussel's creative synthesis of British, North American, and German postmetaphysical and postlinguistic philosophy in the second half of the twentieth century.[20]

Dussel has already moved ahead of this narrative. He has recently published several essays in which he addresses criticisms of his *Ethics of Liberation* (1998), and as he notes in the epilogue to this volume, he is already at work on a book that will develop the political implications of his ethics of liberation.

This anthology is meant to be an invitation. As the description of his work shows, Dussel is an extremely prolific, wide-ranging, and innovative thinker. The essays in this book address several aspects of his work but do not encompass the whole. We hope that these essays will show the diverse sides of Dussel's contributions to philosophy and the various ways in which his work has been taken up. We also hope that they will inspire readers to pursue a more in-depth study of his writings. Our hope is that readers will feel both invited and welcome to delve deeper into the pressing questions that animate all of his thought: the geopolitics of the production of knowledge; the self-perceptions of Western society that obscure its interdependence with its Others; and the persistent, historically effective influence of the "colonial difference," as Mignolo calls it, in the formulation of all categories of social and conceptual analysis. Most importantly, we hope that an acquaintance with Dussel's work will be an invitation to reflect on the insufficiency, the poverty, the "failure," in Levinas's words, of philosophy in light of the increasing inhumanity and impoverishment of our world. The contributors to this volume, despite their varied criticisms, unite with Dussel in the realization that to face the suffering of the other, and to be prepared to heed the interpellation of the Other, requires that we liberate philosophy from its hubris by acknowledging its failures. This must be the first step toward a new stage of enlightenment, one that comes this time not from the centers of colonial power but from the underside of history.

NOTES

1. Ronald Robertson, *Globalization: Social Theory and Global Culture* (London: Sage, 1992), 177–78.

2. This chronology/narrative was developed from the following sources: Enrique Dussel, "Autopercepción intellectual de un procesor histórico," *Anthropos* 180 (September–October 1998): 13–36; Mariano Moreno Villa, "Filosofía de la liberación y personalismo: "Meta–física" desde el reverso del ser: A propósito de la filosofía ética de la liberación de Enrique Dussel" (Ph.D. diss., Universidad de Murcia [Spain], 1993); Germán Marquínez Argote, "Enrique Dussel: Filósofo de la liberación latinoamericana (1934–1975)," in *Introducción a la filosofía de la liberación*, ed. Enrique Dussel, 5th ed. (Bogota: Editorial Nueva América, 1995), 11–57; and Eduardo Mendieta, editor's introduction to *The Underside of Modernity: Apel, Ricoeur, Rorty, Taylor, and the Philosophy of Liberation,* by Enrique Dussel (Atlantic Highlands, N.J.: Humanities, 1996), xiii–xxxi.

3. Dussel, "Autopercepión intellectual," 15.

4. Ibid., 16.

5. Ibid.

6. See Moreno Villa, *Filosofía de la liberación*, 21–25.

7. Dussel, "Autopercepción intellectual," 17.

8. Ibid.

9. Ibid.

10. Ibid., 18.

11. (Buenos Aires: Fernando Garcia Cambeiro, 1973). This book is divided into two major sections. The first section is entitled "Latin American Anthropological Reflections" and has two parts: "First Steps (1964–1970)" and "New Moment (1971–)." The second section is entitled "Latin American Theological Reflections" and is divided in the same way.

12. The edition studied by Eduardo Mendieta still has a postpublication strip that serves as a little dust jacket bearing the subtitle "Beginning of the History of an Anti–Ethics of Latin American Liberation." In effect, this book will become the foundations for chapters 1–2 of his *Ontological Ethics* and volume 1 of his *Toward an Ethics of Latin American Liberation.* See Dussel, "Autopercepción intellectual," 32 n. 19.

13. Cited in Argote, "Enrique Dussel," 22.

14. See the excellent work by Mario Sáenz, *The Identity of Liberation in Latin American Thought: Latin American Historicism and the Phenomenology of Leopoldo Zea* (Lanham, Md.: Lexington, 1999).

15. Dussel, "Autopercepción intellectual," 21.

16. See Roberto Oliveros, "History of the Theology of Liberation," in *Mysterium Liberationis: Fundamental Concepts of Liberation Theology,* ed. Ignacio Ellacuría, S.J., and Jon Sobrino, S.J. (Maryknoll, N.Y.: Orbis, 1993), 20.

17. Dussel, "Autopercepción intellectual," 24.

18. Preparatory or preliminary studies from the late 1970s and 1980s have been gathered in *Historia de la filosofía y filosofía de la liberación* (Bogota: Editorial Nueva América, 1994).

19. See Michael D. Barber, *Ethical Hermeneutics: Rationalism in Enrique Dussel's Philosophy of Liberation* (New York: Fordham University Press, 1998).

20. See Eduardo Mendieta, "Ethics for an Age of Globalization and Exclusion," *Philosophy and Social Criticism* 25, no. 2 (1999): 115–21.

2

Dussel's Philosophy of Liberation: Ethics and the Geopolitics of Knowledge

Walter D. Mignolo

Enrique Dussel's philosophy of liberation project has been extended and transformed during the past thirty years, from his early lectures and publications in 1969–1970 to the recent *Etica de la liberación en la edad de la globalización y de la exclusión* (1998). Although philosophy of liberation goes beyond the central body of Dussel's work, he has been relentlessly thinking about such a project, which I characterize in this chapter as involving ethics and the geopolitics of knowledge. I also distinguish two periods in Dussel's sustained work. The first period is in Argentina from 1969 to 1975. The second is from 1976 to today in his condition as a political exile in Mexico. Like many other intellectuals, Dussel left Argentina in the mid-1970s in reaction to the military dictatorship that lasted from 1973 to 1983. Before leaving, he was a professor of philosophy at the Universidad Nacional de Cuyo. The transition between these two periods is marked by Dussel's serious engagement with the entire work of Karl Marx. In Mexico, he taught two-year-long seminars at the end of the 1970s. One result of this seminar was that Dussel published a trilogy about Marx's work (Dussel 1985, 1988, 1990) and a critical revision of Marxism from Friedrich Engels to Jürgen Habermas, going through Georg Lukács, V. I. Lenin, and Rosa Luxemburg. However, and this is my main argument, it was the encounter with the work of Emmanuel Levinas that gave Dussel's project its consistent formulation and creative dimension.

In what follows, I distinguish liberation philosophy in general from Dussel's own version and interpretation. For Dussel, the "original experience" of liberation philosophy is the awareness and critical uncovering of the massive experience of "domination": a given subjectivity dominating other subjectivity as universal phenomenon. However, the forms of domination (and liberation) in which Dussel is interested are framed in the modern/colonial world. Thus we can understand the relevance in his thinking of 1492 and dependency theory (Cardoso and Faletto 1969) and one of its consequences, the emergence of the concepts of the modern world-system and world-system analysis (Dussel 1996, 213–39; 1998a, 1998b).

For this reason, liberation philosophy for Dussel is linked to the history of Latin America. For him, Latin America is the home and horizon of liberation philosophy. Since the formation of his thinking comes from the late 1960s and early 1970s, questions about Latin American identity (and its consequences, Salazar Bondy 1969; Fals Borda 1970) were and still are very much on his mind. This is another reason that for Dussel, as well as for certain branches of philosophy in Latin America, philosophy cannot be detached from geopolitics. Consequently, the relentless presence of geopolitics in philosophical discussions reveals its absence in the universalism of European philosophy, as is clear in Apel's presentation of discursive ethics and transcendental pragmatics (Apel 1994, 37–56) and in his response to Dussel (Apel 1996, 163–204). Furthermore, I explore this distinction within Dussel's own work and do not compare it with other existing versions of liberation philosophy. My reason for doing so is to recognize and honor Dussel's immense contribution to philosophy and to liberation philosophy. I first identify the epistemic potential of liberation philosophy as articulated by Dussel. Second, I delve into some of what I perceive as Dussel's actually limiting his own "discoveries," chiefly by pointing out and capitalizing on Levinas's blindness to the colonial difference (Dussel's first period) and by reading Marx's concept of "living labor" (*lebendige Arbeit*) through Levinas's "Otherness as exteriority."

1. WHEN AND WHY LEVINAS?

In 1975, the Argentinean publishing house Editorial Bonun released a small book containing two articles, one by Enrique Dussel and the other by Daniel E. Guillot. The title of the book is *Liberación latinoamericana y Emmanuel Levinas*. The text by Dussel came from a lecture he delivered in 1971 at the Universidad de El Salvador in Buenos Aires under the title "Para una fundamentación filosófica de la liberación latinoamericana." Guillot's contribution is a detailed summary of Levinas's work as published to that point (Dussel and Guillot 1975). This was part of a doctoral dissertation in philosophy at the Universidad de Cuyo under the direction of Enrique Dussel. In "Preliminary Words," Dussel also accounts for the when and why of Levinas, as well as the why not: what are the shortcomings that young Dussel (at that time in his mid-thirties) found in Levinas's work?

"Cuando leí por primera vez el libro de Levinas, *Totalité et infini* (1961), se produjo en mi espíritu como un subsersivo desquiciamiento de todo lo hasta entonces aprendido" (When for the first time I read Levinas's *Totality and Infinity* [1961], I experienced an unsettling of every thing I had learned until that time). With this sentence, Dussel introduces his relationship to the work of Levinas. Later, following his encounter and conversation with him in Paris (at the beginning of 1971), Dussel was able to measure more closely the point of encounter and divergence of his own thinking with that of the great French Jewish philosopher. Dussel described this difference as the "great disruption" between Levinas's thought and the young generation of Argentinean philosophers. He locates this great disruption in the following anecdote:

> Levinas told me that the great political experiences of his generation had been the presence of Stalin and Hitler (two dehumanizing totalities and a result of European-Hegelian modernity). But when I told him that the experience not only of my generation, but also of the last half millennium of human history was the *ego* of European modernity, a conquering *ego*, colonialist, imperial in its culture and oppressor of people in the periphery, Levinas recognized that he never thought that "the Other" (*Autrui*) could have been an (Amer)indian, an African or an Asiatic. . . . If Levinas, as a Jewish thinker, was able to find in his own experience a trace of exteriority to critique European thought in its totality (particularly Hegel, Husserl and Heidegger), he had not suffered Europe in its [colonial] totality and Levinas's reference point continued to be Europe in itself. However, for us (people and intellectuals from Latin America, Africa and Asia), from the peripheral world, that have experienced and suffered Europe, our reference point is a peripheral history, positive in itself, although from the perspective of the civilized world peripheral histories were considered barbarian, non-being, uncivilized. (Dussel 1975, 8)

The coloniality of "being" was a philosophical nonexistence and a historical disgrace. Dussel assumed the coloniality of being as "being in exteriority" rather than as "the exteriority of being."

This paragraph shows that the geopolitics of knowledge were already drawn in Dussel's thoughts in the early 1970s. There is more, however. In his reading and conversation with Levinas, Dussel also found the limits of Levinas's eroticism in the face-to-face relationship that confronts not only people across the colonial difference (Europeans face-to-face with Latin Americans [Amerindians or Creoles, whether mestizo, white or black], Africans, Asians) but across genders. In Levinas, Dussel finds that women are attributed a passive role that results in the unintended reproduction of patriarchy. The difference here is in the relation between the erotic and the pedagogic. According to Dussel, in Levinas's work, women remain passive and are relegated to the interior of the house, the dwelling place, and he finds wanting what Levinas has to say about education. Thus Dussel introduces Paolo Freire, whose works in education take a critical and liberating bent beyond the family from the Third World experience. For Freire, education is a project that leads to the recognition of the coloniality of being and to its assumption as a liberating force rather than the shameful place of the nonbeing. It is not so much the fact that Freire is Latin American but that Latin America is part of the geopolitical spectrum on which the colonial difference of the modern world had been inscribed and reproduced. By emphasizing this, Dussel again extends Levinas to the colonial (or Third) world and locates the critique of totality therein. Thus Levinas, according to Dussel, shows in depth the violence of totalitarian politics and by doing so denies the Other as such. Yet Levinas falls short in suggesting a "politics of liberation" as a next step:

> We owe to Levinas the description of the original experience, but we should supersede him regarding the implementations of mediations. Starting from the face-to-face scenario, Levinas is able to critique a totalitarian erotic, a totalitarian pedagogic and a totalitarian politic, although grounding himself ontologically in "Sameness." The Other presents itself as *absolutely* other. . . . it is necessary, instead, to understand that the Other, as other (and not as absolutely other) is not equivocal but ana-logos. It is not univocal either as something that is in the Totality of my world, but it is neither equivocal as absolutely external. "The Other" has the exteriority singular to a person (in Greek, *face*) that is not immediately comprehensible but with time and by conviviality and engagement in solidarity, walking the same path of liberation, they (the "same" and the "other") arrive at an historical communication. (Dussel 1975, 9)

I would suggest that instead of "superseding" Levinas (a view that reproduces a linear progression of knowledge toward the ideal point of arrival, which is indeed embedded in totalitarian thinking), a spatial and regional conception of knowledge be enacted. Thus, while for Heidegger "being" is the totality of Western philosophy dwelling in the "Europe of Nations," Levinas introduces the exteriority of "being" as the fracture within the "Europe of Nations" from the perspective of Jewish experience in the modern/colonial world. Dussel extends the exteriority of "being" to the colonial difference. These three perspectives are not to be seen as superseding each other in search of the final destination but rather as the regionalization of the universality of being from different historical dwellings. The epistemic potential of liberation philosophy cannot consist therefore in the search for a new totality, this time built from a Third World and post- (or neo-) colonial perspective. Liberation philosophy, as we will see in section 3, is one of many projects of intellectual and social decolonization emerging all over the planet since 1970—announcing the crisis of neoliberalism and socialism and their impossibility as abstract universal democratic projects. In the same way that Heidegger's "being" or Levinas's "otherwise than being" cannot subsume the exteriority of the colonial difference that Dussel has uncovered, neither can this exteriority subsume Heidegger's "being" or Levinas's "otherwise than being." The blindness of Heidegger's "being" and Levinas's "otherwise than being" to Dussel's "coloniality of being" (my expression), and the awareness of the latter to the limits of the former, are to be understood precisely as an epistemic potential rather than as a point of arrival. The thinking of "being" from the colonial difference means to open up the coloniality of being as a new dwelling for the liberation of philosophy. What will be retained is Dussel's uncovering of "third world" exteriority, crossed by the colonial difference, which Levinas introduced from his experience of the exteriority of the imperial difference (e.g., the Jewish as the "enemy within" in the history of modern/colonial Europe since the sixteenth century). We have then three parallels and historically located perspectives on philosophy, being, and exteriority.

2. WHEN AND WHY MARX?

Although Marx and Marxism were not alien to Dussel's philosophy of liberation during the first period (how could it have been in Latin America in the late 1960s and early 1970s?), Dussel did not engage it seriously during this time. Yet as soon as he arrived in Mexico in 1977 as a political exile, he engaged in a detailed and prolonged study of Marx's work. This monumental task culminated in three volumes (Dussel 1985, 1988, 1990) and a new perspective of Marx's contribution to the philosophy of liberation and the interpretation of Latin American history and society, as well as his relevance for it. Reinterpreting Marx along with his critics, Dussel proposed the advent of a "second century" of Marx's influence (1983–2083), in which Marx would be in the hand of a humanity (not a political party or the owners club) critical of capitalism and projecting a truly social democracy. In Dussel's view, the "first century" after Marx's death (1883–1983) developed first under the authority of Engels and then under the hegemony of the Second International (Karl Kautsky, Lenin, Luxemburg) and finally the Leninist period of the Third International, which quickly fell under Stalinism. After the death of Stalin, the period of "occidental Marxism," from Lukács to Althusser and Habermas, arrived.

Dussel's innovation is looking at Marx from the historical perspective of Latin America (a particular historical articulation of the colonial difference; see Zea 1974, "Filosofía como liberación") instead of looking at "Marx in Latin America." That is, Dussel undertakes a universal perspective on Marx's works from the basis of a regional perspective, as regional as that of Engels, Lenin, Luxembourg, Habermas, or Althusser. In this regard, Dussel offered a solution to the Marxist impasse exposed by José Aricó (1980), one of the most lucid Marxist thinkers in Latin America and a key figure (along with Oscar del Baro) of the Latin American New Left, that was articulated around the publication of *Pasado y Presente* from 1963 to 1980 (Aricó 1988, 63–82). Aricó analyzed the limits of Marx himself in order to understand the (colonial) situations in the Americas and, consequently, the difficulties of thinking Marx from a Latin American perspective or, in other words, from a particular history of the colonial difference to which Marx was blind. Curiously enough, Aricó's central reflections on Marx were carried out in Mexico, where he (as well as del Barco and many others) was in exile for reasons similar to Dussel's. Aricó was also involved in the book series *Biblioteca del pensamiento socialista,* which included Dussel's three books on Marx. However, there was no public engagement (just cordial relations) between intellectuals of the New Left, grouped around *Pasado y Presente* and Dussel's reading of Marx from liberation philosophy. There were historical reasons (going back to the 1970s in Argentina) that fall outside the scope of this chapter.

From 1977 (Argentinean military dictatorship) to 1990 (the fall of the socialist block), Dussel studied Marx because he had discovered the concept of "living work," which he considers the fundamental concept of Marxist ethics and conceptual architecture. There is, however, a second important point in Dussel's reinterpretation of Marx's work that contests previous interpretations from Lukács to Althusser and Habermas. By reconstructing the stages in the writing of *Das Kapital*, Dussel is able to advance two interrelated theses. Contrary to all previous interpretations of Marx's work that focused on the concept of *totality*, Dussel's maintains that the logico-dialectical grounding of Marx's concept of capital is not totality but *exteriority*; the absolute *exteriority* to the totality of capital as a system is the "living labor."

At this point, it is neither a surprise nor a secret that Dussel reads Marx through Levinas's concepts of "exteriority" as well as "labor." We have already referred to the limits Dussel perceives in Levinas's concept of exteriority, at the same time accepting exteriority as an epistemic, ethic, and political fracture in the articulation and hegemony of Western knowledge. In other words, he is accepting that history of knowledge self-constructed from Greek thoughts to modern science and philosophy. This is a history of knowledge whose foundational epistemology has relegated to the exterior other forms of knowledge and languages (e.g., Chinese, Indian, Arabic, Amerindians) and incorporated them as objects of study or as cultural commodities rather than as epistemic potential.

The concept of "living labor" makes possible the intersection between Marxism and philosophy of liberation as far as philosophy of liberation was logically defined as a form of thinking from the exteriority of European totality (that Dussel would explore later on in *Eurocentrism and Modernity* [Dussel 1995, 1998a]) and the totality of capitalism. In the 1970s, Dussel defined exteriority as the practice of the oppressed. In turn, he categorized the oppressed primarily as the "poor." However, he was thinking not only about oppression of the poor but also about other kinds of oppression, for example, oppression based on gender, sexuality, age, and ethnicity. Lately, following Levinas, Dussel prefers to identify the oppressed as the "victims." How does the "outside" then become the exteriority of "living labor" and why was it so important in Dussel's political and ethical reflections? (See also Chakrabarty 1989, 1993 for a similar, although mutually independent, reading of Marx "after Marxism.")

After reading the four versions of Marx's fundamental work *Das Kapital* (1857 to 1880), Dussel argues that for Marx the "absolute condition of possibility for the existence of capitalism was the transformation of money into capital" (Dussel [1990] 1994b). Dussel advances the strong interpretive hypothesis that the very beginning of *Das Kapital* was indeed a search for an answer to this question. The final answer (and I am here oversimplifying Dussel's argument) was that "living labor," which is neither "labor competence" nor "labor force," is labor "before" being part of capital as an economic system. It is labor but non-capital or, in other words, labor otherwise than capitalism. In this particular sense, it is exterior to the totality of capital, but once it is transformed into "labor competence" or "labor force," it moves from the exteriority to the borders of the system and becomes commodity. In Dussel's interpretation, "living labor" becomes subsumed, and consequently it is negated in its exteriority (e.g., nonvalued or devalued, as *ocium* [free time] is negated and becomes *negocium* [business]). Thus, according to Dussel, Marx develops an argument that answers the question "how is money converted into capital" by saying that "living labor" exterior to the system must be appropriated, subsumed, and placed in the margin of the system. There are then two simultaneous operations in the process of subsuming it. One is the situation Marx described under the known concept of "plus-value": the exchange between labor and money favors the party that has the money, not the party that provides the labor. The other is that in the process of being subsumed, "living labor" is negated and devaluated, pushed out of the totality. At this point, Dussel distinguishes his interpretation from those provided by the canonical interpreters of Marx's work (from Lukács to Althusser). The difference, Dussel maintains, is that all previous interpretation focused on the totality of the system rather than on its exteriority. For Dussel, Marx's starting point and all Marx's works are nourished by an ethical impulse. The transformation of land into private property and the transformation of living labor into pay labor are two instances in which the analysis of the structure of capitalist economy is founded in an ethic.

The intersection between ethic and economy in Dussel's interpretation of Marx offers quite a different perspective from the interpretation advanced by economist and Nobel Prize winner Amartya Sen (1987). Sen assumes and begins with the individual and self-interest in economics. He rightly critiques the liberal and neoliberal belief that self-interests and rational behavior are one and the same thing:

> Why should it be uniquely rational to pursue one's own self-interest to the exclusion of everything else? It may not, of course, be at all absurd to claim that maximization of self interest is not irrational, at least not necessarily so, but to argue that anything other than maximizing self-interest must be irrational seems altogether extraordinary.
>
> The self-interest view of rationality involves *inter alia* a firm rejection of the "ethics-related view of motivation." (Sen 1987, 15)

When he critiques Adam Smith (*The Wealth of the Nations,* 1776), Sen notices that Smith discussed the possibility of famines "arising from economic processes involving the market mechanism" (Sen 1987, 26). Smith's conclusion is that "people are led to starvation and famine through a process over which they themselves have little control" (pp. 26–27). Because of this, Sen argues, Smith was often used and cited by "imperial administrators for justification of refusing to intervene in famines in such diverse places as Ireland, India and China." According to Sen, however, there is nothing to "indicate that Smith's ethical approach to public policy would have precluded intervention in support of the entitlements of the poor. Furthermore, "the neglect of his ethical analysis of sentiment and behavior fits well into the distancing of economics from ethics that has occurred with the development of modern economics" (Sen 1987, 27–28).

While Sen proposes a link between ethics and economics from above (which of course should not be neglected), Dussel's reading of Marx proposes the link between ethics and economics from below (which of course cannot be isolated from the former). Following Dussel's distinction between "reformation" and "transformation" (Dussel 1998b, 528–37), we can say that Sen's goal is an ethic of "reformation" whereas Dussel's is an ethic of "transformation." Sen's ethics start from the assertion that people and land should be subjected to the economic machine and that the economic machine should be ethically programmed. In contrast, Dussel departs from the fact that land and people are not "naturally" subject to capitalist economy. They are "exterior" to the system, the moment in which they are subsumed into the system (e.g., the totality), their exteriority becomes living labor and land and people are then twice marked over. On the one hand, they are marginal to the system because they are exploited; on the other hand, they maintain the trace of their exteriority, which, in Levinas's term, will not be an alternative to capital but "otherwise than capitalism." This is one of the strongest arguments from the perspective of Amerindians in Latin America (e.g., the Zapatistas) and of Native Americans in the United States (Deloria [1991] 1999).

I cannot indulge myself in an extended exploration of the consequences of Dussel's interpretation of Marx, since my goal is to explain the links between Marx(ism) and liberation philosophy. However, I will say this: Dussel's interpretation of Marx, through Levinas, opens up a crack between the opposed and symmetrical philosophies of liberalism and Marxism as inheritors of the Enlightenment's contribution to the formation of the Europe of Nations. If Levinas reflected the "otherwise than being" (while before him Heidegger introduced "being" to counteract the "modern subject" of liberal thinking), such a reflection was more than a critique of Western philosophy—it was a critique from the Jewish history and experience. In the modern world-system, Jewish history is the history of the enemy within, a space inside and outside the system at the same time. To suggest that Levinas's main contribution to philosophy was to think from the crack in which the exterior and the marginal become at the same time part of and yet negated by the system is not too far-fetched. I will go even further and suggest that if Dussel was highly impressed by Levinas's *Totality and Infinity* (1961), it was because he "saw" in Levinas's philosophy a reflection in and from the exteriority and the margins. Dussel introduced the enemy within the modern/colonial world, the colonial experience.

3. COLONIALITY, "THIRD WORLD," AND LIBERATION PHILOSOPHY

The marginal space in which Dussel locates himself is equivalent in logic, but not similar in content, to the historical experience invoked and theorized in Levinas's work. Although Levinas rebounds from what I have called elsewhere the "imperial difference," Dussel is assumed to live in and think from the "colonial difference." Let me explain. While the conflict between Christians and Jews can be traced back to even before the sixteenth century, the expulsion of the Jews from Spain established a landmark in the history of the modern world. The expulsion of the Jews, as well as the Moors, was indeed a constitutive moment of modernity/coloniality. The expulsion of the Jews from Spain (yet not from the rest of Europe) established the imperial differences within the system. The expulsion of the Moors (and simultaneously the encounter with the Amerindians, the initiation of the slave trade from Africa to the Americas, and the Jesuit missions in China since 1582) established the external borders of the modern/colonial world. These events established the colonial difference or, in other words, the colonial structure of the modern/colonial world.

It is not by chance but by historical and logical necessity that Dussel made the sixteenth century a fundamental historical moment in his conception of liberation philosophy. Furthermore, if Dussel's philosophical reflections were grounded in the colonial history of the modern world since the sixteenth century, the historical present in which he embraced liberation philosophy was the moment in which the world had been divided into three sectors: the first, second, and third worlds. The very conception of the Third World was the rearticulation of the colonial difference once the antithesis of liberalism, communism in the Soviet Union, had become a historical reality. The Third World was, in certain ways, the exteriority of a system whose totality was divided between "left" and "right." However, the exteriority of the Third World was a marginal exteriority, since it was also part of the totality, but a part without power. It is my intuition that Dussel perceived the similarities between the exteriority of the Jews in the history of the modern/colonial world (and the Holocaust, which motivated a great deal of Levinas's reflections) and the exteriority of the Third World during the Cold War. The links between geopolitical spaces and the production of knowledge (in this case, philosophy) have been clear to Dussel since the 1970s. In his *Filosofía de la liberación* ([1977] 1980), he included the diagram on page 36.

I would say, then, that there is a strict geopolitical correlation between the Third World and the emergence of liberation philosophy on the one hand, and between liberation philosophy and Levinas's philosophical reflections on "otherwise than being" after the Holocaust on the other. However, I will not say, as Moreno Villa (1998) does, that Dussel's philosophy is "a Third World philosophy for the Third World" and an intent toward "superseding European ontology." I do not think Moreno Villa will assume that Habermas's is an ethic and a political project only for Europe and Germany, in the same way he assumes that Dussel's is for Latin America. I have already made this argument vis-à-vis very complimentary readings of Darcy Ribeiro's theory of civilization, celebrated and recognized as a "Third World theory for the Third World" (Mignolo 1998). If it is possible to maintain statements such as this one, they should be maintained under the condition that we limit production of knowledge to its geohistorical location. Therefore, any theory or philosophy of the First World will be just for the First World and not universal. Marx, as well as Heidegger, Derrida, or Habermas, will

Figure 2.1 Opppresion of the Colonial and Neocolonial Periphery

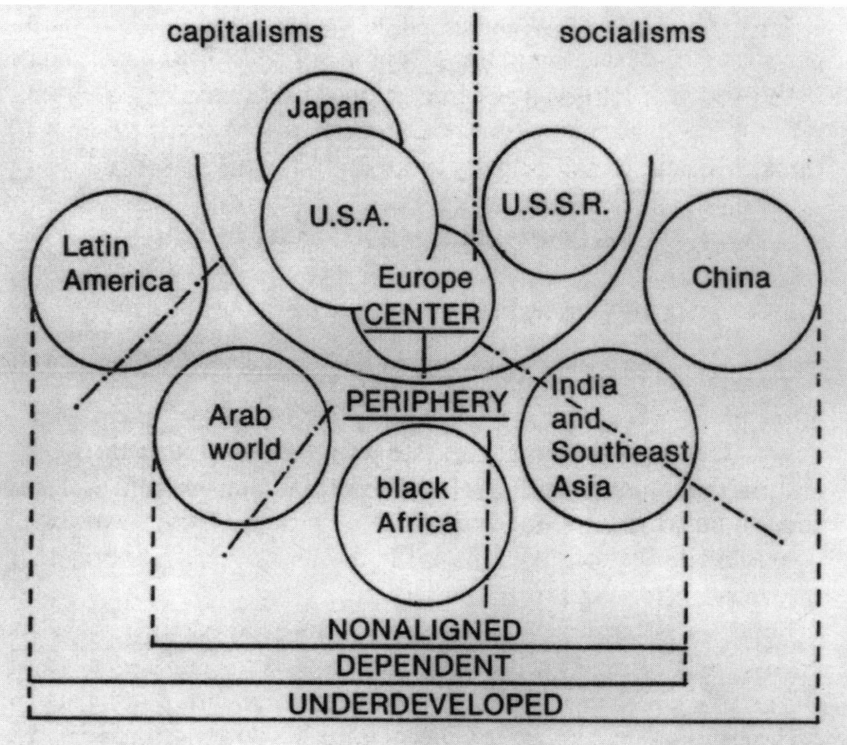

be for the First World only. Of course, such a limitation will never occur and I cannot elaborate here on the implications of such logic. Yet I would like to submit the following: if a philosophy of liberation makes sense, its liberation would be in the first place the liberation of philosophy from its Eurocentric genealogy within the modern/colonial world. One of Dussel's major contributions (whether he admits it or not) is precisely in having opened the gates to a rearticulation of the rationale between knowledge and geohistorical locations. Consequently, instead of maintaining a lineal conception of the history of philosophy and thinking of liberation philosophy as "superseding" European philosophy, I would instead think in terms of space and the geopolitics of knowledge. Thus liberation philosophy contributes to "provincialize" Europe (Chakrabarty 1992) and to show the regional dimension of European philosophy's universality claims. However, from Dussel's geohistorical and geopolitical point of view, it becomes clear that the universal claims of European philosophy are linked to the imperial cosmology of the modern/colonial world (Dussel 1996, 213–39; [1974] 1978).

Dussel's latest book, *Etica de la liberación* (1998), summarizes his long trajectory since the early 1970s. In the first place, his argument has clearly been displaced from the Cold War era to the globalization (post–Cold War) period. The main changes in the argument are the recognition of the emergence of new social actors and the formation of new historical subjects. The working class is no longer configured as Marx initially experienced it, although the process of subsuming living labor and transforming money into capital remains. The "victims" now are better characterized as "dispensable human lives" under the logic of the market, freed from both the civilizing mission and the constraints of socialist utopia. Liberation philosophy thus puts the accent on "transformation" rather than "reformation" (Dussel 1998, 528ff.):

> La praxis de liberación es la acción posible que transforma la realidad (subjetiva y social) teniendo como última referencia siempre a alguna víctima o comunidad de víctimas. La *posibilidad de efectivamente liberar a las víctimas es el criterio sobre el que se funda el principio mas complejo de esta Etica*—que subsume a todos los otros principios en un nivel mas concreto, complejo, real y crítico. [italics mine]
>
> El criterio de transformación ético-crítico es un criterio de factivilidad en referencia a las posibilidades de liberación de la víctima ante los sistemas dominantes: desde la existencia de la víctima como capacidad efectora (el "ser", lo dado). . . .
>
> Por su parte, el Principio-Liberación enuncia el deber-ser que obliga éticamente a realizar dicha transformación, exigencia que es cumplida por la propia comunidad de víctimas, bajo su re-sponsabilidad, y que se origina, práctico-materialmente, como normatividad, desde la existencia de un cierto Poder o Capacidad (el ser) en dicha víctima.
>
> Se trata entonces del enfrentamiento entre un movimiento social organizado de las víctimas y un sistema formal dominante (el feminismo ante el patriarcalismo machista; los asalariados, pobres y excluidos por el desempleo ante el capitalismo que se globaliza; los ecologistas ante los subsistemas que destruyen la vida de la tierra). (1998, 553–54)

These paragraphs summarize the current formulations of Dussel's philosophy of liberation. The main question from my perspective is, What will be the role of liberation philosophy once a diversity of social actors and the constitution of new historical subjects are conceiving, planning, and enacting their own "philosophy" of liberation? How would philosophy of liberation liberate the victims? Is this a new formulation of the organic intellectual who believes the victims need a savior? Are not the victims agents of historical processes and constantly struggling to liberate themselves?

It seems to me that the logico-historical possibilities of liberation philosophy that I underlined above (e.g., a philosophy emerging in the cracks of the modern/colonial world and from the colonial difference) encounter here their historical limits as well as their regional potential (like Levinas). The splendors of philosophy (and an ethic) of liberation have been to open up coloniality of being as a legitimate place for thinking, thus showing the regional limits of the universal production of "modern" knowledge. Its miseries would be to maintain a "universal" vigilant location vis-à-vis the "victims" whose liberation is being reclaimed. Once the philosophy of liberation opens up the space of self-recognition and action for and *from* the "victims," it can no longer "dictate" the routes for social transformation *of* the "victims." The "victims" are no longer all "illiterates," as Dussel's imagination of the "poor" sometimes indicates. Indigenous social movements (ecological movements, feminism, ethnic movements, etc.) in Latin America and elsewhere no longer need a general liberation philosophy as a guidebook, although liberation philosophy will remain as a crucial space for social criticism. In fact, the splendor of liberation philosophy has been to create a particular space for social criticism of capitalism from the Third World, with universal value. The misery would be to reproduce what liberation philosophy revealed in its limits: the dictatorial function of instrumental reasons, both in its liberal and socialist versions.

4. DIVERSITY AS A UNIVERSAL PROJECT (DIVERSALITY): PHILOSOPHY OF LIBERATION AND THE COLONIALITY OF BEING

There was a historical context prompting the outburst of philosophy of liberation. In Latin America, projects of modernization and development after World War II led economists to the conclusion that thinking development and modernization in Latin America had to begin by recognizing the dependent character of the economy in Latin American countries (Jaguaribe 1970). The intersection of the influence of the Cuban Revolution and the critical liberal projects for the development of Latin America prompted the emergence of dependency theory (Cardoso and Faletto 1969, 1979). Both the contributions of CEPAL (Comisión Económica para América Latina), through its major Argentinean theoretician and economist Raúl Prebisch (De La Peña 1980), and dependency theory were an inspiration to I. Wallerstein's conception of the modern world-system building on the dependency of the periphery upon the center. This context explains, on the one hand, Dussel's early and prolonged interest and engagement with world-system theory (Dussel 1998b, 1998c). On the other hand, dependency theory brought to the foreground and into the discussion a concern with the marginal, the poor, and the miserable as the victims of capitalism. This was particularly true in Latin America when development and modernization after World War II implied a massive expansion of the American economy to Latin America in order to counter the effects and consequences of the Cuban Revolution (Ceceña Matorella 1994; Nun 1969). Catholicism and Marxism shared a common concern for the poor, and Dussel's philosophy of liberation grew out of this intersection.

Of course, there was an international context existing simultaneously with the events taking place in Latin America: the second wave of decolonizaton, in Asia and Africa. The first wave was in the Americas (United States, Haiti, and the continental Iberian colonies). Frantz Fanon's *Les damnés de la terre* (Fanon [1961] 1963) was translated by Siglo XXI Editores in Mexico and went through eight editions between 1963 and 1977. Dependency theory and liberation philosophy were the equivalents, in Latin America in the 1970s, of the debates about decolonization in Asia and Africa. The difference was the context in which these discussions were occurring. In Asia and Africa, the illusion and dreams of nation building were the dream of decolonization (Béji 1982; Chatterjee 1997), while in Latin America, where decolonization was 150 years old, the vocabulary was "independent development" and "ethical and intellectual liberation" (Fals Borda [1970] 1987) rather than "decolonization." The coloniality of being was, in different ways, being uncovered. This was a task that Fanon himself had already initiated in 1952 with *Peau noire, masques blancs* (1952). The limits of Marx, Freud, and Nietzsche that Fanon was signaling at that time in his book could not have been read yet as the consequence of the coloniality of being.

These were some of the sub-Continental and global aspects that prompted the emergence of liberation philosophy in the 1970s. My purpose in this section is to situate philosophy of liberation in contemporary projects, debates, and criticism of capitalism and Euro-centrism that have erupted all over the world since the 1970s. I do not intend to be exhaustive. I only intend to point to them for future discussions.

First was Dussel's own intentional critical engagement, mainly with Apel and Habermas but also with Ricoeur and Rorty. In this engagement, Dussel's project was and still is a liberation of philosophy as one of the consequences of philosophy of liberation. With this dialogue (Dussel 1994c), Dussel contributed to show the regional limits of universal pragmatic or of any theory, from the left or the right, that acquired its universality piggybacking the universalization of capitalism. The limits I indicated before for liberation philosophy are, at the same time, the limits that liberation philosophy uncovers for any universalizing project, starting with Christianity itself.

Dussel's dialogical engagement with Apel and Habermas contributed, as I suggested above, to the process of provincializing Europe and to the intellectual decolonization of philosophy and knowledge production. The most radical move of liberation philosophy in this regard could be located in two instances. First, the question is no longer the beginning of philosophy and its entire agenda but the beginning of the modern/colonial world and the role of philosophy in revealing and undoing colonial forms of domination in the modern world. Second, there is the question of the links between ethics and philosophy of liberation as a response to colonial forms of domination, that is, the coloniality of power. By these two moves, it becomes clear that transcendental pragmatic and the ethic of discourse in Apel and Habermas are universal in that their geopolitical foundations are kept in silence and not revealed. The value and relevance of transcendental pragmatic and discourse ethics, consequently, should not be located in their "universatility" but in their regionality. This is a regional philosophy that became the companion of the modern world and, in its severe critique of modernity, remained blind to the colonial horizon of the modern world and reproduced, in a secular world, the good intentions of totalizing designs introduced by Christianity. In this respect, liberation philosophy will be recognized as one of the many projects coming from the Third World linking explicitly place and knowledge, the ratio between historical locations and epistemic production (see also Eze 1997a, 1997b).

In 1981, Ranajit Guha introduced the first collection of essays, which became famous as the Subaltern Studies Series, with the following clarification:

> The word "subaltern" in the title stands for the meaning as given in the *Concise Oxford Dictionary*, that is, "of inferior rank." It will be used in these pages as a name for the general attribute of subordination in South Asian society whether this is expressed in terms of class, caste, age, gender and office or in any other way. ([1981] 1988, 35)

Thus it appears that the extension of the definition of "victims" and "subalterns" is quite similar, since it includes class, gender, and age. To this definition, I would add sexuality and ethnicity, explicitly mentioned by Dussel and easily integrated into Guha's "in any other way." If the semantic extension of the definition is similar, one can say that the term "victims" (and its forerunner, the "poor") is a vocabulary that can be traced back to Christianity, while the term "subaltern" belongs to the vocabulary of Marxism. This is difficult to reconcile if we think of the original moment of Marx and Engels taken position vis-à-vis the church, but perhaps not so distant if we remember Dussel's reading of *Das Kapital* and its emphasis on "living labor." Living labor, in Dussel's interpretation, is that which is exterior to the system and when subsumed remains in the margins and transforms money in capital; in a sense, it is subalternity (although not the "subaltern" as a particular group of people) by excellence. If we agree then that for Dussel, after his extensive reading of Marx in the late 1970s and early 1980s, liberation philosophy is grounded in the exteriority of living labor in capitalistic economy and that such exteriority is the paradigm of subalternity (that includes all the groups mentioned by Guha and Dussel himself), then liberation philosophy and subaltern studies are not as far removed from each other as one might think.

Perhaps the differences between the two should be looked at primarily in the difference of historical rhythms in postindependence Latin America on the one hand and postcolonial (or postpartition) India on the other. Or perhaps the differences are also due to reading Marx and Gramsci together with Foucault and Derrida on the one hand, and Marx and Gramsci together with Levinas on the other. There is also the fact that subaltern studies was mainly a historiographical project, whereas the philosophy of liberation was primarily a philosophical and ethical project. Furthermore, liberation philosophy was produced in the Spanish language, whereas subaltern studies was in English from its very inception. All of this is necessary if we are to think liberation philosophy in Latin America, and subaltern studies in India (and South Asia).

Yet what about Latin American subaltern studies? This project emerged within Latin American studies in the United States, particularly among literary criticism, cultural studies, historiography, and anthropology, at the intersection of the collapse of the Soviet Union and the failure of the Sandinista movement in Nicaragua, with South Asian subaltern studies. In other words, it emerged as a result of an interdisciplinary group instead of a perspective from history or philosophy, as was the case for subaltern studies and liberation philosophy respectively. A question remains, however: Why did the Latin American subaltern studies group engage in discussion with the South Asian group and not with Latin American projects with similar goals, liberation philosophy being one of them? At the beginning of the 1990s, liberation philosophy was difficult to ignore, even among those who disagreed with it. The failure of Sandinism can be explained by Dussel's interpretation of the limits of Marxist readings of Marx, from Lukács to Althusser and the Sandinistas. Perhaps one of the reasons for the connections between South Asian subaltern studies and Latin American subaltern studies was that both had a geopolitical framing, South Asia and Latin America respectively, although the respective ratio between the geohistorical location of their members varied and still varies greatly. Members of South Asian and Latin American subaltern studies are part of an equation between production of knowledge and geohistorical location that places them in a conflictive relation with area studies. Instead, Levinas and Dussel linked place and knowledge differently. In fact, the intersection of place and knowledge was a "given" from which exteriority (of the Jewish in Europe and the coloniality of being in Latin America) was perceived.

If the philosophy of liberation cannot be taken as a new sacred project, it has at least three dimensions on which it would be worthwhile to capitalize:

- Liberation philosophy can be seen as an indirect response to Chakrabarty's dilemma in the domain of historiography. This dilemma stated in a particular way the tensions between place and knowledge, both knowledge as discipline and knowledge "about." Chakrabarty's dilemma was of a disciplinary nature: the history of the Third World cannot be written as a discipline as long as it remains a discipline of the First World (Chakrabarty 1992). From the perspective of liberation philosophy, the way out of this dilemma would be to work in a double articulation: a project of liberation and a critique of the limits of First World philosophy, recognizing, at the same time, the exteriority of living labor. Liberation philosophy, as living labor, is labor that engages critically with the totality of the system, that constantly marks its borders and its limits, instead of being subsumed by and from the perspective of the system. Thus a way out of the dilemma is to turn the analysis of the logic of capital in its appropriation and subalternization of living labor on its head and to claim the exteriority of living labor as a project of liberation.

- As such, liberation philosophy can be conceived as one of many historically located social and intellectual projects of analyzing, denouncing, and overcoming oppressive regimes and social structures, whether they are globally hegemonic (neoliberalism) or locally hegemonic (religious fundamentalism and local patriarchies). If the splendor of liberation philosophy is to contribute to revealing the limits of any abstract universals (from the left or the right) and to open the doors for diversity as a universal project (diversality), then the philosophy of liberation cannot conceive itself as a new universal. As long as forms of domination are multiple, there cannot be a single principle of social transformation, and a grand theory is no longer possible. Yet macrohistories from the perspective of coloniality (not telling the new "truth" of history but revealing the silence of modern historiography) are more and more necessary. In this regard, Dussel's macrohistory of modernity/coloniality, in which he locates the philosophy of liberation project, is comparatively as necessary as it is impossible to have any single macrohistory. Yet the limits of development and modernization no longer require alternative developments, but are alternative to developments, as Boaventura de Sousa Santos (Santos [1995] 1998) and Escobar (1995) have asserted. Consequently, alternatives to capitalism are needed—not capitalism otherwise, but rather otherwise than capitalism. Diversality as a universal project requires a new theory of translation, a theory of translation in multiple directions rather than translations that followed the directionality of power (imperial and colonial), which was conceived and went together with a universal concept of knowledge.
- Liberation philosophy cannot be a monotopic and universal discourse "speaking" the liberation of the diverse constituencies of civil society that can be identified as "oppressed" (racially, sexually, generationally, economically, etc.). The time has come when many of Dussel's "victims" or Guha's "subalterns" can speak by themselves, and both of these scholars know full well that subalterns have difficulties in speaking. The question for the future here is double. First, how can academic work join with the intellectual and social work of liberation being carried out by communities in subaltern (or victim) positions outside the university? Additionally, within the university, how can the philosophy of liberation be just a point of reference rather than a textbook between diverse academic agendas (ethnic studies, queer studies, Latino or Afro-American studies, gender studies, etc.), whose goals are also to link scholarship with social transformation (see, for instance, Alexander and Mohanty 1997; Alcoff 1997, 1999; and Harding 1998)? If the philosophy of liberation owes much to the emergence of new social actors and new historical subjects, it is also obvious that it (or any other project from the left

> or the right) cannot speak for them. The great lesson of liberation philosophy is, perhaps, the liberation of the sacred role assumed by secular science and cultures of scholarship. Liberation philosophy, not just using the philosophy for liberation outside itself, means precisely that thinking will no longer be attached to the chains of Western epistemology from the Greeks to today, traveling through Greek, Latin, German, French, and English. After all, liberation philosophy is a contribution from colonial Spanish in Latin America. As far as philosophy of liberation is a project in the domain of the academy but with a desire to be influential beyond it, it has to be open to the danger of its own transformation. Otherwise, it could become a new version or a dogmatic version of liberal or socialist ideas that concluded with forms of totalitarianism that were far beyond the good intentions foregrounding the original project. Liberation philosophy would be subjected to the same charges that Vine Deloria Jr., writing and reflecting from the experience of Native American histories, makes concerning liberation theology. It is something that is good to have as a reformative project, although we shall not stop there. The aim should be to turn liberation against theology instead of assuming theology as a ground for liberation. (Deloria ([1977] 1999)

I perceive philosophy of liberation as one of many critical and ethical projects that have emerged in the past forty years, and are still emerging, in response to the increasing oppression of capitalism, globalization, and neoliberalism. These include critical projects for social transformation that can complement, but never be replaced by, noble critical and ethical projects of reformation, such as the theology of liberation, the work of NGOs, or public policy implemented by the state. As a critical project in philosophy, liberation philosophy should be in solidarity with the project of the postcolonial "negative critic" proposed and being executed by African philosophers. First, what both projects have in common is the history and awareness of colonialism, or, in other terms, the need (as an imperial imposition) to deal with philosophy. However, this is the need to deal with philosophy "out of place," in Africa or Latin America—although not only in Latin America, since Cornel West has demonstrated how in Anglo America there is, from Emerson to Rorty going through C. S. Peirce and Dewey, a constant evasion of (Continental) philosophy (West 1989). However, in African and Latin American philosophy, the concern with colonialism, coloniality of power, and the colonial difference is, for obvious historical reasons, much more acute than in the Anglo-American tradition. Second, the "negative critic" as a project emanating from the variegated experiences of different countries with European colonialisms (Eze 1997b, 1–21) runs parallel to Dussel's constant reference to the colonization of the Americas, mainly by the Spaniards and secondarily by the Portuguese. The historical rhythms of (post)colonial processes are certainly different. Africa was mainly colonized by northern European countries and its decolonization took place in the second half of the twentieth century, whereas in the Americas, decolonization took place at the end of the eighteenth century. In 1776, the United States achieved independence; in 1804 the Haitian Revolution occurred; and between 1810 and 1830, several continental Latin American countries became independent. However, the frame of the modern/colonial world since the sixteenth century is common to both traditions. Eze, for instance, asserts that by the term "colonialism" we should understand the indescribable crisis disproportionately suffered by the African peoples in their tragic encounter with the European world from the beginning of the fifteenth century through the end of the nineteenth into the first half of the twentieth century. This was a period marked by the horror and violence of the transatlantic slave trade, the imperial occupation of most sections of Africa and the forced administration of its peoples, and the resilient and enduring ideologies and practices of European cultural superiority (ethnocentrism) and "racial" supremacy (racism) (Eze 1997a, 4).

Both Dussel's philosophy of liberation and the African philosophy of the "negative critic" take issue with the imperial underpinning of Continental philosophy, from Kant and Hegel to Apel, Derrida, Habermas, and Foucault (Bernasconi 1997). Serequeberhan, for example, confronts the limits of Focault's reading of Kant's "What is Enlightenment?" To Foucault's credit, says Serequeberhan, he indicates that Kant's emancipatory project "has a domineering and tyrannical effect in 'respect to others,'" that is, non-European people." However, Foucault never asked why that was the case and "neither pursues nor responds to the question" (Serequeberhan 1997, 147). Eze, from his part, confronts Heidegger's assumptions about Africa and the "Negro" intelligence: "Nature has its history. But then *Negroes* would also have history. Or does nature then have no history? It can enter into the past as something transitory, but not everything that fades away enters into history" (Heidegger, quoted in Eze 1997a, 13). Eze also confronts Habermas concerning the typologies of Africa and the African worldview that Habermas develops in his *Theory of Communicative Action,* in which he discusses reason and the rationalization of society (Eze 1997a, 13). Basically, Africa is absent from Habermas's typology of rationalities. He contemplates Judaism, Christianity, and Greek philosophy as forms of Occidental rationality, and Hinduism, Buddhism, Confucianism, and Taoism as Oriental forms of rationality. Not only is sub-Saharan Africa absent but so is North Africa, since Islam has also been forgotten in Habermas's typology. Dussel, as I have mentioned, has engaged himself in a similar critical dialogue with Continental philosophers (Dussel 1994c, 1996), with motivations similar to the ones that animate the African philosophers. Bernasconi has recognized these motivations as the "challenge of African to Continental Philosophy" (Bernasconi 1997).

5. CLOSING REMARKS

In closing, I would like to also bring into this picture of diverse critical engagement with Occidental (to use Habermas's term) philosophy and concept of rationality, the contributions of Osage lawyer, activist, and thinker Vine Deloria Jr. In an early article on theology of liberation (Deloria [1977] 1999) he observed that "liberation theology assumes that the common experience of oppression is sufficient to create the desire for a new coalition of dissident minorities. Adherents of this movement indiscriminately classify all minorities . . . in a single category of people seeking liberation" ([1977] 1999, 100). One of the consequences of this is that liberation theology, thus conceived, is a reformist project that remains under the control of an abstract universal (a Christian conception of liberation): the diversity of singular projects emanating from the personal perspective of oppressed groups. Deloria adds that liberation theology "does not seek to destroy the roots of oppression, but merely to change the manner in which oppression manifests itself" ([1977] 1999, 100). In a more recent article on vision and community ([1990] 1999, 108), Deloria contrasts and compares Christian and secular Western "vision" with that of Native Americans:

> The basic philosophical difference between the American tribal religions and the world religions, Christianity being the world religion most likely to come into direct contact with the tribal religions, is the difference between time and space, between time and places, between remembered history and sacred location. At this point Christianity and by extension liberation theology, is in mortal danger. ([1990] 1999, 116)

From Native American perspectives, the difference between white and Indian people lies in the fact that, according to a Crow Indian chief, white people have ideas while Indian people have visions. Visions require action and action manifests itself in the community, whereas ideas have a limited relevance. An idea never reaches the entire community, since "it only reaches those who have the ability to grasp it and the rest of the community is left struggling for understanding" ([1990] 1999, 117). Thus a radical liberation theology, which will join critical liberation philosophy, should question the basic assumptions of Occidental rationality such as the continuing concept of time, human description of nature as absolute knowledge, or "that inductive and deductive reasoning are the primary tools for gaining knowledge" ([1977] 1999, 107). As we have seen, this is not just a claim from a Native American perspective (which will put us again on the reproduction of dichotomies) nor an inverted "us" versus "them" (which will continue reproducing separatism), but a critical engagement with Occidental categories of rationality from the perspective of Native American visions, African critical philosophy, and Latin American liberation philosophy. The multiplication of "dichotomies" concludes in a diversity of understanding, in a diversity or universal projects (diversality) engaging Occidental rationality from local histories and colonized/subaltern knowledges.

Instead of saying that philosophy of liberation is a "new" paradigm and reproducing the sense of "newness" and the linear history of modern epistemology, I would suggest thinking in terms of space and complementary solidarities instead of superseding the old and bringing forth (again!) a new paradigm, thus translating the logic of development in economy to all cultural orders. Instead, I would say that liberation philosophy invites us to think otherwise, that is, to think in the spatial simultaneity of local histories, as well as social and intellectual projects responding to global designs (e.g., neoliberalism or a planetary revolution of the working class) from the experiences of the colonial difference (the force that produces Dussel's victims and poor) and colonial subalternities in the modern/colonial world order.

If there is a "new" paradigm, of which philosophy of liberation is an important and pioneering member, this paradigm is not mono-topic but pluri-topic; it is di- or pluri-versal rather than universal. We have seen some of this diversality emerging from dwelling in the colonial difference: Third World femininism and women of color, subaltern studies, postcoloniality and African philosophy, and Native American critique of Euro-centrism and Christianity. In Latin America, Amerindian (Yampara Huarachi 1992) as well as Creole (Rengifo Vásquez 1991; Valladolid Rivera 1998) intellectuals have been reflecting on the contribution of Amerindian thought and tradition as a critique of development and modernization. When the Amerindian or Native American perspective, enacted when Amerindian, Native American, or Creole intellectuals enter the picture, appears, there are two critiques that appear almost instantaneously: one is the reproduction of dichotomies (e.g., Amerindian versus European cosmologies); the other is the New Age bent of such discourses. Curiously enough, the first criticism does not take into account the fact that such dichotomies were prompted and constructed by the European colonial discourse. Of course, they will not be reproduced. Yet, at the same time, it is necessary to tell the dichotomous story from the Indian perspective as well. Second, dichotomies abound; they are multiplying all over the planet, between Eurocentric values and Asian and African histories and cultures, between Eurocentric values and Amerindian and Afro-Americans in Latin America and the Caribbean as well as the United States. As far as the "New Age look" is concerned, we have two choices. One has already been made. This is to devalue (as anthropologists and leftist intellectuals are doing) or to celebrate (like the media, bourgeois "discovery" of Amerindian medicine and art, etc.) Native Americans and Amerindian-based discourses because of their idealistic perspective. The other alternative, opened up by critical positions such as philosophy of liberation, is to enact a critique of Western knowledge from the colonial exteriority that Dussel has uncovered for us (Dussel [1992] 1995). This is the exteriority of the colonial difference shared by Amerindians and Native Americans, Afro-Americans, women of color, and Third World women, and from where they are already acting and responding. If nothing else (and this is not a small achievement), one of the great contributions of liberation philosophy has been to initiate *the* liberation *of* philosophy and epistemology. The task of the future will be to push philosophy of liberation to the limits of its own foundation; toward an "otherwise" than philosophy as the ultimate horizon for liberation or, even better, decolonization of knowledge and of the social order. "Otherwise than the (coloniality of) being" will be the horizon for projects of social transformation transcending reformative ones oriented toward searching "being otherwise."

REFERENCES

Alcoff, Linda Martín. 1997. "The Politics of Postmodern Feminism, Revisited." *Cultural Critique* 36 (Spring 1997): 5-27.

———. 1999. "Latina/o Identity Politics." In *The Good Citizen*, edited by D. Batstone and E. Mendieta, 93-112. New York: Routledge.

Alexander, M. J., and Ch. T. Mohanty, eds. 1997. *Feminist Genealogies, Colonial Legacies, Democratic Futures*. Bloomington: Indiana University Press.

Apel, Karl-Otto. 1994. "La pragmática transcendental y los problemas éticos." In *Debate en torno a la ética del discurso de Apel: Diálogo filosófico norte-sur desde América latina,* edited by E. Dussel, 37-56. Mexico: Siglo XXI Editores.

———.1996. "Response by Karl-Otto Apel: Discourse Ethics before the Challenge of Liberation Philosophy." In *The Underside of Modernity: Apel, Ricoeur, Rorty, Taylor, and the Philosophy of Liberation*, translated by E. Mendieta, 163-204. New York: Humanities Press International.

Aricó, José. 1980. *Marx y América Latina*. Lima: Centro de Estudios para el Desarrollo y la Participación.

———.1988. "La experiencia de *Pasado y Presente*." In *La cola del diablo: Itinerario de Gramsci en América Latina*, 63-82. Caracas: Nueva Sociedad.

Béji, Hélé. 1982. *Désenchantement national: Essai sur la décolonization*. Paris: Francois Maspero.

Bernasconi, Robert. 1997. "African Philosophy's Challenge to Continental Philosophy." In *Postcolonial African Philosophy: A Critical Reader,* edited by E. C. Eze, 183-96. London: Blackwell.

Cardoso, F. E., and E. Faletto. 1969. *Dependencia y desarrollo en América Latina: Ensayo de interpretación sociológica.* Mexico: Siglo XXI Editores.

———.1979. *Dependency and Development in Latin America*. Berkeley: University of California Press.

Castro-Gómez, Santiago. 1997. *Crítica de la razón latinoamericana*. Barcelona: Puvill.

Ceceña Matorella, Ana Esther. 1994. "Los miserables en la teoría social latinoamericana." In *La teoría social latinoamericana.* Vol. 2, *Subdesarrollo y dependencia,* edited by R. M. Marini and M. Millán, 237-262. Mexico: Ediciones del Caballito.

Cerutti Guldberg, Horacio. 1983. *Filosofía de la liberación latinoamericana*. Mexico: Fondo de Cultura Económica.

Chakrabarty, Dipesh. 1989. *Rethinking Working-Class History: Bengal, 1890-1940*. Princeton: Princeton University Press.

———.1992. "Postcoloniality and the Artifice of History: Who Speaks for 'Indian' Pasts?" *Representations* 37: 1-26.

———.1993. "Marx after Marxism: Subaltern Histories and the Question of Difference." *Poligraph* 6-7: 10-16.

Chatterjee, Partha. 1997. *A Possible India: Essays in Political Criticism*. New Delhi: Oxford India Paperbacks.

De La Peña, Sergio. 1980. "Las ideas principales de la CEPAL." In *Pensamiento latinoamericano: CEPAL,* edited by R. Prebisch y A. Pinto, 14-35. Mexico: Instituto de Investigación Económica y Universidad Nacional Autónoma de Mexico.

Deloria, Vine, Jr. [1971] 1994. *God Is Red: A Native View of Religion*. Golden, Colo.: Fulcrum.

——. [1977] 1999a. "On Liberation." In *For This Land: Writings on Religion in America*, 100-107. New York: Routledge.

——. [1991] 1999b. "Reflection and Revelation: Knowing Land, Places, and Ourselves." In *For This Land: Writings on Religion in America*, 250-60. New York: Routledge.

Dussel, E. [1974] 1978. *Ethics and the Theology of Liberation*. Translated by B. F. McWilliams. New York: Basic.

——. [1977] 1980. *Philosophy of Liberation*. Translated by A. Martinez and Ch. Morkovsky. New York: Orbis.

——. 1985. *La producción teórica de Marx: Un comentario a los "Grundrisse."* Mexico: Siglo XXI Editores.

——. 1988. *Hacia un Marx desconocido: Un comentario de los "Manuscritos del 61-63."* Mexico: Siglo XXI Editores.

——. 1990a. "Marx's Economic Manuscripts of 1861-63 and the 'Concept' of Dependency." *Latin American Perspectives* 17, no. 2: 62-101.

——. 1990b. *El último Marx (1863-1882) y la liberación latinoamericana*. Mexico: Siglo XXI Editores.

——. [1987] 1994a. "Trabajo vivo y filosofía de la liberación." In *Historia de la filosofía y filosofía de la liberación*, 205-220. Bogota: Editorial Nueva América.

——. [1990] 1994b. "Las cuatro redacciones de 'El Capital' (1857-1880)." In *Historia de la filosofía y filosofía de la liberación*. Bogota: Editorial Nueva América, 221-52.

——. 1994c. "Una década Argentina (1966-1976) y el origen de la filosofía de la liberación." In *Historia de la filosofía y filosofía de la liberación*, 55-96. Bogota: Editorial América.

——. 1995. "Eurocentrism and Modernity (Introduction to the Frankfurt Lectures)." In *The Postmodern Debate in Latin America*, edited by J. Berverley, J. Oviedo, and M. Aronna, 34-54. Durham, N.C.: Duke University Press.

——. [1992] 1995. *The Inventory of the Americas: Eclipse of "the Other" and the Myth of Modernity.* Translated by M. D. Barber. New York: Continuum.

——. 1996. "Response by Enrique Dussel: World System, Politics, and the Economics of Liberation Philosophy." In *The Underside of Modernity: Apel, Ricoeur, Rorty, Taylor, and the Philosophy of Liberation*, translated by E. Mendieta, 213-239. New York: Humanities Press International.

——. 1998a. "Beyond Eurocentrism." In *The Cultures of Globalization,* edited by F. Jameson and M. Miyoshi, 5-35. Durham, N.C.: Duke University Press.

——. 1998b. "En búsqueda del sentido (Origen y desarrollo de una filosofía de la liberación." *Revista anthropos* 180 (September-October): 13-36.

——. 1998c. *Etica de la liberación en la edad de la globalización y de la exclusión*. Mexico: Universidad Nacional Autónoma de México.

Dussel, Enrique, ed. 1994. *Debate en torno a la ética del discurso de Apel: Diálogo filosófico norte-sur desde América latina.* Mexico: Siglo XXI Editores.

Dussel, E., and D. E. Guillot. 1975. *Liberación latinoamerica y Emmanuel Levinas*. Buenos Aires: Editorial Bonum.

Escobar, Arturo. 1995. *Encountering Development: The Making and Unmaking of the Third World*. Princeton: Princeton University Press.

Eze, Emmanuel Chukwudi. 1997a. "The Color of Reason: The Idea of 'Race' in Kant's Anthropology." In *Postcolonial African Philosophy: A Critical Reader,* 103-40. Oxford: Blackwell.

——. 1997b. "Philosophy and the (Post)colonial." In *Postcolonial African Philosophy: A Critical Reader,* 1-22. Oxford: Blackwell.

Fals Borda, Orlando. [1970] 1987. *Ciencia propia y colonialismo intelectual*. Bogota: Carlos Valencia Editores.

Fanon, Frantz. [1961] 1963. *Los condenados de la tierra*. Mexico: Fondo de Cultura Económica.

———. *Peau noire, masques blancs*. Paris: Du Seuil.

Guha, Ranajit. 1988. Preface to *Selected Subaltern Studies*. New York: Oxford University Press.

Harding, Sandra. 1998. *Is Science Multi-Cultural? Postcolonialisms, Feminisms, and Epistemologies*. Bloomington: Indiana University Press.

Jaguaribe, Helio, ed. 1970. *La dependencia política-económica de América Latina*. Mexico: Siglo XXI Editores.

Levinas, Emmanuel. [1961] 1969. *Totality and Infinity: An Essay on Exteriority*. Translated by A. Lingis. Pittsburgh: Duquesne University Press.

———. [1974] 1981. *Otherwise Than Being: Or Beyond Essence*. Translated by A. Lingis. New York: Kluwer.

Mignolo, Walter D. 1998. "Globalization, Civilization Processes, and the Relocation of Languages and Cultures." In *The Cultures of Globalization*, edited by F. Jameson and M. Miyoshi, 35–52. Durham, N.C.: Duke University Press.

Mohanty, Ch. T., A. Russo, and L. Torres, eds. 1991. *Third World Women and the Politics of Feminism*. Bloomington: Indiana University Press.

Moreno Villa, M. 1998. "Husserl, Heidegger, Levinas y la filosofía de la liberación." *Revista anthropos* 180: 47–57.

Nun, José. 1969. "Superpoblación relativa, ejército industrial de reserva y masa marginal." *Revista latinoamericana de sociologia* 5, no. 2: 165–80.

Rengifo Vásquez Grimaldo. 1991. "Es posible un desarrollo alternativo? Desaprender la modernidad para aprender lo andino: La tecnologia y sus efectos en el desarrollo rural." *Revista Unitas* 4.

Salazar Bondy, Augusto. 1969. *¿Existe una filosofía en nuestra América?* Mexico: Siglo XXI Editores.

Santos, Boaventura de Sousa. [1995] 1998. *De la mano de Alicia: Lo social y lo político en la postmodernidad.* Translated by C. Bernal and M. G. Villegas. Bogota: Universidad de los Andes y Siglo del Hombre Editores.

Schelkshorn, Hans. 1994. "Introducción: Discurso y liberación (un acercamiento crítico a la 'ética del discurso' en Apel y Habermas y a la 'ética de la liberación de Dussel')." In *Debate en torno a la ética del discurso de Apel: Diálogo filosófica norte-sur desde América latina,* edited by E. Dussel, 11-36. Mexico: Siglo XXI Editores.

Sen, Amartya. 1987. *On Ethics and Economics*. New York: Blackwell.

Serequeberhan, Tsenay. 1997. "The Critique of Eurocentrism and the Practice of African Philosophy." In *Postcolonial African Philosophy: A Critical Reader,* edited by E. Ch. Eze, 141-161. Oxford: Blackwell.

Valladolid Rivera, Julio. 1998. "Andean Peasant Agriculture: Nurturing a Diversity of Life in the *Chacra*." In *The Spirit of Regeneration: Andean Culture Confronting Western Notions of Development* edited by F. Apfel-Marglin, 51-88. London: Zed.

Wallerstein, Immanuel. 1995. "World-Systems Analysis: The Second Phase." In *Unthinking the Social Sciences: The Limits of Nineteenth-Century Paradigms*, 266-72. New York: Polity.

Warrior, Robert Allen. 1995. *Tribal Secrets: Recovering American Indian Intellectual Traditions*. Minneapolis: University of Minnesota Press.

West, Cornel. 1989. *The American Evasion of Philosophy: A Genealogy of Pragmatism.* Madison: University of Wisconsin Press.
Yampara Huarachi, Simón. 1992. "Economía comunitaria aymara." In *La cosmovisión Aymara*. Edited by H. V. den Berg and N. Schiffers. La Paz: Hisbol, Biblioteca Andina.
Zea, Leopoldo. 1974. "La filosofía latinoamericana como filosofía de la liberación." In *Dependencia y liberación en la cultura latinoamericana*, 57-76. Mexico: Joaquín Mortiz.

3

The Material Principle and the Formal Principle in Dussel's Ethics

James L. Marsh

In this chapter I reflect on Enrique Dussel's *Etica de la liberación en la edad de la globalización y la exclusión*. It is very likely Dussel's greatest book—his most comprehensive, most original, and most rigorous—a culmination and a synthesis of work that he has been carrying on for years in the ethics and politics of liberation. In earlier work he was responding to and using primarily the work of Heidegger and Levinas. Since then, Dussel has confronted and critically appropriated, among other thinkers, the political economy of Marx and the discourse ethics of Apel and Habermas.[1] This latest work synthesizes Heidegger and Levinas with Marx and Apel–Habermas, early with late Dussel. Since the inauguration of his project for an ethics of liberation, Dussel has been concerned with the reality of economic globalization and the way that it negatively affects the Third World. Very early in his work, therefore, Dussel uses the theme, derived from Levinas, of the marginalized, excluded, exploited individual and collective other, relatively external to a system of economic, political, and social domination now centered in North America, Europe, and Japan. Ethics, Dussel insists in his early and late works, must be done from the perspective of the Other. But now that sense of the Other is richly mediated by Marxist hermeneutics, Habermasian-Apelian discourse ethics, and Dussel's own material ethical principle in a "critically modernist" or "transmodern," not postmodern, manner.[2]

Following Dussel, we can say that there is a preferential option for the poor, oppressed, and marginalized that can be argued for in a rigorous philosophical manner, which is necessary if we are going to be in the truth and stay in the truth. Otherwise we are most likely philosophizing from the perspective of the oppressive center that claims to be in the truth but actually is not.[3]

This current, superb work, then, is marked by a systematic development of Dussel's ethics, worked out in the form of a very comprehensive, thoroughgoing, far-reaching dialogue with the history of philosophy, ethics, and critical theory. His ethics is in two parts, a foundational and a critical–liberatory. Part 1 is in turn divided into three parts, each covered in a chapter: the material principle, the formal, communicative principle, and the feasibility principle. Part 2, using these principles as positively established, erects a negative critique of national and international capitalism, applying each principle in turn. Thus chapter 4, the first chapter of part 2, shows how such capitalism violates the material principle, chapter 5 how it violates the formal principle, and chapter 6 how it violates the principle of feasibility. On the basis of this negative critique, we are in a position to construct a positive, legitimately utopian alternative to the present system. The present system of national and international capitalism, because it is antilife, antiparticipatory, and unfeasible for the majority of people living under it, must be transformed, not merely reformed, into a system that is truly life enhancing and affirming, genuinely communal and democratic, and really feasible technically and ethically for all of its inhabitants.

Because I will be focusing on the distinction and relation between the material and formal principle in Dussel's ethics, I will be concentrating in this chapter primarily on Dussel's chapters 1–2. After exposing Dussel's conception of the principles, I will develop some of the implications of these principles as they are carried out and applied in part 2 of his work. Then I will briefly reflect critically on the scope and validity of Dussel's achievement. This should be of great interest because Dussel relativizes the role of discourse ethics in Apel and Habermas, while not denying the validity of such ethics. But in Dussel's scheme, discourse ethics is preceded by a material, ethical principle—a principle of life—and it is followed by a principle of feasibility, which integrates formal and material ethics in reflecting on the human good to be achieved in just institutions.

THE MATERIAL PRINCIPLE

Dussel starts chapter 1 with the following sentence: "This is an ethic of life, that is to say, human life is the content of ethics."[4] The project of a critical ethic is to effect a critique based on the dignity of each human life that is victimized, oppressed, or excluded. The material principle is "the obligation to produce, reproduce, and develop the concrete human life of each human subject in community."[5] This principle is universal because each human culture is a way of trying to achieve the happiness proper to the good life as such. Each society in its economic, political, and cultural domains has at bottom and ultimately the content of the production, reproduction, and development of human life. The economy, for example, produces goods that sustain and enhance physical life, and cultural institutions such as art museums contribute to the development of aesthetic life. Human life, therefore, has various interrelated levels—physical, emotional, economic, aesthetic, political, intellectual, and religious.[6]

Dussel here distinguishes between "material" with an *a,* which denotes the content of human life on various levels, and "materiel" with an *e,* which refers only to the physical level. Dussel's sense of material is the first sense, which he argues is also Marx's sense; Marx also makes human life the ethical criterion in the light of which capitalism is criticized as unjust and unhappy. Dussel takes over the norm and critique from Marx and extends them into a critique of capitalism as a neoimperialist, international system in a way that Marx did not develop fully. Like Marx, Dussel emphasizes the concrete, embodied, incarnate character of human life, but not in a way that denies the distinctiveness of the aesthetic, ethical, intellectual, and spiritual levels founded on such incarnate being, expressing it, relating back to it, interpreting it, and transforming it.[7]

The material principle has two levels, or aspects, a descriptive and an ethical. It first of all functions as a criterion of theoretical truth or, as Dussel puts it, a universal, material criterion of practical truth. Dussel argues as follows: The ethics of liberation claims that one is able to make true judgments of fact concerning the life of each human being in community. These judgments do not proceed from an instrumental or a formal reason but from a substantive reason reflecting on the production, reproduction, and development of human life. Consider a judgment, 1, "John is eating." When we reflect on the presuppositions of such a judgment, we see that the proper name, "John," refers to an embodied human subject in community, who is distinct in kind from inanimate things, plants, and animals. We realize that John is consciously, rationally, and responsibly choosing to eat in order to live. We pass easily to the second judgment, 2, "John, who is a living, responsible, human subject, is eating." There is a fundamental recognition here of the concrete human subject, John, but this recognition is different from the one that Honneth makes because it focuses more than he does on concrete human life and its needs.[8]

The descriptive judgment is important because it allows us right away to reflect on the compatibility between a theoretical judgment oriented to life and a system of instrumental rationality that may or may not be compatible with such judgments. Contemporary capitalism is such a system; well over 20 million people a year die under its dominion from starvation. Because such a system turns out to be incompatible with the judgment "John eats," there is a logical incompatibility between capitalism and the theoretical judgment that John eats. We can see this point even prior to reflecting on the properly ethical level of Dussel's philosophy.[9]

We will move to that level now. It is necessary, Dussel says, to effect a dialectical passage from the descriptive to the ethical level, from mere *ser* to *debe-ser,* from the judgments "John is eating" and "John, who is a living, responsible, human subject, is eating," to ethical judgments. Thus we move to judgment 2b, "in order to live, it is necessary to eat," and 2c, "if John does not eat, he will die, commit suicide." From these judgments, judgment 2d follows, "as responsible for his life, he ought not to allow himself to die, or it will be suicide." Therefore judgment 3 follows, "John ought to continue eating."[10]

We have moved, then, from a judgment of biological necessity, 2c, "If John does not eat, he will die, commit suicide," to a judgment of ethical obligation, 3,

"John ought to continue eating." This is a transition from a natural exigency of eating in order to live to the ethical responsibility of the subject who is obligated to eat in order not to die, *debe-comer-para-no-morir.*[11] This "ought" shows itself to be both a material and ethical exigency, and it shows how fundamental ethical judgments about life are. Ethics is not only primarily judgments of value concerning culture or politics; it bears fundamentally on the survival and well-being of the self, the human being as self-conscious, cultural, and responsible for herself. The ecological crisis is an example. Here we have a situation in which human beings either deal responsibly and critically with the effects of rampant capitalism or commit collective suicide.[12]

Such suicide, however, cannot be argued for without self-contradiction, for we implicitly or explicitly value life, on the basis of which we argue for collective suicide. We cannot value our judgment without the life that is its presupposition. Moreover, we should remember, again, that life is on many levels—corporeal, emotional, cultural, political, economic, religious. The material principle includes all of these levels in its purview, and it is the presupposition for the further stages of liberation ethics such as the formal procedural, feasibility, critical, antihegemonic, and liberatory.[13]

One might ask, however, whether the argument as I have presented it does not commit the naturalistic fallacy in making an illegitimate transition from "is" to "ought." Is not Dussel risking returning to a pre-Kantian level that falls behind what Apel and Habermas have already attained?[14] To his credit, Dussel honestly faces up to this question. He answers that the charge of committing a naturalistic fallacy would be valid if he were executing a formal deduction from materialistic premises to ethical conclusion in the manner of Frege or Russell. This argument would indeed be a naturalistic fallacy, but this is not what Dussel is doing. Rather, he is executing a dialectical grounding, *fundamentacio dialectica,*[15] on the level of content, not form, showing how the "ought" is already implicitly contained in the "is." Because our lived body is already making evaluations about what is good and what is bad, what is healthy and what is unhealthy, and because our lived body spontaneously desires to live, ethical reasoning simply unfolds and makes explicit the spontaneous evaluation already going on. Ethical reasoning simply takes up and subsumes and integrates this spontaneous bodily evaluation into a complex human context; the evaluation is not simple or merely animalistic. We will return in our critical evaluation to see how convincing this argumentation is.[16]

THE FORMAL PRINCIPLE

The question now arises concerning the application of the material principle itself. Because human beings themselves are reflexive and self-conscious and responsible, the application cannot be automatic or immediate. What is necessary is a co-principle, a co-determining principle that "produces, from the truth of the material principle, the validity by means of argumentation that grounds the ends, means, and values to be effected."[17] Thus application is different from a private, monological phronesis because we are now in an intersubjective discursive context of dialogue. Such application also has broader meaning than the usual one insofar as it will function discursively in each of the four further substages of Dussel's ethic. In stage 5, for example, stage 2 of part 2 of his ethics, he will use discursive, formal reasons to establish an antihegemonic community of victims, which brings the established socioeconomic system into question and shows its untruth.[18]

Dussel goes on to say that if the content of ethics grounds the material principle of ethics, the formal aspect of morality founds the fundamental principle of universality and moral consensus. Elsewhere Dussel says that the function of formal morality is that of grounding and applying, *fundamentar y applicar,*[19] in the concrete the norms, ethical judgments, and diverse moments of material ethics. Without the basic complementarity of the moral norm, ethical decisions do not acquire material validity, and they can be affected by egoism, solipsism, and violent authoritarianism. There is a tension here between a more narrow sense of the moral principle, in light of which it merely applies a material principle already established, and a broader sense, in which it both grounds and applies the material principle. I will return to this tension in my critical remarks.

What the above implies is that truth and validity are co-determining. There is no adequate truth without validity. Even a judgment made by myself, "John is eating," can be intersubjectively, argumentatively defended. On the other hand, there is no adequate validity without truth, for intersubjective agreement is about something with content, the truth of a scientific theory, for example, or a moral or legal proposition. Otherwise the achieved agreement would mean little to us. Truth and formal validity, therefore, are related but distinct, both in regard to reference, reality or intersubjective agreement, and the type of rationality, material or formally discursive.[20]

Dussel distinguishes further between an intersubjective criterion of validity and a formal, moral universal principle. The criterion of validity is that which governs the process of achieving actual intersubjective agreement concerning true enunciations in accordance with the better argument in community. All the validity claims—truth, rightness, sincerity, and clarity—have been obeyed, no illegitimate coercion or violence has been used, each of the participants has had equal chance to express feelings, propositions, and arguments, and no one has been excluded from the discussion.[21]

The moral principle of universal validity says that if we argue intelligently, as members of a community of communication, we ought to be responsible in our argumentation as mediation of material truth in order to produce, reproduce, and develop the human life of subjects with respect to other human subjects perceived as equal. If we are consistent in our claims, concerns about life and dignity have to translate into struggling for formal validity and being open to accepting the argument of others whom we have already on the level of practical, material truth recognized as equal. The argument is now transformed into a moral obligation.[22]

How does this formal principle interact with the material principle in practice? Let us consider the judgment "these human beings are living." We can say, because of the material principle, that they ought to live. "They ought not to allow themselves to die or be killed by anybody." Then follows the descriptive judgment, "this person kills person Z with act Y." Then because this person X is responsible for person Z, in light of the material principle, "this person should not kill person Z with act Y." Or another way of putting the point is "this person committed to killing Z commits a bad act."[23]

Moreover, when we bring the formal criterion of universality into play, we see that arbitrary, unprovoked killing of one person by another cannot be made a moral norm. If we try to do so, then we see that this norm is not valid morally because each person affected by it cannot participate symmetrically in the corresponding discussion. If I am dead, I cannot discuss, and if I am killed arbitrarily without discussion or from having been excluded from a discussion in which the decision was made to kill me, then I have been unjustly excluded from discussion, and my life has been unjustly taken. The validity of the principle of morality links up with the material principle to produce, reproduce, and develop each human life in community. Because one human life has been taken arbitrarily, the material principle as universal has been violated; and because the decision was made to take my life in a discussion that excluded me partially or totally, the principle of morality has been violated.

If I try to argue against killing or against some other kinds of violent exclusion, then descriptively it is true that "I can say now that I am arguing." But from the descriptive claim, one can infer, because of the formal, moral principle, that "I think that I ought now to participate and argue."[24] But if this claim is true, it follows that "I ought not to be killed" because I cannot argue if I am dead.

How is this line of reflection similar to and yet different from that of Apel or Habermas? First, Dussel accepts, as they do, the validity of the moral criterion and the moral principle. Where he mainly disagrees with them, second, is in their tendency to reduce truth to validity, the material principle to the moral principle and, thus, not to distinguish adequately the material principle from the moral principle.

This difference has many interesting consequences. One of them is that one cannot, Dussel thinks, give priority to the right over the good, as Apel and Habermas do; rather, they are co-determinate. To be concerned with concrete human life is to be concerned with the needs and goods of that life as well as what is right for that life. Another consequence is that Dussel's liberation ethics can supply motivation for acting ethically in a way that discourse ethics cannot. Because the legitimate happiness of the human subject in community is a legitimate and obligatory theme of ethics, then the frustration of that happiness and well-being by an unjust social system is also a legitimate and obligatory moral concern. As Dussel will show later in his work, because capitalism is both alienating (in the sense of producing unhappiness) and unjust, capitalism needs to be transformed qualitatively and not merely reformed.[25]

One final consequence of the difference between Dussel and Apel–Habermas is that without a material principle, discourse ethics lands in a fundamental contradiction, a performative contradiction. Discourse ethics rests on a symmetry condition: each participant should be able to argue equally with every other participant. If one or more participants is materially deprived, however, lacking food, housing, education, medical care, and so on, then he is not able to participate as an equal. The required moral symmetry of communication is violated and rendered inoperative by a real, lived, material inequality of living conditions.

The formal principle, therefore, requires the material principle as the condition of its own possibility. Otherwise we face a contradiction between required moral symmetry and the real inequality in living conditions. Dussel refers here to the "interpellative speech act" through which the materially excluded person appeals to those in the speech community to become open to the materially excluded Other. Otherwise the speech community is not genuinely universal and thus contradicts the formal requirement of universality.[26]

FEASIBILITY AND OTHER CONSEQUENCES

Dussel pursues his inquiry into ethics by articulating a principle of feasibility, *factibilidad.* This principle unites the formal and material principles in formulating a notion of the good that articulates itself on three levels: a material level, a formal level, and a level of realization in which we try to establish a concrete social totality as good because it produces, reproduces, and develops human life in the most adequate manner and because it allows all persons to participate equally in the economic, political, and cultural institutions of their society. On the level of realization, there are at least three moments—judgments of fact using instrumental reason to reflect on appropriate means to achieve appropriate goals, strategic reason reflecting on the best way to persuade or manipulate people to choose means and ends, and ethical reason using the material and formal principles to evaluate instrumental and strategic reason ethically.[27]

Feasibility rests on possibility, and possibility can take different forms—logical, empirical, technical, and ethical. The latter in the series presupposes the former. If something is empirically possible, then it must be logically possible. If something is technically possible, then it must be empirically possible. If something is ethically possible, then it must be technically possible. I do not have an ethical obligation to do what is logically, empirically, or technically impossible. On the other hand, the former in the series does not imply the latter. Something can be logically possible without being empirically possible, empirically possible without being technically possible, and technically possible without being ethically possible or desirable.[28]

Corresponding to possibility is impossibility. A socioeconomic system is impossible if one or more of these criteria, logical, empirical, technical, or ethical, is violated. Feasibility in the broadest sense confronts instrumental and strategic reason with material and formal ethical principles. A social system that is logically, empirically, and technically possible might be ethically impossible, in the sense that many or most of the people living under this system are not able to live and develop adequately and to participate equally and fully. Currently the principle of free market competition works for the top 10–20 percent of the population but not for the starving majority; or it works for the North but not the South. A system is ethically impossible if it cannot produce, reproduce, and develop the human lives of all in the community and if it does not allow all to participate equally and fully. Capitalism in this sense, although it is logically, empirically, and technically possible, is ethically impossible.[29]

A somewhat simple example is the following. (1) "This hungry human being asks me for alms"; this is a judgment of fact. After reflecting or discussing the issue with other people, I decide that giving alms is logically, empirically, and technically feasible. (2) "It is feasible to give alms to this hungry person." After further reflection, I decide that giving alms is compatible with the production, reproduction, and development of my life and hers. Judgment 3 is the result: "Giving alms to this person is compatible with the production, reproduction, and development of her life." After further reflection I make the following decision, 4, "I have decided to give this person alms," and finally I conclude that not to give alms is irresponsible. (5) "I ought to give the agreed-upon alms to this hungry person."[30]

Now, of course, this is a relatively simple, easy example. In part 2 of his ethics, the properly critical and liberating part, Dussel becomes more complex. I want to give a brief example of his thinking here and indicate the power, insight, and fruitfulness of his ethics. First, we make a judgment of fact, 1, "here now is a victim." Such a person can be unemployed, hungry, homeless, uneducated, or any combination of these. We then move to another judgment of fact, 2, "this situation does not permit the victim to live adequately, negates his dignity as a human being, and excludes him from discourse." The cause of this situation is social policies that exclude or exploit; an example is the policy of the New York rapid transit system discouraging and forbidding begging. This judgment leads to a judgment about a social system X, 3, "this person in misery is a victim of system X." A further judgment follows immediately, 4, "I recognize this victim as a human being with dignity and as Other to system X." Such recognition is a judgment of fact, not yet ethical, not yet employing an "ought," a *debe-ser.* That occurs in judgment 5, building on and presupposing the material and formal principles, "this recognition situates me as responsible for the victim excluded by system X."

This taking responsibility for the ethical life of the Other will only be properly, fully ethically critical if it not only proceeds from a recognition of the Other as equal but also sees him as a victim of a system that keeps him hungry, unemployed, uneducated, homeless, and so on. The ethical ought occurs when I make the judgment, 6, "I am compelled by the ethical ought because I am responsible for him, to take responsibility for this victim." As part of a communication community that has left me well off materially and allows me to participate fully and equally, I respond to the call of the Other, excluded, marginalized, and exploited by this system.

Consequently, I move to judgment 7, "being responsible before system X for the victim I ought (it is an ethical obligation) to criticize such a system because it causes negativity to such a victim." We can sum all this up by saying in judgment 8 "that I ought not to act in such a manner that my action causes or creates victims because we are responsible for her death, you and I, and consequently we are responsible for this murder."[31]

We need to move further, however, for we still have not moved to the level of feasibility and the necessity of transforming and not just reforming the socioeconomic system. I will sketch this argument in several steps, which occur in Dussel's discourse of liberation in the last subpart of *Ethics* II.

1. A victim suffers the negativity M, which puts at risk in some manner his life.
2. The system Z causes M in X.
3. The subsystem Y of system Z is the cause of M in X (Again, think of the rapid transit system of capitalist New York City as a cause of hunger because of its new policy on begging).
4. In order to eliminate M in X, we have to avoid Y.
5. In order to avoid Y, transforming Z in this way, mediations A, B, C, (technical, economic, political, pedagogical, etc.) are necessary.
6. These mediations are feasible here and now.
7. Therefore Y can be averted and, to that extent, Z transformed.
8. Y cannot be avoided without completely destroying system Z.
9. In order to avoid M and its cause Y, we must transform totally Z into W.
10. In W the victim X will no longer suffer M.
11. Mediations D, E, F, and so on are able to be effected to bring about W.
12. These mediations are feasible here and now.
13. Therefore W should be brought about.[32] (Again, for the sake of clarity, the rapid transit system causing hunger to its victims cannot be changed fully for the better without transforming capitalist New York City into socialist New York City. Because of material, formal, and feasibility principles I have an ethical obligation to work against capitalism and to transform it completely into democratic socialism.)

As we have seen already and as Dussel has developed in other books, capitalism is the system Z that needs to be transformed, not merely reformed. Capitalism is a system in which it is ethically impossible to produce, reproduce, and develop the human lives of all of the people living within it or under it. As already noted, there are over 20 million people who die every year in the worldwide capitalist system just from hunger: a yearly "worldwide Auschwitz," to use Dussel's phrase from a conference held in Mexico City in September 1997.[33]

The principle of liberation, therefore, the most comprehensive and concrete principle in Dussel's ethics, subsumes the material, formal, and feasibility principles from part 1 of his ethics into a critique of the reigning socioeconomic system—capitalism. Such a principle is explicitly deontological and expresses a negative and positive task. Negatively I ought to criticize and transform the oppressive system, Z above, and positively I ought to construct new norms, actions, microstructures, institutions, and systems of ethicity, system W in the above example. This new system will be good, *bueno,* in the most concrete, comprehensive sense; and the norms, actions, microstructures, and particular institutions will be good in a more narrow, partial sense. Thus the good at the end of the *Ethics* II is related to the good at the end of *Ethics* I as realization to anticipation, full to empty, concrete to abstract, realized "ought" to postulated "ought."[34]

CRITICAL REFLECTION

We are now in a position to reflect critically in a positive and negative manner on Dussel's achievement. I personally find what he has done to be enormously impressive. In one sense, he has put the ethical-political Humpty Dumpty back together again. Opposites such as right and good, deontology and teleology, justification and application, duty and happiness, universal and particular, which have fallen apart in contemporary thought, he has integrated. As one who is engaged in a similar project, I cannot but be greatly sympathetic and largely in agreement at least in broad outline with what he has done. And there are other thinkers such as Paul Ricoeur in *Oneself As Another* who are proceeding along a similar path.[35]

When we consider the way in which postmodernism and Habermasian critical theory are at an impasse in the United States, each with its own kind of one-sidedness (e.g., Derrida's prophetic critique of the new world order in *Specters of Marx* but with a very inadequate notion of reason and Habermas's very developed notion of reason but very uncritical capitulation to late capitalism), we see that Dussel criticizes, relativizes, and subsumes both projects. He integrates a prophetic critique of the capitalist system with a material and formal notion of reason, a very developed sense of the oppressed Other with an account of the normative foundations in the light of which we can say that the other is illegitimately oppressed, and a very concrete sense of hermeneutical specificity with a material and formal sense of universality.

Both postmodernism and Habermasian critical theory, Dussel argues, are Eurocentric. Postmodernism reflects the bad conscience of a North American and European academic and intellectual who is bright enough to know that something is deeply wrong with our institutional arrangements but is not perceptive enough and honest enough to bring into question the socioeconomic system that is the source of his privilege. Postmodernism is a kind of safe and easy way to engage in radical talk without really being radical, a kind of "critical criticism" very similar to the left Hegelians Marx criticized over a hundred years ago. Only now the ideology is dominantly French and North American rather than German. And, of course, in making reason the target of the critique rather than the socioeconomic system that is the real cause of alienation and oppression and exploitation, postmodernism deprives itself of the only adequate resource available for critical transcendence. Postmodernism twists in the wind uneasily, praising a liberation it cannot deliver and claiming a legitimacy it cannot justify. It is the false coin of liberation masquerading as the true coin.[36]

Habermasian critical theory, on the other hand, on an abstract ethical and philosophical level achieves universality and thus overcomes Euro-centricism in principle but caves into it on concrete hermeneutical and political levels. It leaves the role of the South, the Third World, in the formation of Europe unthematized hermeneutically, and it leaves neoimperialism uncriticized ethically and politically. Habermas's support of the Gulf War is an extreme, obvious example of this tendency, but it runs throughout his work and causes it to be reformist, not revolutionary or transforming in the way that is necessary. Apelian-Habermasian critical theory, we might say, in terms of delivering on its real critical and revolutionary promise, ends not with a bang but with a whimper. And I say this while fully recognizing the achievements of such theory on more abstract philosophical, ethical, and hermeneutical levels.[37]

What Dussel has articulated, most fully in this book and partially in others, is a new version of critical theory that trumps both postmodernism and Apelian-Habermasian critical theory while retaining the valid insights of both. Dussel's version of critical liberation includes a much fuller use of Marx, a radical rather than a merely reformist critique of late capitalism, national and international; an insistence on the lived, incarnate, existential free subject as opposed to the overly linguistified subject in both postmodernism and critical theory; a linking of the formal with the material, right with good, duty with happiness, universal with particular; and a taking of our bearings from the excluded and exploited Third World other rather than social movements or the proletariat in the North. These last are certainly not denied by Dussel but subsumed within a grander planetary ethic. Again, as someone in the North who has been pursuing a similar, critical theoretical path for the past twenty years, I cannot but register a significant amount of agreement.[38]

And so, with all of this positive response and agreement, I want to pursue one line of questioning with Dussel that is at least in part more negatively critical. Such a line of thinking does not invalidate what he has done but invites him to go deeper and use more resources already present in his thought. My first question to Dussel is whether he has done full justice to Apel's and Habermas's formal principle by presenting it merely or primarily as an application of the material principle. Most of the time it is in terms of mere application that Dussel speaks, although occasionally, as we have already seen, Dussel links application with grounding, *fundamentar.*[39] Habermas wants to insist on the role of justification with any norm that presents itself as a moral norm; such justification occurs in the light of validity claims, the universality principle (U) saying that every legitimate norm implies that all concerned can accept the consequences and the side effects its universal acceptance can be anticipated to have for the satisfaction of everyone's interests (and that these consequences are preferred to those known alternative possibilities for regulation); and, based on U, the discourse principle (D) saying that only those norms can claim to be valid that meet (or could meet) with the approval of all concerned in their capacity as participants in a practical discourse.

Second, application, according to Habermas drawing on Günther, utilizes a principle of appropriateness, which says that the application of moral norms must consult all relevant differences among subjects. An example would be my promising a friend that I will meet him at a party, but another friend falls sick and needs my care. Considering all relevant circumstances and norms, I ought to visit my sick friend. The promise to go to the party can be set in abeyance.[40]

Third, not only does Dussel not capture this distinction between justification and application in its full richness and nuance as Habermas understands it, but he underestimates the role communicative action plays in the justification of the material principle itself. Recall that we went through a several-step process, starting with "John is eating" and ending with "John should continue to eat." Such a process is rationative and communicative and uses communicative action to establish and justify, and not simply to apply the material principle.

Fourth, Dussel, to be fair, does not exactly deny what I am saying all the time. At times, as we have seen, he refers to the material principle and formal principle as co-equal and co-determinative, and the formal principle as not merely applying but grounding the material principle in its universality and rational cogency. Other times, however, he seems to assert the priority of the material principle to the formal principle and to affirm a pre-originary ethical recognition of the other as prior to any discursive validation. Consider that "recognition of the other, thanks to the pre-originary, ethical reason is prior to critique and prior to argument (to discursive or dialogical reason); this is in the origin of the process and is the affirmation of the victim as subject, which is negated or ignored in the system as subject."[41]

In this part of the book Dussel is being very Levinasian and less Marxist and Habermasian, and there may be a tension between and among these influences and sources of his thought. It is certainly true to say that concrete perception of the Other is prior to any critical or dialogical encounter with the Other in a relative sense, although my perception is certainly informed by prior discursive encounters with others. If the Other is not present as embodied, concrete Other, then I cannot talk with her or engage her ethically. But Dussel conflates this epistemic priority with an ethical one. I must see the Other in a prediscursive way as an equal and a victim before I begin to dialogue. I would submit that I can only see the Other as equal and as illegitimately marginalized in the context of a hermeneutics and an ethics that is already operative at least prethematically in my encounters with the Other. Indeed Dussel himself talks this way when he talks about the Other's interpellative speech act calling into question those within the Apelian-Habermasian community of communication, claiming to be inclusive but not really being so. Without the prior validity of the communicative ethic of the community, the interpellative speech act loses its cogency. Indeed, there is a movement from formal to material here to which I wish to return. As anyone who has seen beggars totally ignored by passengers on a New York subway can attest, what I am talking about is not empty possibility. I think the ethical call of the Other is always mediated hermeneutically and ethically, not immediately. If, as is the case, passengers on the subway have bought into the notion of the poor as lazy welfare chiselers, then they will see the beggar epistemically but will feel no obligation to give anything.[42]

Building on all of these points, we can ask whether Dussel's argument for the material principle does avoid the naturalistic fallacy. I have my doubts. I think that Dussel intends to avoid it. I recognize the importance of distinguishing between a deductive argument and a concrete, dialectical one. Nonetheless, with all of this said, does the argument finally convince us? How do we get from "John is eating" to "John should continue eating"? I confess that I am not convinced by his argument, backed by a long discussion of human physiology, that spontaneous, bodily, prediscursive processes engage in spontaneous evaluations and already see some things as values and others as disvalues. The question here would be, Why should such bodily values be ethical, moral values in the full post-Kantian, communicative sense?

It is possible, of course, that with further elaboration Dussel can pull this argument off. I think, however, that he has other resources in his arsenal for unequivocally and clearly making a stronger argument and avoiding the naturalistic fallacy. Here I think that he would have to take seriously the strand of his argument insisting that the formal principle is co-determining with the material principle, a claim that is in tension with and perhaps contradictory to his claim concerning the priority of the material principle over the formal principle and his claim concerning the preoriginary, prediscursive ethical recognition of the Other, Dussel at his most Levinasian.

Here the move I make is to start with communicative action and the correlative principles U and D and move to the material principle. The argument would look like this:

1. There is a communication community A composed of at least three persons, B, C, and D.

2. As interacting with one another in community, they ought to follow and do follow the validity claims, comprehensibility, sincerity, truth, and rightness.
3. As a communication community and in fidelity to such validity claims, A affirms itself as a moral community by affirming U and D.
4. Person D, however, because of material deprivation (lack of education, housing, food, clothing, medical care, etc.), cannot participate fully or equally in A.
5. Person D, therefore, makes an interpellative speech act to community A. "Because I should be able to participate fully and equally by your criteria U and D, I should be supplied with the material prerequisites of such participation."
6. Therefore community A, in order to be performatively consistent with itself as a communication community affirming U and D, should commit itself to producing, reproducing, and developing the human life of each subject in the community.

Some brief comments on this argument are in order. First, as I have already said, it is a line of argument or is similar to a line of argument that Dussel himself has employed at times. Second, the argument is really consistent with his claim that the formal principle is co-determining with the material principle. On a pragmatic level communicative action is used to argue for that material principle; on an explicit, thematic level of argument, the formal principle or principles can be used as premises and starting points to reach the material principle. The material principle, on the other hand, supplies the presuppositions, ground, and content that make full participation possible. Third, the movement from the fact of communicative action to U and D, premises 1–3, is unproblematic; both Dussel and Apel-Habermas agree with this movement.

Fourth, the movement from 4 to 6, from the lack of material prerequisites to the material principle, is not a movement from "is" to "ought" but from formal ought to an ought of content, from a formally grounded and oriented communication to one of flesh and blood grounded in material content. The naturalistic fallacy is, therefore, avoided. Fifth, the necessity to move from form to content is again one of being consistent logically, performatively, and morally. If I really am committed to full participation, then I must be committed to the material grounds necessary for full participation. Otherwise I am in logical, performative, and moral contradiction with myself. Last, it is not an objection to say, as Dussel might say, that such a move makes the material principle less important or formidable than the formal principle. Since when, I would say in reply, is a conclusion less important than its premises? What my argumentative move does is take seriously Dussel's claim that the material and formal principles are co-determining.[43]

CONCLUSION

I insist again that the above disagreement and reconstruction are but a relatively minor cavil about a magnificent, stunning work. And I think that we should remind ourselves again that Dussel is engaged in no mere academic exercise here. Rather, this is a book written in an international context in which Third World peoples are literally fighting for their very lives, and the United States is the imperial power leading the charge in such oppression. I am, therefore, going to conclude with a quotation from the last pages of Dussel's book. It brings home the real importance of what he is saying and also shows him to be a writer not only of great cogency, insight, and synthetic breadth but also tremendous rhetorical conviction, persuasiveness, and power.

> This globalization is that of a formal, performative system (the value that valorizes itself, the money that produces money, D—D'; fetishism of capital) which raises itself up as the criterion of truth, validity, and feasibility and destroys human life, trampling on the dignity of millions of human beings and not recognizing their equality or much less affirming itself as co-responsible for the alterity of the excluded and accepting only the hypocritical juridical exigency of carrying out the duty of paying an international debt (fictitious) of poor, peripheral nations, even if the debtor people perishes, *fiat justitiam, pereat mundus*. It is a massive assassination; it is the beginning of a collective suicide.
>
> It is for this reason that we believe it necessary to erect a principle that is absolutely universal, which is completely negated by the prevailing system which globalizes itself; the duty of producing and reproducing the life of each human subject, especially the victims of this mortal system, which excludes them as ethical subjects and only includes the increase of the value of exchange. It is a fetishization process that has carried out a total inversion.[44]

NOTES

1. Enrique Dussel, *Etica de la liberación en la edad de la globalización y de la exclusión* (Madrid: Editorial Trotta, 1998), hereafter referred to as *EL*. For a work in English translation that summarizes and gives the gist of the earlier ethics, see *Philosophy of Liberation*, trans. Aquilina Martinez and Christine Morkovsky (Maryknoll, N.Y.: Orbis, 1985).
2. "Critical modernist" is my term; "transmodern" is Dussel's term. See *EL*, p. 64.
3. Ibid., pp. 71–75.
4. Ibid., p. 91. "Esta es una ética de la vida, es decir, la vida humana es el contenido de la ética."
5. Ibid. "El principio de la obligación de producir, reproducir y desarrollar la vida humana concreta de cada sujeto ético en communicad."

6. Ibid., pp. 91–92.

7. Ibid., pp. 131–32.

8. Ibid., p. 134. Axel Honneth, *The Struggle for Recognition: The Moral Grammar of Social Conflicts*, trans. Joel Anderson (Cambridge: MIT Press, 1996).

9. Ibid., pp. 135–36. Jack Nelson-Pallmeyer, *Brave New World Order* (Maryknoll, N.Y.: Orbis, 1992), pp. 4–5.

10. *EL,* p. 139.

11. Ibid., pp. 139–40.

12. Ibid., p. 140.

13. Ibid., pp. 140–42.

14. This was a question explicitly raised by Karl-Otto Apel in a conference on liberation philosophy and critical theory hosted by Dussel in Mexico City in late September 1997.

15. *EL,* p. 104.

16. Ibid., pp. 93–106.

17. Ibid., p. 143. "Aalcanza, desde la verdad del principio material, la validez por medio de la argumentacion, fundamentacion racional de los fines, valores, y medios a operarse."

18. Ibid., pp. 411–73.

19. Ibid., p. 201.

20. Ibid., pp. 205–6.

21. Ibid., pp. 202–6.

22. Ibid., pp. 213–14.

23. Ibid., pp. 208–9.

24. Ibid., pp. 210–13.

25. Ibid., pp. 180–201.

26. Ibid., pp. 303–4, 309–12, 460–64.

27. Ibid., pp. 235–37.

28. Ibid., pp. 265–73.

29. Ibid., pp. 267–68.

30. Ibid., pp. 268–69.

31. Ibid., pp. 368–77.

32. Ibid., pp. 554–55.

33. Ibid., pp. 310–11.

34. Ibid., pp. 558–59, 563–56.

35. See my *Critique, Action, and Liberation* (Albany: SUNY Press, 1994), pp. 113–24. Paul Ricoeur, *Oneself As Another*, trans. Kathleen Blamey (Chicago: Chicago University Press, 1992).

36. *EL,* pp. 166–76.

37. Ibid., pp. 166–76. Jürgen Habermas, *The Past As Future*, trans. Max Pensky (Lincoln: University of Nebraska Press, 1994), pp. 5–31.

38. Ibid., pp. 166–76. In addition to *Critique, Action, and Liberation*, two other books that are part of my own project are *Post–Cartesian Meditations* (New York: Fordham University Press, 1988); and *Process, Praxis, and Transcendence* (Albany, N.Y.: SUNY Press, 1999).

39. *EL,* p. 201.

40. *Critique, Action, and Liberation*, p. 382 n. 48. Klaus Gunther, *The Sense of Appropriateness*, trans. John Farrell (Albany: SUNY Press, 1993), pp. 229–55. For Habermas's use of Gunther, see his *Justification and Application*, trans. Ciaran P. Cronin (Cambridge: MIT Press, 1993), pp. 13–14.

41. "Reconocimiento del Otro, gracias al ejercicio de la *razon ética pre–originariaé* . . . es anterior a la crítica y anterior al argumento (a la razon discursiva o dialogica); est en el origen del proceso y es ya afirmación de la víctima como sujeto, que es negada or ignorada en el sistema como sujeto . . ." (p. 30).

42. See my own discussion of this issue in *Critique, Action, and Liberation*, in which I draw positively on Levinas but also criticize him, pp. 174–76, 181–86.

43. See *Critique, Action, and Liberation*, pp. 132–47, where I make my own version of this argument from form to material content. The material principle for me is embodied in the Principle of Generic Consistency (PGC), which says that I should act in accord with the generic rights and well-being of others as well as myself; and Freedom as Self-Development (FSD), which says that I should promote in myself and others the freedom to develop oneself through one's action and to realize one's projects through activity in the course of which one forms one's character and capacities.

44. *EL*, pp. 567–68.

4

Can "Liberation Ethics" Be Assimilated under "Discourse Ethics"?

Karl-Otto Apel

Like a flash of illumination, the following point of departure for a discussion occurred to me during the first encounter between discourse ethics and the ethics of liberation in November 1989 in Freiburg: Enrique Dussel, after my presentation entitled "Discourse Ethics As an Ethics of Responsibility,"[1] remarked wryly that about 75 percent of the inhabitants of this earth—he meant the poor of the Third World—have so far not been able to participate in all discourses, including those that concern them. Apparently, this was intended as a well-directed challenge, or even a central objection, to the starting point of discourse ethics. At that moment, I responded to this objection extemporaneously something like this: Unfortunately, what Mr. Dussel has said is true. But this is no objection to the grounding principle of discourse ethics, rather, a particularly illuminating example of the necessity of the distinction between part A and part B of discourse ethics.

I had introduced this distinction in my presentation, and previously in my book *Discourse and Responsibility*,[2] in order to render intelligible the problem of the historical transition to "postconventional morality." In this context, the necessity of a part B of discourse ethics resulted from the responsibility–ethical recognition of the fact that the conditions of application for the basic procedural norms of part A of discourse ethics (e.g., for the demand for a purely discursive solution to all conflicts of interest among human beings) are not, or not yet, given in the world in which we live. Admittedly, among my examples of this problem, only the problem of the (appropriate) legal conditions which, at least on a global scale, have not yet been generated. The primarily economic conflict between the North and the South did not figure in the first position. For example, we still have the problem of the persistence of a "natural condition" of warlike conflict among states.

At the time, I saw the practical concern of discourse ethics—as did Jürgen Habermas—to be primarily the substitution of *strategic* solutions to violence with regulating conflicts of interest through the procedures of a discursive formation of consensus about validity claims. However, in order to make these procedures of conflict resolution possible, we also had to be concerned with, so to speak, unburdening human beings from *strategic self-assertion* through a legal and peaceful order on a global scale. We had to render the discursive resolution of their conflicts of interest, so to speak, *acceptable* to them.[3]

At that time I was of the opinion—this time differing from Habermas[4]—that the basic principle of discourse ethics (for which there is in my view a transcendental-pragmatic, ultimate foundation [*Letztbegründung*])[5] does not only include the *formal-deontological* principle of grounding norms in practical discourses but also a *teleologically* oriented duty. This duty signifies *coresponsibility for the historically situated production of the institutional conditions of practical discourses* and thus, for example, for the production of a legal and peaceful order on a global scale. For this reason, I was willing to grant to the oppressed and to those deprived of rights on this globe the a priori moral privilege, so to speak, of the strategic—if necessary, also revolutionary—enforcement of their vital interests, even prior to the deontologically basic norm of strategy-free conflict resolution in practical discourses. This moral privilege of the oppressed, or their political representatives, is certainly, however, in turn, like all validity claims, subject to the regulative and thus also limiting condition of its capacity for consensus for the members of an ideal—and counterfactually anticipated—community of discourse.

No matter how difficult, or even impossible, the real formation of consensus among the opponents of the conflicts of interest may be, there is nonetheless always—for as long as this problem can be the object of philosophical consideration, as for example in the current discussion—the basic possibility to represent already here and now, in a real community of discourse, the counterfactually anticipated consensus of an ideal community of discourse about the moral privileges of the oppressed and those deprived of rights.

This much—to indicate vaguely—about the architecture of parts A and B of discourse ethics already formed the background of my spontaneous response to Dussel's "objection" in 1989. What is the relevance of this response today, after a few discussion sessions between discourse ethics and the ethics of liberation?

Dussel has meanwhile elaborated further his challenge to discourse ethics. He has done so with arguments that apparently reach far beyond the problems of part B of discourse ethics—for example, with the argument that what matters in the end in ethics is not the regulative idea of the progressive production of an "ideal community of communication" but the idea of the production of an "ideal community of life" of human beings. The latter would not, or not only, require a transcendental pragmatics of language or a discourse ethics but a "transcendental economics" that could be developed on the basis of Karl Marx. Further, Dussel elaborates the argument that a transcendental-pragmatic discourse ethics could at best refute the skeptic on the level of the academic discourses of philosophy but that it was entirely powerless when facing the real opponent of the ethics of liberation: the cynic who would not even begin to engage in the argumentative discourse concerning moral claims about rights. I will come back to these arguments.

I myself have, in the meantime, further elaborated the architecture of the differentiation between part A and part B of discourse ethics. I did so with regard to viewpoints that were determined, among other things, by the challenge of the ethics of liberation (especially by Dussel's and Franz Hinkelammert's recourse to economics)[6] but also by the challenge from another party: Karl Homann's ethics of a market economy.[7] I exposed myself consciously to this confrontation with alternatives of economically oriented ethics, which are still prominent today, and I believe that I learned a good deal in this confrontation.

What are the consequences of my late coming to terms with estimating the relation between discourse ethics and the ethics of liberation? First, I have to confess that I still view my spontaneous response of 1989 to Dussel's challenge as essentially correct. Of course, in what follows, I have to give special reasons for this in relation to Dussel's new arguments. Before I tackle this, I have to indicate what in my view are the results of my progressive explication of the distinction between part A and part B of discourse ethics.

1. THE RESULTS OF THE ELABORATION OF THE DISTINCTION BETWEEN "PART A" AND "PART B" OF DISCOURSE ETHICS IN REGARD TO THE INSTITUTIONAL OR SYSTEM-RELATED IMPLEMENTATION OF MORAL NORMS

I believe that I have learned the following conclusion from the confrontation with the problems of law,[8] of the economy,[9] and, in this year, again with the problems of politics—indeed, in this anniversary year of Kant's project Toward Eternal Peace.[10] This conclusion is that one should not exclusively (or even only primarily) thematize the problem of part B of discourse ethics from the viewpoint of an *interpersonal ethics of action*, or one that is, so to speak, situated beyond institutions.

This viewpoint is probably still the primary one for the ethical orientation of most human beings. This is because it corresponds to a religious tradition as well as to its secularization in, say, existentialism and in the phenomenology of the I-Thou relationship. Concerning the problem of an ethics of responsibility—and thus also the problem of part B of discourse ethics—I myself was for a long time inspired by Jean-Paul Sartre and even more by Max Weber's distinction—in "Politics as a Vocation"—between the "ethics of conviction" *[Gesinnungsethik]* and the "ethics of responsibility." Thus for a long time I viewed the problem of the mediation between discursive and strategic conflict resolution as one of the situated decisions of actions of individual persons, who would have to be held immediately responsible for those decisions.

I still do not wish to disavow this perspective. There remains, of course, the problem of the solitary decision of the politician who cannot—in the world as it is under the pressure of the responsibility for success—orient himself according to the pacifism of the Sermon on the Mount or Kant's recommendation for the "moral politician" according to the motto "*fiat iustitia, perat mundus.*"[11]

There is, as well, the example of the problem of the father and breadwinner who in a corrupt society cannot perform the moral action of paying his taxes alone or of renouncing the bribery of state officials, if he thereby ruins his family.

However, the existential sharpening of these kinds of problems—problems of the necessary deviation of responsible action from the ideally universalizable or consensus-capable *[konsensfähigen]* action—only seems concrete. For it suggests that the problems of part B of discourse ethics deal with mere exceptions to the application of part A of discourse ethics, similar to the case of the allowed or disallowed lie of necessity which, as is well-known, was discussed as the controversy between Kant and Benjamin Constant.[12]

Yet this confrontation between, on the one hand, nonsituated, universalizable maxims of action and, on the other, situated maxims of action passes over the social reality of institutions or functional systems of actions and their quasi-self-evident game rules *[quasi-selbstverständliche Spielregeln]*. What is lacking here is a kind of sociological enlightenment—even with regard to those cases in which a single person, owing to his postconventional moral competence,[13] can reflect upon and transcend the habits and rules of institutions; here, the situated decisions turn for this person into existential problems.

Even in these cases, the moral problem of a responsible decision to act can only be reflected upon in adequate form if we take into account that there are always already rules and customs of behavior that are morally expected in the complex sociocultural reality in which human beings live. In our times in particular, human beings do not normally live in a "face-to-face proximity" and in an immediate encounter of the other[14]—be it in the sense of love and of respect, be it in the sense of the struggle for life and death. Thus they do not live in those situations of the immediate I-Thou relation that religiously inspired ethics in particular usually suppose. In the life world, human beings must always already satisfy roles of status and occupation, and through these they are also always already justified to a considerable extent in the behavior that can be expected.

(One would now have to describe in greater detail what this can mean in typical cases, for example, for a soldier who, as a soldier, kills enemies but not prisoners and does not rape women; or for a diplomat who, on duty, deals strategically with the expression or concealment of a truth known to him but does not deceive his wife or a private business partner; or for a mother who, as a mother, steals food for her children, or for an entrepreneur who, as an entrepreneur, forces competitors into bankruptcy, etc.)

At this point, however, I do not wish to return to the train of thought *[Denkspur]* of the Hegelian concept of "ethical life *[Sittlichkeit]*" or, as a historical extension of this train of thought, to advocate the reduction of morality to the respective customs of the different (sociocultural) life forms. Rather, I would like to present for discussion, as itself a *problem of a universally valid ethics*, the tension between, on the one hand, the "postconventional" claim to universality of a personalistically oriented ethics of humanity and, on the other, the morally relevant rules and habits of institutions and social systems. The problem seems to me to be the following: is it possible, and even necessary, that a universalist ethics, which advocates as ultimately valid *[letztgültig]* the principle of universalizable reciprocity or respect of all human beings as, in principle, persons having equal rights, still recognizes the mediation of the validity of all moral norms—not only by the demands of the specific situation but the prior mediation by the rules of different institutions or social systems of a complex sociocultural reality?

1.1 In my view, this question is to be answered in advance in the negative (only) if we hold two false premises (which tend toward opposition) because the necessity and peculiarity of the institutional or system-related implementation of moral norms cannot be understood under these premises.

1. The first of the false premises consists in the speculative-utopian assumption that the *externalization* and *alienation* of the face-to-face relations between persons, an alienation that is necessarily connected with all institutions or functional social systems, is to be abolished completely. This seems to me to be the message of the Marxist utopia of the "realm of freedom" and even more of the Dusselian utopia, inspired by Marx and Levinas, of *proximidad.*[15] In my view, not only would, in this case, the alienation and reification of human relations in a capitalist free market have to be abolished—in favor, for example, of a community of producers and of distribution that is not mediated by any intercourse of exchange. But also, the alienation and reification of human relations in a state economy of command (of whatever type) would have to be abolished as well. It seems to me that this tendency (which is without doubt religiously and philosophically fascinating) toward the abolition of all "alienation," even if only understood as a regulative idea, is irreconcilable with any human *cultural development.*

In my view, this insight, which is directed against an anarchist utopianism, in no way leads to an uncritical affirmation of all institutions as a quasi-nature of human culture.

2. The second premise—under which the *mediation* of morality by a *universalist ethics* and through institutions and social systems that cannot be adequately understood—is exactly the opposite of the first premise. It consists in what is propagated today, sometimes carelessly, as the "morality of institutions," or, more precisely, the "development of morality alongside institutions," with a complete rejection of every transcendental, ultimate foundation of ethics. To my knowledge, only Arnold Gehlen, in his cultural anthropology, advocated this position consistently in this century. He left no doubt that, in his opinion, human freedom could only grow out of *institutional alienation.* And he was willing to recognize as rationally unquestionable and as a normative-moral authority any functioning order of power—at that moment, the order of fascism and later, among others, also the order of the Soviet empire. The position of the "morality of institutions," or of the "development of morality alongside institutions," which I called careless and is, for example, advocated in Karl Homann's and Franz Blome-Drees's

ethics of economy, appears far less harmful. For one notices, at a closer look, that this position shows an *ambiguity of foundation* that is hard to disentangle.

To begin with, Homann distinguishes the "moves of the game" from the "rules of the game" of action in the system of the market economy, and he attributes priority to the "rules of the game" as the "locus of morality." Therewith, he also supposes that the rules of the game can be altered as morally unsatisfactory and in many cases should be altered. Morality thus becomes a matter of the politico-legal framework order of the economy. But for Homann, this does not mean that one would now have to fall back on an ethical, ultimate foundation for the politico-legal framework in order to ensure its legitimation. Rather, the framework order of the market economy is in turn to be legitimized only by *institutional metarules:* The order is to emerge—according to the institutional rules of (Western) democracy—out of the factical decisions of the state citizens who bear this framework order. According to Homann, this grounding through *factical decisions*—in the end, through the *factical social contract* that is the basis of the constitution of a democratic, legal state—is supposed to already fulfill the demand for "solidarity" among all human beings, as intended by Christian ethics or by Kant. Going beyond this, such as taking recourse to a *philosophical principle of justice,* would for Homann (as for James M. Buchanan, whom Homann is following here) end up in *dogmatic metaphysics.*[16]

It is difficult today to keep one's head above water on this point, for in my view it has to be admitted that all the sites of rules Homann mentions can be and must be considered institutional mediations of morality in the complex reality of modern society. Do these institutional sites of mediation not in turn, however, require legitimation and perhaps critique on the basis of an *independent principle of morality?* Even if, as Homann claims, the game rules of the market economy could be proved to be factically capable of consensus as rules of a "welfare market economy" according to the rules of Western democracies—and that means capable of consensus not only in the sense of a "two-thirds society" but for all citizens of the respective states—even in this case the systems of rules in question—those of the capitalist market economy and of its democratic metarules—would by no means already be definitively justified in the sense of a universalist ethics. For one always, from the perspective of universalist ethics, has to take into account that a factical consensus of human beings (e.g., a nationally limited consensus) occurs at the *expense of an affected third party,* for example—as Dussel could object—at the expense of the poor of the Third World.

At this point, the "parallel logic" of the necessary convergence of economic-strategic and moral (qua utilitarian) rationality—which Buchanan and Homann, as already Thomas Hobbes and Adam Smith, presuppose as a priori valid—apparently meets its limit. In my view, one does not need to have recourse to metaphysics in order to see this, unless one considered metaphysical the *principle of the necessary capability for consensus of moral norms for all those affected* (also, for example, for the next generations). At least the transcendental-pragmatic discourse ethics would protest against this.[17]

But with this rejection of Homann's "parallel logic" of economic-strategic and moral-utilitarian logic rationality, I have not, of course, excluded a priori that the complexity of the rule systems of the welfare market economy, of democracy, and of the legal or constitutional state with an optimal realization on a global scale, could not in fact be acceptable to all those affected. It is at least more acceptable than the combination of socialist statism and so-called democratic centralism. I would even regard this possibility with Homann as a likely one—not on the level of a transcendental-pragmatic *foundation* of discourse ethics but on the level of fallible social-philosophical hypotheses. But they would on principle and always have to be checked against the *metainstitutional standard of discourse ethics*, that is, the *principle of the universal capability for consensus of all those affected*.

1.2 Therewith, I have arrived at the possibility that I had in view from the beginning: the possibility of a positive response to the question as to the possible—and, in the sense of part B of discourse ethics, even necessary—recognition of the mediation of the validity of all moral norms by the game rules of institutions or functional social systems. This question can and in fact must be answered in the positive if the two following provisos are taken into account:

1. The mediation of the responsible *validity of compliance [Befolgungsgültigkeit]*[18] of moral norms by so-called institutional "forces of circumstance" *[Sachzwänge]* may precisely not, as Homann suggests, be understood as the necessary "development of morality" through the institutional "implementation" of norms, independently of every transcendental, ultimate foundation of ethics. Rather, the institution-independent, legitimizing, and critical function of the transcendental-pragmatic, ultimate foundation of discourse ethics has to remain in effect at all times in the sense indicated above.

2. It follows from the first proviso that the norms of morality, which are dependent on institutions or systems as well as these institutions and systems themselves, can never definitively form the measure of human morality; rather, they are in principle *revisable*. However, already those material norms at which human beings can arrive without the presupposition of institutional forces of circumstance, on the basis of ideal practical discourses alone—that is, the presupposition of the principle of consensus-formation of part A of discourse ethics—are revisable. In this case, the fundamental incompleteness of our knowledge about the consequences of following norms—and that means our ideal dependence on the consensus of an unlimited community of argumentation—would still require revisability. But in the case of the necessary mediation of the validity of norms through institutions or social systems, we have the additional possibility that the institutions or social systems could prove to be morally unacceptable before the forum of *transcendental discourse*, which functions as the *ultimate metainstitution*.

This possibility exists regardless of the fact that the necessity of the institutional implementation of moral norms has to be recognized. Thus the institution of war, for example, is not acceptable before the forum of the transcendental-pragmatic, ultimate foundation of discourse ethics. Nonetheless, an implementation of our norms of action in the sense of the institution of war can today belong to the uncircumventable demands of an ethics of responsibility. In short, we can see that the necessity of the institutional implementation of morality belongs to part B of discourse ethics. As the "force of circumstance" of the institutional mediation, it constitutes part B even before the situation-dependent force of an ethics of responsibility in the sense of Max Weber or Jean-Paul Sartre. However, in both cases the ultimately founded principle of discourse ethics remains the site of a proviso in the face of the circumstantial forces—either the forces of the institutions or the forces of the situations—which are not capable of consensus and necessitate for our responsible action deviations from the discursive principle of problem solving.

1.3 The *structure of the necessary and acceptable mediation of morality by institutions,* which is here indicated in formal abstractness, is just as far removed from the utopianism of the abolition of all institutional mediations of human "relations" as it is from the surrender of these relations to the "development" of institutions or social systems, which factically prevails in the cultural revolution. I shall attempt to illustrate this more closely with regard to the very different functions of institutions or social systems.

1.3.1 Let us begin with the function of politics in its broadest and most general sense. The condition that Kant aimed at exactly two hundred years ago, the condition of "perpetual peace" in a "cosmopolitan" legal order, a federation of "republics"—today we would speak of democracies—has not yet been attained. And this means that we still have to reckon with politics as a dimension that has not been domesticated by *law,* a *dimension of the strategic self-assertion of systems of power,* be it states and associations of states or be it power groups within states, all the way down to the self-assertion of ethnic groups, families, and even individuals against state power, semistate power, or criminal violence. Today there can still be situations on all these levels in which the *exercise of power* in the sense of part B of discourse ethics is inevitable and justified—that is, as long as such exercise of power at the same time knows itself to be obligated, to collaborate in its long-term self-supersession in favor of discursive conflict solutions. In short, and exemplified in an extreme case, in the context of a "just war," as well as in the context of justified self-defense or the defense of a family, killing can still be an implementation of morality in the sense of the rules of politics in its broadest sense, an implementation that is justified in the sense of the ethics of responsibility.

Does it, however, follow from this concession to the *politically* related variety of the ethics of institutions, that the *prohibition of killing*—which no doubt, just like the *recognition of equality* (and thus of *equal human dignity*) of all discourse partners, belongs to the basic norms of discourse ethics, norms that can be ultimately founded[19]—has been superseded definitively with regard to its political implementation in favor of the institutional "development of morality"? According to Homann, this would have to be the case because he does not grant to the transcendental, ultimate foundation of morality the function of a proviso in view of the institutional implementation of morality. (The economic force of circumstance of the shipment of weapons into areas in crisis, for example, can certainly be suspended, according to Homann, by changing the rules of export for all. However, such a change could not be founded on the continuous validity of an institution-independent basic norm of morality but would itself only be an institutionally conditioned, further development of morality. The analogy to the political implementation of the basic norm of nonkilling is obvious.)

By contrast, the problem is more complicated according to the architecture that I suggest, the architecture of the complementarity of part A and part B of discourse ethics: To be sure, given the (still) existing conditions of power politics, one cannot or should not responsibly act according to the quasi-Kantian principle of the universalizability of discourse ethics—as if one were a member of the "kingdom of ends" or of the "ideal community of communication." But this ideal principle remains in effect, and it even prevails in the functional forces of circumstance and the corresponding norms of the system of political self-assertion by subordinating the latter to a superordinate, moral long-term strategy, for example, in the sense of the Kantian project Toward Perpetual Peace. In other words, the norms of politics that are related to institutions—and thus quite valid for compliance—and which (as of yet) still contradict the basic norms of part A of discourse ethics (e.g., the duty of soldiers to kill) are not genuine, deontological norms. Rather, in order to be justified deontologically at all in the present, they must always at the same time subordinate action to the teleological duty of changing the political systems and conditions in view of the long-term generation of the conditions of a cosmopolitan order of law and peace.

This postulated combination of *deontologically* and *teleologically* oriented morality presents itself, no doubt, as puzzling from the viewpoint of the currently prevalent analytic metaethics. In my view, this is solely due to the fact that analytic metaethics begins with conceptual distinctions that abstract from the *historicity* of the basic human condition or suppose a fictive zero point of history (or the possibility of a new beginning). By contrast, the transcendental-pragmatic version of discourse ethics—already with regard to the issue of its ultimate foundation—begins with the historicity of the basic human condition. This is revealed in the fact that discourse ethics presupposes, along with the uncircumventability of argumentation, the dialectical jointure of the a priori of the real community of communication (and its historically conditioned preunderstanding of the world) and of the a priori of the *ideal* community of communication, which is counterfactually assumed in all universal validity claims. With respect to the procedural norms of the postulated ideal practical discourses of its part A, discourse ethics bases itself on the latter presupposition, and it is thus deontological and it *abstracts from history.* By contrast, in the regulative principles of its part B, discourse ethics, as a *historically situated ethics of responsibility,* takes into account the difference between the a priori of the ideal and the a priori of the real community of communication.

1.3.2 In the context of our problem, the systemic function of *law*—which is distinct from the function of political systems of power—came into view with the Kantian project of the long-term generation of *a legal order of peace within states and among states.* However, the systemic function of law can only be realized if political power places itself at the service of law. If this occurs—as is already *the* case today in the form of the monopoly of power of the individual, functioning *states of law [Rechtsstaaten]*—it then shows itself that for the implementation of moral norms, the systemic function of law is the exact opposite of the systemic function of *politics.* While politics (note: in every form of state or government) imposes on all groups organized in the state the circumstantial necessity *[Sachzwang] of the responsibility for its self-assertion,* the law to which the state, so to speak, lends its power, is able to *relieve* the individual groups subject to the state from the responsible exertion of their strategic self-assertion. Through this relief, the state is able to approximate the empowering of individuals and groups to resolve their conflicts discursively and consensually, outside taking legal steps or the path of legally regulated negotiations.

In short, the institutions of the legal system make the functionally decisive contribution, so that human beings can afford morality in the sense of part A of discourse ethics. Under the conditions of the law enforced by the state, the *morality of conflict resolution through practical discourses,* relieved of strategic risk responsibility, becomes *acceptable* to human beings.

Thus, one can say (to some extent, with Habermas)[20] that morality—that is, the morality that is relieved of the political (historically situated!) responsibility of success, the universalist-deontological morality in the sense of the procedural norms of ideal practical discourses (in my terminology: morality in the sense of part A of discourse ethics)—is "equiprimordial" with the establishment of politically enforceable law. (For two reasons I would not, however, with Habermas, equate this condition with the condition of the "principle of democracy." First, I would not do this because the principle of democracy implies too many historically contingent presuppositions of Western, modern development. Second and more importantly, I would not do this because the principle of democracy has never had *merely* the function of the enforcement of universally [and thus internationally] oriented law but, like every *politically* relevant principle of organization, has always had to fulfill a function in the framework of the *self-assertion of a particular system of power.* That this is so is revealed today, for example, in discussions concerning the law of asylum in European democracies. Such discussions can never be rendered intelligible from the viewpoint of the "specification of the principle of discourse" in the sense of the universalizable *principle of law* alone. Rather, they must take into account *specifically political* concerns—in part also for reasons of the ethics of responsibility.)

In my view, it should not be concluded, however, from this equiprimordiality of the differentiation of the functions of law and of morality in the sense of post-conventional dimensions of practical discourses—historically speaking, from the preceding, unified function of "ethical life *[Sittlichkeit]*" in Hegel's sense—that *law and morality,* in the sense of the systematic question of their legitimation, could be understood *in general as equal specifications of a morally neutral* principle of discourse (as Habermas has recently argued).[21] Rather, in my view, in the *transcendental principle of discourse,* the *equal coresponsibility* for the politico-legal realization of the conditions of practical discourses on a global scale (and hence, for example, a cosmopolitan legal order of peace in Kant's sense) is recognized as *morally binding* along with the morally relevant equality of all possible partners of discourse. For this reason, in the transcendental principle of discourse, part B of discourse ethics is cofounded as well. This is the part that cannot yet count on the successful differentiation of law and the morality of part A but finds in this telos the regulative idea of its historically situated responsibility. Yet another conclusion follows: the differentiation of the legal system, which is equiprimordial with the *morality of part A,* finds its expression in the special character of legal norms, namely, in their enforceability through sanctions. This function—as a morally legitimizable exertion of force—itself belongs to part B of this ethics. More precisely, this function can be legitimized as an *institutionally related implementation of morality* only in part B of this ethics, namely, under the presupposition that while in this world we may not count on the conditions of an ideal community of communication, we can come significantly closer to these conditions by way of the detour through the institutionalization of *compulsory norms of law,* especially if these conditions of law can be established on a global scale. (In the democratic, legal state, the system of law can and must create the conditions allowing its own function to be subjected to control and critique through the morally oriented discourses of the "reasoning public" in Kant's sense.)

After these remarks about the norm-implementing functions of politics and law, which can be justified in the sense of part B of discourse ethics, we can now return to the function of the economic system mentioned above.

1.3.3 If one sees the defining function of the *free market* system in the *competition of the sellers of commodities,* whose result is the qualitative improvement and the price reduction of the commodities, which is in turn the interest of the consumers, then the morally relevant point of the implementation of norms in the free market system appears to be the exact opposite of that point in the *legal system.* Human beings are here not relieved of strategic action through institutionalized norms, but, on the contrary, they are forced to strategic action, possibly against their inclinations. However, this is the case under the further institutional presupposition that strategic action is, so to speak, domesticated through the game rules (which are valid for all) of the politico-legal framework order of the economy.

From this structural characteristic results the following double aspect for the moral evaluation of the *market economy.* Strategic action, to which all participants in the market are forced in the sense of their *self-assertion,* appears—according to all basic intuitions of traditional, especially, for example, Christian ethics—distant from morality, if not hostile to it, because the motives of action, at least according to their form, have to be egoistic here.

However, precisely this formal-egoistic conduct is—already according to the basic insight of the moral philosopher Adam Smith and entirely according to the epistemological-economic insight of F. A. von Hayek—the motor of the powerful efficiency of a (capitalist) market economy in the sense of the exploratory acquisition of information about possible resources and possible needs for goods. By way of this orienting mechanism, which depends on the function of nonfalsified price signals, a knowledge about resources and the need of goods, available locally to the respective market participants, is offered. As can be seen especially from the state socialist practice of statism in this century, this knowledge is never available to any central agency of planning and regulation.[22]

Thus the conduct of market participants, which is prima facie hostile to morality, is the source of the market economy's enormous social *function of maximizing utility.* This function, however, only generates benefits for those who can participate in the market with sufficient buying power, while the remainder is, under certain conditions, deprived of all resources, according to the liberalist presupposition that the pure market economy holds the monopoly of supply. Thus the pure system of the capitalist market economy leads to the consequence that the goal of increasing the *total utility* and the goal of *justice*—goals that were traditionally united in the concept of the *common good [Gemeinwohl]*—fall apart. (In my opinion, this is reflected in the philosophical *aporia of modern utilitarianism,* which not accidentally developed at the same time as the market economy.)

Thus a division obtains between potential market participants—which today means humankind. It is a division between economically relevant bearers of "demand" and those who cannot transform their possibly vital *needs [Bedürfnisse]* into economic demand *[Bedarf]* due to a lack of buying power: the "paupers" or the "poor" (rediscovered since the beginning of the nineteenth century). This division occurs at first within the countries with a capitalist market economy, and then, especially at present, in the relation of the First to the Third World. If this description is correct, the decision as to the moral evaluation of the market economy is necessarily made on the level of the acceptance or nonacceptance of the politico-legal order of the market economy by those who subject themselves to this order in the sense of the institutional mediation of their morality. For the (possibly very *selective*) utility of the market economy can only be evaluated on this level with respect to its *distributive utility for all affected parties,* that is, with respect to its justice. John Rawls's second principle of justice could possibly be a useful criterion of evaluation here. According to this principle, deviations from distributive, equal utility are acceptable for as long as the worst-off are still better off than in an alternative order.

As I elaborated above, the presupposed acceptance or nonacceptance of the politico-legal order cannot, however, find its ultimate basis in the *factical formation of consent* within a particular society. For such a basis of consent—even if democratic—could never by itself guarantee the capacity for consent of the order for all affected parties, and thus it could never correspond to the basic principle of discourse ethics.

2. THE QUESTION OF THE ACCEPTABILITY OF THE CURRENTLY EXISTING COMPLEXITY OF THE INSTITUTIONAL OR SYSTEM-RELATED IMPLEMENTATION OF MORALITY TO THE ETHICS OF LIBERATION AND TO DISCOURSE ETHICS: IS A CONSENSUS BETWEEN THE TWO POSSIBLE?

Obviously, with this question, and after my brief discussion of the problem of the institutional implementation of moral norms—which in my view is inevitable and acceptable—I have arrived at the point at which I can enter anew the confrontation with Enrique Dussel. I enter this confrontation in order to show the extent to which the concern of the ethics of liberation is a concern of part B of discourse ethics. For my previous elaborations obviously result in the question of whether the complexity of the institutional or systemic mediations of morality, which I outlined above, could be acceptable in the contemporary world for Dussel or for the poor of this world, who are represented by the ethics of liberation.

I would like to declare at the beginning that I do *not* consider acceptable the currently existing reality of the complexity outlined above. To begin with, I do not consider it acceptable because—as Dussel correctly remarked at the beginning—the poor of the Third World could hardly participate in a democratic consensus-forming discourse about the framework order of the economy. Up to this point, there should be a consensus between Dussel and myself, and probably also between the two of us and Homann. And this means from my perspective that there is a task here, the task to change (existing) circumstances in the sense of part B of discourse ethics (as a historically situated ethics of responsibility).

In this regard, I already clarified in my last contribution to the discussion[23] that I do not at all consider Dussel's distinction between the confrontation with the "skeptic" and the confrontation with the "cynic" as external to discourse ethics. Rather, this distinction offers an especially instructive point of entry into the problem of the *politico-strategic* dimension of part B of discourse ethics. For this dimension in its most poignant form indeed results from a distinction that is itself discourse-ethical, the distinction between those *with whom* one can discuss—to whom the skeptic belongs *per definitionem*—and those *about whom* one can discuss at best, because they reject discourse for strategic reasons. The cynic represents the latter. However, I also warned the ethics of liberation to equate without further ado the "North"—insofar as it appears as the opponent in negotiations—with the cynic, because that is in my view neither ethically nor strategically (in the interest of the assertion of the interests of the poor) tenable.

However, if the ethical demand for the alteration of (existing) conditions should be capable of consensus, then, of course, the crucial question of a globally understood *economic ethics* arises: Can the condition be altered through *reforms* in the sense of their acceptability for all those affected—for example, by realizing the idea of a *social market economy?* Or do we need—still in the sense of Karl Marx—the abolition of the commodity-exchange relations of the capitalist market economy and their replacement by a direct organization of distribution through the "community of producers"?

I understand Dussel's work, including his most recent utterances, as a vote for this socialist alternative, that is, as a plea for a "transcendental economics" that is essentially based on the "labor theory of value" of Marx's *Capital.*

In my very preliminary and tentative introduction[24] to the discussion of the ethics of liberation, I permitted myself to argue against this conception of Dussel, and in this context also directly against the Marxian *labor theory of value* and its consequences. Before I return to this argumentation, however, at this point I have to examine more closely the aforementioned new arguments of Dussel about the relation between the fundamental methodological presuppositions of discourse ethics and the ethics of liberation.

2.1 Looking back at my exposition of the theme in the introduction to the discussion with Dussel, I find that the correction of an apparent methodological misunderstanding seems necessary. In this context, I argued against the plausibility of the Marxian and of Dusselian conceptions not on the basis, and in the name of, the *transcendental-pragmatically grounded discourse ethics* but on the basis of an *anthropological and social-philosophical discourse.* In my view, the latter already presupposes the transcendental-pragmatic theory of discourse, but it presents of itself only *fallible hypotheses.* Here, I must first of all briefly examine a terminological point of difference between Dussel and myself.

In my view, there cannot be a "transcendental economics" because economics cannot be responsible for the answer to the question as to the conditions of its own intersubjective validity as a theory. One may very well concede to Dussel that economics—insofar as it is thematically concerned with the conditions of the bodily existence of human beings—is *ontologically* more fundamental than any *theory of discourse,* which, of course, already ontologically presupposes the bodily existence of human beings. But this consideration—which can lead, in the sense of *historical materialism,* to playing off the priority of the bodily existence of human beings against the "superstructural" phenomenon of thought (or of discourse)—only shows that Kant's *transcendental question* has not been understood any more. (In my view, one must indeed direct this charge already against the young Marx).[25] In my view, when dealing with the transcendental question of philosophy, one cannot compare, and play off against each other, bodily existence and (transcendental) discourse as innerworldly states of affairs. For—to put it succinctly—one can quite well think, or conduct a valid or invalid discourse, about *[über]* human life and its conditions, but one cannot live about *[über]* thought or discourse. This linguistic experiment demonstrates that what is uncircumventable *[das Nichthintergehbare]* in the transcendental sense cannot be life or *bodily existence,* no matter how fundamental they may be from an *ontological* perspective. "To be the participant of a community of producers or of life is [indeed, from my perspective as well] the first condition for the arguing subject as a *living subject.*" [26] In my view, however, this ontological-anthropological truth—which, by the way, will have to be supplemented—in no way alters the transcendental-philosophical, foundational primacy of discourse theory.

In my view, we find here the *methodologically* decisive problem in the possible confrontation between *transcendental-pragmatic* discourse ethics and Dussel's *ethics of liberation.* Transcendental pragmatics presents itself, according to its self-understanding, as a speech-pragmatic and intersubjectivist transformation and radicalization of Kant's mentalist transcendental philosophy. From the viewpoint of this *transcendental pragmatics,* the question as to the *rational foundation of an intersubjectively valid ethics* cannot be answered by the phenomena of the *encounter with the destitution of the other* (Dussel with Levinas), no matter how impressive they are.

The *question of foundation* can only be answered through recourse to the "self-agreement" (Kant) of reason, which is demonstrable *[ausweisbar]* in a self-reflexive discourse. The self-agreement of reason, however, implies as a "communicative rationality" ("discourse rationality") that the "interpellation of the other" (Dussel), that is, the validity "claim" of every possible discourse partner, is to be taken into account unconditionally.

This is a demand of our autonomous (i.e., in Kant's sense of giving oneself the moral law) reason, a demand that is discursively-communicatively explicated. For this reason, this demand can secure a priori (in the sense of the transcendental-reflexive ultimate foundation of morality) that one cannot dismiss the purely phenomenologically understood appeal of the "interpellation of the other." This interpellation, linguistic or prelinguistic, can be linguistically explicated, but it cannot be dismissed as "heteronomous" and thus as an unreasonable demand *[Zumutung]* without moral obligation, as would otherwise always be the case. However, this also means that the "interpellation of the other," say concretely of the Third World poor, must be brought to validity by those affected themselves or by their advocates (e.g., the theologians of liberation and the philosophers) in the discourses about this topic, however deficient or deformed, while taking into account all pertinent knowledge of the sciences. (In my view, a methodologically relevant gap opens up here today between those ethics that are, in Levinas's sense, phenomenologically oriented and discourse ethics, insofar as the latter must insist on the, at least partially possible, settlement of all differences of interests and of opinion in discourses that are as rational as possible.)

On the basis of this indication of a *complementarity* of the starting points *[Ansätze]* of *discourse ethics* and of the *ethics of liberation*—starting points that are irreducible to one another—one might think that one could arrive relatively quickly at a discussion that is oriented toward cooperation. It would be a discussion about the concrete and more urgent but also, for the philosopher, more difficult question of how, in today's world, justice can be done to the claims of the others who are excluded from the discourse of the dominant community of communication (more, but not very much more, concretely, the poor of the Third World). Unfortunately, however, there cannot yet be any talk of the possible agreement that I just indicated, an agreement about the starting point of the discussion. I had to convince myself of this lack of agreement in particular by reading Dussel's essay "The Priority of the Ethics of Liberation over Discourse Ethics."[27] Precisely the thesis of complementarity which had already solidified with me to an operative illusion, is here rejected passionately in favor of an equalization of the real *foundation* with the "revelation" of the claims of the other, transcending reason in the event of the "encounter" with the other.[28]

To be sure, Dussel assures us of his agreement "with the estimation that valid argumentation and thus also the ethics of liberation would be impossible if we did not succeed in rejecting the skeptic."[29] But he does not see that the transcendental-pragmatic way of grounding ethics through reflection on the unchallengeable conditions of argumentation—to which also belong the moral-normative conditions in the sense of the recognition of the claims of all partners in argumentation—is an indispensable presupposition also for "the ethical grounding of the praxis of liberation of the dominated and excluded," if it is to be rationally compelling. This is so because only in this way—that is, the way of the prior recognition of the excluded others as potential partners of argumentation—can the obligation to consider virtual "acts of interpellation" of these others be rendered obvious. For Dussel, the transcendental-pragmatic ultimate foundation of moral norms is in general only a subordinate methodological self-grounding of ethical argumentation "on the level of the community of philosophers and scientists"—a special ethics of argumentation, so to speak.[30]

Dussel does not see that the methodological detour via the securing *(Vergewisserung)* of what even the most radical skeptic cannot challenge without self-contradiction has its significance for the *ethical foundation of the praxis of liberation itself* in procuring in advance a legitimation that is required for the interpretation of every particular case of the "interpellation of the Other." This legitimation renders it impossible to perceive, and thus not to recognize as morally relevant, the *claims of the Other* from the perspective of a dominant worldview of a self-enclosed internal morality (a "totality" in Levinas's sense).

Instead, Dussel claims that the original ethical rationality lies solely "in the practical recognition *[Erkennen]* that . . . constitutes the *Other* as a person, as an

Other. . . ." Thus, this rationality exists "*prior to every argumentation*" (Dussel's emphasis) and "thus also prior to the Apelian process of transcendentalizing and grounding."[31] He claims further that it is the "original ethical rationality . . . that represents the rational way to relate to Otherness, to the distinct rationality of the Other and not (as in Apel) to the difference-in-identity." For, Dussel argues, "from my/our world . . . and in it, the Other *reveals* himself as transcendent. . . . The ethical-practical experience of the 'face-to-face,' the respect toward the Other who is recognized as an autonomous person, is not primarily an experience of the understanding of being, but a 'letting-the-other-be,' poised in expectation of his 'revelation.'"[32]

By contrast, according to Dussel, "every universal morality, including that of Apel and Habermas," has to articulate itself "always within a pre-given, conventional "ethical life *[Sittlichkeit]*," for example, the European-North American, conservative, liberal or social-democratic ethical life." For "it would be naive to believe that the critical European philosopher could situate himself in a postconventional manner in his everyday life without admitting that his concrete 'reactions' are those of a member of Western culture—in this point, one has to agree fully with Charles Taylor."[33]

Beginning from the conclusion, so to speak, just like Dussel, I passed through, and thus do not need to be enlightened about, the reflection on the a priori of facticity, of historicity, and of the *sociocultural conditionedness of our everyday understanding of the world,* a reflection that reaches from Heidegger to the communitarianism of the present. However, I have not been converted to a historicism-relativism in my constant confrontation with this *hermeneutic-neopragmatic-communitarian turn* in, and since, my book *Transformation of Philosophy* (1973). And this means the following with regard to the current problem under discussion between Dussel and myself.

I am not exactly sure how far, in a concrete case, the dependence of Dussel's and my everyday reactions on that *conventional ethical life* (or on the "morality" of a "totality" that closes itself off from the outside) goes. At least, both of us could reflect on this ethicality critically and philosophically. (Philosophers, and later social scientists too, have been capable of this reflection since the Axial Age *[Achsenzeit]* of ancient high cultures,[34] to which belonged not only the Greek origin of Occidental culture. And this *postconventional* competence of thinking about morality and law, which has since that time never been lost, has also expressed itself in our institutions, especially in the constitutional tradition of basic rights and of human rights, a tradition that is today in the process of global instantiation. All of this holds despite the fact that, according to Lawrence Kohlberg's estimation, even at present only about 80 percent of the U.S. population factically reaches the level of the postconventional competence of moral judgment.)

On the other hand, however, I know at least the following on the basis of transcendental-pragmatic reflection: In the current discussion between Dussel and myself about the concern and the mutual relation of discourse ethics and the ethics of liberation, it cannot be a matter of one of those "reactions" that are entirely dependent on conventional ethicality. If this were the case, I would have to articulate myself according to Dussel within the European–North American tradition (i.e., according to Dussel, within the "totality" that excludes the other of the Third World), whereas he supposedly articulates himself within an entirely different ethicality. Dussel summarizes this latter ethicality as "Semitic" and characterizes it in the following way: "The Bantu-African, Primitive-Egyptian (since 4000 B.C.), Mesopotamian-Semitic world like that of Hammurabi, the world of the Phoenicians, Aramians, Hebrews, Christians, up to the Muslims."[35]

Here, I cannot and will not examine more closely Dussel's audacious ethnohistorical delimitations. (From the perspective of the conception of the "Axial Age," matters appear in a somewhat different way, especially in the historical retrospective on the synthesis of Greek and Semitic thought, which persists since the time of the Church Fathers in the Christian West and in Islam and which, in my view, presents the real articulatory background of all of Dussel's writings.)

In any case, it is clear that the current discussion between Dussel and myself could not take place under Dusselian presuppositions (self-enclosing conventional "totalities" of morality on the one hand, "transcendence of the Other" on the other). (Already at this point, a performative contradiction, in the sense of transcendental pragmatics, arises.) In practice, this would mean that a philosophically led understanding *[Verständigung]* between cultures—let alone the serious effort at a "multicultural" world society of the affirmative tolerance within the limits of a formal morality of equality that would be binding for all, and a world society of the equal coresponsibility of all for the solution to the problems of mankind—would have no chance. In regard to the real problems of the relation between the Third and the First Worlds, we would again get into the—philosophically prefabricated!—dead end that, in my view, already results if one equates, without further ado, the representatives of the North in their structure of thought with the philosophical construct of the "cynic."

What is decisive in this situation (in which one could only face, with Samuel P. Huntington, the "clash of civilizations") is in my view the serious philosophical attempt to *reflexively reappropriate [einholen]* the *current dialogue* (argumentative discourse) in view of its normative conditions before all definitive estimation of the possibility of the *dialogue with the other.* One has always already entered this current dialogue (even in his lonely thinking, the philosopher has always already entered this discourse), and one always already, necessarily, counts on the principled possibility of understanding, even of consensus about validity claims.

In my view, this attempt is lacking in Dussel's argumentation, as sketched above. But it is not only lacking in him but, in my view, in all those thinkers who today set the tone and presuppose, and *only* presuppose, to use Heidegger's language, the "existential prestructure" of "the being-in-the-world that understands," that is, the "ontological prestructure of the understanding of being" in the sense of the "thrown projection" of a historically conditioned mode of understanding the world (in the sense of the later Wittgenstein, a "form of life"). For a long time now I have made an effort not to reject this starting point but to demonstrate it as being in principle incomplete. For this sketch of the "prestructure" of the being-in-the-world that understands the reflection on that part of the "prestructure" that enabled philosophers to analyze the prestructure in Heidegger's (and Gadamer's) sense in intersubjectively valid form, and to render conscious on this level of reflection the problem of the multiplicity and difference, and even opposition, of the modes of the ontological understanding of being.

If the *reflexive self-reappropriation,* as indicated above, of the inescapable starting point of every philosophy succeeds (the *transcendental*-pragmatic and *transcendental*-hermeneutic turn of thought), then, in my view, we can detect the aforementioned, historically situated jointure of two a prioris as the foundational situation of ethics. This is a jointure of the *a priori of the real community of communication* (the unchallengeable belonging to a particular, historically conditioned tradition of a preunderstanding of the world, including an understanding of morality), and the *a priori of the ideal community of communication,* which is necessarily anticipated counterfactually by the universal validity claims of every criticizable, philosophical argumentation. One side of the dialectical jointure conditions the danger of a cynical self-enclosure of a moral "totality" against all claims of outside parties (the factically oppressed and exploited others), a danger that Dussel rightly makes the object of a permanent ideology-critique in view of *Euro-centrism.* By contrast, the other side of the jointure (which today, however, hardly any "pragmatic" thinkers of the North recognize as the necessary orientation of normative thought) stretches out in advance a horizon of understanding the Other with regard to his possible "claims." This horizon grounds in part A of discourse ethics the procedural norms of "practical discourses" about possible conflicts of interest (which in my view would be possible under the condition of a cosmopolitan order of law). Furthermore, this horizon opens up in part B of discourse ethics a possible justification of all imaginable strategies of "liberation" in the sense of the progressive realization of the conditions of applications of part A of discourse ethics.

Of course, in its a priori of the coresponsibility of all discourse partners for the discovery and consideration of all claims of virtual discourse partners, this transcendental grounding renders itself in advance dependent on the factical *experiential evidences* in regard to the necessary interpellation of the other. (This interpellation consists not only in the possible face-to-face experiences of the destitution of the Third World poor—and in the corresponding experience with practically excluded ones within one's own "moral totality"!—but also, as remarked earlier, in the merely imaginable claims of coming generations.) Nonetheless, the experiential evidences that are here presupposed are anticipated in advance, and they are placed in advance under a basic norm of intersubjectivity in the sense of a *universalized reciprocity* with regard to the ethical *interpretability* of these evidences (in the sense of principled equality of all interests as virtual validity claims in practical discourses under the regulative ideal of the effort for the consensus of all those affected). (This basic norm is, as mentioned above, already recognized in a thinking with intersubjective validity claims, and, in this sense, it has nothing to do with the strategic reciprocity of the *do, ut des,* which belongs to a different, abstractly limited type of rationality.) This basic norm, as a horizon of interpretation, is, to be sure, referred in advance to the *emotional* and *sensual affectability in the encounter with the other*—so to speak, as a "context of discovery" of every applicable discourse ethics. But in my view, this basic norm cuts off a priori the interpretation that wishes to originally ground the idea of justice (and the coresponsibility that belongs to it) on the basis of the in itself "infinite" claim of the "transcendent Other," a claim that is experienced as "heteronomous" and is thus "context-free" and without comparison.[36]

As a basic norm of *transcendental hermeneutics,* it respects, along with the hermeneutic tradition since Friedrich Schleiermacher, the principle *individuum est ineffabile* and thus *the nonanticipatable otherness*, or "exteriority," of every other in relation to my or our "thrown projection of the understanding of being" and thus, if you will, in relation to every "ontology" (in Heidegger's sense). But it does not, as a post-Hegelian and post-Peircean insight, engage in the performatively contradictory attempt to think that which is *in principle unthinkable,* or that which is only thinkable as unknowable (Kant's "thing in itself"), as the essence of reality of the other and his claims. Instead, it supposes, with Charles Peirce, the definition of the real as the regulative idea of the knowable, which, however, cannot ever be fully known *[erkannt].* In my view, this definition does justice both to the demand for understanding *[Verständigung],* which is implied in the basic norm of morality, or for hermeneutic understanding *[Verstehen],* and to the related critical modesty in the sense of the awareness of the *otherness of the other.* And this definition is also thoroughly sufficient to render intelligible that the other, as the representative of a foreign culture, can confront the conventional understanding of being of a "moral totality" (e.g., of the "North" in Dussel's sense) with his genuine claims and their presuppositions in the sense of the understanding of being, and as a transcendent site of putting the former in question. However, it is not sufficient to oppose *a wholly different thinking, a different reason* to the *logos* of Occidental philosophy as a whole, more precisely, to the *logos* claimed by Hegel, which is, as is the *logos* of the understanding of being in Heidegger's sense, oriented not toward the "prestructure" of the "thrown projection" of "being-in-the-world," but rather toward the *self-reflection of argumentative discourse.* As critically related to Hegel, this definition only brings to validity the *openness of possible experience* of every potential, human dialogue, which in principle cannot be "superseded" *(aufgehoben)* in the monologue of a thinker.

In my view, the preceding remarks can be summarized in the following way: as the *transcendental-hermeneutic foundation* of the normative conditions of the interpretation of possible experiential evidences regarding the possible "claims" of the other or of others, the *transcendental-pragmatic foundation* of the basic norm of morality stretches out, so to speak, the prior horizon for the discourse–ethical consideration of all of Dussel's "interpellations" of the poor as those who have previously been excluded from all relevant discourses. This foundation can in principle transcend the horizon of the conventional understanding of morality of a self-enclosing "totality." It can provide the bridge to the concern of the ethics of liberation because it does not, in contradistinction to almost all currently dominant starting points for an ethics in the West or in the North, begin with the "strong valuations" (C. Taylor) of a particular tradition of community, and even less with the strategic self-interests of isolated individuals. Instead, it begins with the *a priori of the ideal community of communication,* which is presupposed by every real community of communication qua community of discourse. As a regulative idea, this a priori transcends every particular "moral totality" (already in the foundational part A of discourse ethics). Furthermore, (in the foundational part B of discourse ethics) it can render intelligible the difference between the presuppositions of self-enclosing "moral totalities," a difference that arises in the conflict between cultures, and especially in the conflict between the North and the South. It can also render intelligible the ideal demand for understanding *(Verständigung)* in an unlimited ideal community of communication, and it can ground the long-term overcoming of obstacles to understanding as a duty to progress.

With regard to this second dimension of the possible application of discourse ethics to the problems of the ethics of liberation, I have, in the present contribution, put forward the thesis that we are here essentially dealing with the ethical acceptability of the *implementation of moral norms.* This implementation is in principle inevitable, but it is still not without reservations in a particular case. It is an implementation *according to the game rules of social institutions or the functional action systems of society.* And I have also already explained that the currently existing global reality of the institutional mediation of morality cannot be acceptable to those in the Third World. From this point of view, for me the primary problem that arises in the confrontation with Dussel's ethics of liberation is that of the acceptability or nonacceptability of the system of a (capitalist) market economy. I would now like to present some reflections on this problem that may clarify my earlier reservations about the recourse of liberation ethics to Marx.

2.2 In the aforementioned introduction I found myself compelled to argue against Dussel's recourse to the Marxian *thesis of the value of labor* in *Capital* and its consequences (socialism as the only alternative to the "destruction of nature and human beings") in a sense that is not grounded on transcendental economy but on anthropology and social philosophy.

Here, I would only like to return to one of the main points of my argumentation. In my view, one has not sufficiently understood the argument, first presented by Habermas,[37] that Marx does not sufficiently take into account the difference between "labor" and "interaction." One has not understood it sufficiently if one refers, correctly, to the fact that Marx always also, in conjunction with the function of the "material exchange with nature" through labor, takes into account the *association of the subjects of labor in the community of producers.* The following passage, for example, is indeed characteristic of Marx's perspective:

> Let us finally imagine, for a change, an association of free men, working with the means of production held in common, and expending their many different forms of labour-power in full self-awareness as one single social labour force. *All the characteristics of Robinson's labour are repeated here, but with the difference that they are social instead of individual.* All Robinson's products were exclusively the result of his own personal labour and they were therefore directly *objects of utility* for him personally. The total product of our imagined association is a *social product.* One part of this product serves as fresh means of production and remains social. But another part is consumed by the members of the association as means of subsistence. . . . *The social relations of the individual producers, both towards their labor and the products of their labor,* are here transparent in their simplicity, for production as well as distribution.[38]

It becomes very clear in this and in many similar passages that for Marx, the consideration of the societal relations of human beings comes down to the *replacement of individual subjects of labor by a collective subject—the community of associated producers.* This community, in partial analogy to Robinson's appropriation of his products of labor, is supposed to distribute the total product of labor as "objects of utility"—or "concrete use values"—to the members of the community of producers. On the other hand, however, this community, now in opposition to Robinson, is supposed to reuse a part of the social product as a means of production. In this way, Marx suggests, the relation among human beings, their work, and their products of labor remain "transparent and simple." But this appearance stems, in my view, from the fact that Marx says almost nothing about the *interaction* that has to take place between human beings from the start in *complementarity to labor* qua "material exchange with nature." Instead, Marx only speaks of the "regulation" of labor and the "distribution" of the products of labor through the collective subject of the community of producers.

What is missing here is, in my view, not only the *aspect of interaction* that one may call, with Habermas—in a certain idealization of life world interaction—"consensual interaction." What is missing, first, is the aspect of *strategic interaction* between human beings that is enacted in the *exchange of goods* and in related *negotiations.* This aspect of interaction is, in my view, and I am here following the opinion of almost all anthropologists, based in the life world and equiprimordial with labor, and that means prior to the differentiation of the system of the market economy. If one now takes into consideration this anthropological *equiprimordiality of the complementary functions of labor and interaction qua exchange,* then Marx's thesis is extremely implausible (as the advocates of the "limit-use theory" *[Grenznutzentheorie]* have pointed out correctly). It is the thesis that the market (in the sense of the capitalist system of the economy) abstracts completely from the (concrete) use value of goods—in favor of exchange value, which is only measured by the expended labor time.

Marx's insight into the tendency toward *alienation* and *reification* of human relations in the institutions of the market economy (in the sense of the "fetishism" of commodity relations) remains in my view correct and ingenious. But this "alienation" and "reification" cannot be removed completely if only because it is not only based on the *necessity of the institutionalization of labor* but also on the *necessity of the institutionalization of (strategic) relations of exchange.* If one overlooks, as Marx does, this second dimension of the differentiation of the social subsystems of the economy, then one cannot sufficiently appreciate the positive achievements of market economy. These are achievements in terms of the *commercial mediation between scarce resources and potential demand.*

With this remark, I do not want to dispute or play down the precarious fact that the commercial mediation between *resources* and *demand* in no way takes into consideration the concrete (and vital) *needs* of human beings themselves. The market system of the economy indeed abstracts from these needs—but not from the "use values" of goods in general. As a market system, it takes into consideration only the—by all means "concrete"—"use values" of goods for the *bearers of demand* (who are supposed to possess buying power) but not the concrete needs of human beings. (In my view, the relevant correction of Marx's thesis of the nonconsideration of the "concrete use values" by the "exchange values" of the capitalist market economy would have to be formulated approximately in this way by a limit-use theory. Thus the "labor theory of value" would still retain a part of its significance, namely, for those cases in which we can disregard the commercial achievement of supply *[Versorgungsleistung]* through the market (the discovery and mediation of resources and demand), and in which only the technological level of production of the national economies that are competing with one another or are dependent on regular exchange, has any weight. In these cases, the state of affairs of the "unequal exchange," as analyzed by Marxist economists, can in my view really be obtained.)[39]

Primarily because of the achievement of supply, as efficient as it is selective, of the market with regard to the concrete needs of human beings, the market economy is, as I have indicated above, dependent on a *compensatory function of economic and social politics* on the level of the *framework order of the economy.* This order ought to be acceptable to all those involved. In our time, this compensatory function must be fulfilled on a global scale, and that means in the face of the division of people who profit from the market economy and those who are excluded from the monopoly of supply by the market economy. Unfortunately, I am not able to offer any concrete prescriptions for the possible politico-economic solution to this task. However, I also do not see that any such solutions could be offered by the *ethics of liberation.* In any case, Marx's utopia of the *su-*

persession of the market economy seems to me to be as implausible today as the *liberal or neoliberal utopia,* which expects the best possible fulfillment of the demand for "social justice" from the "invisible hand" of the market economy alone. (Of course, we have to distinguish from this the substitution of the ethical idea of social justice by the social Darwinist idea of the inevitable prevailing of the capitalist market economy along the lines of the "survival of the fittest," as suggested by F. A. von Hayek. This solution can in my view no longer be seen as morally acceptable in the sense of Adam Smith.)

Thus I can by all means—against Hinkelammert's imputation[40]—agree with him (and with L. Kolakowski) that we should resist the utopian "extortion by reference to the only alternative"—either in the sense of Marxism or in the sense of neoliberalism.

Nonetheless, this should not prevent us from considering the concern of the ethics of liberation—just like the concern of an ecological ethics or an ethics of peace aimed at the generation of a cosmopolitan order of law—as a current dimension of application of discourse ethics, primarily its part B.

NOTES

Translated by Matthias Lütkehermölle.

1. Cf. Karl-Otto Apel, "Diskursethik als Verantwortungsethik—Eine postmetaphysische Transformation der Ethik Kants," in *Ethik und Befreiung,* ed. Raúl Fornet–Betancourt (Aachen: Augustinus–Buchhandlung 1990), pp. 10–40. See Dussel's response in "Die 'Lebensgemeinschaft' und die 'Interpellation der Armen': Die Praxis der Befreiung," in *Ethik und Befreiung,* pp. 69–96.

2. Cf. Karl-Otto Apel, *Diskurs und Verantwortung* (Frankfurt/M: Suhrkamp, 1988), esp. pp. 134ff.

3. Cf. ibid.; Apel, "Diskursethik vor der Problematik von Recht und Politik: Können die Rationalitätsdifferenzen zwischen Moralität, Recht, und Politik selbst noch durch die Diskursethik normativ–rational gerechtfertigt werden?" in *Zur Anwendung der Diskursethik in Politik, Recht, und Wissenschaft,* ed. Karl-Otto Apel and M. Kettner (Frankfurt/M: Suhrkamp, 1992), pp. 29–61.

4. See Jürgen Habermas, *Justification and Application: Remarks on Discourse Ethics,* trans. Ciaran P. Cronin (Cambridge: MIT Press, 1993), pp. 84ff.

5. Translator's note: Apel's central concept of the *Letztbegründung* of moral norms, which carries connotations of "justification," is usually translated as "ultimate foundation." *Begründung* and its verbal forms have been translated as "foundation," "founding," or "grounding," depending on the context. Apel has in mind a "reflexive grounding" that turns on the speaker's self-reflective awareness of what he or she is doing when raising or questioning validity claims in arguments. This self-reflection reveals those presuppositions of argumentation that Apel characterizes as *nicht hintergehbar* (literally, "what cannot be gotten behind," "what is uncircumventable"). This latter term has been translated as "inescapable" for consistency.

6. Cf. Franz J. Hinkelammert, "Die Marxsche Wertlehre und die Philosophie der Befreiung: Einige Probleme der Diskursethik und der Marxismuskritik Apels," in *Für En-*

rique Dussel, ed. Raúl Fornet-Betancourt (Aachen: Augustinus–Buchhandlung, 1995), pp. 35–74; Hinkelammert, "Diskursethik und Verantwortungsethik: Eine kritische Stellungnahme" (Brazil: Unisinos, 1993), 29.9–1.10; Hinkelammert, "Gebrauchswert, Nutzenpräferenz, und postmodernes Denken: Die Wertlehre in der Wirtschaftstheorie und ihre Stelle im Denken über die Gesellschaft" (unpublished manuscript); Hinkelammert, *Kritik der utopischen Vernunft* (Mainz: Matthias–Grünewald–Verlag, 1994).

7. See Karl Homann and F. Blome-Drees, *Wirtschafts– und Unternehmensethik* (Göttingen: Vandenhoek & Ruprecht [UTB], 1992). With reference to this, see Karl-Otto Apel, "Institutionenethik oder Diskursethik als Verantwortungsethik? Das Problem der institutionellen Implementation moralischen Normen in Fallen des Systems der Marketwirtschaft," in *25 Jahren Diskursethik,* ed. J. P. Harpes (Luxemburg: Lit-Verlag, 1995).

8. Cf. Apel, "Diskursethik vor der Problematik von Recht und Politik."

9. Cf. Apel, "Institutionenethik oder Diskursethik als Verantwortungsethik."

10. See Karl-Otto Apel, "Kant's 'Toward Perpetual Peace' as Historical Prognosis from the Point of View of Moral Duty," in *Perpetual Peace: Essays on Kant's Cosmopolitan Ideal,* ed. James Bohman and Matthias Lutz-Bachmann (Cambridge: MIT Press, 1997), pp. 79–110.

11. Immanuel Kant, "Perpetual Peace: A Philosophical Sketch," in *Political Writings,* ed. Hans Reiss, trans. H. B. Nisbet (Cambridge: Cambridge University Press, 1990), p. 123.

12. See Immanuel Kant, "On a Supposed Right to Lie Because of Philanthropic Concerns," in *Grounding for the Metaphysics of Morals and On a Supposed Right to Lie Because of Philanthropic Concerns,* trans. James W. Ellington (Indianapolis: Hackett, 1992), pp. 63–67.

13. Cf. L. Kohlberg, *The Philosophy of Moral Development* (San Francisco: Harper & Row, 1981). On Kohlberg, see Karl-Otto Apel, "Die tranzendentalpragmatische Begründung der Kommunikationsethik und das Problem der höchsten Stufe einer Entwicklungslogik des moralischen Bewußtseins," in *Diskurs und Verantwortung* (Frankfurt/M: Suhrkamp, 1988), pp. 306–69.

14. Translator's note: Dussel and thus Apel adopt the phrase "the other" from Levinas. In standard English translations of Levinas's work, Levinas's *autre/Autre* is rendered as "other," whereas *autrui/Autrui*, referring to the personal other, is translated by "Other."

15. Cf. Enrique Dussel, *Philosophy of Liberation,* trans. Aquilina Martinez and Christine Morkovsky (Maryknoll, N.Y.: Orbis, 1985), sec. 2.1, "Proximity." See also H. Schelkshorn, *Ethik der Befreiung: Einführung in die Philosophie Enrique Dussels* (Freiburg: Herder, 1992), chap. 4.

16. Cf. Homann and Blome-Drees, *Wirtschafts– und Unternehmensethik*, pp. 55, 67. The cite on page 67 refers to James M. Buchanan, "Constitutional Democracy, Individual Liberty, and Political Equality," in *Jahrbuch für Neue Politische Ökonomie* 4 (1985): 35–47. Cf. also K. Homann and A. Suchanek, "Wirtschaftsethik—Angewandte Ethik oder Beitrag zur Grundlagendiskussion?" in *Ökonomische Theorie und Ethik*, ed. B. Biervert and M. Held (Frankfurt/M: Campus, 1987), pp. 101–21. Cf. my response in "Diskursethik als Verantwortungsethik und das Problem der ökonomischen Rationalität," in *Diskurs und Verantwortung,* pp. 270–305; Apel, "Institutionenethik oder Diskursethik als Verantwortungsethik."

17. Cf. Karl-Otto Apel, "Can an Ultimate Foundation of Knowledge be Non–Metaphysical?" *Journal of Speculative Philosophy* 7, no. 3 (1993): 171–90.

18. I am relying here on the distinction (proposed by M. Niquet) between the "validity" of norms (in the sense of the principle of universality, which is related to the ideal formation of consensus) and its "validity of compliance" (in the sense of the responsibility related to factical situations). Cf. M. Niquet, "Verantwortung und Moralstrategie: Überlegungen zu einem Typus praktisch–moralischer Vernunft," in *Die eine Vernunft und die vielen Rationalitäten,* ed. K.-O. Apel and M. Kettner (Frankfurt/M: Suhrkamp, 1995).

19. The concept I am using here—the concept of the "basic norms" that can be ultimately founded—meets with difficulties, in particular under the presupposition of a principle of discourse ethics that can be ultimately founded and that delegates the foundation of all *material* (and thus "substantial") norms to the "practical discourses" of those involved (or their representatives). But in my view, these difficulties are only of a conventional–linguistic kind and are conditioned by the habitual terminology of metaethics, which does not do justice to the *transcendental–pragmatic* problematic of foundation anyway. In my view, the following factor is more important than a smooth applicability of the habitual dichotomies (such as "formal" vs. "material" or "substantial").

Both the legitimate question as to the content of meaning *[Sinngehalt]* of the "procedural norms" of ideal "practical discourses" and especially the insight that this content of meaning can be *specified* in the form of such "norms"—which cannot be founded in "practical discourses" because they belong to the *conditions of possibility* of ideal practical discourses—require a terminology in the sense of the "basic norms" I have in mind.

These norms correspond to Kant's "indispensable duties" whose nonfulfillment would be irreconcilable with the "agreement of reason with itself," insofar as they cannot be denied in the ideal discourse without performative self–contradiction. Nonetheless, the "validity of compliance" (e.g., not killing, not lying, not instrumentalizing the Other strategically, etc.) by no means follows from this in the real world. The validity of compliance would only follow if it can be assumed that all others are also *complying* with the valid basic norms; otherwise, part B of discourse ethics is in effect, which is equiprimordial with part A in view of the difference between the a priori of the ideal community of communication and the a priori of the real community of communication.

20. See Jürgen Habermas, *Between Facts and Norms: Contributions to a Discourse Theory of Law and Democracy,* trans. William Rehg (Cambridge: MIT Press, 1996), pp. 104ff.

21. Ibid.

22. Cf. Friedrich August von Hayek, *Individualismus und wirtschaftliche Ordnung,* 2d ed. (Salzburg: Neugebauer, 1976); see also his *Die Verfassung der Freiheit* (Tübingen: Mohr, 1971); and *Recht, Gesetzgebung, und Freiheit*, 3 vols. (Munich: Verlag Moderne Industrie, 1980–81).

23. Cf. Karl-Otto Apel, "Die Diskursethik vor der Herausforderung der lateinamerikanischen Philosophie der Befreiung," in *Konvergenz oder Divergenz,* pp. 17–38.

24. Cf. Karl-Otto Apel, "Die Diskursethik vor der Herausforderung der Dritten Welt, pt. 1, Vorüberlegungen," in *Diskursethik oder Befreiungsethik?* pp. 16–54.

25. Cf. D. Böhler, *Metakritik der Marxschen Ideologiekritik* (Frankfurt/M: Suhrkamp, 1971).

26. Dussel, "Die Priorität der Befreiungsethik gegenüber der Diskursethik," in *Anerkennung der Anderen,* ed. Edmund Arens (Freiburg: Herder, 1995), p. 126 passim.

27. Ibid., pp. 113–37.

28. Ibid., pp. 130f.

29. Ibid., p. 133.
30. Ibid.
31. Ibid., p. 118.
32. Ibid., pp. 130f.
33. Ibid.
34. See Karl Jaspers, *The Origin and Goal of History,* trans. Michael Bullock (New Haven: Yale University Press, 1953). See also S. N. Eisenstadt, ed., *Kulturen der Achsenzeit: Ihre Ursprünge und ihre Vielfalt*, 2 vols. (Frankfurt/M: Suhrkamp, 1987); *Kulturen der Achsenzeit II,* 3 vols. (Frankfurt/M: Suhrkamp, 1992). See further H. Rötz, *Die chinesische Ethik der Achsenzeit* (Frankfurt/M: Suhrkamp, 1992). Translator's note: In Jaspers's historico-philosophical project, *Achsenzeit* refers to a turning point of world history. Since this turning point, which Jaspers locates between 800 and 200 B.C., world history becomes an integrated and comprehensive event. The concept is directed polemically against the traditional Christian concept of universal history, which neglects the plurality of cultures but maintains the idea of humanity as a historical unity.
35. Dussel, "Die Priorität der Befreiungsethik gegenüber der Diskursethik," p. 132 n. 54.
36. For this reason, the Levinasian starting point of a "heteronomous" grounding of ethics, which Dussel follows, is probably in the end irreconcilable with the starting point of transcendental pragmatics. As far as I can see, Levinas himself could not solve, in a manner satisfactory to himself, the problem of justice with this starting point, as presented in his first major work, *Totalité et infini* (1961). The problem of justice presupposes a priori a context of the comparison, and thus also the possibility of the *autonomous recognition of the equality,* of all claims of the potential *Other.* I dare doubt that he succeeded in solving this problem in later writings (e.g., in *Autrement que'être; ou, Au-delà de l'essence,* 1974) by way of the introduction of the "third party" as the "Other of the other." Cf. Stéphane Mosès, "Gerechtigkeit und Gemeinschaft bei Emmanuel Levinas," in *Gemeinschaft und Gerechtigkeit,* ed. M. Brumlik and H. Brunkhorst (Frankfurt/M: Fischer, 1993).
37. Jürgen Habermas, "Labor and Interaction: Remarks on Hegel's Jena *Philosophy of Mind,*" in *Theory and Practice,* ed. John Viertel (Boston: Beacon, 1973).
38. Karl Marx, *Capital,* vol. 1, trans. Ben Fowkes (New York: Vintage, 1977), pp. 171f. Apel's emphasis.
39. Cf. also Enrique Dussel, "Die 'Essenz' der Dependenz: Die Beherrschung unterentwickelter durch hochentwickelte Bourgeoisien und die Übertragung von Mehrwert," *Dialektik* 2 (1993): 99–106.
40. Cf. Franz Hinkelammert, introduction to *Kritik der utopischen Vernunft: Eine Auseinandersetzung mit den Hauptströmungen der modernen Gesellschaftstheorie* (Mainz: Matthias–Grünewald-Verlag, 1994); Hinkelammert, "Gebrauchswert, Nutzenpräferenz, und postmodernes Denken," in *Die Diskursethik und ihre lateinamerikanische Kritik,* ed. Raúl Fornet-Betancourt (Aachen: Augustinus-Buchhandlung, 1993); Hinkelammert, "Etica do discurso e etica de la responsabilidade: Uma tomada de posiçâo critica," in *Etica do discurso e filosofía de libertaçâo: Modelos complementares,* ed. A. Sidekum (Sao Leopoldo, Brazil: Ed. Unisinos, 1994).

5

Discourse and Liberation: Toward a Critical Coordination of Discourse Ethics and Dussel's Ethics of Liberation

Hans Schelkshorn

The discourse theory of ethics developed by Jürgen Habermas and Karl-Otto Apel and the liberation ethics of Enrique Dussel have come to attain representative status for the respective political contexts out of which they arise. The passionate discussions they have provoked confirm their significant position. Discourse ethics continues the European tradition of universal morality at a purified level; it integrates critically the two waves of Enlightenment that European history has crossed. On the other side, the Latin American "philosophy of liberation" marks the temporary climax of a development toward a genuine Latin American thinking. The first (though failed) impulses of this development lie in the independence movements of Latin American colonies in the nineteenth century. In this chapter, however, I refer only to Dussel's conception,[1] which is one among the many different lines of "philosophy of liberation"[2] because it lends itself very well to a critical comparison with discourse ethics.

I will not try to develop a systematic comparison between discourse and liberation ethics. This chapter should be understood as a contribution to a dialogue that has been going on recently between Karl-Otto Apel and Enrique Dussel.[3] I intend to compare their two moral theories in such a way that the strong and the weak points of each ethics become manifest in the light of the other.

Dussel's "philosophy of liberation" and Apel's "transcendental pragmatics" claim to have reformulated the Aristotelian project of a "first philosophy." I do not consider this question nor the concomitant problem of an ultimate foundation *(Letztbegründung)* of ethics.

1. CONTEXTS AND PROVOCATIONS

Moral theory responds to certain problems of morality, for instance, the ecological question, which led Hans Jonas to develop a new foundation of ethics. It also responds when moral claims themselves become questionable, as was the case with Freud's unmasking of the claims of conscience. It is therefore advisable to first look at the different contexts of discourse and liberation ethics.

1.1. Discourse ethics as an ethics in the context of science and technology

At the beginning of the important article "Das Apriori der Kommunikationsgemeinschaft und die Grundlage der Ethik,"[4] Apel outlines the "paradoxes of the problem situation" that moral theory is faced with today. On the one hand, the global expansion of modern science and technology has generated moral problems of planetary extension. Today, therefore, we need a macroethics more than ever. On the other hand, the identification of rationality with value-free science dissolves the fundamentals of ethics within general validity. Just as religion migrated into the realm of private subjectivity, unable to obtain its own rationality in front of the dominion of scientific reason, so has ethics. Orthodox Marxism attempted to bridge the gap between subjective action and objective science, but the price was a deterministic concept of history that fulfilled the totalitarian tendency of positivistic reason. According to Apel, the philosophies of the Western societies have reproduced that duality in the division of labor between analytical and hermeneutic philosophy, thus resulting in the privatization of morality. Politics likewise falls within the competence of instrumental rationality, which in turn is based on conventions that can only be "grounded" through irrational decisions. A rational discussion of aims is no longer possible.

Apel therefore develops his discourse in a situation in which the general validity of morality threatens to collapse in the tongs of analytic philosophy and hermeneutics. The moral skepticism that represents the common sense of the two main streams of philosophy in the twentieth century has become the central provocation for discourse ethics.

For this reason its strategy of foundation aims at a *fundamentum inconcussum* by reflection on the conditions of doubt continuing Descartes's ideas on the level of linguistic pragmatics. The surprising point of this strategy is that the moral principle of universalization doubted by moral skepticism is already affirmed in the act of doubting as a form of argumentation. Argumentation is impossible without the moral presuppositions of renunciation of violence and the acceptance of the equality of rights. With the strategy of the performative elenchus, Apel tries to make visible the secret moral pillars in the illuminated dome of value-free science and the colorful greenhouse of hermeneutics.

1.2. Ethics of liberation as an ethics in the context of dependence and underdevelopment

In the early 1970s, as Apel started his new theoretical path, Dussel developed in Argentina the "ethics of liberation." Dussel reflects the same planetary process that Apel has defined as the expansion of science and technology, but from a political and economic perspective. Colonialism and the neocolonial dependence of

Latin America, and the whole Third World in general, is the central provocation of Dussel's moral theory. At the theoretical level, Dussel is faced with the critique of the Western model of development by the "theory of dependence." Although rumors of the crisis or even the end of the *dependencia* theory goes around today, it seems to me that the enduring merit of the *dependencia* theory was to break the charm of *desarollismo* (developmentalism) and to definitively put on the agenda the question of an independent and genuine path of development for the peoples of the Third World. This question could not remain on the borders of the social sciences but became a theme of philosophy as well. Salazar Bondy has pointed out precisely the specific epistemological provocation of the theory of dependence. He diagnosed Latin American Euro-centrism as a reflection of its political and economic dependence.[5] According to Bondy the imitative thinking of Latin American philosophy is at the same time victim and perpetrator of oppression. Inasmuch as philosophy is alienated from its own culture and reality by Eurocentic imitation, it stabilizes and deepens the cultural alienation of oppressed people. Philosophy discovers itself as an ideological moment of a global system of domination. The philosophy of liberation is an effort to escape this involvement in a credible way.

Against this background Dussel himself feels forced to develop a new foundation for philosophy. He has fulfilled this task in two steps, first, by a radical critique of the universalistic claims of European reason and, second, by searching for a critical standpoint that is unquestionable by ideological critique. Although we cannot completely escape the ambiguity of history in the perspective of the ethics of liberation, solidarity with the poor allows the most critical position with regard to the structures of oppression and ideological justification of the "real communication community." The standpoint from which the vicious circle of alienated and, at the same time, alienating thinking can be partly overcome is the life of the oppressed, who are excluded by the system. The ethics of liberation tries to escape its involvement in cultural imperialism through its preferential option for the poor. That means that the process of liberation of Third World peoples becomes the central theme of the philosophical discourse. Latin American philosophy seeks its authenticity by understanding itself as a critical and solidaristic reflection on the every day struggle for liberation of the oppressed in the periphery.

2. JUSTICE THROUGH PRACTICAL DISCOURSE AND RESPONSIBILITY AS LIBERATION: THE TWO CENTRAL INTUITIONS OF DISCOURSE ETHICS AND THE ETHICS OF LIBERATION

The basic principle of discourse ethics is related to rational adjudication between conflicting interests and claims. "Rational" means that only the strength of the better arguments should decide the conflict. According to Wolfgang Kuhlmann the basic constellation is "the conflict of interests and claims between subjects of reason of approximately equal strength and competence and of equal rights."[6]

Discourse ethics reconstructs and grounds the moral intuition of universal justice with reference to a consciousness of the fallibilistic status of scientific theories and the experience of cultural relativism. Material questions, therefore, can be answered only preliminarily; their validity is justified by the consensus of the concerned—the community of investigators within the scientific discourse, the affected and concerned in a conflict situation within practical discourses. In this way discourse ethics helps expose and conceptualize an essential aspect of the factical moral consciousness of Western societies.

The ethics of liberation departs from a different standard situation, namely, the situation of domination, of the denied discourse, and of the instrumentalization and exploitation of human beings. The original situation is the encounter with the poor, the provocation of the oppressed. Discourse ethics assigns this moral experience to the ethics of sympathy and compassion, associating with it irrationality and even instinctive reflex.[7] According to my interpretation, the ethics of liberation reconstructs the intuitions of the traditional ethics of compassion and love on the actual level of consciousness. The traditional forms of compassion are corrected radically (e.g., the reduction of compassion to private relations) to the practice of alms, to paternal care, or to partiality without the correcting idea of justice. The most important elements of the transformation of the ethics of care are:

1. A metaphysics of Otherness: any man or woman isn't only an example of universal humankind (difference of a prior unity) but, because of his or her liberty, is a being of radical heterogeneity and *distinction* (in opposition to simple difference); correcting the personalistic tradition of philosophy, Dussel removes the category of the Other from its private idyll—the Other is not only the private friend but also the Other gender, the Other generation, the Other social class, the Other nation, the Other culture. The strongest moral claim lies on the Other outside of the social totality—the orphans outside the families, the poor outside the welfare state, the old outside the society based on efficiency, the strangers outside their native country;
2. A theory of understanding: the only way to understand the exteriority of the Other is through the experience of encounter, proximity;[8]
3. A theory of the praxis of liberation: the cry of the oppressed demands justice; the sense of liberation is differentiated from Hegel's master and slave dialectic and from a specific sense of emancipation that neglects the economic dimension of oppression.

The paradigm for an authentic liberation is the biblical Exodus, and it has three central elements:

1. The point of departure is domination as the negation of the constitutive and historical exteriority of the Other, the instrumentalization of his or her face;

domination is the denial of the face-to-face relation and the totalization of the I or We;
2. Exodus as the outbreak from the system of domination; the process of self-finding that means the detachment of introjected power and the affirmation and reconstruction of one's own identity;
3. The construction of a new order in which the oppressed could live as an original and a different person in equality with others.

The ethics of liberation transforms the intuitions of the ethics of compassion into an ethics of commiseration[9] on the level of modern political consciousness. The demands of the poor are responded to through an analysis of the structural causes of poverty and, departing from this analysis, the construction of a more just order of society. In our day, the intuitions of the ethics of compassion can be reformulated only as a political ethics—an ethics of commiseration without any paternalization. The encounter with the poor has to be transformed into the solidaristic commitment with the poor on their way toward liberation. Whether liberation is a reform of the system or becomes a revolution depends on the historical situation. Thus the ethics of liberation corrects and integrates the legitimate aims of a revolutionary morality without either a deterministic or a utopian theory of history. Liberation is a historical process without the guide rope of dialectical laws of history.

3. CRITICAL COORDINATION OF DISCOURSE ETHICS AND THE ETHICS OF LIBERATION

We are now ready to compare discourse ethics and the ethics of liberation. First, Apel searches, in the face of the universal relativism of actual philosophy, for an irrefutable base on which the absoluteness and universality of theoretical and practical reason can be grounded. Dussel's problem is more complex: on the one hand, his appropriation of Heidegger and Ricoeur allows him to break with the totalitarian universality of European reason and find a legitimate way to an autochthonous cultural life world; on the other hand he does not want to sacrifice the absoluteness of ethics to hermeneutical *culturalismo* lest the critique of the exploitation should lose the ground under its feet. Therefore Dussel and Apel have the same problem with hermeneutic philosophy: both want to ground the absoluteness of ethics in a way that the plurality of the life worlds is not oppressed by a totalitarian universalistic thinking. Apel finds the solution in a transformation and renewal of transcendental reflection. The hermeneutic description of cultural life worlds presupposes a transcendental anticipation of an ideal communication community that preserves philosophy from a free fall into total relativism. Dussel avoids relativism by recourse to Emmanuel Levinas: the unconditionality of moral claims that is grounded in the liberty and the exteriority of the Other, which can be oppressed but never completely controlled. Even if the Other is killed, he or she keeps his or her secret forever. The demands of the Other, of the poor, transform the attitude of phenomenological description. The phenomenological concept of "experience" (which is quite different from scientific objectification) includes an understanding in which the horizon of the interpreter is widened by phenomena, but the "epiphany," or irruption of the poor, provokes the phenomenological description to a moral decision, to a solidaristic attitude of the interpreter with the poor. This is—if I have understood rightly—the sense of Dussel's phrase "from phenomenology to liberation."[10]

Against this background, it becomes obvious that Apel's strategy cannot immediately solve Dussel's problems, and vice versa. While Apel finds himself in a theoretical universe that is cleaned of every ethical element, Dussel responds to a situation in which philosophical discourse finds itself already implicated in the ideological justification and legitimation of oppression, and participation in the cultural alienation of his own people. In spite of these differences Apel and Dussel have a common aim: both of them want to develop ethics as macroethics—Apel because of the planetary expansion of modern science and technology, Dussel because of the global dimension of the North–South conflict. Both of them try to ground a planetary ethics without any ethnocentrism. Both discourse ethics and the ethics of liberation intend to preserve the absoluteness of ethics in such a way that the cultural forms of the good life are not destroyed. How these common intentions can be realized shows their respective corrections to Kant's categorical imperative.

3.1. The search for successful universality: Corrections to the categorical imperative

Discourse ethics and the ethics of liberation share the thesis that has acquired an almost commonsense character in actual philosophy, namely, that Kant's formulation of the categorical imperative cannot serve moral universality as he intended it. The complete reversibility of standpoints, of "universal role taking," which Kant demanded, remains imprisoned in the nets of a given life world, if it is merely monologically realized in *foro interno* by an individual. It is therefore possible that members of different life worlds may universalize different norms without subjective compulsion.

Discourse ethics responds to this problem through its demand for practical discourses, in which all concerned should solve their conflicting claims and interests consensually. Moral theory restricts itself to the reconstruction of the "moral point of view"—the viewpoint of impartiality outlined only by rules of discourse formation, rules that constitute the indispensable conditions of argumentation in order to enable a fair solution of conflicts. The tree of philosophical ethics, after the purgatory of science and hermeneutics, has lost almost all its leaves of substantial morality. All that remains is the structure of a procedural principle as guarantee for a just solution of conflicts. But the profit of this extreme formalism is that moral theory can integrate the fallibilism of science and the cultural relativism of hermeneutics without giving up the absoluteness of ethics. Discourse ethics restricts the field of moral questions to the narrow area of conflicts between various forms of "good life" that are not touched in their substance. Delegating controversial questions to the practical discourses of the concerned and affected, discourse ethics avoids the trap of any universalistic morality, namely, the universalization of particular norms. This should also be a debatable conception of a planetary ethics for the philosophies of the Third World.

But how does the ethics of liberation solve the problem of successful universalization? In his critique of Kant,[11] Dussel refers to the historical and cultural relativity of human subjectivity that marks the limits of every concrete universalization. Every universalization, therefore, is factually limited. But delimitation implies exclusion. Because the mere "idea" of unlimited universality cannot overcome the factual limitation of concrete universalization, Dussel tries to open the factual totality of society from the perspective of the excluded person(s) (in the sense of the concrete negation). The demands of the oppressed, of those "beyond" the system, tear the veil off the pretended universality of a concrete society. The irruption of the poor unmasks the factual consensus in its ideological character. The "monological" universalization (of an individual, a group, a class, a people, a culture, etc.) is broken concretely by the liberating praxis of the oppressed.

From the perspective of the ethics of liberation the process toward successful universality is not a process like an approximation to an ideal, like a developing, evolving, and unfolding of a communication community. It is instead an anadialectical process of the praxis of liberation. The oppressed Other irrupts into the system and opens it to a more extensive totality where there will be new poor who will through new liberation movements fight again against the limits of the new existing Totality. The "vehicle" on the way to successful universality is not only practical discourse but also the liberating praxis of the oppressed.

3.2. The problem of monological discourses and the analogical understanding of the Other

Discourse ethics and the ethics of liberation share the intention to overcome monological universalization through real interactions. With regard to discourse ethics, however, W. Lütterfelds has shown the possibility of monological understanding even within practical discourses.[12] The understanding of alien argumentation is dependent on one's own horizon of understanding in which something can count as "reason." Thus the reasons proposed by the Other remain my own reasons, and therefore discourse ethics would continue monological universalization despite the demand for practical discourses. Lütterfelds draws the conclusion that the "egological base"[13] of real argumentation cannot be eliminated. But he ends with the thesis that a theory of discourse which takes into account the contradiction between monological and universal reason is "still missing."[14] Apel has answered rightly that the recourse to the "egological base" of argumentation is "unnecessary" because it was never left. However, Apel has not answered the unsolved problem of real argumentation pointed out by Lütterfelds: How can alien argumentation break out of its own horizon of understanding in such a way that the idea of consensus does not become a mere idea which conceals dissent as already liquified. Habermas has outlined consensus as depending on "empathetic sensitivity by each person to everyone else."[15] But the problem remains unaffected, as unexplained, if the question of how can we think of nonmonological empathy is not cleared up. My thesis is that Dussel's theory of an analogical understanding of the Other could complement discourse ethics on this point.[16]

The material core of practical discourses includes interests and needs, which should be examined with respect to their universalizability. Although "arguments transcend per se beyond particular life-worlds,"[17] the reasons that the involved and affected advance for their claims are rooted in their particular life worlds, their concrete backgrounds of plausibility. The idea of consensus not becoming a chimera depends entirely on the possibility of understanding the claims of the Other from his own life world. Dussel's theory of knowledge is specifically related to this problem. The point of departure is the constitutive heterogeneity of the Other in her life world; the "irruption of the Other," the immediate encounter of "face-to-face" inaugurates the process of understanding. The constitutive moral act, even prior to verbal understanding, is to open oneself to the Other, which means to break out of one's own horizon, to break out of the plausibility of one's own life world (detotalization). Because the plausibility of verbal information and exchanges is rooted in its own history and life world, it is not possible to understand the Other completely. The world of the Other can never become my own. Therefore personal understanding depends on the revelation of the Other; it demands an involvement with the life world of the Other. The "egological base" is not left at any time because I can understand anything only by relating it to my own horizon; but this horizon is broadened, expanded more and more through the encounter with the Other. Thus the Otherness of the Other emerges with the continuing decentralization of the I or the We; the exteriority of the Other, which could not be "comprehended" within the framework of the initial preunderstanding, now appears without lifting its mystery.

Discourse ethics and the ethics of liberation seem to describe the same thing from different sides; therefore, they stress different aspects. Apel's point of departure is the situation of argumentation. He shows that in this situation the Otherness of the Other is already accepted. Argumentation implies and presupposes respect for the Other. Dussel's point of departure is the situation of domination, of the refusal to respect the Other. Therefore the acceptance of the Other, of the oppressed, the detotalization of the I or We, moves into the center of moral theory. Argumentation appears only as a consequence of this original moral act. The theory follows the way from domination over interpellation and respect for the Other to the understanding of her appellation and argumentation.

But Dussel's thesis of the constitutive exteriority of the Other does not intend to glorify "dissent," as Lyotard has done. On the contrary, according to Dussel, the quality of factual consensus depends on the commitment to enter the life world of the Other and to begin to understand the Otherness of the Other.[18] This cannot substitute the cognitivistic moment of justice in the sense of weighing claims without respect for persons. There is no justice without a deep understanding of the Otherness of the Other—of her history, her life world, her horizon of plausibility for her claims.

3.3. "Solidarity" and the problem of partiality

Up to now discourse ethics has defended the principle of justice as the integral core of moral theory on two fronts: against Jonas's ethics of responsibility[19] and in the context of the Kohlberg-Gilligan controversy.[20] Whereas W. Kuhlmann[21] concedes a "surplus" in Jonas's concept of responsibility that cannot be fulfilled by an ethics of justice, Apel and Habermas try to strictly deduce responsibility and solidarity from the discourse-ethical principle of justice. Discourse partners in practical discourses not only commit themselves to the moral principles of argumentation (e.g., the equality of the dialogue partners, their right to a fair say, etc.) but also commit themselves to "coresponsibility" in the sense of a "solidaristic responsibility for the settlement of problems."[22] Habermas accentuates this coresponsibility as the other side of justice in the sense of the "maintenance of the integrity of this form of life,"[23] in which dialogue partners must be interested to the same extent that they must be also interested in the freedom to respond to raised validity claims. Here I neglect the question of whether the intentions of Gilligan and Jonas are integrated by discourse ethics in this way. From the perspective of liberation ethics, this question has to be suspended.

Apel's notion of "coresponsibility" and Habermas's concept of "solidarity" presuppose that we must only protect and extend the already existing social ties of the real community of argumentation in light of ideal universality (the aspect of emancipation). The ethics of liberation develops its concept of responsibility in a situation in which the social tie is torn, human communication is interrupted. Indeed, in this situation the universal idea of justice is also present, and thus we have to concede to Habermas: "Without these idealizing presuppositions, no one, no matter how repressive the social structure under which she lives, can act with an orientation to reaching understanding."[24] But the praxis of solidarity and the function of actions oriented to understanding changes in the context of domination: solidarity turns into partiality for the oppressed. Partiality means that the legitimacy of claims is anticipated because it cannot be vindicated (redeemed) consensually in a situation of domination. Processes of understanding therefore need the oppressed's consciousness of their own situation, through which the internalized role of servant is transformed, challenged, and fought against, and through which a new identity is established. These processes can be described better through the different aspects of the reproduction of the life world, as they have been outlined by Habermas (cultural tradition, social integration, socialization),[25] but with the important difference that in this context we must speak not solely of the "reproduction" but also of the "reconstitution" of the life world of the "oppressed."[26] The oppressed begin to identify with themselves. They begin to discover their own history (tradition), which was unknown to the dominant public until now. They free themselves from the societal norms that justified their oppression (coordination of actions), they begin to live in the moral norms of their own tradition, in communities of resistance, thus building up new identities. A practical discourse such as Apel demands presupposes the exodus of the oppressed, the exodus from their role as servants. If the identity of one of the partners of dialogue is broken by oppression, discourse itself turns into its opposite.

The partial anticipation of universality, however, has to be vindicated at a given time. This problem was not treated adequately by Dussel. Successful liberation leads to a new totality based on justice. In this situation the claims of the formerly oppressed have to be redeemed too in a practical discourse of all concerned in order to avoid the dialectic between the dominator and the dominated. The ethics of liberation has not developed suitable categories for this problem. On this point the contribution of discourse ethics is extremely worthy. The limits of liberation ethics become immediately obvious if the evidence of domination is not strong enough. In that case the option for partiality (i.e., the preferential option for the poor) must be open to a rational discourse of all concerned. Whoever insists here on the evidence of domination places himself in the field of dogmatism. What looks like cynicism in the context of the suffering of the people in the Third World becomes more relevant with regard to terrorist organizations like the Red Army Faction in Western Germany. Dogmatism is the latent danger of partiality,[27] cynicism the danger of an ethics that demands practical discourses without consideration of the political and economic conditions that would make possible their implementation.

3.4. The labor theory of value versus the procedural principle of justice: The problem of "material" justice

Liberation ethics has complemented the principle of partiality with a theory of economic justice, thus also reformulating Marx's labor theory of value.[28] Dussel is aware that this would be interpreted in Europe as an understandable but anachronistic Third World fascination with Marxism.[29] Despite the many controversies within critical theory, there is a consensus among the main philosophers, including Habermas, that alienation cannot be described primarily in terms of economic categories. Delegating even principles of a just distribution to practical discourses,[30] the proceduralism of discourse ethics implies a critique of the Marxist labor theory of value. Habermas[31] raises two main objections to the labor theory of value that represent a certain consensus in Western Europe: Marx did not distinguish sufficiently between class-specific institutionalization and the positive structural differentiation that capitalism also is. Marx therefore did not possess criteria to differentiate between the rationalization and reification of posttraditional life worlds. The theory of value presupposes (1) a premodern romantic form of economy and is (2) a productivistic theory because it interprets alienation below the level of interaction.

These objections are only partially correct with regard to Dussel's theory of value, especially if we neglect the question of the right philology of Marx. According to Dussel, any production stands in the context of interaction. Its telos is the reproduction of human life, which is always a life in community. In its abstract sense economy is a practical-productive relationship—there is a relationship between persons mediated by a product of labor. The theory of value is not a complete phenomenology of the relationship between humans and nature. It accentuates only those aspects that should be relevant for economic justice. Therefore the product is defined only under the perspective of the self-objectification in human work; the "value" of a product is measured by the quantity of the "objectified life." The two axes of the theory of value are, first, the difference between the value of the product and the value of the working person—the "origin of all values"—who must not be degraded to a mere value. Second is a theory of a just exchange within the criteria of the quantity of objectified life. An unjust exchange must not be considered as an unfortunate circulation of material objects but as a loss of "life."

Maybe the crucial question concerns the function that this theory can obtain. In Dussel's ethics of liberation the labor theory of value seems to be a fourth formulation of the categorical imperative in economic terms. The imperative must "treat the other not only instrumentally but respect him/her as a person" and can be translated into the terms of the labor theory of value: "treat the other not only as value but respect him/her as the 'origin of values.'" Respect for the Other has to stand the test of just exchange.

Thus the labor theory of value is the criterion of all economic systems. Its validity cannot be limited to a premodern form of production.[32] Liberation ethics receives the theory of value for two main reasons: it is related to the most serious problems of the Third World, its economic exploitation; and the labor theory of value allows liberation ethics to connect itself with the experience of the poor who must offer their working power for the cheapest salaries. Although they work very hard, separated from their families and their village, the poor are not able to reproduce their material and social life. Thus the theory of value fits very well with the preferential option for the poor. Clearly, the labor theory of value not only has the function of a moral criterion but also suggests a model for a new economic system that meets Habermas's objections.

As historical experience shows, we cannot deduce an economic system from the theory of value; we can only—perhaps—diagnose economical injustice. But economical systems are not unlimitedly available. The peasant revolts at the end of the Middle Ages failed because the oppressed were missing a practical and effective alternative to the dominant economic system. The economic crisis was not primarily the effect of a moral failure, since its roots lay in the whole feudal system. Therefore the conflict could not be solved by the reconstitution of the "old right."[33] This is not a pleading for an amoral systems theory. But it seems to me that other criteria than those of the labor theory of value are legitimate in the discussion about economic systems, for instance, the teleological criteria of efficiency or Rawls's principle of fairness. It is understandable that Dussel is afraid to disguise real misery with these abstractive theories. Liberation ethics has rightly criticized the systems theoretical viewpoint of the economic sciences. But the moral impulse of liberation ethics threatens to vaporize without practical alternatives. Today there exists a disillusionment with the history of the alternatives. On the other hand the revival of the neoliberal *desarrollismo* shows how the social sciences move in a circle. No strategy has reached more than punctual successes, which displays the universal helplessness like shop windows. But the poor cannot afford this theoretical skepticism while struggling for their survival. It is the indisputable merit of liberation ethics to have asserted the justified claims of the poor on the level of an ethical reflection.

3.5. Apel's complementarity principle and the ethics of liberation

Both moral theories obviously presuppose a specific historical situation to which their categories are related. Discourse ethics is aware of this fact. The procedural principle depends on a "form of life that *meets it half-way*"[34]—not in regard to its validity but to its realization. Apel himself speaks of a "limit"[35] of discourse ethics. At this point we can observe bridges between these two moral theories. When faced with "the facts of misery," "moral questions are open." As Habermas says, "Wherever this is the case, wherever existing conditions make a mockery of the demands of universalist morality, moral issues turn into issues of political ethics."[36] Apel admits that "as members of an oppressed class or race, they possess *a priori* a *moral privilege vis-à-vis* the *socially privileged,* a right to bring about equality even prior to acknowledging the rules that only have to be accepted once real equality exists."[37] Habermas notes that "the issue of revolutionary morality (which incidentally has never been satisfactorily discussed by Marxists, Eastern or Western) is fortunately not an urgent one in our type of society."[38] But Apel understands that the real life worlds of constitutional states are still shot through with power interests. Therefore the application of discourse ethics is still a serious problem even within democratic social structures. This is why Apel introduces the complementarity principle (part B) into discourse ethics that would mediate between strategic and consensual action. On the other hand, liberation ethics does not reduce its realm of validity to the situations of obvious oppression because every society has its oppressed, its poor.

At this point Apel and Dussel treat the same sort of problems side-by-side but with different instruments. Apel works with types of rationality; the strategic rationality of action—excluded in part A of discourse ethics—now receives an important role under the rule of the procedural principles of argumentation: to serve life and to establish institutions for practical discourses. Dussel's theoretical instruments are rooted in a personalistic philosophy. They reconstruct the historical "logic" of human relationships. Every social totality, from the intimacy between man and woman up through the totalities of peoples and states, builds up a horizon that excludes and oppresses the Other. Therefore, solidarity has to transcend the real regnant social totality and reach to those who are outside. The "anadialectic" describes the historical logic of totalization and detotalization, of domination and liberation, of subsumption and irruption of the Other. It is obvious that these two theoretical instruments are not contradictory; they are close to each other and could be complementary.

The praxis of liberation has to decide continuously between mere strategic and consensual action, and real practical discourse is always limited in regard to time and to the members who can really participate and so on, meaning that every factual discourse is limited. It is almost unavoidable that factual discourse implies consensus at the cost of third parties. Negating the factual consensus by the concrete negation of the poor, preferential solidarity corrects the idea of a mere linear and evolutionary realization of the ideal communication community. At this point liberation ethics converges with an objection of Albrecht Wellmer against discourse ethics. Exclusions of women, foreigners, blacks, and gays, for example, rooted in collective patterns of interpretation that can hardly be corrected with reasons "but with the *pressure* of a struggle for recognition and under the *influence* of new experiences."[39] Thus the liberating action of the excluded provokes the experiences that are the basis of a consensual elimination of inequality.

3.6. The utopian horizon

Discourse and liberation ethics try to reconstruct the anticipations that are included in moral intuitions. They agree completely that the vanishing point of moral practice does not prescribe a historical project but only the horizon in which all projects can be criticized. This is the conclusion reached by the critique of utopia in the last decades. Transcendental anticipation breaks the totalitarian dynamics of utopia by overcoming the absoluteness of any historical project. Although Apel and Dussel agree about the function of counterfactual anticipations as "regulative ideas," they differ about the contents of moral anticipations. Discourse ethics describes the ideal communication community through the idea of complete understanding. Dussel has objected that Apel reduces the ideal community to a community of language, in opposition to a community of bodies.[40] In my opinion this does not mark the crucial difference[41] because, in fact, discourse ethics treats the dimension of the human body in the context of the question of ideology.

According to Apel, complete understanding implicates the linguistification of the unconscious or "natural" elements of communication. This demands a temporary objectification of the Other, but any objectification must be integrated into a dialogue that is oriented to mutual understanding. Therefore the ideal communication community includes as the "transcendental presupposition of every critique of ideology" the "postulate of a non-distorted and in basically unlimited verbalization of extra-linguistic communicative competence," and that means the "overcoming of what is merely 'natural.'"[42] This postulate seems to exceed even the critique that Wellmer formulated against the scientistic tendency of the ideal communication community. Wellmer speaks of the idea of "a definitive language," "the original dream of logical empiricism," "complete transparency."[43] Human liberty threatens to disappear in the "permanent daylight" (Nietzsche) of reason. Faced with this idea, Dussel asserts the exteriority of human liberty as the abysmal source of human vivacity, which cannot be absorbed by the light of transparency. Therefore the specific ethical anticipation is the "proximity" between human persons; the proximity with timeless synchrony, full with the richness of freedom, so that the Other remains with respect to the one, the regnant totality, an eschatological exteriority. The proximity of persons, not the crystalline clearness of arguments, mobilizes moral praxis.

Consensus cannot be the adequate moral anticipation. In contrast to theoretical discourse, consensus is only an element within moral practice that seeks to restore distorted relationship and communication. Therefore, the adequate ethical anticipation has to be reconstructed from the other side of the practical discourse, from the side of solidarity, as Habermas says. The anticipation of solidarity is not the consensual clearness of arguments but the proximity between humans. Whether in the face-to-face of the child–mother relationship in nursing, or the sex-to-sex of the man–woman relationship in love, or the shoulder-to-shoulder of colleagues in an assembly that is deciding the fate of a country, or the word-hearing of the teacher–pupil relationship in the apprenticeship of living, proximity is the word that best expresses the essence of persons, their first (archeological) and last (eschatological) fullness.[44]

5. CHALLENGES, SUCCESSES, AND THE SELF-UNDERSTANDING OF DISCOURSE AND LIBERATION ETHICS

If one were to place the two moral theories into the original context of the other, their strengths and weaknesses would become immediately obvious. The ethics of liberation seems to be insecure in the face of theoretical skepticism. The evidence of the option for the poor—which needs no arguments in the context of real misery—loses a bit of its plausibility in a theoretical space in which claims are proved on the basis of whether they can be doubted or not. On the other hand, the strict transcendental reflections of discourse ethics threaten to ignore the pressing questions that arise in the context of misery and oppression, though the foundation seems to be unassailable in the secured rooms of academic discussions. Obviously discourse and liberation ethics are developed in regard to different standards of foundation by which they want to be measured. Dussel tries to expose and ground the original ethical practice in front of the relationships of domination in all life worlds and cultures, the proximity of face-to-face. Apel searches for a situation that is unavoidable for the moral skeptic, the well-known situation of argumentation with its unavoidable moral presuppositions. Without discussing here the question of an Ultimate Foundation of ethics, we can relate these two types of theoretical grounding of morality. Insofar as the ethics of liberation competes with other moral theories, it works in an argumentative situation in which it cannot avoid the presuppositions that discourse ethics has already outlined. Therefore, in regard to the foundation of the philosophical theory, it seems to me that the transcendental reflection of Apel reaches deeper than liberation ethics. However, liberation ethics is not defeated because moral theory could be restricted to the small field of unquestionable sentences. Responsibility is not identical with this principle of justice, as Kuhlmann has shown.[45]

The limits of discourse ethics become evident where claims cannot be asserted. Kuhlmann speaks of groups "whose membership is denied because of their competence: sick persons, negros, jews etc.)." He speaks of the problems of the embryo, the question of abortion, and our relationship to nature.[46] These dimensions of responsibility do not necessarily mean the supererogatory practice of love; they belong to fundamental moral intuitions that every society needs in order to preserve humanity. Surely it is possible to construct bridges to these problems by discourse ethics too, but even Kuhlmann concedes that they are more or less unsteady.[47] Liberation ethics tries to reconstruct precisely this responsibility from the experience of the exteriority of the Other who suffers silently oppression, the exteriority of the unborn—they who have no voice—or even the exteriority of "dumb" nature.[48]

Thus we come to the question of the theoretical extension of discourse and liberation ethics. The thesis I tried to represent and defend here was that the ethics of liberation reconstructs a certain aspect of an ethics of responsibility and solidarity, integrating from this perspective the intuitions of justice. On the other hand, discourse ethics grounds responsibility and solidarity as the other side of justice. Neither one can be reduced to the other, as I tried to show with some examples. A last word on the self-understanding of these moral theories: According to its theoretical position, discourse ethics delegates all questions of ethical contents to their discussions within their respective life worlds. It restricts itself to the justification (and to reminding us) of the moral "point of view." Material positions have to be regarded only as contributions in an open discourse. This modesty of philosophical moral theory is correct in view of the fact that moral judgments depend more and more on the data that science may provide. But this modesty may be a virtue only in a situation in which institutions for practical discourses have already been established.

Under totalitarian conditions, the material implications of discourse ethics are obvious.[49] In such a situation the deduction of the procedural principle loses its function of being a mere contribution, and it receives unavoidably a prophetical character, for instance, statements against censorship, against being convicted without a fair trial, and so on. Here is a bridge to understanding a little bit better the often breathtaking categorical resoluteness of liberation ethics. Pressed by the daily death of the poor in the Third World, the academic modesty of discourse ethics becomes questionable for liberation ethics. The adequate form to do philosophy is as prophetical philosophy, as the reduplicated "cry" of the poor.[50] Dussel's philosophy of liberation intends, just as Apel also attempts, to "inspire the practice of men by a dialogical constitution of sense,"[51] with the difference that now it is inspired through the liberating action of the oppressed. The philosophy of liberation understands itself as an "analectic pedagogy of liberation,"[52] not as paternalistic avant-garde, not as a revolutionary idea that has to take root in the masses, but as a critical assistance, in solidarity, of the poor on their way toward liberation:

> To think of everything in the light of the provocative word of the people—the poor, the castrated woman, the child, the culturally dominated youth, the aged person discarded by the consumer society—shouldering infinite responsibility and in the presence of the Infinite; that is philosophy of liberation.[53]

NOTES

This chapter was translated from the original German and revised by Eduardo Mendieta.

1. Among the publications of Enrique Dussel, I want to refer above all to his five volumes on the ethics of liberation: *Para una ética de la liberación latinoamericana,* vols. 1–2 (Buenos Aires: Siglo XXI Editores, 1973); vol. 3 (Mexico: Edicol, 1977); vols. 4–5 (Bogota: Usted, 1979–1980).

2. See H. Cerutti Guldberg, *Filosofía de la liberación latinoamericana* (Mexico: FCE, 1983). This is the most comprehensive but not impartial description of the first phase of the philosophy of liberation in Latin America.

3. The first dialogue in Freiburg, Germany (November 1989), is documented in *Ethik und Befreiung: Dokumentation der Tagung: Philosophie der Befreiung: Begründungen von Ethik in Deutschland und Lateinamerika,* ed. Raúl Fornet-Betancourt (Aachen: Augustinus–Buchhandlung, 1990).

4. Karl-Otto Apel, *Toward a Transformation of Philosophy,* trans. Glyn Adey and David Frisby (London: Routledge & Kegan Paul, 1980), pp. 225ff.: "The *a priori* of the communication community and the foundations of ethics: the problem of a rational foundation of ethics in the scientific age."

5. See A. Salazar Bondy, *¿Existe una filosofía en nuestra América?* (Mexico: Siglo XXI Editores, 1968), pp. 131ff.

6. W. Kuhlmann, "Prinzip Verantwortung versus Diskursethik," *Archivio di filosofía* 55 (1987): 99. Translation from the author.

7. See Karl-Otto Apel, "Die Herausforderung des Menschen als Herausforderung an die praktische Vernunft," in *Funkkolleg Praktische Philosophie/Ethik: Dialoge* (Frankfurt/M: Suhrkamp, 1984), 1:49–69; Apel, "Grenzen der Diskursethik? Versuch einer Zwischenbilanz," *Zeitschrift für philosophische Forschung* 40 (1986): 25. Translation in Karl-Otto Apel, *Ethics and the Theory of Rationality: Selected Essays*, vol. 2, ed. Eduardo

Mendieta (Atlantic Highlands, N.J.: Humanities, 1996). Includes an introduction by Eduardo Mendieta a preface by Karl-Otto Apel.

8. See Enrique Dussel, *Philosophy of Liberation* (Maryknoll, N.Y.: Orbis, 1985), para. 4.3.

9. Ibid., para. 2.6.8.2.

10. Ibid., chap. 2.

11. See Enrique Dussel, *Para una destrucción de la historia de la ética* (Argentina: Mendoza, 1973), pp. 75–118; Dussel, *Para una ética de la liberación,* 2:67–69.

12. W. Lütterfelds, "Die monologische Struktur des kategorischen Imperativs und Fichtes Korrektur der Diskursethik" *Zeitschrift für philosophische Forschung* 40 (1986): 90ff.

13. Ibid., p. 103.

14. Ibid.

15. Jürgen Habermas, "Morality and Ethical Life: Does Hegel's Critique of Kant Apply to Discourse Ethics?" in *Moral Consciousness and Communicative Action*, trans. Christian Lenhardt and Shierry Weber Nicholsen (Cambridge: MIT Press, 1990), p. 202.

16. See Enrique Dussel, *Método para una filosofía de la liberación* (Salamanca: SIGUEME, 1974), pp. 181–93; and Dussel, *Para una ética de la liberación*, 2:52–59.

17. Jürgen Habermas, "Justice and Solidarity: On the Discussion Concerning 'Stage 6,'" *Philosophical Forum* 21, no. 1–2 (1989–1990): 48. Translation slightly modified by editor.

18. Apel and Habermas have developed very similar theories of understanding with regard to the foundations of the human and social sciences, albeit not in the context of moral theory. See Karl-Otto Apel, *Understanding and Explanation: A Transcendental Pragmatic Perspective*, trans. Georgia Warnke (Cambridge: MIT Press, 1984); and Jürgen Habermas, *Theory of Communicative Action*, trans. Thomas McCarthy (Boston: Beacon, 1984), 1:102–41.

19. See Karl-Otto Apel, "Verantwortung heute—Nur noch Prinzip der Bewahrung und Selbstbeschränkung oder immer noch der Befreiung und Verwirklichung von Humanität?" in *Diskurs und Verantwortung* (Frankfurt/M: Suhrkamp, 1988), pp. 179–216; W. Kuhlmann, "Prinzip Verantwortung versus Diskursethik," *Archivio di filosofia* 55 (1987): 89–116.

20. See Habermas, *Moral Consciousness and Communicative Action,* pp. 171ff. n. 16; Habermas, "Justice and Solidarity," n. 16; and Apel, *Diskurs und Verantwortung*, pp. 137ff., 452ff.

21. See Kuhlmann, "Prinzip Verantwortung versus Diskursethik," pp. 114ff.; n. 6.

22. See Karl-Otto Apel, "Normatively Grounding 'Critical Theory' through Recourse to the Lifeworld? A Transcendental–Pragmatic Attempt to Think with Habermas against Habermas," in *Philosophical Interventions in the Unfinished Project of Enlightenment*, trans. William Rehg, ed. A. Honneth et al. (Cambridge: MIT Press, 1992), pp. 140ff.; Apel, *Diskurs und Verantwortung,* p. 451.

23. Habermas, "Justice and Solidarity," p. 47.

24. Ibid., p. 48.

25. Jürgen Habermas, *Theory of Communicative Action*, trans. Thomas McCarthy (Boston: Beacon, 1987), 2:140ff.

26. See ibid., p. 143 (schema 22), where Habermas lists the phenomena that come up when the life world comes into crisis. These observations correspond in many aspects to Dussel's description of the life world of the poor.

27. This is the cause of the strained relation between the ethics of liberation and the scientific discussion on the development of the Third World. That the philosophy of liberation departs from a situation of domination is but a correction and further development of the theory of dependence, and in no way its abandoning, as has been the case in Europe. It is obvious that this situation builds limits for the dialogue between both moral theories.

28. See Dussel's works on Marx: *Filosofía de la producción* (Bogota: Nueva América, 1983); *La producción teórica: Un commentario a los "Grundrisse"* (Mexico: Siglo XXI Editores, 1985); *Hacia un Marx desconocido: Un commentario de los "Manuscritos del 61–63"* (Mexico: Siglo XXI Editores, 1988); *El último Marx (1863–82) y la liberación latinoamericana* (Mexico: Siglo XXI Editores, 1990).

29. Dussel, "Die 'Lebensgemeinschaft' und die 'Interpellation des Armen,'" in *Ethik und Befreiung*, p. 78 n. 3.

30. Habermas, *Moral Consciousness and Communicative Action*, pp. 65ff.

31. See Habermas, *Theory of Communicative Action,* 2:338ff.; Habermas, "A Reply to My Critics," in *Habermas: Critical Debates,* ed. John B. Thompson and David Held (London: Macmillan, 1982), pp. 223ff.

32. Compare A. Honneth, "Arbeit und instrumentelles Handeln," in *Arbeit, Handlung, Normativität: Theorien des Historischen Materialismus,* ed. A. Honneth and U. Jaeggi (Frankfurt/M: Suhrkamp, 1980), pp. 185–233.

33. See L. Bauer and H. Matis, *Geburt der Neuzeit: Vom Feudalsystem zur Marktgesellschaft* (Munich: Fischer, 1988), p. 58.

34. Habermas, "Morality and Ethical Life," p. 207.

35. Apel, "The A Priori of the Communication Community," p. 278.

36. Habermas, "Morality and Ethical Life," p. 209.

37. Apel, "The A Priori of the Communication Community," p. 179.

38. Habermas, "Morality and Ethical Life," p. 209.

39. A. Wellmer, *The Persistence of Modernity: Essays on Aesthetics, Ethics, and Postmodernism*, trans. David Midgley (Cambridge: MIT Press, 1991), p. 198.

40. Enrique Dussel, "Die 'Lebensgemeinschaft' und die 'Interpellation des Armen': Die Praxis der Befreiung," in *Ethik und Befreiung,* pp. 78–84 n. 3.

41. Dussel's critique is correct with regard to the themes of the factual application of the discourse ethics, where the global economic problems are not treated sufficiently.

42. Apel, *Toward a Transformation of Philosophy,* p. 224 n. 105.

43. Wellmer, *Persistence of Modernity*, pp. 174ff.

44. See Dussel, *Philosophy of Liberation,* para. 2.1.4.3, n. 8.

45. See Kuhlmann, "Prinzip Verantwortung versus Diskursethik," pp. 114f., n. 8.

46. Ibid., p. 115.

47. Ibid.

48. See Habermas, "Morality and Ethical Life," pp. 210–11: "It is just as difficult to answer the basic objection of ecological ethics: How does discourse ethics, which is limited to subjects capable of speech and action, respond to the fact that mute creatures are also vulnerable? Compassion for tortured animals and the pain caused by the destruction of biotopes are surely manifestations of moral intuitions that cannot be fully satisfied by the collective narcissism of what in the final analysis is an anthropocentric way of looking at things."

49. See A. Honneth, "Diskursethik und implizites Gerechtigkeitsprinzip: Eine Diskussionsbemerkung," in *Moralität und Sittlichkeit: Das Problem Hegels und die Diskursethik,* ed. W. Kuhlmann (Frankfurt/M: Suhrkamp, 1986), pp. 183–94.

50. Dussel, *Método de la liberación,* p. 195 n. 15.

51. Karl-Otto Apel, *Transformation der Philosophie* (Frankfurt/M: Suhrkamp, 1973), 1:220.

52. See Dussel, *Método para una filosofía de la liberación,* p. 194 n. 15.

53. Dussel, *Philosophy of Liberation,* para. 5.9.5.1, n. 8.

6

Beyond Universal History: Dussel's Critique of Globalization

Eduardo Mendieta

Geopolitics has always determined the cartography according to which history is written.[1] As Adrienne Rich put it, "a place on the map is a place in history."[2] Conversely, a time in history is also a place on a map. This is more than a question of perspective, for it insists that history happens more forcefully, authentically, as if for the first time, in certain places, with the concomitant that other places are relegated outside history to the supplemental, to the epigonic. Universal history, as has been practiced in the "West," exemplifies this claim.[3] One may argue that the genre of universal history began with Augustine's *City of God*. But here history is a thin veil for divine history. Nonetheless, it is Augustine's idea of world history as *Heilsgeschichte* (salvation history) that inspired a whole tradition of speculation about the logic and telos of history.[4] Since Guizot, Condorcet, Smith, Hegel, Marx, and Dilthey, history has been concerned with the elucidation and discernment of those processes and forces that explain humanity's history and future. Although Christendom stands behind many of these historians' speculations, most of them have secularized salvation history into Europe's civilizing mission. For many of these great philosophers of history, the issue of history was the question of "universal history," that is, of the unity of human historical experience. Their general contention was that this unity could be explained in terms of a series of processes or determining logics. These invariably turned out to be European, Western processes and logics: secularization, modernization, industrialization, juridification, *Entzauberung* (disenchantment), bureaucratization, and so on.[5] These, in turn, were allegedly absent, stagnant, lacking from non-Western societies—or at the very least still to be brought to them via diffusion, contact, and exchange. Not unexpectedly, it was the West that would catalyze innovation in these non-Western societies. In this way, salvation history became the West's civilizing mission, the "white man's burden." Universal history, however, emerged in the eighteenth and nineteenth centuries as the ideology of European world hegemony. This is the time when European colonialism and imperialism attained their farthest global reaches. Universal history, therefore, became the apologia for Western expansionism by writing the history of humanity in terms of any one, or several, of the following tropes: civilization and/or culture, freedom, the state, technology, civil society, urbanization, and so on—ideals and ciphers that stood for Europe and the West.[6] The type of universal history practiced in the West, in short, became a way of writing about the "West" and the "rest" in a way that defined the latter by "clusters of absences" that turned out to be what the former possessed in abundance and exclusively.[7]

The project of universal history, however, entered into crisis in the early part of the twentieth century. Two world wars made it extremely difficult and suspect to project certain aspects of Western culture as possessing universal validity.[8] The moral and evaluative aspects, taken from the Christian idea of a salvation history, of universal histories, became highly questionable and indefensible. Europe itself plunged into a deep moral identity crisis. Lord Acton was to be the last great universal historian, even as his work remained incomplete.[9] A new brand of history was to be inaugurated by Arnold Toynbee. His historical project began as a rejection of universal history as had been understood by writers from François Guizot to Lord Acton. Toynbee was to inaugurate what is today called "world history": a history of the world in terms of the history of civilizations that rise and fall with the ebb of time.[10] The West, in this new historical practice, became one of the many civilizations to have its time on the historical stage. The West was neither the most advanced nor the most moral nor even the summation and synthesis of all prior cultures and civilization. Toynbee began to see history through a decentered and decentering historical perspective in which the West could no longer claim a place of privilege or prestige.[11] This orientation was to be furthered by William McNeill, the best-known American practitioner of world history. For McNeill, who is the author of the *Rise of the West: A History of the Human Community,*[12] however, Toynbee's approach remained too parochial and not global or planetary enough. More recently, McNeill has leveled the same criticism at his own work.[13]

Today, the proliferating discourses of globalization project themselves as a new version of universal history.[14] As with the universal histories of eighteenth- and nineteenth-century historians, the discourses of globalization emphasize certain civilizational forces that purportedly collapse all parochialism and cultural chauvinisms. With globalization theory we seem to be returning to the orientations of the Marquis de Condorcet, Adam Smith, David Hume, Immanuel Kant, Karl Marx, or Max Weber, all of whom could think of history only in terms of the planetarization of certain concepts, processes, organizational principles, and so on. These, in turn, were taken to be unique, endemic, and autochthonous to Europe and the West. Globalization has become the West's new cartography, according to which history's map is traced by the planetarization of the free market, laissez-faire liberalism, mass consumption, and mass culture.[15]

In this chapter I challenge the ways in which globalization is offered as a new apologia for, and of, the West. I begin with an analysis of several recent theories of globalization. This analysis, although summary and sketchy, will suffice to illustrate the ideological character of some of these theories of globalization. I then proceed to sketch the ways in which these theories have failed on several counts, namely, with respect to the questions of ethics and history, and their respective but linked relationships to globalization. My central contention is that globalization has raised the stakes on what kinds of analysis can and should be provided. Globalization demands of us not just greater attentiveness to detail but also greater circumspection concerning our conceptual apparatuses. I suggest that we need to pay greater attention to the way globalization fits into history and to how "Western" history looks when seen from a global perspective. Most importantly, however, globalization appears as an ethical challenge, and this is why I take up Dussel's challenge. Therefore, in the final section I discuss the ways in which Dussel offers us a critical discourse about globalization that directly addresses the failures of its recent discourses.

THEORIZING GLOBALIZATION

Globalization can be understood in a variety of ways. It can be seen as a purely economic project or the realization of one. This is, for instance, the view held by Richard J. Barnett and John Cavanaugh, who speak of globalization as the realization of global dreams by imperial corporation.[16] For them, globalization is the planetarization of a global bazaar, with its concomitant K-Mart realism aesthetic, the global casino economy, the global labor market, and the global shopping mall. Benjamin Barber shares some aspects of Barnett and Cavanaugh's approach. In Barber's case, however, globalization is merely the confrontation between "McWorld" and jihad—ciphers of economic processes that register as cultural epiphenomena—which results in the evisceration of politics by economics.[17] For Barber, the challenge of globalization is the threat to the possibility of civic participation: "Globalism is mandated by profit not citizenship."[18]

Globalization can also be seen as a cultural phenomenon, or the final fusing of economy and culture. Fredric Jameson has suggested that one of the distinctive qualities of postmodernity is that it registers this economization of the cultural and the culturization of economy. In other words, as culture becomes economy, the latter turns into the former. Globalization as Americanization is the epitome of this mutation of the one into the other.[19] In a recent article, Jameson has extended this analysis to globalization.[20] Arjun Appadurai, on the other hand, who could also be included under this rubric of interpreting globalization as a cultural process, is more interested in how sociopolitical processes unleashed by economic imperatives have turned into cultural projects that surpass and cunningly outwit these imperatives themselves. For Appadurai, globalization is a new space for a new social imaginary that works through the nation-state but also against it and beyond it as well. In the last instance, Appadurai is interested in the constitution of a new social imaginary that can no longer be matched or reduced to economic goals and processes alone.[21]

There are also political readings of globalization. This we find represented in the work of Jürgen Habermas and Malcolm Waters,[22] although I will only discuss the former. For Habermas, globalization is the extension to the entire globe of the highest achievements of the Enlightenment and critical modernity. To this extent, globalization appears to be an extension of modernity, if not its final denouement. In two recent essays, Habermas has directly addressed the question of globalization.[23] He has suggested that globalization does indeed consist in a series of economic and political challenges but that the appropriate answers to them require instituting at a global level the rule of law and one of the greatest achievements of the twentieth century, namely, the welfare state. In fact, in the face of the many quandaries and problems that besiege European nation-states, the appropriate answer is to reach out to the law.[24] Law becomes the civilizing element. Indeed, Habermas talks about the juridification of politics, at a global level, as the answer to the conflicts brought about by growing cultural ethnocentrism and the atavistic reactions by societies that are trying to survive the onslaught of Europeanization and westernization. As Habermas puts it, "The only means of countering the factual oppression exercised by the dictatorships of developing nations is a juridification of politics *[Verrechtlichung der Politik]*. The integration problems that every highly complex society has to master can be solved by means of modern law, however, only if *legitimate* law helps to generate that abstract form of civic solidarity that stands and falls with the realization of basic rights."[25]

Then there is a systems theoretic perspective on globalization, which I think is represented best by Ronald Robertson, Niklas Luhmann,[26] and Martin Albrow;[27] for brevity's sake I will discuss only the first. Roland Robertson, the theorist who has most consistently contributed to our understanding of globalization, reads globalization as a profound challenge to the basic categories of sociology.[28] For Robertson, globalization results from the diachronic and synchronic interactions within a "global field" that is constituted by four axes, or components: (1) selves, (2) national societies, (3) a world-system of societies, and (4) humankind. Synchronically, each one of these components has developed and transformed in relationship with one another. Diachronically, they stand in tension and mutual codetermination. More concretely, however, we ought to see the development of a global system, that is, a system that is increasingly interdependent and is aware of this integration, in the following way:[29]

1. The individual self (1) is to be understood as a member of a community and/or nation-state that through its culture of citizenship endows that individual with inalienable rights; but these rights often stand in contrast to and in tension with other inalienable rights and conceptions of self of other so-

cieties (3); even the individual is to be seen, in the last instance, as a particular instance of humanity as such (4).

2. A national community (2) stands in a particularly contentious relationship to its members (1), who are seen as either rights carriers or members of a culture and language community. This national community, in turn, sees itself as a member of a community of national communities (3), one that makes claim to such status on the grounds that it provides to its members a status closest to those made by and for humanity on its behalf.
3. A global system of nations (3) is established through the coordination, attenuation, and acknowledgment of sovereignty on the part of individual communities (Kant's project in *Perpetual Peace* is a perfect example). This system elaborates, maintains, and legislates a certain set of expectations with respect to the ways in which people are treated as citizens within their respective body politics (1). The Nuremberg Trials are a perfect example, as well as the many challenges of nations before the World Court. Finally, the ability of a global system of nations to legislate on human rights offers a test of feasibility for many humanitarian projects (3). Robertson calls this a reality check.
4. Humanity, in turn, is defined not just in terms of certain religio-philosophical perspectives but also in terms of concrete rights of persons qua human beings (1). These rights are sometimes granted by nation-states, but they are nevertheless possessed or claimable by all human beings (2). These rights in turn are enforced and are given weight by international arrangements and pressures (3).

These four components of the global field exert a relativizing force on one another. Thus selves are relativized with reference to the notion of humanity, and humanity in turn is made relative with respect to specific embodiments of selves. Individuals, as selves, stand in a problematic relationship to the nation-states that either nurtures and enables them or disables them. Similarly, nation-states are relativized when viewed from the perspective of humanity and other nation-states. Robertson has given nice expression to these forces of relativization with a schema in which arrows cross while extending from each corner of a square, whose right angles are made up of each component. Interestingly, Robertson notes, one of the most salient characteristics of this global field is that it both relativizes and further enhances the "identity" of each component. Robertson suggests that globalization is in fact the institutionalization of identity declarations, as much by individuals, nation-states, and world systems of nations as by humanity in general.

This dynamic of relativization and the institutionalization of identity declaration is further stylized by Robertson in an insightful formulation. Globalization, for Robertson, consists in a twofold process "involving the interpenetration of the universalization of particularism and the particularization of universalism."[30] To this extent, globalization results as much in a quest for universalism as for particularism. Globalization thus involves the universalization of particularism, not just the particularization of universalism.[31] In other words, under globalization, all societies must be both unique and individual, but they must be able to make universal claims about their uniqueness, particularity, and difference. Robertson is quick to note that the West is not exempt from this dissolving and integrating force of globalization. The West is just one of the many cultures in the world, one which, like all others, must present itself before the world court of universalism.

In contrast to Barnett, Cavanagh, and Barber, Robertson suggests that globalization is prior to modernity and, further, that the imperatives for globalization are, to a large extent, dictated by cultural or systemic-sociological imperatives and not by economic or political ones.[32] For Robertson, globalization is driven by the logic of social systems as systems of agency to which economics and politics are subsidiary. As he summarizes: "Globalization theory turns world-systems theory nearly on its head—by focusing, first, on *cultural* aspects of the world 'system' and, second, by systematic study of *internal* civilizational and societal attributes which shape orientations to the world as a whole and forms of participation of civilizations and societies in the global-human circumstance."[33]

Some of these different takes on globalization, however, have tried to elucidate the links that exist between globalization and history, history and ethics, and ethics and globalization, with varying degrees of success and self-consciousness.[34] Had they succeeded in their effort, they would have realized that many of their assumptions, as well as ideals and models, were Eurocentric and ethnocentric. In contrast, Dussel's *Ethics of Liberation in the Age of Globalization and Exclusion*[35] is the most comprehensive, thorough, and systematic analysis of the relationship between ethics, globalization, and history. Before I discuss Dussel's magisterial contribution, I would like to briefly flesh out the relevance of these conjunctives.

Globalization and History

Under this rubric I gather the question concerning the relationship between globalization and history. Is globalization a result or a catalyst of modernity? Can we subsume globalization into the dialectic of modernization, and to that extent is the latter a product of the spirit of the West alone? Could we in fact view globalization as reflexive modernity, as is suggested by Ulrich Beck, Scott Lash, and Anthony Giddens?[36] And concomitantly, can we then view globalization as a project, modernity's project elevated to a planetary scale? On the other hand, if globalization entails the corrosion of all developmental projects and the agents that heralded them, such as the state and the economy, how then do we do history in a global age? It is not clear what relationship exists between a global age and a global history.[37]

History and Ethics

This dyad, although analyzed extensively, has not been framed appropriately with reference to global history. Ethical perspectives, on the one hand, are always the result of particular histories. An ethos is coagulated history, so to speak. Aristotelians and Hegelians share this view. History also unleashes processes that challenge established ethicities (*Sittlichkeiten*), and, insofar as histories are projects, certain ethical perspectives become the result of certain epochal shifts. We can see Protestantism, and its resultant ethos of privatization and individualism, in this light. This brings up the question, to what extent, for instance, can we speak of a new planetary ethical consciousness that surpasses the reaches of local and culturally based ethical perspectives? It must be acknowledged that this question has been at the center of Karl-Otto Apel's[38] and Jürgen Habermas's work.[39] Yet their views on a postconventional moral consciousness are too rooted in a particular view of socialization processes that seem endemic and unique to the West. If we take globalization to entail the relativization of other cultures as well as of the West itself, then we cannot work on the assumption that a global moral perspective can only be forthcoming from a globalization of Western formalism and neo-Kantianism. In short, we must ask what global history stands behind what new global ethos, and whether we can speak of a global ethos that challenges as well as actualizes what was inchoate in up to now relatively inward-looking ethicities.

Ethics and Globalization

Globalization, as Jameson has suggested, ought to be taken as a philosophical problem. Robertson, as noted, has suggested that globalization ought to be taken as a major challenge to the basic categories of social analysis. Globalization should also be taken as an ethical problem. For globalization at the very least has meant the growing gap between rich and poor, developed and underdeveloped, linked up and unconnected to the flows of information, money, and power, which, like a storm, elevates some to heights of obscene wealth while plunging others into abysmal levels of subhuman existence. Globalization, similarly, has also meant the relativization of cultures and their views about what human agents can and ought to do. If we begin with the simplistic realization that an ethical perspective consists of the coordination of the concepts of an ethical agent, a criteria for the discernment of the validity of ethical judgments, and the guiding light provided by cultural goods that acts as moral compasses, then we must ask what ethical systems are allowed by a global age in which agents, judgments, and cultural goods have been destabilized, rendered fluid and suspect, and in which the reach of individuals and even communities is thwarted by global processes that even if locally unleashed have unforeseen planetary consequences. At the very minimum we must begin with the realization that globalization commands that we visualize new categories of ethical analysis.

THE WORLD-SYSTEM OF INCLUSION THROUGH EXCLUSION: ENRIQUE DUSSEL'S CRITIQUE OF GLOBALIZATION

It is my contention that Dussel's work addresses these challenges. His *Ethics of Liberation in an Age of Globalization and Exclusion* is a contribution of paramount importance because it explicitly and in an unprecedented fashion links up these dyads: globalization and history, history and ethics, and ethics and globalization. I will present his work as being guided by these dyads.

Globalization and History

Above all, Dussel seeks to dislodge the ethnocentric and Eurocentric views that inform most of contemporary philosophy. He does this first by demonstrating that modernity must be read as the result not of an autochthonous dynamic of European culture but rather as the result of the management of a world-system by the West. In order to demonstrate this thesis, Dussel periodizes world history into four stages of the "interregional system" (see table 6.1).[40]

The thrust of Dussel's argument is that the West assumes a hegemonic position vis-à-vis other cultures only through its becoming the center of a world-system that is inaugurated with the discovery of the New World. In contrast to the standard chronologies and metahistorical philosophical justifications for the success of the "miracle of the West" or the "rise of the West" (celebrated since Hegel and informing Marx, Weber, Parsons, Habermas, and many recent world historians), Dussel argues that the "triumph" of the West can be understood appropriately only when we take into consideration the management of the world-system that allows the West to obtain a differential advantage over the East and Africa. In Dussel's view, the willfully myopic conceptualization and chronology that informs most contemporary Eurocentric philosophy has resulted in part from a series of conflations, first, from conflating the formulation of the "new theorical paradigm (modernity) with its historical origin, as well as with the crisis and eventual demise of the medieval paradigm."[41] Second, from conflating European ontogenesis, so to speak, with world phylogenesis in such a way that a mirroring *(espejismo)* effect takes place in which what were effects of a positioning within a world-system are taken to be intrinsic advantages that belong to the very spirit of the West.[42] Most importantly, however, by reframing the question of modernity in terms of Europe's centrality within a world-system, Dussel is able to talk about the "underside" of this purportedly "civilizing" project. Modernity emerges from Dussel's reframing of it as a project that entails a "sacrificial logic," one in which the perpetuator of the sacrifice is exculpated and left blameless for the demise and on-

Table 6.1 Schematic Representation of the Four Stages of the "Interregional System," Which Begins to Unfold As "World System" after 1492

Stage	*Diachronic Name of the Interregional System*	*Poles around a Center*
I	Egyptian-Mesopotamian (since the fourth millennium B.C.): §0.1	Without center: Egypt & Mesopotamia
II	"Indo-European" (since 200 B.C.): §0.1	Center: Persian region, Hellenic world (Seleucid & Ptolemaic) since the fourth century B.C. Eastern extreme: China Southeastern: Indian kingdoms Western: Mediterranean New World
III	Asiatic-Afro-Mediterranean (since the fourth century A.D.): §0.4	Center of commercial connections: Persian region & the Turín & Tarim, later the Muslim world (since the seventh century A.D.) Productive center: China Southwestern: Bantú Africa Western: Byzantine–Russian World Extreme West: Western Europe
IV	World-System (after 1492 A.D.): §§0.5-0.6	Center: Western Europe (today U.S.A. & Japan, from 1945 to 1989 with Russia) Periphery: Latin America, Bantú Africa, Muslim world, India, southwestern Asia, eastern Europe Semi-autonomous: China & Russia (since 1989)

Source: Enrique Dussel, *Etica de la liberación en la edad de la globalización y de la exclusión* (Madrid: Editorial Trotta, 1998), 21.

slaught that it unleashes on a world and its cultures, which are to be managed, civilized, bureaucratized, and secularized. Modernity, whether incomplete or already exhausted, cannot be understood comprehensively unless we give voice to the victims of this project.[43]

History and Ethics

Analogously to Hegel and Charles Taylor, Dussel views ethical systems through the lens of history. He is also related to Habermas and Apel in that he views ethics not just as the actualization of a form of life but also as the unfolding of formal aspects of moral thinking that, in coordination with ethical and cultural goods, lead ethicities to higher levels of abstraction, formalization, and universalization. His work thus is interested in demonstrating how the ethical material and moral formal levels of ethical consciousness are historically conditioned. He discerns in the first stage of the interregional system the dawning of an ethical consciousness that departs from the recognition of the material, corporeal individuality of the ethical agent. In the Egyptian Book of the Dead and the Code of Hammurabi, to mention just a few documents from the first interregional system, we find enshrined, according to Dussel, the respect and reverence for the dignified unity of the ethical-corporeal subject. This subject is addressed in his or her individuality, in his or her suffering and vulnerable corporeality.

During the second stage of the interregional system, which is marked by the rise of the military empires of the Bronze and Iron Ages, Dussel discerns the rise of metaphysical and anthropological dualism. For this dualism, matter, the body, living corporeality is a blemish, a fault, a prison, a hindrance. The poles of this ethical orientation are the rejection of corporeal life and the quest after the One. Thus in Dussel's view, from Greece and Rome to the Persians, the kingdoms of India and Taoist China, arose a metaphysics of the absolute as One and a dualist anthropology inaugurated an ascetic ethics. This ethics of the negation and overcoming of corporeal materiality meant the superseding of material plurality as a return—a *Heilweg*—to the originary unity of the fountainhead (Plotinus being the epitome of this voyage toward the divine).

In the third stage of the interregional system, the ethical perspective of the Egyptian–Mesopotamian stage of the system reasserts itself. Partly through Christianity and Islam, an ethics of the suffering ethical-corporeal subject is proclaimed. Buddhism, Islam, and Christianity are reformation movements formulated in light of the empires that dominated antiquity.

With the fourth stage of the interregional system, we return to the ethicities of the second interregional system, during which the great empires of antiquity rose and brought about the unification of the Eurasian and African continental masses. The difference is that for the first time we have a world-system in which the relatively autonomous regions of the world are subsumed into a system in which there is a center and a periphery. The center acts as manager and metropolis, the periphery as backwater and colonial outpost. In analogy to the second stage of the interregional system, anthropological dualism is reaffirmed and the subject is conceptualized as a disembodied epistemic subjectivity. The ethical subject is reduced to an appendage of the epistemic subject.[44]

Ethics and Globalization

Perhaps like no other living philosopher, with the exception of Karl-Otto Apel, Enrique Dussel has been insisting since the early 1960s on an ethical consideration and analysis of both modernity and globalization. For Dussel, the processes of global integration, at first understood by him through the prism of underdevelopment theory, represent not just historical or socioeconomic challenges, challenges that could be met by the conceptual tools that would refashion the edifice of social science. For him, modernity/globalization represents an ethical challenge of the first order. What secularization, urbanization, industrialization, and colonialism meant as ethical challenges for European philosophers during the last five hundred years of the world-system, globalization means for Dussel. It is a point of departure for all ethical speculation. For Dussel, globalization profiles itself as an ethical problem in two senses, or under two registers. First, we cannot, and must not, circumvent, turn away from, minimize, or simply neglect the brutal fact that three-fourths of humanity lives in massive poverty. In absolute numbers, people today are poorer and are more likely to become victims of famine, drought, and interregional or global conflicts.[45] In absolute numbers, developing nations are less likely to jump-start their economies into the kind of development that would allow them to meet even the most minimal standards of dignified human living. Children and women, moreover, are the general victims of this spiraling into the abyss of subhuman levels of existence.[46] Ecologically, culturally, economically, and politically, the Third World, fast becoming a Fourth World (to borrow from Samir Amin),[47] is succumbing to the logic of finance capitalism—a logic of chaos, disorder, and economic russian roulette (although Cornel West's term "gangsterization" just as appropriately describes the present world economy).[48] For Dussel, globalization spells the material, discursive, cultural, and philosophical exclusion of the majority of the world's peoples (most located south of the equator), just as a rhetoric of inclusion and interconnectivity announces their purported participation and coresponsibility for a globalized planet. Globalization, in short, means for Dussel what Hans-Peter Martin and Harald Schumman have called the "20:80 society," in which only 20 percent of the world will suffice to produce all that is needed, and the remaining 80 percent will be entirely superfluous, supplemental, a burden, a perpetual lumpen proletariat. To this it should be added that of this 20 percent, only the top 5 percent will enjoy the riches produced by world society.[49]

The second sense in which globalization is an ethical challenge for Dussel concerns the development of appropriate ethical categories that will ground an ethics for the age of globalization and exclusion. At the core of Dussel's *Etica de la liberación en la edad de globalización y de la exclusión* lies precisely the resolution to this challenge. In light of the threat to life (understood by Dussel in its plethora of manifestations, i.e., culture, thought, ecosystems) that globalization entails, all contemporary ethics must begin with an affirmation of life. Ethics, in Dussel's view, thus departs from a recognition of the materiality of human agents, who are always first and foremost members of a community of life. Second, life in its human plurality, one that is recognized with greater appreciation due to a global awareness, requires an arbitration, negotiation, and discernment between different and competing moral goods projected by different and competing forms of life (the historical encounter between civilizations or cultures, each of which is generally informed by a mythico-ethical core). Finally, the ethical, as what must be done in light of the preservation and nurturing of human life, must concern itself with what is feasible, what is materially and logically possible. These fundamental points of departure are summarized and expressed as principles for a foundational ethics: the material principle (practical truth) that enjoins respect for and preservation of life; the discursive principle of formal validity (formal morality); and the principle of feasibility (strategic-instrumental rationality). In this way, Dussel offers a middle path between Aristotelian-Hegelian historicist communitarianism and Kantian-Rawlsian idealist transcendentalist proceduralist universalism. These three principles concern foundational ethics. They in turn are, and must be, complemented by the principles that inform a critical ethics.

A critical ethics is an ethics that departs not just from the affirmation of life but life already under threat, life denied. Ethics thus must contain two necessary aspects: the negative (abstract and universal) and the positive (concrete and particular). It is the latter that critical ethics elaborates. Paralleling but now articulating in a positive way, the principles of a critical ethics are enunciated thus: every system, practice, and norm that makes the life of any or all humans impossible must be criticized. Every system that produces victims must be submitted to ethical censure. The *locus criticus* of ethics is thus the victim. This is the critical material principle. Inasmuch as all systems are blind to their victims (they are not recognized as victims, much less as victims of their own logic), the imperative to include all possible individuals affected by the decisions they make in all of their deliberations demands that all systems criticize their practices of inclusion and/or exclusion. When the victims of any system, practice, or norm recognize their victimization, the system is under compulsion to give privileged attention to their critique of the system, lest the principle of abstract validity be broached (i.e., a system turns dogmatic and cynical). To this extent, the critical principle of abstract formalization and justification turns into the principle of the hermeneutical-ethical privilege of the victim. Finally, from every critique that arises from the recognition of the ways in which any given system makes life impossible and from the imperative to submit every system's practices to validation and justification by all must inescapably result in the commandment to liberate the victims of the system from the conditions that oppress them and make their life an impossibility. This last is the liberation principle that gives positive form to what was merely affirmed formally and negatively in the abstract and general principles of foundational ethics.

In Dussel's view, then, the appropriate and necessary ethics for an age of globalization and exclusion must begin with the affirmation of life and must include a recognition of the plurality of ethical goods that must be submitted to a universalization test (whether these goods could be universalized by a community of discourse under conditions in which these discourses would not be vitiated by systematic exclusion), while at the same time recognizing what is both materially possible and feasible. But since every social system, practice, and norm is by definition imperfect, all ethical reflection must at the same time seek out the victims of the system, and the ways in which they enunciate a critique of the system, while also seeking to liberate these victims from their situation of negativity, privation, and lack.

NOTES

I would like to thank Linda Martín Alcoff, Santiago Castro-Gómez, and Martin Woessner for their insightful comments.

1. The classic statement of this insight is found in Marshall G.S. Hodgson, "In the Center of the Map: Nations See Themselves As the Hub Of History," in *Rethinking World History: Essays on Europe, Islam, and World History,* ed. Edmund Burke III (Cambridge: Cambridge University Press, 1993), 29–34. See also Lewis Martin and Kaeren E. Wigen, *The Myth of Continents: A Critique of Metageography* (Berkeley: University of California Press, 1997).

2. These words appear in Adrienne Rich, "Notes toward a Politics of Location," in *Blood, Bread, and Poetry: Selected Prose, 1979–1985* (New York: Norton, 1986), 212.

3. The "West" is to be taken as signaling a set of representations and not a "real" geographical entity. One of the central themes of this essay is precisely how the West comes to constitute its identity through the practices of historical representation. What I want to underscore is the need to question our practices of narrating the history of the world as a means to privileging certain ways of representing and constituting the West that at the same time entail the erasure of other geohistorical markers and entities. For a succinct but precise presentation of this issue, see Thomas C. Patterson, *Inventing Western Civilization* (New York: Monthly Review Press, 1997).

4. See Karl Löwith, *Meaning in History* (Chicago: University of Chicago Press, 1949).

5. See Immanuel Wallerstein et al., *Open the Social Sciences: Report of the Gulbenkian Commission on the Restructuring of the Social Sciences* (Stanford: Stanford University Press, 1996), esp. chap. 2.

6. See J. M. Blaut, *The Colonizer's Model of the World: Geographical Diffusionism and Eurocentric History* (New York: Guilford, 1992), esp. chaps. 1–2. See also Samir Amin, *Eurocentrism* (London: Zed, 1989).

7. For the idea of "cluster of absences," see Bryan S. Turner, *Marx and the End of Orientalism* (London: Croon Helm, 1986), 81, quoted in Andre Gunder Frank, *ReOrient: Global Economy in the Asian Age* (Berkeley: University of California Press, 1998), 17

8. See Manfred Kossok, "From Universal History to Global History," in *Conceptualizing Global History,* ed. Bruce Mazlish and Ralph Buultjens (Boulder: Westview, 1993), 93–111. See also Gilbert Allardyce, "Toward World History: American Historians and the Coming of the World History Course," *Journal of World History* 1 (1990): 23–76.

9. See William H. McNeill, *Mythistory and Other Essays* (Chicago: University of Chicago Press, 1986), chap. 6, "Lord Acton."

10. See William McNeill, "Basic Assumptions of Toynbee's *A Study of History,*" in *Mythistory and Other Essays*, 125–46.

11. See Arnold Toynbee, *The World and the West* (New York: Oxford University Press, 1953).

12. William H. McNeill, *The Rise of the West: A History of the Human Community* (Chicago: University of Chicago Press, 1963).

13. See William H. McNeill, "The Rise of the West after Twenty–Five Years," *Journal of World History* 1, no. 1 (1990): 1–21. See also R. I. Moore, "World History," in *Companion to Historiography,* ed. Michael Bentley (London: Routledge, 1997), 941–59.

14. My argument is similar (although aimed at a different group of theorists) to the one made by Frederick Buell, who argues acutely that globalization has become a nationalist postnationalist discourse. Buell writes: "I am taking the position that the demise of the nation has been greatly exaggerated and that the recent U.S. culture is characterized less by insurgent postnationalism (however much it is being invoked now by dissident-progressive cultural movements) than by the invention of a new breed of cultural nationalism—a form of cultural nationalism for post-national circumstances" ("Nationalist Postnationalism: Globalist Discourse in Contemporary American Culture," *American Quarterly* 50, no. 3 [1988]: 548–91, at 550). I go further than Buell and argue that globalization has become the discourse of the West that replaces the already exhausted discourses on modernity/postmodernity. Still, Buell offers a historicization of the rise of discourses about globalization within American culture that is insightful and indispensable.

15. I think the proliferation of these discourses about globalization has reached such levels of differentiation and complexity that we need a typology. I have ventured such a typology in "Society's Religion: The Rise of Social Theory, Globalization, and the Invention of Religion," in *The Religions of Globalization,* ed. Dwight N. Hopkins et al. (Durham: Duke University Press, forthcoming). There I argue that theories of globalization can be divided into three types: 1. mono-metastructural (Wallerstein, Amin, Barber, etc.), 2. matrix rearrangement and differentiation (Robertson, Turner, and Appadurai), and 3. metatheoretical reflexivity (Luhman, Münch, Clark). Given what I argue in this chapter, I think that Dussel should be put under the third type of globalization theory. Further, I find the typology offered by Held, McGrew, Goldblatt, and Perraton pedagogically useful but not perspicacious; see their impressive *Global Transformations: Politics, Economics, and Culture* (Stanford: Stanford University Press, 1999).

16. Richard J. Barnett and John Cavanagh, *Global Dreams: Imperial Corporations and the New World Order* (New York: Simon & Schuster, 1994). See also their nice summary of their work in Mazlish and Buultjens, eds., *Conceptualizing Global History*.

17. Benjamin R. Barber, *Jihad vs. McWorld: How Globalism and Tribalism Are Reshaping the World* (New York: Ballantine, 1995).

18. Ibid., 24.

19. See his collection of essays eponymously subtitled after the classic essay "The Cultural Logic of Late Capitalism" in *Postmodernism or, The Cultural Logic of Late Capitalism* (Durham, N.C.: Duke University Press, 1991).

20. Fredric Jameson, "Notes on Globalization As a Philosophical Issue," in *The Cultures of Globalization,* ed. Fredric Jameson and Masao Miyoshi (Durham: Duke University Press, 1998), 54–77.

21. Arjun Appadurai, *Modernity at Large: Cultural Dimensions of Globalization* (Minneapolis: University of Minnesota Press, 1996).

22. Malcolm Waters, *Globalization* (New York: Routledge, 1995).

23. Jürgen Habermas, *Die postnationale Konstellation: Politische Essays* (Frankfurt/M: Suhrkamp, 1998). See the essays under part 2, "Die postnationale Konstellation," two of which have already appeared in translation. "Aus Katastrophen lernen? Ein zeitdiagnostischer Rückblick auf das kurze 20. Jahrhundert" has appeared in *Constellations: An International Journal of Critical and Democratic Theory* 5, no. 3 (1998): 307–20; "Zur Legitimation durch Menschenrechte" has appeared in *Philosophy and Social Criticism* 24, no. 2–3 (1998): 157–71.

24. Appropriately Habermas has circumscribed his reflections on globalization within the horizon of Europe's fate in light of European unification and the disintegration of the Soviet Union. At the same time, this is certainly disappointing in its narrowness. What is an otherwise brilliant phenomenological description of the physiognomy of modernity turns into a hypostatization of Europe's experience of it. Compare Habermas's recent collection, *Kleine politische Schriften*; Habermas, *Die Normalität einer Berliner Republik* (Frankfurt/M: Suhrkamp, 1995); and Habermas, *Vergangenheit als Zukunft* (Zürich: Pendo–Verlag, 1990).

25. See Jürgen Habermas, "Remarks on Legitimation through Human Rights," *Philosophy and Social Criticism* 24, no. 3–4 (1998): 167.

26. See Niklas Luhmann, *Die Gesellschaft der Gesellschaft*, 2 vols. (Frankfurt/M: Suhrkamp, 1997). See also Luhmann, *Observations on Modernity*, trans. William Whobrey (Stanford: Stanford University Press, 1998).

27. Martin Albrow, *The Global Age: State and Society beyond Modernity* (Stanford: Stanford University Press, 1997). Albrow sees globalization as entailing the end of modernity or of a particular type of discourse about society that we have come to associate with it.

28. Roland Roberton, *Globalization: Social Theory and Global Culture* (London: Sage, 1992).

29. Ibid., 25–31.

30. Ibid., 100.

31. Ibid., 130.

32. Here Robertson seems to agree with some world systems theorists (e.g., Wallerstein and Frank). Yet the world system propounders connect the world system to the emergence of capitalism in such a way that globalization is the imposition of a global capitalist system since 1492. Andre Gunder Frank has began to take distance from this capitalistic–Eurocentric perspective. See Andre Gunder Frank and Barry K. Gills, "The 5,000 year World System," in *The World System: Five Hundred Years or Five Thousand Years?* ed. Andre Gunder Frank and Barry K. Gills (New York: Routledge, 1993); see also Andre Gunder Frank, *ReOrient*. A recent intervention in the discourse about a world systems approach

is the fascinating work by Robert P. Clark, *The Global Imperative: An Interpretative History of the Spread of Humankind* (Boulder: Westview, 1997). Whereas Wallerstein, Frank, and Amin write the history of the world-system in terms of center-periphery, accumulation-expropriation, and so on, Clark pivots his narrative around the notion of entropy.

33. Robertson, *Globalization,* 133.

34. Self-conscious attempts at theorizing globalization in historical terms have been made by the world-systems theorists as well as the Annales School historians—Wallerstein and Frank as well as Braudel, Chaunu, and others.

35. Enrique Dussel, *Etica de la Liberación en la edad de globalización y de la exclusión* (Madrid: Editorial Trotta, 1998). See my review essay "Ethics for an Age of Globalization and Exclusion," *Philosophy and Social Criticism* 25, no. 2 (1999): 115–21.

36. Ulrich Beck, Anthony Giddens, and Scott Lash, *Reflexive Modernization: Politics, Tradition, and Aesthetics in the Modern Social Order* (Stanford: Stanford University Press, 1994). See also Ulrich Beck, *Was ist Globalisierung? Irrtümer des Globalismus—Antworten auf Globalisierung* (Frankfurt/M: Suhrkamp, 1998). This book is part of a series edited by Beck entitled Edition Zweite Moderne (Second Modernity Edition).

37. See the excellent essay by Michael Geyer and Charles Bright, "World History in a Global Age," in *American Historical Review,* October 1995, 1034–60. See also the introduction to Mazlish and Buultjens, *Conceptualizing Global History*; and Andre Gunder Frank, "A Plea for World System History," *Journal of World History* 2, no. 1 (Spring 1991): 1–28.

38. See Karl-Otto Apel, "The Problem of Justice in a Multicultural Society: The Response of Discourse Ethics," in *Questioning Ethics: Contemporary Debates in Philosophy,* ed. Richard Kearney and Mark Dooley (London: Routledge, 1999); and Apel, "Globalization and the Need for Universal Ethics" (unpublished manuscript, 1998). See also his contribution (chapter 4) in this volume.

39. See Jürgen Habermas, *The Inclusion of the Other: Studies in Political Theory*, ed. Ciaran Cronin and Pablo De Greiff (Cambridge: MIT Press, 1998), esp. chaps. 1, 3, 4, 8; Habermas, *Die postnationale Konstellation.*

40. Enrique Dussel, *Etica de la liberación,* 21. All translations from this work are mine.

41. Dussel, *Etica de la liberación,* 621.

42. Ibid.

43. These arguments have been more extensively elaborated by Dussel in *The Underside of Modernity: Apel, Ricoeur, Rorty, Taylor, and the Philosophy of Liberation*, ed. and trans. Eduardo Mendieta (Atlantic Highlands, N.J.: Humanities, 1996). See also "Beyond Eurocentrism: The World-System and the Limits of Modernity," in *Cultures of Globalization,* 3–31; Dussel, *The Invention of the Americas: Eclipse of "the Other" and the Myth of Modernity,* trans. Michael D. Barber (New York: Continuum, 1995).

44. While the *Etica de la liberación* contains the most succinct version of this Dusselian narrative, it is by no means the first time he has offered it. In fact, this history of ethicities has been a recurrent theme of Dussel's work. It begins with his earliest works, such as *El humanismo semita: Estructuras intencionales radicales del pueblo de Israel y otros semitas* (Buenos Aires: EUDEBA, 1969), finished in 1964; Dussel, *El dualismo en la antropología de la cristiandad: Desde los orígenes hasta antes de la conquista de América* (Buenos Aires: Ed. Guadalupe, 1974), finished in 1968; and *El humanismo helénico* (Buenos Aires: EUDEBA, 1975). This book was written in 1961 but was not published until 1975 because of censure by the Videla dictatorship. There is a wonderful collection of

Dussel's essays on the topic of Latin America in world history, and the elaboration of his notion of mythico-ethical cores of civilizations: *Oito ensaios: Sobre cultura latinoamericana e libertacao*, trans. Sandra Trabucco Valenzuela (São Paulo: Paulinas, 1997). On the chronology of Dussel's works, see his recent autobiographical essay: Enrique Dussel, "Autopercepción intelectual de un proceso histórico," *Revista Anthropos*: *Huellas del conocimiento* 180 (September–October 1998): 13–36. This issue of the prestigious Spanish magazine *Anthropos* is dedicated to Dussel's work. See also Hans Schelkshorn, *Ethik der Befreiung: Einführung in die Philosophie Enrique Dussels* (Vienna: Herder, 1992).

45. See Roger Burbach, Olando Núñez, and Boris Kagarlitsky, *Globalization and Its Discontents: The Rise of Postmodern Socialism* (London: Pluto, 1996), esp. chap. 1, "New World Disorder."

46. See the excellent collection *The Gendered New World Order: Militarism, Development, and the Environment,* ed. Jennifer Turpin and Lois Ann Lorentzen (New York: Routledge, 1996).

47. See Samir Amin, *Capitalism in the Age of Globalization* (London: Zed, 1996).

48. Cornel West, "The Moral Obligations of Living in a Democratic Society," in *The Good Citizen,* ed. David Batstone and Eduardo Mendieta (New York: Routledge, 1999), 6.

49. See Hans-Peter Martin and Harald Schumann, *The Global Trap: Globalization and the Assault on Prosperity and Democracy*, trans. Patrick Camiller (London: Zed, 1997), 1ff.

7

Burnt Offerings to Rationality: A Feminist Reading of the Construction of Indigenous Peoples in Dussel's Theory of Modernity

Lynda Lange

In his book *The Invention of the Americas* (1995), the philosopher Enrique Dussel makes an important and interesting contribution to the critical analysis of European modernity and colonization that includes an approach to the critique of modern philosophy. From his location in South America, he is responding particularly to the history of the Spanish conquest of South and Central America, a conquest Tsvetan Todorov terms the worst genocide the world has ever seen (1984, 5). Dussel aligns his postcolonial theory with feminism, noting the intersection of colonization and patriarchy that makes women a special part of the spoils of conquest for European men, although he does not elaborate on questions concerning women or refer to feminist texts.[1] However, reading Dussel from the perspective of a democratic feminist critic, I find many similarities between his approach to postcolonial criticism and that of some feminist criticism, similarities that encourage us to make use of his work for the task of "postcolonial feminism."

His position with regard to the ongoing confrontation between modernism and postmodernism is of interest to feminist critics who are convinced of the cultural and gender bias in many modernist concepts and values but are also concerned about the negative implications for political action that seem to flow from certain types of postmodernism. More would be in moral agreement with efforts to respect non-European cultures and avoid a Eurocentric approach to the history of modernity than would agree to such postmodern views as that truth and value cannot be communicated across cultures or across such differences in life forms as gender and/or sexual orientation. There are broad similarities between the variety of politicized critiques of "philosophy" extant right now, such as feminist critique, antiracist critique, queer critique, and post/colonial critique. They all seek to expose the biases of philosophical concepts and especially to show how philosophical concepts presented as universal may be implicitly particular to the degree that they are shaped by the socioeconomic and cultural locations of their inventors. They all seek to show, to use Nancy Tuana's (1992) useful critical concept, who is "located in the text," that is, who is talking to whom, about whom.

However, I believe that there are noteworthy differences among these critiques, which make their implications for both philosophy and political practice different as well. I am not referring to differences between feminist, antiracist, and other approaches, which are also important, but to philosophical and epistemological differences that may be found within any of these approaches. Dussel's work makes an interesting case study for illustrating this point. In addition, because Dussel's work is much less well-known in North America than the work of Europeans in the same areas, I am also concerned simply to present his ideas and to discuss how we can best understand what he is doing and what it may imply for us.

Dussel shares the radical, politically positive edge of postmodernism, which is to affirm the dignity and validity of the Other. In fact, he used to call himself a postmodernist. However, he now presents a theory of modernity (that he terms "transmodern"), which affirms "that rationality can establish a dialogue with the reason of the Other, as an alterative reason" (Dussel 1995, 132). At the same time, it seems to me that he deepens our appreciation of the difficulty of overcoming a Eurocentric perspective in a manner that is as relevant to "white European feminism" as it is to masculinist Euro-centrism. He could be thought of as saying something like: Yes, it is in principle possible to overcome Euro-centrism by rational and imaginative means, but it is harder than you may think.

According to Dussel, not only proponents or defenders of the ethos of European modernity but also many of its postmodern or postcolonial critics remain Eurocentric insofar as they presuppose, whether positively or negatively, that there is an inner dynamic of European modernity that has caused it to have superior power or effectiveness over non-European peoples. So, for example, a classical affirmation of European superiority considered as beneficial is that of Max Weber, that only on "Western soil" have there been cultural phenomena that have produced signs of "evolutionary advance and universal validity" (*Sociologie, Westgeschichtliche Analyzen, Politik,* quoted in Dussel 1995, 10). This may be contrasted with a postcolonial view that also presupposes a purely inner dynamic of European modernity, for example, that of the African-Caribbean humanist Aimé Cesaire, that "Europe is indefensible" and that at the end of all the mere "boastfulness," as he terms it, colonization is a poison "instilled into the veins of Europe and, slowly but surely, the continent proceeds toward *savagery*" (1972, 13). Although writing from a perspective in the African diaspora, Cesaire had in mind, among other things, the Holocaust of the mid-twentieth century, which occurred within Europe's own boundaries. According to Dussel, however, the power of modernity (which he does not mean to deny) is the *result* and not the *cause* of the centrality of Europe in a world or global system. The success of violent conquest and colonization of the Americas and Africa gave Western Europe a formidable advantage over the non-Christian East. European modernity therefore originates, and is constituted by, a dialectical relationship with non-Europe.

Although this view of the constitution of European modernity has been propounded in other disciplines, for example, the work of Blaut in geography (1992), Dussel suggests it can be applied specifically to the nature of modern European philosophy as such.

Dussel holds the view (contrary to many postmoderns) that it is not modern philosophical or scientific *rationality* that has been an instrument of terror but a distinctively modern Eurocentric *irrational myth* that has resulted in the terror of what he calls "sacrificial violence." Dussel therefore distinguishes two concurrent paradigms of modernity. One is the rational, emancipatory conceptual content of modernity. The other is the negative and irrational myth, in which Dussel traces the justification of colonial violence to a "developmental fallacy." This fallacy rests on the view that Europe is the endpoint of a universal developmental process, toward which all other peoples must and will go. It is especially relevant for philosophers (feminist and otherwise) that he finds this "irrational myth" exemplified by philosophy itself. It should not be viewed, therefore, as "cultural myth," with reference to which modern philosophy has stood as a critic on the basis of reason. Dussel's positioning of the "irrational myth of modernity" is contrary to modern philosophy's positioning of itself as distinct from and opposed to "myth." This is intriguing as a criticism from one who now distances himself from postmodernism.

Dussel maintains that the developmental fallacy is still present in much philosophy. However, in my view, even the bare bones of his theory, as presented so far, implies an intention to recuperate philosophic reason. In this light, postcolonial critique cannot be leveled in a general way at modern philosophy *as such*; it can only be aimed at particular texts. Dussel's work suggests that it is not the case that philosophy *cannot* stand as a critic of culture on the basis of reason, but that for the most part it *does not*. He therefore avoids what I call a "pan-critical" effect of postmodernism that disables the very notion of philosophy, in much the same manner as it may disable political action motivated by social criticism based on humanistic reason. Avoiding this pan-critical effect makes it possible to consider postcolonial, feminist, and other politicized critiques of "philosophy" to be themselves "philosophy" (or so I maintain).

How can a postcolonial critique of texts be effected? First, it may be shown that Europeans saw non-Europeans in terms of their own categories, in itself hardly a surprise. However, without a presumption of European supremacy, a possible result of this observation is the identification of European categories of thought as historically particular, by means of comparisons with other cultural paradigms with noncorresponding categories. If we take this line of thought seriously, it implies that from different perspectives, the world is quite literally *perceived,* and not just *interpreted,* as cut up in different ways.[2] This view can amount to a claim that a European category posited as "universal" is actually "particular" to European intellectual culture. Dussel argues that Europeans saw non-Europeans exclusively in terms of their own categories of thought, especially in the early stages of contact in the sixteenth century. The Spanish perception of the indigenous peoples of the Americas was entirely self-referential: they literally did not perceive the Other as other but rather as deficient examples of the same. According to Dussel, the Spanish could not, therefore, be said to have "discovered" them. Instead, they "invented" them, first as Asians and then as undeveloped inferior peoples who would benefit from the arrival of the Europeans. In the first century of encounter, Spanish self-referentiality was so strong that even the dazzling evidence of urban development among the Aztecs and Incas that was *superior* to what the Spanish would have known in Europe failed to suggest to them that these peoples might be best thought of as different from them rather than as inferior to them. Then again, while the label "Indians" for the peoples of the Americas can be explained as an initial mistake, what depth of self-referentiality explains why the name stuck for five hundred years?

South and Central America were therefore "invented" as undeveloped, regardless of the actual levels of development of different peoples, which the evidence indicates varied greatly. This invention was then given a brutal epistemological guarantee, as major cities were reduced to rubble, the people forced into slave labor, and the population decimated to a small fraction of its previous size.[3]

Another strategy for a postcolonial critique is to show the action in texts of relations of domination and subordination. Nancy Tuana's concept of "location in the text," developed for feminist criticism, may be used to analyze to whom a text is speaking and about whom it speaks. Those spoken about but not directly addressed are subordinated in the text to those for whom the text is intended. Thus theory about indigenous peoples of the Americas and Africa was developed by Europeans for other Europeans, and never in discursive communication with indigenous peoples themselves. Dussel may also be thought of as identifying what is called in cultural studies "the gaze," although he does not use that term himself. The gaze exemplifies the fundamental asymmetry between those who look, stare boldly, and identify, and those who are stared at and labeled. It's a bit like putting something on a board with a pin—there is no question of interraction between subjectivities. In the case of people, this asymmetry, which may be identified in both texts and social practices, is a type of profound inequality very familiar to feminist critics. Nothing the indigenous peoples could do counted as evidence of a high stage of development or political sophistication or true morality, since in European eyes they lacked these things by definition.

There are other strategies that may illuminate a critical postcolonial understanding in one way or another. Dussel employs those (such as the ones described above) that lend themselves to political understanding and political action. A more ready affinity with political action is a feature of his work that sets him apart from some more clearly postmodern approaches.

A subtlety of Dussel's approach is that he does not deny that there were (and are) different levels of development, which may be considered different levels of value, for example, in the technology of production or in the complexity or sophistication of social governance. He avoids the extreme of the postmodern impulse that will brook no comparison but that of "difference." Nevertheless, he denies that the European model of development is the only one. A particular limitation of the developmental fallacy is that it presupposes that humans are inferior at less complex stages of development, and even that the peoples of less developed cultures are *to blame* for their condition. Dussel quotes Kant from 1784: "Enlightenment is the exit of humanity . . . from a state of culpable immaturity. . . . Laziness and cowardliness are the causes which bind the great part of humanity in the frivolous state of immaturity" ("Answering the Question: What Is Enlightenment?" quoted in Dussel 1995, 19–20). Although he is a critic of Enlightenment thinking, Dussel is a humanist in his affirmation that human development (by which I think he means simply whatever it is that makes us different from other beings) was pretty much fully achieved in its present form in Neolithic cultures. In my own view, while cultures may vary in type and complexity, it is a fallacy of composition to presume that *individuals* in a less complex culture are less fully human or less capable of development than individuals in more complex cultures.

Regarding the action in texts of relations of domination and subordination, Dussel points particularly to the inadequacy of "communicative ethics" (mentioning Habermas and Apel), which does not take into account the profound asymmetry in the *effectiveness* of speech and argument created by domination. This critique is similar to one that has been raised from a feminist perspective by Alison Jaggar regarding the speech of women. Dussel usefully identifies what are termed the "conditions of entry" into a discursive community, calling attention to the very harsh and thorough exclusion of indigenous peoples from dominant European discursive communities, an exclusion that was not significantly breached until after the mid-twentieth century. The significance of conditions of entry in Dussel's thought will be revisited on closer examination of the developmental fallacy, in which it is the "conditions of entry" to discursive community that can be seen as key points of inconsistency with the imagined ideals of European discursive communities. Dussel maintains a modernist (or at least "non-postmodernist") distinction between rationally held belief (which can be mistaken) and irrational myth. However, part of the power of his work for me is the way he shows that the point at which "rational belief" slips over into "irrational myth" can be difficult to discern.

ARGUING A MYTH

Looking more closely at the claim of irrationality regarding European beliefs about development entails examining the argumentative stages of the myth of modernity. The case of Juan Ginés de Sepúlveda, a Spanish philosopher and theologian of the sixteenth century, illustrates how this irrationality might be spelled out in a particular thinker's ideas.

According to Dussel, in its secondary and mythic content, modernity justifies an irrational praxis of violence, despite its ideal of discursive community in which coercion is unacceptable. First and foremost, Europe understands itself as more developed, its civilization as superior to others. It lacks awareness of its own historical specificity. This self-image can be accounted for by Europe's practical centrality in a world system *in conjunction with* its own highly developed notions of "universality," "impartiality," and "objectivity."

In light of that fundamental first stage, a second argumentative step is that a culture's abandonment of its "barbarous" differences spells "progress, development, well-being, and emancipation for that culture" (Dussel 1995, 66). Thus one may defend Europe's domination over other cultures as, in Dussel's words, "a necessary pedagogic violence," which may take the form of a "just war." The other culture's anguish is justified as the necessary price of civilization and modernization, as well as expiation for its culpable immaturity. Since barbarians always resist this civilizing process, modern praxis is compelled, quite rightly, to exercise violence as a last resort in order to overcome obstacles to modernization. However, the barbarian is at fault for opposing the civilizing process. Civilizing heroes may then justify the treatment of their victims as "a sacrifice," "a quasi-ritual act," for the salvation of the victims. Dussel terms them "holocausts of a salvific sacrifice," using the term "holocaust" in its ancient general meaning of "a sacrificial offering the whole of which is consumed by fire; hence, a complete or thorough sacrifice or destruction" (Webster's *New International Dictionary*). Finally, the suffering and sacrifice of backward and immature peoples is regarded as the inevitable cost of modernization. As Dussel puts it, "the myth of modernity declares the Other the culpable cause of its own victimization and absolves the modern subject of any guilt for the victimizing act" (Dussel 1995, 64).

Considering philosophy, in the case of Hegel, for example, Dussel's main point is not, as might be expected, that Hegel's philosophy helped inspire and justify colonialism. (This is certainly part of what he seeks to show and is in itself hard to take issue with.) Dussel's more original argument, however, is that Hegel's philosophy should be understood as a *result* of Europe's successful colonization of non-European peoples, not as a basic ideological source of certain attitudes. The conquest of Mexico was the beginning of a process that made a philosopher like Hegel possible because Europe's de facto domination made possible a seemingly reasonable and commonsense belief that Europe was the center of the world and the point of reference for everything else. Consider the following quotations from Hegel (various works, quoted at greater length by Dussel 1995, 20–22).

> Universal history goes from East to West. Europe is absolutely the *end of universal history.*

> Regarding America, especially Mexico or Peru, and its degree of civilization, our information indicates that its culture expires the moment the Spirit draws near. . . . The inferiority of these individuals in every respect is entirely evident.

> Africa . . . does not properly have a history. For this reason, we abandon Africa, we will mention it no more.

What if an intellectual from West Africa, or the middle of South America, wrote the same things with reference to those cultures and their relation to other cultures and locations? Far from attracting widespread study of a difficult text, it would be taken as the ravings of a lunatic, would it not? Whatever we may think of Dussel's work, should we not, indeed, be asking, What are the conditions that enable someone to think this way and be taken seriously?

Apart from philosophy and apart from consideration of the especially rapacious activity of the early Spanish occupation, there is ample evidence that the majority of European missionaries and colonial administrators throughout the Americas and Africa believed it necessary to destroy indigenous cultures, even at the cost of great suffering, before the people could be "civilized," educated, and prepared to adopt a saving Christianity. Dussel maintains that the modern belief that within the discursive community only argumentation is appropriate was undisputed in principle in fifteenth-century Spain. He emphasizes that the justification of violent recruitment into "Europe" (as an ethos) must therefore be about *how one enters* the discursive community, not about how one behaves within it.

The Spanish conquistadores of the sixteenth century thought of themselves as evangelists and liberators; or at least this was a self-image that was culturally available to them should they feel a need for self-justification. Given the most cursory knowledge of what they did to the indigenous peoples, this self-image is now, on the face of it, almost incomprehensible. Yet there is not only a plausible historical account of it, but in light of Dussel's analysis, there is even an account to be offered of links between this attitude and modern humanism and individualism, showing how some of their fundamental philosophical principles can be implicated in the irrational myth of modernity.

How can violent conquerors be evangelists and liberators? In the early eighth century, a movement began for the Christian Spanish "reconquest" of what is now Spain from the powerful Muslim Moors. This process took a full seven hundred years, several centuries longer than the period of modernity now under discussion! According to Dussel, over the centuries a Spanish judicial-military culture developed of *conquista* (conquest), with a highly positive identity for conquistadores (those who conquer). The reconquest was completed in 1492, and the conquistadores were liberators of the Spanish people and proponents of Christianity against powerful unbelievers. The Spaniards at once expelled all the Jews from Spain, along with the Moors, in the same year as the storied "discovery" of America. Nothing intervened in the transfer of conquistador values to their dealings with peoples initially perceived as "Eastern," like the Moors, and without question unrepentant unbelievers.

Dussel finds a "definitive and classical" expression of the irrational myth of modernity in the thought of the theologian Juan Ginés de Sepúlveda. Dussel considers him a modern humanist, since he simultaneously expresses the irrational myth of modernity and the rational and positive content of modernity as Dussel sees it. Sepúlveda engaged in a famous controversy with Bartolomé de Las Casas. Although Las Casas embraced the value of Christian evangelization of the indigenous peoples in America, he was nevertheless an advocate for them against the forces of violent conquest and exploitation. In 1550 Sepúlveda published a defense of "the just cause of war against the Indians."[4]

Sepúlveda's approach is a mixture of Aristotelianism, humanism, and even modern liberal individualism (a not uncommon mix in early and late modern philosophy). According to the historian Anthony Pagden (1987), there were other voices in this controversy besides Sepúlveda and Las Casas. Important theologians rejected Aristotle's concept of "natural slavery," on which Sepúlveda relies. However, Dussel's focus on Sepúlveda's thought is sadly justified because it was Sepúlveda's point of view that carried the day. Moreover, it is sobering to note that Sepúlveda was the most "modern and enlightened" theologian in the debate, not least because of his use of ancient philosophy. His theological colleagues criticized him for his more historical and philosophical approach, and it was the more traditional theologians who argued for the inherent rights of the Indians of the Americas in virtue of their humanity. Sepúlveda's appropriation of Aristotle enables him to argue that the Indians are "natural servants" and that therefore it is good and right for them to be governed by those who are rational, more perfectly developed as human beings, and better. The potential affinity between the resistance of women and the resistance of other oppressed groups may be seen in Sepúlveda's smooth Aristotelian amalgamation of a great range of forms of domination in the single figure of the elite European male.

> This war and conquest are just first of all because these barbaric, uneducated, and inhuman [Indians] are by nature servants. Naturally, they refuse the governance which more prudent, powerful, and perfect human beings offer and which would result in their great benefit. By natural right and for the good of all, the material ought to obey the form, the body the soul, the appetite the reason, the brutes the human being, the woman her husband, the imperfect the perfect, and the worse the better. (Dussel 1995, 63)

While this may not sound very humanistic (much less liberal) in the late twentieth century, central values of modern liberal moral and political philosophy, for example, that all individuals are of equal moral worth and equally entitled to autonomy in virtue of their intrinsic rationality have virtually always been held as hypothetical. These values have been limited by stipulation of the nature of rationality (i.e., *if* an individual is of a certain type, *then* . . .) and virtually all modern philosophers have believed that some groups of humans failed to meet the criteria. These groups have encompassed women, people without property, non-Christians, and people of color. All these exclusions continue to require contestation.

Sepúlveda is quite clear that even considering the splendid cities of the Aztecs and Incas, their irrationality is evident in the fact that they are not entitled to own property and bequeath it to their biological heirs, and in their failure to resist the authority of the rulers who have so much power over them. In other words, according to Dussel, they have failed to embrace modernity's supreme characteristics—subjective liberty and autonomous resistance to the arbitrariness of rulers (Dussel 1995, 65). Critique of arbitrary forms of power is rightly identified as a central modern and humanist idea. In addition, even the most severe postmodern critics seem to take it for granted. This makes it all the more disconcerting to see what Sepúlveda does with this same modern principle.

Sepúlveda justifies violence as a means of bringing indigenous peoples into the modern European discursive community, even though rational autonomy and subjective liberty are core ideals of that community, and most especially the philosophical community. How? In contrast with Aristotle, it is a modern ideal of equality that power over others, to be legitimate and morally acceptable, should not just be rationally justified by elite philosophers, but in principle justifiable to all members of a society in terms of some version of the "rational self-interest" of each. In modern secular philosophy, equality is premised on the innate rational ability of each person to determine his or her own self-interest, rather than have it imposed by someone else, no matter how well-intentioned. Power should not be mere successful coercion or custom and tradition that have not been evaluated and found acceptable. The consent of those who live under power is supposed to follow from power's justification in terms of their own good, as those who are rational consent to what is rational, by definition. However, as mentioned above, modernist ideals of equality have from the beginning been qualified by stipulations of what rationality is, and there have always been some types of people presumed to be exceptions to this "universal" ideal. What of them? The ideal of consent may continue to be given lip service. However, their consent or lack of consent ceases to be a primary consideration. It becomes rather *a goal*: how can "we" who are rational get "them" to see the light and consent?

Sepúlveda has linked the rational justification of power to particular substantive claims about rationality that are recognizably modern and individualistic, wedding these claims to Aristotelian claims of inherent inequality of rational capacity. In his view, if those marked for appropriate power are not actually in positions of power, they are justified in using force to bring about arrangements that will enable them to govern, much as parents fence in their children and supervise their activities "for their own good."

From our perspective, the most striking error in this argument regarding indigenous peoples is the Aristotelian concept that there can be such a thing as "natural human slaves or servants." However, Dussel's critical analysis works even if this Aristotelian element is eliminated because the developmental fallacy does not actually require the notion of inherent inferiority. There was controversy in sixteenth-century Spain over whether the Indians were inherently (and therefore permanently) inferior to Europeans, or whether they simply lacked the education and culture that would enable them to become as "civilized" as Europeans. If the view were taken, as it was by many, that the Indians belonged to such a benighted culture and belief system that they would never *willingly* embrace European values (even though in principle they were capable of doing so), then initial coercion in setting them along that path could still be justified. As a justification for coercive interference in indigenous cultures, the argument then becomes recognizable as the attitude, for example, of governments in the United States and Canada in subsequent centuries.[5]

In my view, it could even be said that these attitudes come too close to well-intentioned late twentieth-century beliefs about the mission of liberal political ethos to be easily dismissed as a self-evidently wrong product of a colonial age.[6] Contemporary movements for self-government by indigenous peoples in North America have been criticized by their most sympathetic supporters for failing to be as crucially concerned about subjective liberty or individual rights as Western liberals are. So, the argument runs, should they be "allowed" self-government before they agree, for example, to European feminist standards of gender equality or accept as primary principles of liberal individualist rights and freedoms? These standards may well cut across the cultural distinctiveness that is the basis of their desire for self-government. There is a fine line between support (moral or practical) for the aspirations of women or other oppressed groups in societies simultaneously struggling for self-determination, and the denial of self-determination to the group as a whole. The latter means keeping control, with the unacknowledged implication that the society in question is somehow less able to resolve its inner conflicts than "we Europeans" are to solve our own inner conflicts and that the society actually benefits from our continuing control. There is no reason (except a very naive notion of "progress") to suppose that the colonizers and missionaries of modern Europe were, on the whole, less consciously well-intentioned than we are now.

For Sepúlveda, the nonarbitrariness of power is justified by the rational nature of those holding power. They are those with the capacity, or *power*, to promote the highest forms of human development and therefore uplift those in whom this capacity or power is not present. There is, therefore, an equivocation on the term "power." It may refer to an inherent quality or a de facto social position. Because indigenous leaders clearly held power as a matter of fact, it cannot be power alone that justifies itself from a modernist point of view. As a result, it is the very concept of rationality embraced by Sepúlveda that seems to justify the assumption of power by whatever means are necessary, on the part of those with the "rational" and "right" view of society.

In the relations to Europeans in which they were placed, indigenous peoples could thus only attempt to demonstrate their rationality, and therefore their right to subjective liberty and consent, by the contradictory means of voluntarily accepting the domination of the Spaniards! In the light of overarching principles, they are to be "forced to be free." Yet this notion is itself contradicted. Given the terms of their entry, they will actually be inducted into European forms of subordination (or as Dussel would put it, "internalized," "covered over"), analogously to working or propertyless people, women, some internal ethnic and religious minorities, and so on. To a very large extent, this has actually been the fate of the indigenous peoples of the Americas, a self-fulfilling prophecy of an irrational notion of development that has oppressively constrained them in a "no-win" situation in relation to those of European origin.

Dussel's analysis suggests that irrationality and self-contradiction can be recognized in the developmental fallacy of modernity even when viewed "from inside," that is, by the standards of the rational, emancipatory paradigm of modernity. He does not want to step away from problems of justification in the spirit of postmodernism wherein one "discourse" may be set beside another but there can be no overarching standards or values by which to compare them. However, looking closely at how someone like Sepúlveda justified violent domination of whole peoples—someone who held the modern value that only argumentation is appropriate in discursive community—raises some doubts in my mind about Dussel's neat separation of the rational, emancipatory, conceptual content of modernity and the negative and irrational myth of development. These two paradigms of modernity seem to be more entangled than Dussel wants to admit.

Dussel abjures the term "postmodern," presumably because it carries some unwanted epistemological and political associations. However, it seems that his analysis of modernity would be supported by a characteristically postmodern observation: the belief that one possesses "universal truth" of any sort may function as a powerful background support to any impulse to enforce a particular view of rationality, tending to silence those who do not embrace it. Although he does not want the term, his nuanced conclusions could still be called "postmodern" inasmuch as they provide an alternative to the features of modernism that have abetted colonization and modern patriarchy by crowning them with self-affirming philosophies. However, Dussel wants to retrieve the possibility of cross-cultural "truth," so as to be able to say that the destruction of colonization was wrong and to offer a positive vision for the future.

> This book serves only as a historico-philosophical introduction to an intercultural dialogue that will encompass diverse political, economic, theological, and epistemological standpoints. Such a dialogue endeavors to construct not an abstract universality, but an analogic and concrete world in which all cultures, philosophies, and theologies will make their contribution toward a future, pluralist humanity. (Dussel 1995, 132)

At this stage in my thinking, Dussel's analysis suggests to me that it is unproductive to counterpose "modernism" and "postmodernism" too strongly. Dussel seems to hold out the belief that the critical detachment of philosophy is at least possible, but his analysis also conveys an important cautionary observation. Authentic recognition of those Other to our own culture is more difficult than we may imagine, and the obstacles to it may include what we hold as best among our values, rather than what we more readily recognize as our cultural potential for bias.

Included in what we hold as best may be our feminist convictions, even when they are applied (we may assume with good intentions) to groups of women much less privileged than Western middle-class women. For example, Dussel's analysis is consistent with, and further illuminates, the argument of Chandra Mohanty (1991) regarding feminists' treatment of Third World women. Mohanty argues that an initial positioning of "women" as a homogeneous category, which has been characteristic of both liberal and radical feminism in the West, leads to the creation of another homogeneous category: Third World women. The implicit self-presentation of Western feminist women as secular, rational, and knowledgeable about the "real" issues, by comparison with Third World women thought to be more oppressed by religion, family, and tradition, betrays a modernist assumption of superior subjectivity. Mohanty points out that the discursive self-presentation of Western feminists as "liberated" and "having control over their own lives" would be problematic without the foil of Third World women because it does not correspond to the reality of First World women. I would also note that the discursive strategy of positioning oneself as the more conscious component of a basically homogeneous oppressed group stands in the way of material and political analysis of the extent to which First World women benefit from imperialism themselves.

Mohanty also stresses that there is great diversity among women of the Third World, not just by culture but also by class and other forms of social power. As a result, her critique includes the more privileged women of the Third World who write about lower-class, poor, or rural women using the same Western-influenced discursive formations. She differentiates among women not by "identity" but by material circumstances, cultural context, and politics. Like Dussel, therefore, her analysis does not tend to posit "cultural differences" that we can hope to do no more than "appreciate" but rather suggests the possibility, at least, of general critical analysis that helps motivate political action.

From the perspective of democratic feminism, the enormity of the holocaust of the indigenous peoples of the Americas once again reminds us that it is impossible to conceive of any meaningful polarity between "women" and "men" as such. Paying attention to differences of class, race, and colonization inevitably shows that, even from within their own relative oppression, in these supposedly postcolonial times, middle- and upper-class women of European origin still have vastly more privilege and power than many groups of women and men combined.

NOTES

This chapter was originally prepared for Globalization from Below, a conference of the Radical Philosophy Association, November 14–17, 1996, and subsequently published in *Hypatia* 13, no. 3 (Summer 1998). It is reprinted here with permission of the journal's editors and the publishers.

1. "In satisfying a frequently sadistic voluptuousness, Spaniards vented their purely masculine libido through the erotic subjugation of the Other as Indian women" (Dussel 1995, 46).

2. Although this type of claim may be freighted with political significance, it will not be news to anyone who has studied W. V. O. Quine, the early Richard Rorty, or Paul Churchland in the fields of epistemology and philosophy of science in the last several decades.

3. The point regarding the epistemological guarantee was made by Anandi Hattiangadi in a graduate seminar of mine.

4. Ginés de Sepúlveda's *De la justa causa de la guerra contra los indios* was published in Rome in 1550. Dussel's references are to the Spanish edition published in Mexico by Fondo de Cultura Económica, 1987.

5. In twentieth-century Canada, the forcible removal of Native American children from their homes and communities to residential schools was driven by this logic. Taking them away from the "backward" influence of their own culture and compelling them to learn European language and culture is a good example of the operation of "necessary pedagogical violence" meant to induct them into "Europe."

6. Dussel himself saw this attitude in operation in the United States during the Gulf War (Dussel 1995, 64). It appeared that extreme violence—indeed, a self-proclaimed "storm" of violence—was the just exercise of those whose ostensible principle was subjective freedom.

REFERENCES

Blaut, J. M. 1992. *1492: The Debate on Colonialism, Eurocentrism, and History*. Trenton, N.J.: Africa World Press.

Cesaire, Aimé. 1972. *Discourse on Colonialism*. New York: Monthly Review Press.

Dussel, Enrique. 1995. *The Invention of the Americas: Eclipse of "the Other" and the Myth of Modernity*. Translated by Michael D. Barber. New York: Continuum.

Mohanty, Chandra Talpade. 1991. "Under Western Eyes: Feminist Scholarship and Colonial Discourses." In *Third World Women and the Politics of Feminism*. Edited by Chandra Mohanty, Ann Russo, and Lourdes Torres. Bloomington: Indiana University Press.

Pagden, Anthony. 1987. "Dispossessing the Barbarian: The Language of Spanish Thomism and the Debate over the Property Rights of the American Indians." In *The Languages of Political Theory in Early-Modern Europe*. Edited by Anthony Pagden. Cambridge: Cambridge University Press.

Todorov, Tsvetan. 1984. *The Conquest of America: The Question of the Other*. New York: Harper & Row.

Tuana, Nancy. 1992. *Women and the History of Philosophy*. New York: Paragon.

8

Thinking *Otherwise*: Dussel, Liberation Theology, and Feminism

Elina Vuola

In this chapter, I approach Enrique Dussel's thinking in the context of Latin American liberation theology. Several liberation theologians use the concept the Other *(el Otro)* to clarify the difference of liberation theology from "traditional" theology. The question of the Other is most systematically elaborated by Dussel. He is usually counted among the liberation theologians, and rightly so, but his most important contributions are in the area of philosophy and history. He is one of the founders of the Latin American philosophy of liberation *(filosofía de la liberación),* which has close affinities with liberation theology—a movement that since its beginning has been divided into several camps, Dussel presenting one of them.[1] One of the basic—if not the most important—concepts and starting points for the philosophy of liberation is the concept of the Other, the question of alterity. Related to this is the question of who is the philosophizing subject. Dussel bases his use of the concept on the philosophy of Emmanuel Levinas, modifying it with the tools of Marxism and dependency theory.

I do not claim to have an expert knowledge of Dussel, whose thinking has undergone several major shifts. I am mainly interested in his influence on liberation theology, and thus my analysis focuses on his earlier texts. My specific interest in both liberation theology and Dussel is informed by a feminist analysis and critique: I argue that there are certain thinking habits in most liberation theologians, including Dussel, that has made the inclusion of feminist critique in liberation theology problematic.[2] This again has to do with the subject of liberation theology, the Other, the poor. Dussel's influence on liberation theology and its philosophical sibling has been enormous. Many of his ideas are shared by his colleagues, explicitly or implicitly: an analysis of Dussel's philosophy and ethics thus tells us something about liberation theology as a current of thought.

Dussel was one of the first male Latin American intellectuals, at least in philosophy and theology, to take up the issue of women's liberation. It is important, however, to note that some of his ideas developed in very specific contexts and have since changed. I am above all concerned with his influence on liberation theology and its openness and capability to discuss feminist concerns. Many of Dussel's early views developed from systematic philosophical and historical reasons. Many of these views are still shared by other liberation theologies.

I remember sitting next to Dussel some years ago in the mountains of Norway, facing a deep blue mountain lake and a glacier, discussing my dissertation project with him. I recognized his openness to discuss critical issues such as feminism in the context of liberation theology. Thus my critique here may appear unjustified—those who dare to say something are those being criticized. Dussel is a case in point: he is one of the few liberation theologians who addresses issues of gender, male–female relationship, and sexism. My critique rises from an empathetic demand to take a more critical look at the status of our truth claims. This demand, as will become clear in my article, is directed at myself and at all feminists who advocate taking women more seriously.

SUBJECT(S) OF LIBERATION THEOLOGY

In this chapter, I look at liberation theology as a current of thought and not at Dussel specifically. More than in the case of the homogeneous "poor," the oppressed themselves are now becoming the subjects of theology. The encounter/disencounter with the poor is constitutive for the praxis liberation theologians speak about. The option for the poor, the solidarity with the Other, is at the heart of liberation theology. Still, it is another matter when this Other announces herself or himself as a subject and wants to participate in the very definition of theology. From the point of view of the Other, she or he is no Other.[3] Thus the whole discourse on solidarity with the poor and the option for them is deepened and challenged when the objects of this option become subjects. To put it bluntly, the oldest Others of Western theology have continued being Others in liberation theology as well.

Who can represent "the people," "the poor"? What do liberation theologians mean when they speak for the poor? Academic liberation theologians prefer understanding themselves as "organic intellectuals" in the Gramscian way. According to Juan Luis Segundo, liberation theologians have accepted being organic intellectuals, understanding their tasks to be the representation of the community, the articulation of a foundation for their intra- and extracommunal demands, and providing for them the fundamentals of a conscientization that is appropriate to their possibilities of knowledge and analysis of reality.[4] "There is no doubt that liberation theology, in its simplest and most basic forms, plays an important and, in some extraordinary cases, decisive role in satisfying these needs." Segundo "translates" the theologian's role into "teaching to analyze reality." This, according to some, is a crucial shift in the role of the intellectual (theologian) from individual scholarly authority to reflective community advocate.[5] Even if true, it also entails problems having to do with the question of who speaks for whom, and in what way.[6]

Obviously, the option for the poor and its theological, epistemological, spiritual, and political consequences can be seen as the major innovation of liberation theology. But a radical and critical question about the subject of theology goes further. The differentiation and extension of the concept "poor" is accepted nowadays by practically all liberation theologians. They have consciously taken "the dominated and dependent Latin America" as their starting point, but they have not been as critical of other "places" that define their theologizing, such as race and gender.[7] This is why the growing dialogue between different liberation theologies is so important. It does not mean weakening the basic options and innovations of liberation theology or ridiculing them. To the contrary, it means taking them more seriously.

The poor as subjects of liberation theology carry the Marxist heritage, referring primarily to production and class consciousness. Recent social scientific research on Latin American social movements stresses the importance of moving beyond the centrality of class concept in interpreting the success or failure of these movements.[8] According to David Slater, the major problem with Marxist class analysis concerns the failure to theorize subjectivity and identity.[9] He reminds us that nowhere has the critique of a notion of a unified subject been so effectively developed as in feminist theory.[10] Referring to Chantal Mouffe, Slater states that each social agent is inscribed in a range of social relations connected to gender, race, nationality, locality, and so on. Every social agent is the site of many subject positions. An oppressed subject can also, simultaneously, be an oppressing subject.[11]

This kind of perspective offers us one explanation for the conflicting interests and power struggles inside social movements, which can very well be applied to liberation theology too. The poor as a one-sided (seen primarily as a class) and homogeneous concept needs to be challenged by the "multiple subject positions of each agent in the struggle."

Dussel has in fact been critical of the tendency to see the poor primarily as a class. His most important single theoretical tool has been the Other.

ENRIQUE DUSSEL AND THE OTHER

According to Dussel, "a philosophy of liberation is rising from the periphery, from the oppressed, from the shadow that the light of Being has not been able to illumine. Our thinking sets out from non-being, nothingness, otherness, exteriority, the mystery of no-sense. It is, then, 'barbarian philosophy.'"[12]

Another important term in Dussel's early philosophical work is Totality *(la Totalidad).* It is not merely understood in the classical sense of "the ordered Whole" or as the a priori ultimate horizon of meaning without which it is impossible to attach meaning to any object, including the human being. His anadialectical (*ana,* beyond) method is a way to go beyond the dominant Totality, which in a historical sense is that of Europe and North America: "'The Same' (*Lo Mismo*), as a Totality, is closed in a circle that rotates eternally without novelty. The apparent novelty of a moment in its dialectic, in its movement, is accidental. . . . 'The Same' devours historical temporality and ends up being the Neutral 'since always.'"[13] Modern thinking has been introducing the Other in "the Same" to the extent that the Totality, as the only possible substance, makes any real alterity impossible.[14]

What makes it possible to think—or rethink—the Totality outside its boundaries, outside its logic, is the Otherness. The irruption of the Other into the Totality reveals not just its boundaries but also its irrationality and, ultimately, its violence. The dominant Totality is incapable of acknowledging the existence of the Other in his alterity/difference.[15] The basic concretizations of the alterity are to be found in the relationships male–female, parent–child (also teacher–student) and brother–brother (including nation–nation). These correspond to three different levels: the erotic, the pedagogical, and the political.[16]

For Dussel, Otherness is basically a category that refers to domination, or to the dominant–dominated relationship in which the Other is the dominated party, and to the potential liberation of this oppressive relationship. For example, women are the Other not just in relation to men but in relation to the Totality as well. For the historical reasons of their oppression and domination, women are the principal protagonists of liberation, at least in the realm of female–male relationships.[17]

Since ethics and philosophy are not separable for Dussel,[18] his basic ethical thesis is that "to affirm the Other and serve him is the good act, and to dominate him is the evil act."[19] This is the absolute criterion of metaphysics and ethics.[20] The Same, like Totality, is the *being* and its knowledge is the *truth* (e.g., the *ego cogito* of Descartes, the Absolute Knowledge of Hegel, and the Eternal Return of the Same of Nietzsche). Thus the one who-is-not (the Other) has to be dominated and ultimately eliminated.[21] If the negation of the Other is the ultimate wrong, the ultimate good is his affirmation through love-for-justice *(amor-de-justicia).*[22] The radical goodness for Dussel is the conversion to the oppressed Other—be it in racial, political, economic, or sexual terms. To have "ethical conscience" is to listen-to-the-voice-of-the-Other, the voice that demands justice. Not to have ethical conscience means killing the Other. This is the same as to say that the Other is silent.[23] The "illiteracy" of the dominant culture interprets the Other as a "silent thing" without taking into account the necessity of listening.[24]

The Other manifests himself as a face exterior to the ontological horizon: beyond the established and institutionalized Totality. The Other as exteriority is a condition for a metaphysical possibility of an authentic, creative, new future.[25] In a specific Latin American context, this means that the Other, for us, is Latin America in respect to the European Totality, the poor and oppressed Latin American people in respect to the dominating oligarchies."[26] Dussel's anadialectical method starts from the Other as somebody oppressed but free, as somebody beyond the Totality.[27] He puts it very concretely: "The face of the dominated poor Indian, of the oppressed mestizo, of the Latin American people, is the 'theme' of Latin American philosophy."[28] This means "the end of the pretended universality of Europe,"[29] the ability to "judge the Totality as overcome and dead,"[30] and a justification of the liberation of the oppressed. The Totality now appears as an ontic system, one more system, a given system at one moment of history, one of many, and, finally, as an ideological system.[31]

WOMAN AS THE OTHER

In many ways the Other appears as a more open and inclusive category than "the poor" in liberation theology. Implicitly, they are congruent in the writings of most liberation theologians. However, the poor become more particularized and specified as the Other. Nevertheless, it does not solve the problem of identity: Who is the Other to whom? Who is the one defining others as Others? Is the Other also a subject for himself and herself?

According to Dussel, the conquest of America was an erotic enterprise as well as being political, economic, and cultural. The mestization of the American peoples is the result of the violence of the European conquistador.[32] The modern ego of the conquistador also reveals itself as a phallic ego that is violent by nature. While the conquistador murders the male Indian or subdues him into servitude, he sleeps with the female, sometimes in the presence of the husband.[33] "Spaniards vented their purely masculine libido through the erotic subjugation of the Other as Indian woman," says Dussel.[34] This "unilateral machismo"[35] leads both to alienating erotics[36] and to the birth of modernity based on irrational praxis of violence.[37] If the conquest of America was the start of the modern era, as is often claimed, then, according to Dussel, we have to overcome modernity not by a postmodern attack on reason but by opposing modernity's irrational violence based on the reason of the Other.[38]

> To deny modernity's innocence and to affirm the alterity of the Other, the inculpable victim, reveals the other face hidden and yet essential to modernity. This Other encompasses the peripheral colonial world, the sacrificed Indian, the enslaved black, the oppressed woman, the subjugated child, and the alienated popular culture—all victims of modernity's irrational action in contradiction to its own rational ideal.[39]

Here the Other is the racially, culturally, politically, and sexually oppressed. As already noted, Dussel (as well as other philosophers and theologians of liberation) was strongly influenced by Emmanuel Levinas and his idea of the Other.[40] Besides his historical-philosophical texts in which the woman appears as one concretization of Otherness, Dussel also writes on more practically orientated questions. He is one of the few male liberation theologians to touch on issues of sexual ethics and the church. He speaks of women as sexual objects educated to oppression,[41] but at the same time he has a surprisingly negative understanding of feminism.[42]

> Woman's liberation supposes that she is able to discern adequately her distinct functions, analogically diverse. One function is that of being a woman in the couple. Another is that of procreator of her son (*hijo*). Another is that of an educator. Another one is being a sister among sisters in the political society. And if one does not know how to discern each of these functions, tremendous errors are committed.[43]

Dussel differentiates among "femininity," "woman," and "human person." A woman does not equate with femininity, but a woman as a human being "carries with privilege the human femininity."[44] Men and women equally share human personality but femininity is different from masculinity, even though there is something of the feminine in a man and something of the masculine in a woman.[45]

What Dussel calls "the metaphysics of femininity"[46] is a dialectical notion that is not understandable in itself, but in relation to masculinity (the erotic heterosexual relationship), to the son (maternity), and to the brother (political realm).[47] All this is included in masculinity as well (woman–man relationship, paternity, and political brother–sister relationship).[48] Dussel is careful not to absolutize what he calls femininity and not to identify it exclusively with the woman (nor human person with the male).

The difficulty in giving new meanings to these concepts (femininity and masculinity) while operating in the binary system they imply as concepts becomes clear when Dussel becomes more concrete: "The woman, human person, carries femininity essentially at the sexed, erotic level in the couple, in front of the man, human person as well, who carries his masculinity at the same level. The differences are clear and equality in distinction (*igualdad en la distinción*) must be defended concretely in all the details."[49] In other texts, he says that "what feminism proposes to us is an asexual angelism, even though it may not seem so, since it proposes to us the disappearance of sexual alterity and that each of us would fulfill love with himself. . . . No. The liberation of the woman is not through indistinction, but exactly through distinction."[50] "Liberation is not merely negation of domination by the negation of sexual diversity (as when feminism champions homosexuality, test-tube babies, etc.). Liberation is real sexual distinction."[51]

Many feminist theorists take a critical distance to Dussel's kind of use of the term "Otherness," or "alterity." Stanley and Wise reject a notion of "self and Other" that the self supposedly defines itself against and in opposition to.[52] The Finnish philosopher Sara Heinämaa explains how, for Simone de Beauvoir, the absolute alterity of a woman—the absoluteness of her alterity—means the attempt of man to negate his own carnality, the "impurity" of his existence. Thus woman as the absolute Other is a male projection. In this situation, the man in fact does not encounter the woman. Woman's alterity is not equivalent to woman's being for herself.[53]

DUSSEL AND OTHERS: CRITIQUES

The Dussel citations above could be from almost any recent Vatican document on women. It is exactly the "equality in distinction," taken as naturally and uncritically as Dussel does (in the 1970s), that has been criticized by Catholic feminist theologians.[54] Dussel's use of such problematic concepts as femininity and masculinity seems to imply a tendency toward traditional definitions of both actual gender relations and "a female/male essence." Or rather, as the recent discussion in feminist theory on difference makes clear, it is not notions of difference (whether between men and women or between women) in itself that would imply difference in value or certain hierarchical relations. It is the supposed naturality of difference and its social and political consequences that have been the targets of feminist critique.

Dussel's implicit references to the naturality of the gender difference take him close to official Catholic statements in which "different but equal" and "complementarity" of the differences form the basis of traditional arguments for clearly sexist notions of women and their role in society and church (maternity as women's principal vocation, the absolute refusal to ordain women, etc.).[55] (By saying this, I do not intend to demonstrate that Dussel in fact would represent the official Catholic view. What I am saying is that both Dussel and most liberation theologians come close to a Catholic understanding of sexual difference and, possibly, its consequences in sexual ethics. This happens in an atmosphere in which the official teaching is not seriously or explicitly challenged, and this again cannot happen without profound changes in the traditional image of women and the male-female relationship. Many Catholic feminists have in fact done this, but they are very seldom if ever quoted [or even read] by their male colleagues.)

Thus it should come as no surprise that Dussel proposes "women's liberation" as an alternative concept for "feminism," which he understands in quite negative terms. He misunderstands that both historically and conceptually "women's liberation" has been equated with "feminism" for feminist women, on his own continent as well. However, it must be remembered that many early Latin American feminists shared this differentiation, thus understanding feminism as something foreign to their reality, preferring to use the term "women's liberation." This is not the case in the 1990s. In the early 1970s, Dussel had an idea of feminism as something that suppresses the difference between man and woman and inevitably leads to a homosexual definition of erotic relationships.[56] This, again, would lead (inevitably) to the suppression of biological motherhood.[57]

When speaking of feminism, Dussel explicitly refers to North American and European feminism.[58] This means two things. First, by seeing feminism as something concerning primarily—or even only—First World women, Dussel can ignore it by using anti-imperialist arguments (feminism being "bourgeois" or "foreign"). This way of avoiding the challenge of Latin American feminism is identified by Latin American feminist theologians as one expression of patriarchalism in liberation theology.[59] Second, by speaking of feminism only as a European and North American phenomenon, Latin American male intellectuals ignore the history of Latin American feminism, which has deep roots in the continent. This is especially questionable in the case of Dussel, who as a historian has mainly been interested in rewriting Latin American history, "the unwritten history," giving credit to "indigenous" forms of rebellion and cultural self-assurance.[60]

It is interesting to find this categorical and conservative understanding in Dussel: feminists "wanting to be men" (even though he uses "men" for "human beings") and effacing sexual difference (defined in very traditional terms) in favor of "asexual angelism"[61] and not being feminine (which is practically the same as undoing sexual difference in his terms), since he elsewhere so enthusiastically commits himself to women's liberation.

Many of the points he takes up are implicitly present in the texts of other liberation theologians. As Latin American feminist liberation theologians have pointed out, the whole issue of feminism being omitted in liberation theology is due to the very reasons that Dussel states explicitly: seeing feminism primarily as a phenomenon foreign to Latin American reality and preferring an uncritical and undifferentiated use of concepts such as women and femininity. Thus it is not totally incorrect to see Dussel's views as expressing a more widespread opinion among the liberation theologians. This attitude to feminism has changed as the Latin American feminist movement has grown. Nonetheless, even today there is still very little dialogue between feminist theorists and Latin American intellectuals, including liberation theologians. Feminist writings are not known, nor are they quoted.

According to Horacio Cerutti Guldberg, the methodological center of Dussel's philosophy, the existence of the space *(ámbito)* of anthropological Otherness, is very close to a proposal of an ontological difference between "the Third World" and "the center" (Europe).[62] In the male–female relationship, this would translate into an understanding of an ontological difference between men and women, between a "male" and "female" nature, which, as we have seen, is pretty much what Dussel supposes. Again, he is not alone: there are even many feminists who consciously or unconsciously share this bipolar understanding of gender relations.

Of special interest is Cerutti Guldberg's critique of the "people" as the supposed subject of the philosophy of liberation. It is worth remembering that Dussel himself participates in both the theological and philosophical formulations of the Other, the poor, and the people as the starting point for Latin American thinking. According to Cerutti Guldberg, the role of the intellectual as the prophet is problematic. The intellectual is the master, the knower, the thinker, whereas the Other (the poor, etc.) is necessarily the disciple who is incapable of thinking for himself or herself.[63] The gap between the philosopher (or theologian) and the Other (the poor, the oppressed) is evident. If philosophy is understood as *ancilla theologiae,* as Dussel according to Cerutti Guldberg understands it, and theology as the ultimate verification of truth ("philosophy as access to transcendency" in Dussel's words), this results in "salvationalist philosophy," which for Cerutti Guldberg is unacceptable.[64]

For Cerutti Guldberg, this kind of thinking makes itself immune to criticism, since it "conceives itself as the most profound level of all criticism and as incapable of being criticized because it is 'exteriority' *(exterioridad)*. . . . the only guarantee possible for a permanently renewed interpellation is to postulate an absolute 'exteriority' (God). All 'analectical' philosophy is a philosophy in the service of a theology redefined as a 'popular theology.'"[65]

A critique similar to Cerutti Guldberg's is presented by Ofelia Schutte, who understands the philosophy of liberation as an intellectual movement based on a phenomenological analysis of reality but politicizes it and involves specific Catholic influence as well.[66] Schutte argues that Dussel's philosophical system rests on the primacy of a fusion of ethics and metaphysics, ultimately based on the premise of the origin of all things in God, the Absolute, as "wholly Other."[67] This appeal to God and religion makes it possible for Dussel to "justify his vision of the moral superiority of the periphery over against the center, since the periphery represents the voice of the poor and the oppressed."[68] The postulation of an absolutely untainted source for truth claims is problematic. Ethically, of Dussel's two principles—totality (evil) and alterity (good)—the latter ceases to refer to an otherness or a difference in the postmodern sense but comes to designate the ground for a new absolute.[69] Dussel's philosophy seeks to derive its fundamental principles from faith rather than scientific knowledge.[70]

Schutte warns of authoritarianism in Dussel's philosophical system, since before one is entitled to speak or to make an ethical claim, one must portray oneself as representative of the Other (God, the Third World, the people, etc.).[71] Also, the "people" *(el pueblo)* is represented as weak and in need of help from superior forces, such as God and his prophets. The people remains an object that is thought about rather than a group of persons endowed with the capacity to think for themselves.[72] Here Schutte coincides with Cerutti Guldberg's critique of Dussel and with my critique of the liberation theologians, whose understanding of themselves as "organic intellectuals" may lead them to position themselves above and outside the people they want to speak for. She even says that "the subject of liberation, in his or her ethical and metaphysical condition as 'other,' is always in need and helpless in Dussel's theory. . . . Thus the structure of Dussel's theory is built around a subject who must show his or her pain, who must say 'help me.'. . ."[73] The "people" as a singular collective subject fails to denote the diversity and/or conflicting interests of those who make up "the people." The meaning of "the people" can easily slip from the context of an empirical reference to that of a normatively constructed ideal.[74]

In short, Schutte's critique of not only Dussel but certain tendencies in the philosophy of liberation and, implicitly, in liberation theology, rest on the assumption that

> the theoretical apparatus they [Dussel and others] bring to the problem of the oppression of the Latin American people is not sufficiently liberated itself to guarantee the liberation of others. We need a good (critical) theory which can also serve as

> a theory of liberation. Such a theory cannot rest essentially on the principle of alterity and on the conflict between the center and the periphery, for we have seen that these principles alone do not escape the dualistic, hierarchical, authoritarian, and dogmatic structures which have characterized other oppressive ideological systems in the past.[75]

According to Schutte, there are three levels of absolutism in Dussel's thinking: political, religious, and a combination of these two into an absolute ethics of service to the Other.[76] Dussel's "yes-to-the-Other" is the absolute criterion of a political ethic.[77]

Even though both Schutte and Cerutti Guldberg discuss primarily the philosophy of liberation (not liberation theology) and concentrate especially on Dussel, much of their critique can be extended to (other) liberation theologians as well. The problem here is that only a few liberation theologians have even tried to theorize these issues from a perspective other than their own, which, as we have seen, grants "the poor," or the Other, a status that raises critical questions. Dussel is important here, since he is both a philosopher and a theologian of liberation.

As I see it, there are similar difficulties in feminist theology when "women's experience" is uncritically raised as the sole criterion of theology and ethics, and in parts of secular feminist theory when foundational theoretical presuppositions (such as "man" and "woman") are not critically discussed at all or when these theories consciously part from an understanding of women's epistemological privilege only by virtue of their oppressed position qua women. This is an extremely important and complicated discussion.[78] I do not see a feminist theoretical or practical "package" that as such could be "brought" into liberation theology. The argument for this is not that the respective differences between liberation theology and feminism would make it impossible but rather that they share similar kinds of theoretical assumptions that many feel uncomfortable with, not as much for political as for theoretical reasons.

However, bringing a (self-)critical feminist perspective into the discussion helps us to see that the theoretical discussion on the subject of liberation theology and philosophy has some practical consequences. One area in which the issues of subjectivity, gender, and religion clash is that of sexual ethics, especially in the context of the marginalized poor of Latin America.[79]

LIBERATION THEOLOGIANS AND SEXUAL ETHICS

Latin American liberation theology can be seen as an intent to bridge dogma and morality, faith, and Christian praxis. Even though there is no distinctive ethical theory, the central questions of liberation theology are of an ethical nature. Thus, in an ideal situation, faith and ethics would not be separate. Theological reflection in itself would be an ethical act.

Those few Latin American theologians who consider themselves ethicists in the context of liberation theology affirm this. According to Francisco Moreno Rejón,

> It is not exaggerated to affirm that in its disposition as well as in its methodology, [liberation theology] is the most moral of all theologies. In effect, on the one hand, it requires of the theologian the commitment to reflect from and on the praxis of Christian life. On the other hand, its methodology postulates the praxis as the starting point and as the goal of the hermeneutical circle. Therefore, we are faced with a theology in which the ethical connotations are something substantial and not merely peripheral derivations.[80]

According to Moreno Rejón, most Latin American moral theologians share the basic methodology and theses of liberation theology.[81] The perspective of the poor is the starting point for any ethical theory within liberation theology as well.[82] The option for the poor means incorporating the poor, the nonpersons, as the preferential interlocutors in theological–moral reflection.[83] However, it is almost impossible to find any explicit reference to issues of sexual ethics in the general presentations of the "ethics of liberation." The poor do not appear as reproductive, gendered beings, nor are the implications of poverty to women discussed.

Antônio Moser, a Brazilian Franciscan brother, has an article on sexuality in the "Summa" of liberation theology (*Mysterium Liberationis,* in which all the classical themes of theology are dealt with from a liberation theological perspective).[84] But there is very little in Moser's article that explains how liberation theology proposes a perspective or a sexual ethic that differs from mainstream Catholic teaching. Affirming the goodness of sexuality as God's gift,[85] expressing concern for sexual liberty,[86] and critiquing the most negative attitudes toward human sexuality is nothing new in the history of theology.[87] According to Moser, liberation theology could offer a sociopolitical aspect to the discussion on sexuality.[88]

What are these sociopolitical dimensions of sexuality that liberation theology could help to illuminate? First, according to Moser, sexual instrumentalization and alienation result from an ideology that aims at keeping large proportions of people in the margins of decision-making processes (sexuality in the service of social and political status quo).[89] The commercialization of sex, especially of the female body, is another aspect of this ideological manipulation of sexuality.[90] Further, there are other problems, such as campaigns in favor of birth control that use the "ghost of demographic explosion" as an excuse for all kinds of brutalities—indiscriminate distribution of contraceptives, mass sterilizations, and incentives to abortion.[91] There are hidden ideological reasons behind these campaigns: they are directed to certain races and the most impoverished people. According to Moser,

> the secret presupposition is that these races and the most impoverished sectors of society, which are predominantly concentrated in the Third World, are those responsible for the economic, social and political problems. This is why they have to be dec-

imated in a skilled and progressive manner. With this, the real problem, located in the unjust distribution of goods, remains in the shadow.[92]

Much of what Moser says is in perfect mutual agreement with official Catholic teaching on sexual ethics. The praxis starting point of liberation theology in the context of sexual ethics is not used for an analysis of uneven power structures (except in terms of Third World–First World inequity), sexual and domestic violence, machismo, or the real reproductive realities of poor women, including the lack of access to safe birth control and the high rate of illegal abortions.

DUSSEL AND SEXUAL ETHICS

As noted earlier, Enrique Dussel is exceptional among liberation theologians in speaking explicitly on issues of sexual ethics. His Catholic background may be reflected in how he theorizes sexual difference (masculinity–femininity). It seems that in issues of sexual ethics too he comes close to official church teaching, even though his argumentation may be different from that of the Vatican. There have also been changes in his thinking.

Dussel's ethical system presupposes heterosexuality as normal and normative human sexuality, without explicitly stating it. Dussel has a negative understanding of homosexuality as a "Totality" in which men are not men nor women women.[93] His rejection of homosexuality is combined with a rejection of feminism, defined as something that undoes the natural difference between male and female, leading to a homosexual definition of the erotic relationship.[94] Thus "the most extreme feminism, born and bred in the opulent North Atlantic world, interprets sexuality from Totality."[95] Undoing the difference, this extreme feminism proposes homosexual autoeroticism in which nobody depends on anyone. This could mean lesbianism and rejection of childbearing, as well as individualism and hedonism. Thus it is the counterpart of machismo.[96] Homosexuality is "indifferentiation," which cannot be the aim of erotic liberation.[97] He even says that "feminist homosexuality ends up summing up all perversions." It is, among other things, "radical loss of sense of the reality of the Other and total schizophrenia."[98]

In a later text in which Dussel wants to make a critical evaluation of his philosophy of liberation, looking backward, he presents a somewhat different view on homosexuality. He states that a homosexual person "must be respected in the dignity of his/her personality."[99] He seems to depart from his earlier understanding of the impossibility of encountering the Other in a homosexual relation, the Other being defined exclusively in terms of heterosexual, genital sexual difference. There is the possibility of respect for the Other in a homosexual relationship too. Nevertheless, he considers homosexuality and abortion situations of "minor evil," which makes him an exception among the liberation theologians.[100]

When it comes to contraception and abortion, Dussel does not directly condemn them in the official Catholic way. Nevertheless, in his *Filosofía de la lib-*

eración, he speaks of filicide, child murder, as alienation. The liberation of woman makes it possible that "the couple permits the appearance of offspring."[101] He also says that "the child is the exteriority of all erotics, its metaphysical surpassing, its real fulfillment."[102] Similarly, he says that

> the couple can again totalize itself, close itself in a hedonism without transcendence, without fecundity. . . . The totalized couple negates the child because it invades as the Other who provokes to justice, interpellates for distinct rights and relaunches the couple into real history, responsible and fertile. The couple, because of its "pulsation to totalization," would like to make its voluptuousity eternal without third parties.[103]

This is clearly the official Catholic position that sexual pleasure without the possibility of procreation is morally wrong. According to Dussel, normal and human sexuality is openness to a child. Fecundity is the seal of love.[104] Although it does not become totally clear what Dussel means by all this, it is possible to read it, in the context of his general framework, as a rather traditional Catholic view.[105]

In his earlier texts, Dussel mentions abortion explicitly only in the context of child murder:

> The physical or cultural death of the child is pedagogical alienation. The child is killed in the womb of the mother by abortion or in the womb of the people by cultural repression. This repression, evidently, will always be carried out in the name of freedom, and by means of the best pedagogical methods."[106]

In 1992, Dussel revised some of his earlier theses on abortion as well. There are two absolute rights—the right of the woman to her personality and body and the right of the new being to life—confronting each other. This dilemma can be solved through the old doctrine of "minor evil." Dussel bases his reasoning on the ethical responsibility of the woman as moral subject who has the primary responsibility of decision.[107] Here he comes close to many feminist ethicists who claim that it is the inability to see the woman as a moral subject that is behind an absolute condemnation of abortion. Thus the critique presented by Schutte is not totally justified when she says, "he [Dussel] has equated abortion with murder (filicide)."[108] As we saw, this reading is possible, but it is not the dogmatic stance of Dussel, whatever we think of his general reasoning on issues of sexual ethics.

Dussel's overall unproblematized and uncritical use of such central concepts as the Other, alterity, difference, femininity and masculinity, and so on, produces both the incoherence and the antifeminism in his ethics. Traditional Catholic teaching, especially on issues of sexual ethics, apparently has a strong influence on his thinking. In his later texts, he nevertheless seems to be more aware of his earlier political conservatism and its possible consequences.

Dussel exemplifies a general rhetoric approval of women's liberation as part of the larger liberation project of Latin America (even though, as we saw, his artificial distinction between women's liberation and feminism is not what Latin American feminists would appreciate). But when put face-to-face with the concrete living conditions of women—and feminist theory and practice—his thinking appears abstract and contradictory, if not conservative. According to Schutte—and here I agree with her—"the process of appealing to the logic of exteriority can easily constitute an evasion when it comes to analyzing the actual social relations of domination and the corresponding struggles for freedom found in human existence."[109]

The formal approval of gender equality and condemnation of antisexual elements in the Christian tradition do not make Catholic liberation theologians reinterpret the official teaching on issues of sexual ethics of their church. The same can, of course, be said of Catholic theology in general, including the magisterium.[110]

Moral theology, or "ethics of liberation," in the context of liberation theology or liberation theology as such, first, does not address issues of sexual ethics extensively; second, when it is addressed, the reasoning strongly follows traditional, official teaching, which also has been affirmed by the Latin American Catholic bishops.[111] This is true at least for the Catholic theologians. There is an apparent conflict between the abstract reasoning in sexual ethical issues and the supposed praxis starting point, in which concrete problems of the poor form the base for ethics as well as theology. This again seems to point toward the lack of alternative reinterpretations in the area of theological anthropology, especially concerning male–female relationships and sexuality. "The poor" as a homogeneous, primarily productive (not reproductive, gendered) category may even prevent such reinterpretations in liberation theology.

THEOLOGY OF (WHOSE) LIFE?

Liberation theology today has also been interpreted as theology of life *(teología de la vida)*. This is done in a context in which the massive, real death of people in the Third World is seen as idolatry. Concrete human life must be defended against the powers of death, which the liberation theologians usually situate in "the North."[112] According to Pablo Richard, one of the major proponents of liberation theology as a theology of life, the Third World is becoming a nonworld, since the Third World in the classical sense is now less and less needed even for the production of cheap labor and raw materials.[113] The alternative between development and liberation has changed into a radical alternative between life and death. The only option for liberation theology is to affirm life for everyone *(vida para todos)*. The option for the poor translates into the option for life.[114] The fundamental ethical imperative in Latin America is human life, which in practice refers to work, bread, roof, education, justice, and security.[115] The fundamental criterion for ethical discernment is the human life of the real concrete man *(el hombre)*.[116]

In a later text, Richard speaks of the same issue in absolute terms: liberation theology must take the "radical and absolute option for life."[117] "Human life thus becomes a real criterion for discernment and an absolute and universal imperative,"[118] and "the denial of life is denial of truth, goodness, and beauty."[119] The theology of life must "guarantee the reproduction of human life and of nature."[120] In the realm of ethics, "human life is an absolute value."[121] Theologically, the soul is not saved from the body, as it was in Hellenistic philosophy, but rather the human being (body and soul) is saved from death.[122]

Liberation theology as theology of life takes seriously the concrete, corporeal life of human beings in situations of oppression and death. It is not possible to discuss this perspective here in detail, but I want to point out one possible interpretation of this position. Official church documents (e.g., the CELAM Santo Domingo document of 1992) have adopted liberation theological language in issues of sexual ethics when the bishops speak of contraceptive imperialism *(imperialismo anticonceptivo)* against Latin America.[123] Some liberation theologians, such as Antônio Moser, combine this official Catholic view with the "pro-life" language of liberation theology, seeing birth control and abortion as the imperialist weapons of death against the Latin American poor. The silence of other liberation theologians on issues of sexual ethics, combined with a radical and absolutist overall defense of human life, opens up the possibility of reading liberation theologians as supporting the official Vatican teaching.[124]

Actually, in an article to a German audience, Pablo Richard comes quite close to such a view. He criticizes the way of thinking that sees massive and effective birth control as the solution to the problem (of poverty) in the Third World: "This solution does not have any other use than hiding the real problem and justifying the present power of death. This solution follows the logic of death of the dominating system."[125] He states that family planning is necessary, but "in Latin America, all birth control programs until today have been planned, financed, and finally, forced, by the USA."[126] This explains the deep distrust of all birth control politics from outside or from above.[127] In the same context, he takes up the central issue of defense of life in liberation theology: "The option for life means saying no to death, not accepting death, not permitting even a child to starve; it means radical and unyielded opposition to the death of the poor, not accepting the death of the poor."[128] What he does not notice is how the death of poor women is intimately and directly connected to issues of unsafe or unavailable contraception, illegal abortions, and a high fertility rate.

If "concrete human life" and life of the poor that liberation theologians want to defend is not further concretized, problematized, and differentiated, they may find themselves in rather surprising company. Does the defense of the life of the poor also translate into the defense of the life of poor women? If yes, the fact that poor women die of causes directly related to reproduction has to be taken seriously. This, of course, is one argument in favor of explicating sexual ethics within liberation theology from the perspective of those who suffer most from the consequences of the current situation—poor women.

Dussel's—as well as other liberation theologians'—general method and elaboration of concepts such as Otherness may yield useful results in terms of a productive paradigm and a concern with life at an abstract level, but when it comes to "everyday life" *(la vida cotidiana),* they end in rather useless abstractions, even conservative pronouncements.

LATIN AMERICAN FEMINIST THEOLOGICAL ANTHROPOLOGY

Latin American feminist theologians are not much more explicit than their male colleagues on issues of sexual ethics.[129] Ivone Gebara from Brazil has been the first (and until today the only) liberation theologian, male or female, to publicly favor the decriminalization of abortion. In October 1993 she stated in an interview by the Brazilian magazine *Veja* that a mother who is not psychologically strong enough to face up to a pregnancy has the right to interrupt it.[130] According to Gebara,

> Catholic morality does not reach rich women. They abort, having the economic resources to guarantee a surgical intervention in human conditions. Therefore, the law which the church defends is detrimental to poor women. The abortion must be decriminalized and legalized. Even more, it must be realized at the expense of the state. Abortion is today the fifth cause of feminine mortality in Brazil. Those who die are the poorest women.[131]

Abortion is not a sin.[132]

She also states that what made her change her opinion on the issue was her experience living with the poor women of Camaragibe, an impoverished region on the outskirts of Recife, where she worked as a nun. After being ordered to retract her statement, she clarified her position in an article, "La legalización del aborto vista desde el caleidoscopio social,"[133] in which she says that her practical starting point is the reality of poor women who are the primary victims of the "violence against life" that numerous illegal abortions bring about.[134] A society that cannot guarantee employment, health, housing, and schools is "an abortive society" that forces women to choose between their work and their pregnancy. The maternal death that is associated with millions of abortions is not denounced in the same way as the "innocent life" lost in an abortion.[135] She says her position is a denunciation of institutionalized violence, abuse, and hypocrisy, a position stemming from the defense of life.[136] She uses the same language that her male colleagues use—that poverty is an issue of life and death—but in reproductive issues she seems to understand life quite differently from other liberation theologians. It is the life of poor women that is at stake.

Gebara does not discuss the Catholic teaching on birth control, nor does she enter into a theological debate with the magisterium. Her position is very pragmatic and, as such, similar to a feminist position on abortion anywhere: there are always situations in which women resort to abortions. The issue is whether these are realized under decent conditions or not. Women die of illegal abortions. Nowhere has criminalization of abortion solved the problem.

Gebara, together with María Clara Bingemer, sees theological anthropology as central for a Latin American feminist liberation theology.[137] This means at least four necessary changes in traditional theology: a shift from a male-centered to a human-centered anthropology, from a dualistic to a unifying anthropology, from an idealist to a realist anthropology, and from a one-dimensional to a pluridimensional anthropology.[138] They reject the binary model of specifically female/feminine and male/masculine modes of being and prefer speaking of a feminist anthropology that is closely connected to the present historic moment "in which women's consciousness is breaking into awareness of their age-old oppression and their age-old stance of compliance with and subjection to the oppressive structures of society and particularly of religion."[139] This, together with the understanding of the option for the poor as an option for poor woman,[140] is the larger framework for Gebara's public defense of legalization of abortion.

Gebara states that Christian churches' fear of the human body, especially the female body, has led to the fear of sexuality. Traditional Christian anthropology is an anthropology of verbal equality but with a patriarchal and hierarchical stamp.[141] The human body must become a new starting point for moral theology.[142] This implies accepting a unitary anthropology that intends to exceed dualisms and include the ambiguities inherent in human existence and history.[143] A new theology of sexuality should grow from a revised theology of creation, which must take into account the scientific knowledge of modern times and start from "the wonder of the body."[144]

Like other feminist liberation theologians, María Pilar Aquino stresses the importance of restoring human corporeality, especially in its humiliated female form. This corporeal dimension is nothing less than existence itself. In Latin America, human existence is being threatened every day by malnutrition, sickness, unemployment, and hunger. Women, especially, also live this threat to their existence as sexual beings, their sexuality being violated and destroyed.[145]

According to Ana María Portugal, the historical weight of Catholicism makes it very difficult to touch issues as controversial as sexuality and abortion, even in presumably secular sectors of society or in groups that support feminist demands for birth control and legalization of abortion in theory.[146] The same is true of liberation theology, which has "a profoundly masculine look in avoiding a clear pronouncement on the validity of sexual demands such as the right to birth control and voluntary abortion, pleasant sexuality as well as the question of women's ordination."[147] If it is difficult to imagine a radical questioning of the church, it is even more problematic in the case of liberation theology, since all inner critique is easily seen as "reactionary" or "counterproductive." All early feminist demands concerning abortion and birth control in Latin America were met with hostility from these groups, which explained that these problems were alien to Latin American reality.[148] Even many feminist groups have been careful in taking up the issue of abortion, for the fear of losing support among poor religious women.[149]

When liberation theologians speak of "the radical and absolute option for life"[150] and of human life being "an absolute value,"[151] they do not specify what they mean by "life." This is important for the abortion issue, since the principle of absolute right to life informs the Catholic and the pro-life Protestant view. It is not my intention to discuss the abortion debate here. I merely want to point out that if liberation theologians want to create a coherent ethics that includes sexual ethics, this kind of specification will be necessary.

Most feminists, including Ivone Gebara, when speaking of the reproductive realities of poor women, consider the issue of life and death from another angle. Illegal abortions, too many pregnancies too often, and undernourishment are the main causes of death of poor women all over the Third World. There will be no solution as long as the life of the woman and the life of her (potential) child are pitted against each other.[152]

According to Beverly Wildung Harrison, a theologically trained ethicist, almost nothing, especially in the literature of Christian ethics, has been written on the morality of abortion that fully reflects women's experience.[153] Much of what has been written reflects an open misogyny and a lack of concern for women.[154] Misogyny in Christian discussions of abortion is evidenced clearly in the fact that the abortion decision is never treated in the way it arises, as part of the female agent's life process.[155] According to Harrison, the discussion of abortion treats abortion as if it were an isolated act or deed having no relation to the lived world other than its involvement with prospective birth.[156] For her, as well as for most other feminist ethicists, "the well-being of a woman and the value of her life plan always must be recognized as of intrinsic value in any appeal to intrinsic value in a moral analysis of abortion."[157]

Harrison joins secular feminist opinions of reproductive rights when she states that

> under the most adverse conditions, women have had to try to control our fertility—everywhere, always. Women's relation to procreation irrevocably marks and shapes our lives. . . . Women's lack of social power, in all recorded history, has made this struggle to control procreation a life-bending, often life-destroying one for a large percentage of females.[158]

What both secular and religious feminists share is their emphasis on the real-life conditions of real women, especially the most vulnerable of them. Conceptually, this is very much what Latin American feminist liberation theologians mean by *la vida cotidiana* (everyday life), although they do not discuss it in the context of sexual ethics. Nevertheless, much of what Harrison says on the contradiction between the abstract discussion of life, especially in the context of abortion, on the one hand, and the inability to speak of women's life in concrete terms, on the other hand, also applies to those liberation theologians who defend the life of the poor in rather abstract terms. The poorer the women we are talking about, the more the issues of life, death, and reproduction are bound together.

LA VIDA COTIDIANA

Why does this situation exist? Why is it that issues of sexual ethics are not being discussed critically by Catholic or Protestant liberation theologians, by men or by women? There are some dissident voices, mostly of feminist Christian women who are close to liberation theology but are not necessarily theologians. Overall, silence prevails and thus there is no theological discourse on sexual ethics that could present an adequate alternative to the dominant Catholic discourse and practice. The great majority of Latin American women find no one expressing their most intimate concerns. And liberation theologians who do take up issues of sexual ethics seem to agree with official Catholic teaching.

Older liberation theologians have extra difficulty in addressing issues such as reproduction and sexuality because of their larger perception of society and social and political change. A Marxist-orientated political ethics—which informs many liberation theologians and especially their understanding of praxis—presupposes the change of (economic, political, social) structures. A new ethics of sexuality and a new relationship between men and women would follow these changes almost automatically. Or a hierarchy of necessary changes would be established in which "women's issues" and reproductive questions were seen as less important than macrolevel economic changes.[159] Contemporary Latin America offers us several examples of this dynamic. The most notable and probably the most analyzed case is that of Sandinista Nicaragua.[160] The Latin American left in general has opposed birth control, considering it an imperialist strategy. The influence of leftist party politics on liberation theology can thus be seen here too.

A further reason for the difficulty in creating spaces of critical dialogue on reproductive issues in Latin America in both religious and secular circles, including among many feminists, is to be found in global perspectives on health and population policies. Many Latin American feminists insist on the importance of understanding how international organizations and multinational corporations determine national population policies in their countries.[161] As already noted, liberation theologians tend to see reproductive issues in the larger context of imperialist population control policy, which is aimed primarily at the poor nations. This is an extremely touchy and difficult area, and it is necessary to clarify positions and the arguments supporting them. Many Third World countries, including Latin America, have been targets of aggressive, coercive, international population policies, including forced sterilizations (almost without exception of women), use of suspect hormonal contraceptives, and so on. It is understandable that those critical of Western notions of development—such as liberation theologians—and those defending poor women's right to control their reproductive capacities—such as Third World feminists—suspect any outside control over issues of population, reproduction, and women's health. Nevertheless, there is much confusion. On the one hand, liberation theologians joining the Vatican critique of "contraceptive imperialism" may not want to share the premises behind the critique. On the other hand, Latin American feminists defending women's reproductive rights hardly want to endorse the Vatican policy, although both parties would criticize coercive population politics.

Clearly, Latin American liberation theology speaks of the poor as its context, its locus, its starting point, and the subjects of the praxis, but it understands the poor homogeneously, without taking into account how poverty affects people differently depending, for example, on their race and gender. Practically speaking, preventing the death of poor women has not been an explicit part of liberation theologians' agenda of "defending the life of the poor." To do so implies taking a critical look at how the violence and death produced by poverty affect women differently than men in the area of reproduction. Ninety-nine percent of all maternal deaths in the world occur in the Third World.[162] What makes a difference in Latin America is its being still predominantly Catholic. Catholic teaching on sexual ethics should thus be a special challenge to liberation theologians, who wish to speak about the complex realities of the poor.

There is an implicit presupposition of what is included in "the praxis." As we have seen, it is difficult to include women, especially as reproductive beings, in the supposed collective subject of liberation theology. Feminist (theological) analysis and understanding of a female subject, which is both productive and reproductive, both communitarian and individual, both public and private, reveals this breach in liberation theology. The aspect of *la vida cotidiana,* although not always sufficiently explicated, of Latin American feminist liberation theologians makes it clear that there are central areas of human life that not only challenge liberation theology's understanding of the praxis but question the very usefulness of it as a norm for theology.

The perspective of *la vida cotidiana,* as brought forth by Latin American feminist liberation theologians, may serve as a bridge and critical element between the above-mentioned discourses and practices. Although the concept is not explicitly elaborated in the context of sexual ethics, it nevertheless offers us tools for taking the praxis of the poor women seriously and, possibly, for a critical-constructive sexual ethical agenda in the setting of Latin American feminist liberation theology. Its definite starting point is in seeing the poor women as subjects of both their own lives and Latin American theology.

NOTES

1. For a systematic analysis of the philosophy of liberation, see Cerutti Guldberg 1988–89 and 1992.

2. I elaborate this more substantively in Vuola 1997.

3. Leonardo Boff and Clodovis Boff observe this when they say that "the poor do not usually refer to themselves as 'poor,' which would offend their sense of honor and dignity. It is the non-poor who call them poor." Boff and Boff 1989, 41–42.

4. Segundo 1985, 150. On the theologian as an "organic intellectual," see also Boff 1986, 137–42, 227–52; C. Boff 1991, 89–93; Boff and Boff 1989, 22.

5. Engel and Thistlethwaite 1990, 2.

6. According to Horacio Cerutti Guldberg, the theoretical problems and difficulties included in the option for the poor have generally been obviated. If most liberation theologians' claim that "only the exploited and those who side with them can see the perversity of the system" (referring to José María Vigil), how can one change position or place *(lugar)*, asks Cerutti Guldberg. He criticizes the option for the poor in liberation theology (with the exception of Raúl Vidales) as some kind of guarantee of orthodoxy and orthopraxis, which is not far from "the unsustainable uncriticality of a proletarian science" (Cerutti Guldberg 1996b, 10-12). He also says, "Esta opción, que en verdad es un conjunto de opciones o decisiones existenciales renovadas en diversas coyunturas, no garantiza nada. Posibilita, sitúa, brinda perspectivas, abre horizontes; pero exige una permanente alerta racional y autocrítica para seguir avanzando" (Cerutti Guldberg 1996b, 13). According to Cerutti Guldberg, liberation theologians confuse different levels of analysis, which represents a question of cardinal importance and is difficult to resolve (p. 14).

Cerutti Guldberg takes up the same issue in another text in a little different way: ". . . una identificación cuasi natural entre teoría de liberación y pueblo pobre, una especie de armonía preestablecida y de relación no conflictiva entre el pueblo y el pensamiento de su liberación efectuado por otros . . ." (Cerutti Guldberg 1996a, 3).

7. The supposed collective subject (the poor, the Other) of liberation theology certainly has changed the role of an academic intellectual. Nevertheless, the majority of the most prominent liberation theologians are clerics (with a special meaning in the Catholic Church, in which women's ordination is out of the question and priests do not marry), highly educated, male, and of European descent, that is, "white" in the eyes of the black and indigenous population. The critique of the pretended universality and neutrality of European theology must be extended to liberation theology itself, especially in questions of race and gender.

8. See Slater 1994, 12–13.

9. Ibid., p. 13.

10. Ibid., p. 15.

11. Ibid., pp. 15–17.

12. Dussel 1985a, p. 24.

13. Dussel 1987, 1:97.

14. Ibid., p. 108.

15. Ibid., pp. 118–27.

16. Ibid., p. 128.

17. Dussel 1988, 115. It is the woman who concretizes the alterity in a more radical way because of her historical submission.

18. Dussel 1987, 2:163.

19. Dussel 1988, 183. In the original Spanish text, the Other is defined in male terms (el *Otro*) in spite of the explicit affirmation of women's alterity and their necessary liberation.

20. Ibid.

21. Dussel 1987, 2:14 (emphasis in original).

22. Ibid., p. 37.

23. Ibid., p. 56.

24. Ibid., pp. 56–57.

25. Ibid., pp. 59–60.

26. Ibid., p. 161.

27. Ibid.

28. Ibid., p. 162.
29. Ibid., p. 173.
30. Ibid., p. 176.
31. Ibid., pp. 176–77.
32. Dussel 1974, 118; 1988, 49–57; 1992, 407.
33. Dussel 1995, 46.
34. Ibid.
35. Ibid., p. 138.
36. Ibid., p. 48.
37. Ibid., pp. 136–37.
38. Ibid., p. 137.
39. Ibid.
40. See Dussel 1992, 397. According to Schutte, "The categories of exteriority, totality, and alterity used by Dussel are borrowed directly from the work of the French philosopher Emmanuel Levinas, but these categories are then applied to a different and, indeed, contradictory end, insofar as they are subordinated to a political platform of national-popular liberation" (Schutte 1993, 188). In a recent Finnish dissertation, the philosopher Sara Heinämaa shows how the idea of the woman as the Other is especially clear in Levinas's *Le Temps et l'Autre*. For Levinas, alterity gets its absolute, immediate form in the feminine. Heinämaa points out how Simone de Beauvoir criticizes and reinterprets this understanding of the woman as the Other in *The Second Sex*. According to Heinämaa's interpretation of Beauvoir, woman is not the Other but is comprehended as such. When Levinas writes that woman is a mystery, he forgets to say that she is a mystery to man. His description of woman is nothing else but the enforcement of masculine privilege. See Heinämaa 1996, 142–43.
41. Dussel 1974, 122–23.
42. Ibid., pp. 124–26; Dussel 1990, 25–33. In the foreword to the third edition of his *Filosofía ética de la liberación* (1987), he acknowledges this by saying that he cannot criticize feminism as he did at the beginning of the 1970s.
43. "La liberación de la mujer supone que ésta sepa discernir adecuadamente sus distintas funciones analógicamente diversas. Una función es ser la mujer de la pareja. Otra es ser la procreadora de su hijo. Otra es ser la educadora. Otra es ser una hermana entre los hermanos de la sociedad política. Y si cada una de estas funciones no se saben discernir, se cometen errores tremendos" (Dussel 1990, 28).
44. Dussel 1990, 29.
45. Ibid., pp. 29–30.
46. Ibid., p. 28.
47. Ibid., p. 29. I have consciously used the exact English (masculine) equivalents of *hijo* and *hermano*.
48. Ibid., pp. 30–31.
49. "La mujer, persona humana, porta la femineidad esencialmente en su nivel *sexuado erótico en la pareja,* ante un varón, igualmente persona humana, que porta la masculinidad en ese mismo nivel. Las diferencias son claras y la *igualdad en la distinción* debe ser defendida en concreto en todos los detalles" (Dussel 1990, 32 [emphasis in original]).
50. "El feminismo lo que nos propone es un angelismo asexual, aunque no parezca, porque nos propone que desaparezca la alteridad sexual y que cada uno cumpla consigo el amor. . . . No. *La liberación de la mujer no es por indistinción, sino justamente por distinción*" (Dussel 1974, 125 [emphasis added]).

51. "La liberación no es negación pura de la dominación por la negación de la diversidad sexual (como cuando el feminismo propone la homosexualidad, los hijos en probetas, etc.). *La liberación es distinción real sexual*" (Dussel 1985a, 101 [emphasis added]).

52. Stanley and Wise 1993, 195. See also Benhabib 1992, 148–77; Code 1992, 86, 324 (in which she speaks of women's refusal to remain the Other); Smith 1989, 145–61.

53. Heinämaa 1996, 150–51.

54. See Carr 1990, 123–33; Ruether 1983, 94–99; 1987, 30–45; 1990; 1991.

55. See *Mulieris Dignitatem* 1988, 325–26, 383–84, 398. In this apostolical letter, Pope John Paul II affirms the equality between men and women based on ontological difference. There is a proper feminine "originality," which is expressed in femininity. Masculinity and femininity are different and complementary to each other. A woman should not be masculine and a man should not be feminine. Femininity and masculinity have their origin in the ontological human nature. The former is best expressed in the two dimensions of a woman's vocation, maternity and virginity.

At the end of the letter, the statement on the impossibility of women's ordination in the Catholic Church is based exactly on this theological anthropology in which the priest acts *in persona Christi.* It is essentially a masculine function.

According to Anne Carr, "While there are no longer assertions of the inferiority of women in Christian ecclesiastical or theological discourse, many official Catholic documents affirm a dual anthropology, the complementarity or 'different but equal' status of men and women as inherent in nature, in the created order, and therefore as part of the divine plan" (Carr 1990, 125).

56. This view is still present in the latest edition of his *Liberación de la mujer y erótica latinoamericana* (1990). "La mujer feminista, al ver a la mujer oprimida, pero sin salirse de la 'totalidad' como categoría fundamental, propone que la mujer remonte la corriente e iguale al varón; que suprima la di-ferencia, de tal manera que se hable de 'hombres' sin más, ni de varones, ni de mujeres. Para llegar a eso habría que pensar en la homosexualidad, pues para que nadie dependiera de nadie, la relación debería ser homosexual; la mujer consigo misma, con la mujer; el varón con el varón" (Dussel 1990, 25).

Ironically, here he uses "men" *(hombres)* in the generic meaning of "human beings." In another text, he says clearly; "El feminismo en el fondo lo que quiere son *hombres*; no quiere varones ni mujeres. . . . Cuando digo ahora hombre, quiero decir la especie. El feminismo lucha para que todos seamos hombres, no varones ni mujeres" (Dussel 1974, 124–25 [emphasis in original]).

57. Here Dussel, probably unintentionally, coincides with some radical feminists of the early 1970s who saw biological motherhood as the main obstacle to women's liberation. See Firestone 1971.

58. Dussel 1990, 26.

59. See Aquino 1997, 11.

60. Aquino notes that First World women also often operate with the idea that feminism is nonexistent in Latin America or that it is a mere reproduction of European or North American feminism (Aquino 1997, 11). Dussel not only ignores Latin American feminism but also defines European and North American feminism as something that promotes "in-differentiated individualism typical of English and North American societies," which is a very general and stereotypical statement. See Dussel [1980] 1990, 26.

61. Dussel 1974, 125.

62. Cerutti Guldberg 1992, 236–37. Ironically, seeing Latin America only as a repetitive reflection of Europe in need of liberation, may result in the negation of the history of

Latin American thinking (Cerutti Guldberg 1992, 238). See also Cerutti Guldberg 1988-1989, 49.

63. Cerutti Guldberg 1992, 256–58, 277–78; Cerutti Guldberg 1988–1989, 50–51.

64. Cerutti Guldberg 1992, 279–81. In short, "philosophy, as it is understood by this sub-sector [of philosophy of liberation] is a specific activity of a philosopher, the only one capable of opening himself to the interpellation with the Other, but who does not open himself to the interpellation with social and human sciences. Rather, he dictates to them their epistemic limitations and possibilities. . . . The *counter image* of this philosophy is the dominating North Atlantic thinking and its dominating subject. The subject is not questioned and the philosopher-ethicist appears in his own real life as the norm according to which one can reach alterity and justice" (Cerutti Guldberg 1992, 283–84 [emphasis in original]). I have translated the philosopher as "he," since in the original Cerutti Guldberg uses the male pronoun *(el)* for the philosopher.

65. Cerutti Guldberg 1988–1989, 51–52.

66. Schutte 1991, 275. Actually, Schutte argues that Dussel is aiming at "replacing Marxism theoretically with something else—that something else being a theory of 'liberation' based on a religious metaphysics derived from the Catholic patriarchal tradition and an ethics of 'alterity' borrowed in large part, yet also departing significantly, from the work of the French phenomenologist, Emmanuel Levinas" (Schutte 1991, 276).

67. Schutte 1991, 276.

68. Ibid., p. 277.

69. Schutte 1993, 178–79.

70. Schutte 1991, 278.

71. Ibid., pp. 280–82. Schutte does not discuss a further difficulty in this configuration: How does one become a representative of somebody else? Who gives the philosopher/the theologian the legitimacy of representing somebody else besides himself or herself?

72. Ibid., pp. 281–83.

73. Ibid., p. 283.

74. Schutte 1993, 162.

75. Schutte 1991, 287 (emphasis in original).

76. Schutte 1993, 187–88.

77. Ibid., p. 187, quoting Dussel (emphasis in original).

78. I discuss this in the theological context, claiming that much of the conceptual weakness in feminist theology could be clarified by a deeper dialogue with nontheological feminist theory (in Vuola 1997).

79. When speaking of sexual ethics, I refer mainly to questions concerning *reproductive rights* (not to marriage, divorce, sexuality in general, and so on). Reproductive rights as a concept was originally formulated by women activists or, more precisely, women's groups involved with health issues like reproductive health. The Women's Global Network for Reproductive Rights has defined reproductive rights as women's right to decide whether, when, and how to have children—regardless of nationality, class, ethnicity, race, age, religion, disability, sexuality, or marital status—in the social, economic, and political conditions that make such decisions possible. The struggle for reproductive rights also contains a radical critique of patriarchal society and the dominant development model. Reproductive rights are human rights inseparable from other basic rights. Feminists are united in their insistence that the moral agency of women seeking to shape their procreative lives must be respected. See Andolsen 1996, 249; Dutting 1993, 2; Petchesky 1995, 153.

80. Moreno Rejón 1991, 275. Similarly, see Cuesta 1987, 599; Moser 1984, 258; Vidal 1991.

81. Moreno Rejón 1991, 277.

82. "La ética de liberación afirma expresamente el lugar desde donde se elabora, esto es, su punto de vista, su situación y también cuál es su interlocutor, o sea, su toma de posición. Esto es lo que significa la expresión la *perspectiva del pobre:* explícitamente se pretende mirar la realidad desde el lugar y con los ojos del pobre . . ." (Moreno Rejón 1991, 281 [emphasis in original]).

83. Moreno Rejón 1991, 282; Cuesta 1987, 605.

84. Moser 1991.

85. Ibid., pp. 112–13.

86. Ibid., p. 109.

87. Ibid., pp. 114–15.

88. Ibid., pp. 119–20.

89. Ibid., p. 121.

90. Ibid.

91. "Blandiendo el fantasma de la 'explosión demográfica' y de la consiguiente falta de recursos para atender a las necesidades básicas de todos, se señala el control sistemático de la natalidad como única salida. Y para garantizarlo, todos los medios se consideran válidos: desde la distribución indiscriminada de cualquier tipo de anticonceptivos, hasta la esterilización en masa y el incentivo al aborto" (Moser 1991, 121).

92. Moser 1991, 121–22.

93. Dussel 1985a, 97–98, 81; Dussel 1990, 25–26.

94. Dussel 1990, 25.

95. Dussel 1988, 116.

96. Ibid., pp. 116–17.

97. Ibid., p. 117.

98. ". . . la homosexualidad feminista termina por sumar todas las perversiones, es la univocidad total de la sexualidad, es pérdida radical del sentido de la realidad (una esquizofrenia completa) del Otro, es el final solipsismo del *ego* cartesiano o europeo . . ." (Dussel 1988, 117).

99. Dussel 1992, 407.

100. Ibid., pp. 407–8.

101. Dussel 1985a, 102–3.

102. "El hijo es la exterioridad de toda erótica, su superación metafísica, su cumplimiento real" (Dussel 1985a, 107).

103. ". . . la pareja puede nuevamente totalizarse, cerrarse en un hedonismo sin trascendencia, sin fecundidad. . . . El hijo es negado por la pareja totalizada porque viene a irrumpir como el Otro que pro-voca a la justicia, interpela por derechos dis-tintos y relanza a la pareja a la historia real, responsable, y fecunda. La pareja, por la 'pulsión de totalización,' querría eternizar su voluptuosidad sin terceros" (Dussel 1988, 118).

104. Dussel 1988, 119.

105. Ofelia Schutte also pays attention to this: "Despite his controversial and radical rhetoric, especially in the sphere of politics, Dussel's ethical principles do not contradict the magisterium or teaching authority of the Roman Catholic Church" (Schutte 1991, 277). Schutte's general estimation of Dussel is that he cannot be seen as a critical or progressive thinker, and this is especially true of his view of women. In that respect, Dussel's theory "is as conservative as traditional patriarchal thought" (Schutte 1991, 284).

106. "La muerte física o cultural del hijo es la alienación pedagógica. Al hijo se lo mata en la vientre de la madre por el aborto o en el vientre del pueblo por la represión cultural. Esta represión, es evidente, se efectuará siempre en nombre de la libertad y con los

mejores métodos pedagógicos" (Dussel 1985a, 108). And "en conclusión la maldad del pro-yecto erótico, por su propia totalización, significa alienación del Otro (la mujer en nuestra sociedad machista), y, meta-físicamente infecundidad (muerte del hijo, sea por no desearlo, sea por abortarlo . . .). En cambio, la bondad erótica se despliega como servicio del Otro (en especial liberación de la mujer), y por apertura que esto significa y en esa misma apertura la bondad es *fecundidad"* (Dussel 1988, 108 [emphasis in original]).

107. Dussel 1992, 407.

108. Schutte 1988–1989, 64, referring to Dussel 1985a, 1987, 1988. In 1993, Schutte too recognizes a "modification to some extent" in Dussel's views (Schutte 1993, 202).

109. Schutte 1993, 189. According to Schutte's argument, Dussel's ethics presupposes that the oppressed have to stay in the privileged position of exteriority in order to be able to speak to the established system of domination. Concretely, this could mean that women have to remain in their oppressed position, the poor have to remain poor, in order to maintain Dussel's pure, uncontaminated "exteriority" (Schutte 1993, 189). "One must remain on the periphery if one is to receive the moral blessings associated with alterity" (Schutte 1993, 201).

110. In all recent Vatican documents concerning women, their oppression is stated and condemned, and their equality with men is defended. Nevertheless, this is not applied to the church itself (e.g., women's ordination is not seen as an issue of equality, even though the arguments against it are derived from a theological anthropology that makes women unsuitable for the priesthood). Nor is the link between a theological anthropology that unconditionally accepts women's full humanity and the traditional teaching on sexual ethics made clear.

111. See *Documentos de Medellín* 1969, 26–32, where the validity of the encyclical *Humanae Vitae* is stated. There is nothing especially "Latin American" in this part of the Medellín documents, if "antinatalist demographic politics" is not seen as such. This endorsing of the official Catholic teaching in sexual ethics continues in the documents of Puebla (1979) and Santo Domingo (1992).

In December 1990, the state of Chiapas in Mexico decriminalized abortion in cases of rape and serious genetic or other fetal malformation, as well as for reasons of family planning. As such, the new legislation differs notably from most of Latin America. Chiapas is the poorest state of Mexico, and it is home to the largest part of the indigenous population. In recent years, it has become internationally well-known as the base for the *zapatista* indigenous insurrection movement. The bishop of Chiapas, Samuel Ruiz García, is known for his sympathies for both the *zapatista* cause and liberation theology. Soon after the new legislation, he issued a pastoral letter condemning the decriminalization of abortion. He too pointed out how a demographic population policy (including mass sterilizations) on the part of the United States and international agencies such as the International Monetary Fund can be interpreted as aggression against the predominantly indigenous population of his diocese. He strongly denounces machismo and violence against women, but he also judges some feminist demands as reflecting a similar mentality, as when women consider the new life they are carrying "as their private property." See Ruiz 1994, 435–53. The pastoral letter of bishop Ruiz is one more example of an argument which derives its contents simultaneously from the anti-imperialist discourse of liberation theology in defense of the poor and from the traditional sexual ethical teaching of the Catholic Church.

In the U.N. International Conference on Population and Development in Cairo, September 1994, Latin American bishops—including Ruiz García—followed the Vatican and

Islamic fundamentalists in opposing the proposed conference document, saying that its proposals would hurt the poorest of people, especially indigenous Indians. See Fox 1995, 285, 293.

112. See Richard 1987, 93; 1994, 104.
113. Richard 1991, 3.
114. Ibid.
115. Richard 1981, 56; 1988, 94.
116. Richard 1981, 56.
117. Richard 1994, 94.
118. Ibid., 95.
119. Ibid.
120. Ibid.
121. Ibid., p. 100.
122. Ibid., p. 106.
123. *Nueva evangelización, promoción humana, cultural cristiana* 1992, 62.
124. Actually, Pope John Paul II's eleventh encyclical, *Evangelium Vitae* (The gospel of life), issued in 1995, sets out a moral vision aimed at overcoming what the pope refers to as the modern "culture of death." The encyclical wishes to portray a consistent ethic of life, in which issues of abortion, euthanasia, and capital punishment are treated. See Fox 1995, 317–18.

Thus the language of morality in terms of life and death is present in both the Vatican teaching and liberation theology, and in similar absolutist terms. The context and the contents differ, but less so in issues of sexual ethics than in other areas of moral theology. At least liberation theologians should be conscious of this potential dilemma.

125. Richard 1986, 16.
126. Ibid.
127. Ibid.
128. Ibid., p. 17.
129. According to Phillip Berryman, "compared with their feminist colleagues in North America and Europe, Latin American women theologians are still rather timid, especially on reproductive issues" (Berryman 1995, 118). They do not necessarily have to be "compared" with their colleagues in the industrialized countries. The whole issue must be treated in the historical and cultural context of Latin America—both the reasons why sexual ethics has not been high up on the feminist theological agenda and the ways it might be taken up.
130. Nanne and Bergamo 1993.
131. Ibid.
132. Ibid.
133. Reprinted in *Revista Con-Spirando,* December 1993.
134. Ibid.
135. Ibid.
136. "Mi posición frente a la descriminalización y la legalización del aborto como ciudadana cristiana y miembra de una comunidad religiosa es una forma de denunciar el mal, la violencia institucionalizada, el abuso y la hipocresía que nos envuelven, es una apuesta por la vida, es pues en defensa de la vida" (*Revista Con-Spirando* 1993).
137. See Gebara and Bingemer 1989, 1–19, 91.
138. Ibid., p. 3. Gebara and Bingemer propose this in a Mariological context, but the same anthropological principles can be seen guiding their overall theological approach. The

pluri-dimensional anthropology "takes into account the different dimensions of humankind as it has evolved through history and as countless elements have left their mark on it. The human being is not primarily a definition but rather a history within space and time. . . . human beings are not first good and then corrupted, not first corrupted and then saved, but rather humans are this whole complex reality striving to explain themselves . . ." (Gebara and Bingemer 1989, 10–11).

139. Ibid., p. 14.

140. Gebara 1987.

141. Gebara 1994, 80.

142. Ibid., 77.

143. Ibid., 82.

144. Ibid., 85–86.

145. Aquino 1992, 160.

146. Portugal 1989, 5.

147. Ibid., p. 6.

148. Ibid.

149. Ibid.; Saporta Sternbach et al. 1992, 402.

150. Richard 1994, 94.

151. Ibid., 100.

152. On feminist theological perspectives on abortion, see especially Harrison 1983; Harrison 1985, 115–34 (together with Shirley Cloyes).

153. Harrison 1983, 6.

154. "We have a long way to go before the sanctity of human life will include genuine regard and concern for every female already born . . ." (Harrison 1985, 115).

155. Ibid., p. 123.

156. Harrison 1983, 9.

157. Ibid., p. 16. She also discusses at length how the understanding of when life begins has been changing through the history of theology.

158. Ibid., p. 122.

159. In working with poor women, feminists learned that so-called taboo issues such as sexuality, reproduction, or violence against women were interesting and important to working-class women—as crucial to their survival as the bread-and-butter issues emphasized by the male opposition. Latin American feminists began redefining and expanding the prevailing notion of revolutionary struggle, calling for a revolution in daily life (Saporta Sternbach et al. 1992, 404).

160. See Molyneux 1985, 1988; Randall 1992. The Sandinista government was not only reluctant to confront the Catholic Church, whose hierarchy already supported the political opposition. Many of the Sandinista leaders presented views on contraception and abortion that contrasted with those of feminist organizations supportive of the government. The issue of population growth was seen by President Ortega as one of national interest, with the main problem being U.S. genocide in Nicaragua and the contras.

161. Saporta Sternbach et al. 1992, 403.

162. World Health Organization 1996, 2.

REFERENCES

Andolsen, Barbara Hilkert. 1996. "Rights, Reproductive." In *Dictionary of Feminist Theologies*. Edited by Letty M. Russell and J. Shannon Clarkson. Louisville: Westminster/John Knox.

Aquino, María Pilar. 1993. *Nuestro clamor por la vida: Teología latinoamericana desde la perspectiva de la mujer*. San José: Editorial DEI.

———. 1993. *Our Cry for Life: Feminist Theology from Latin America.* Translated by Dinah Livingstone. Maryknoll, N.Y.: Orbis, 1993.

———. 1997. "Teología feminista latinoamericana." In *Balance y perspectivas de la teología de la liberación*, 1997. Edited by Raúl Fornet-Betancourt. Unpublished manuscript (forthcoming).

Benhabib, Seyla. 1992. *Situating the Self: Gender, Community, and Postmodernism in Contemporary Ethics*. New York: Routledge.

Berryman, Phillip. 1995. "Is Latin America Turning Pluralist? Recent Writings on Religion." *Latin American Research Review* 30, no. 3: 107–22.

Boff, Clodovis. 1991. "Epistemología y método de la teología de la liberación." In *Mysterium Liberationis: Conceptos fundamentales de la teología de la liberación,* edited by Ignacio Ellacuría and Jon Sobrino, 1:79–113. San Salvador: UCA Editores.

Boff, Leonardo. 1986. *Y la iglesia se hizo pueblo: "Eclesiogénesis": La iglesia que nace de la fé del pueblo*. 2d ed. Translated by Jesús García-Abril. Santander: Editorial Sal Terrae.

Boff, Leonardo, and Clodovis Boff. 1989. *Cómo hacer teología de la liberación*. 3d ed. Translated by María Antonieta Villegas. Bogota: Ediciones Paulinas.

———. 1990. *Introducing Liberation Theology*. 4th ed. Translated by Paul Burns. Maryknoll, N.Y.: Orbis.

Carr, Anne E. 1990. *Transforming Grace: Christian Tradition and Women's Experience*. San Francisco: Harper & Row.

Cerutti Guldberg, Horacio. 1988–1989. "Actual Situation and Perspectives of Latin American Philosophy for Liberation." *Philosophical Forum* 20, no. 1–2: 43–61.

———. 1992. *Filosofía de la liberación latinoamericana*. Mexico: Fondo de Cultura Económica.

———. 1995. Introduction to *Filosofías para la liberación: ¿Liberación o filosofar?* Toluca: Universidad Autónoma del Estado de México. Unpublished manuscript (forthcoming).

———. 1996. "Pensamiento y compromiso social." Unpublished manuscript.

Code, Lorraine. 1992. *What Can She Know? Feminist Theory and the Construction of Knowledge*. 2d ed. Ithaca: Cornell University Press.

Cuesta, Bernardo. 1987. "Nuevo enfoque de la moral: La perspectiva de la moral latinoamericana." *Ciencia tomista* 114, no. 3: 595–621.

Documentos de Medellin: IIa Conferencia General del Episcopado Latinoamericano. 1969. San José: Ludovico.

Dussel, Enrique. 1974. "Alienación y liberación de la mujer en la iglesia (Un tema de la erótica teologal)." In *Caminos de liberación latinoamericana*. Buenos Aires: Latinoamérica Libros.

———. 1985a. *Filosofía de la liberación*. 3d ed. Buenos Aires: Ediciones La Aurora.

——. 1985b. *Philosophy of Liberation*. Translated by Aquilina Martinez and Christine Morkovsky. New York: Orbis.
——. 1987. *Filosofía ética de la liberación*. Vols. 1–2. 3d ed. Buenos Aires: Ediciones La Aurora.
——. 1988. *Filosofía ética de la liberación*. Vol. 3. 3d ed. Buenos Aires: Ediciones La Aurora.
——. [1980] 1990. *Liberación de la mujer y erótica latinoamericana*. 4th ed. Bogota: Editorial Nueva América, 1990.
——. 1992. "Filosofía de la liberación como práxis de los oprimidos." *Carthaginensia* 8: 395–413.
——. 1995. *The Invention of the Americas: Eclipse of the Other and the Myth of Modernity*. Translated by Michael D. Barber. New York: Continuum, 1995.
Dutting, Gisela. 1993. "The Concept of Reproductive Rights: Reflections from Experiences." *Women's Global Network for Reproductive Rights Newsletter* 44 (July-September): 2–3.
Engel, Mary Potter, and Susan Brooks Thistlethwaite. 1990. "Introduction: Making the Connections among Liberation Theologies around the World." In *Lift Every Voice: Constructing Christian Theologies from the Underside*, pp. 1–15. San Francisco: Harper & Row.
Firestone, Shulamith. 1971. *The Dialectic of Sex: The Case for Feminist Revolution*. New York: Bantam.
Fox, Thomas C. 1995. *Sexuality and Catholicism*. New York: Braziller.
Gebara, Ivone. 1987. "La opción por el pobre como opción por la mujer pobre." *Concilium* 214: 463–72.
——. 1994. *Teología al ritmo de mujer*. Translated by Miguel Angel Requena Ibáñez. Madrid: San Pablo.
Gebara, Ivone, and María Clara Bingemer. 1989. *Mary: Mother of God, Mother of the Poor*. Translated fby Phillip Berryman. Maryknoll, N.Y.: Orbis.
Harrison, Beverly Wildung. 1983. *Our Right to Choose: Toward a New Ethic of Abortion*. Boston: Beacon.
——. 1985. *Making the Connections: Essays in Feminist Social Ethics*. Edited by by Carol S. Robb. Boston: Beacon.
Heinämaa, Sara. 1996. *Ele, tyyli ja sukupuoli: Merleau–Pontyn ja Beauvoirin ruumiinfenomenologia ja sen merkitys sukupuolikysymykselle*. Tampere: Gaudeamus, 1996.
Molyneux, Maxine. 1985. "Mobilization without Emancipation? Women's Interests, the State, and Revolution in Nicaragua." *Feminist Studies* 11, no. 2: 227–54.
——. 1988. "The Politics of Abortion in Nicaragua: Revolutionary Pragmatism—or Feminism in the Realm of Necessity?" *Feminist Review* 29 (Spring): 114–32.
Moreno Rejón, Francisco. 1991. "Moral fundamental en la teología de la liberación." In *Mysterium Liberationis: Conceptos fundamentales de la teología de la liberación,* edited by Ignacio Ellacuría and Jon Sobrino, 1:273–286. San Salvador: UCA Editores.
Moser, Antônio. 1984. "Como se faz teologia moral no Brazil hoje." *Revista Eclesiástica Brasileira* 174 (June): 243–64.
——. 1991. "Sexualidad." In *Mysterium Liberationis: Conceptos fundamentales de la teología de la liberación,* edited by Ignacio Ellacuría y Jon Sobrino, 2:107–24. San Salvador: UCA Editores.

Mulieris dignitatem: Carta Apostólica del Sumo Pontifice Juan Pablo II sobre la dignidad y la vocación de la mujer con ocasión del año mariano. 1988. In Pope John-Paul II, *Encíclicas y otros documentos*. Vol. 3. San José: Libro Libre.

Nanne, Kaike, and Mónica Bergamo. 1993. "Entrevista a Ivone Gebara: 'El aborto no es pecado.'" Reprinted in *Revista Con–Spirando* 6.

Nueva evangelizacion, promoción humana, cultura cristiana (New evangelization, human development, Christian culture). 1992. IV Conferencia General del Episcopado Latinoamericano, Santo Domingo, 12–28 October. Conclusiones. A conference draft.

Petchesky, Rosalind Pollack. 1995. "From Population Control to Reproductive Rights: Feminist Fault Lines." *Reproductive Health Matters* 6 (November): 152–61.

Portugal, Ana María. 1989. Introduction to *Mujeres e iglesia: Sexualidad y aborto en América Latina,* edited by Ana María Portugal, pp. 1–8. Washington, D.C.: Catholics for a Free Choice; Montevideo: D.F. y Distribuciones Fontamara.

Randall, Margaret. 1992. *Gathering Rage: The Failure of Twentieth-Century Revolutions to Develop a Feminist Agenda*. New York: Monthly Review Press, 1992.

Richard, Pablo. 1981. "La ética como espiritualidad liberadora en la realidad eclesial de América Latina." *Cristianismo y Sociedad* 69–70: 51–59.

———. 1986. "Vorwort: Mit den Augen der Dritten Welt." In *Befreiung von unten lernen: Zentralamerikanische Herausforderung theologischer Praxis.* Edited by Bernd Päschke. Münster: Edition Liberación. Foreword and afterword by Pablo Richard.

———. 1987. *La fuerza espiritual de la iglesia de los pobres*. San José: Editorial DEI, 1987.

———. 1988. "El fundamento material de la espiritualidad." *Christus* 613–14 (March-April): 88–95.

———. 1991. "La teología de la liberación en la nueva coyuntura: Temas y desafíos nuevos para la década de los noventa." *Pasos* 34 (March-April): 1–8.

———. 1994. "A Theology of Life: Rebuilding Hope from the Perspective of the South." In *Spirituality of the Third World: A Cry for Life,* edited by K. C. Abraham and Bernadette Mbuy–Beya, pp. 92–108. Maryknoll, N.Y.: Orbis. Papers and reflections from the Third General Assembly of the Ecumenical Association of Third World Theologians, January 1992, Nairobi, Kenya.

Ruether, Rosemary Radford. 1983. *Sexism and God–Talk: Toward a Feminist Theology*. London: SCM Press, 1983.

———. 1987. *Contemporary Roman Catholicism: Crises and Challenges*. Kansas City: Sheed & Ward, 1987.

———. 1990. "Catholicism, Women, Body, and Sexuality: A Response." In *Women, Religion, and Sexuality: Studies on the Impact of Religious Teaching on Women,* edited by Jeanne Becher, pp. 221–32. Geneva: WCC Publications.

———. 1991. "Diferencia y derechos iguales de las mujeres en la iglesia." *Concilium* 238: 373–82.

Ruiz Garcia, Samuel. 1994. "Documento pastoral sobre el aborto." Reprinted in *Debate feminista*, March, pp. 435–53.

Saporta Sternbach, Nancy, et al. 1992. "Feminisms in Latin America: From Bogotá to San Bernardo." *Signs* 17, no. 2: 393–434.

Schutte, Ofelia. 1988–1989. "Philosophy and Feminism in Latin America: Perspectives on Gender Identity and Culture." *Philosophical Forum* 20, no. 1–2: 62–84.

——. 1991. "Origins and Tendencies of the Philosophy of Liberation in Latin American Thought: A Critique of Dussel's Ethics." *Philosophical Forum* 22, no. 3: 270–95.

——. 1993. *Cultural Identity and Social Liberation in Latin American Thought*. Albany: State University of New York Press.

Segundo, Juan Luis. 1985. *Theology and the Church: A Response to Cardinal Ratzinger and a Warning to the Whole Church*. Translated by John W. Diercksmeier. Minneapolis: Winston.

Slater, David. 1994. "Power and Social Movements in the Other Occident: Latin America in an International Context." *Latin American Perspectives,* Spring, pp. 11–37.

Smith, Ruth L. 1989. "The Evasion of Otherness: A Problem for Feminist Moral Construction." *Union Seminary Quarterly Review* 43, no. 1–4: 145–61.

Stanley, Liz, and Sue Wise. 1993. *Breaking Out Again: Feminist Ontology and Epistemology*. 2d ed. London: Routledge.

Vidal, Marciano. 1991. "Resituar la teología moral a la luz de la teología de la liberación: Aportes fundamentales de la 'ética de la liberación' al discurso teológico–moral general." In *Teología y liberación: Religión, cultura y ética: Ensayos en torno a la obra de Gustavo Gutiérrez,* 3:399–415. Lima: CEP.

Vuola, Elina. 1997. *Limits of Liberation: Praxis As Method in Latin American Liberation Theology and Feminist Theology*. Helsinki: The Finnish Academy of Science and Letters, no. 289.

World Health Organization. 1996. *Revised 1990 Estimates of Maternal Mortality: A New Approach by WHO and UNICEF.* Geneva: WHO.

9

Locating the Absolutely Absolute Other: Toward a Transmodern Christianity

Roberto S. Goizueta

In the early days of the twenty-first century, we are becoming increasingly cognizant of the complex and profoundly ambiguous character of the historical process of globalization. If globalization was heralded as a panacea for the world's social ills not long ago, the Third World debt crisis we are currently witnessing has made us painfully aware of the underside of globalization: billions of human beings are excluded from the process altogether. What is clear is that, whether or not we are willing to admit it, contemporary societies will survive together or they will die together.

The roots of the globalization process can arguably be traced to the conquest of the Americas in 1492, an event that, as Enrique Dussel has so perceptively noted, signaled the birth of the modern period:

> Amerindia is part of "modernity" from the moment of the conquest and colonization (the mestizo world in Latin America is the only one as old as Modernity), since it is the first "barbarian" which Modernity needs in order to define itself. . . . European Modernity is not an *independent*, autopoietic, self-referring system, rather it is a "part" of the "world-system": its *center*. Modernity, then, is a phenomenon that globalizes itself; it begins with the *simultaneous* constitution of Spain with reference to its "periphery." . . . *Simultaneously*, Europe . . . will *constitute itself* as center over a growing "periphery."[1]

From its very origins and of its very essence, modernity needs and demands a center *and* a periphery; conquest is not the consequence but the origin of modernity. "Before the rest of Europe," writes Dussel, "[Spain and Portugal] subjected the Other to conquest and to the dominion of the *center* over the *periphery*. Europe then established itself as the 'center' of the world (in the planetary sense) and brought forth modernity and its myth."[2] The individualism and rationalism so often associated with the origins of modernity are, conversely, merely derivative, legitimating consequences of the center-periphery global structure:

> The "rationalization" of political life (bureaucratization), of capitalist enterprise (administration), of everyday life (Calvinist or Puritan asceticism), the disembodiment of subjectivity . . . the non-ethical character of every economic or political action (understood exclusively as technical engineering), the suppression of practical-communicative reason replaced by instrumental reason, the solipsistic individualism which denies community, etc. . . . are *effects* of the realization of that function proper to Europe as "center" of the world-system.[3]

Though not always as manifestly or explicitly as during the conquest of the Americas, religion has played and will continue to play a crucial role in the process of globalization. Today, cultural and economic "globalization" is accompanied by a resurgence of religious fervor of every stripe, especially in the Third World. And in the United States, a multitude of "spiritualities" are emerging and filling the vacuum created by the decreasing influence of institutional religion, especially mainline Protestant Christianity. (The fastest-growing segment of the publishing business in the United States is the area of "spirituality," broadly defined.) For the first time in recent memory, religious (again, broadly defined) television programs have achieved broad-based popularity and financial success, not just on Sunday mornings but in prime-time programming.

Accompanying the noninstitutional forms of spirituality evident in such programs as *Touched by an Angel,* however, the rise of religious fundamentalism seems anomalous in its emphasis on precisely the kinds of religious institutions and traditions that noninstitutional and New Age spiritualities eschew. These latter reflect a smorgasbord, or pastiche, of religious influences, while the former put forth fervid apologias for rigidly defined and interpreted religious traditions; the "wishy-washiness" of one exists alongside the often triumphalistic self-righteousness of the other. The old Chinese blessing has been realized: we do indeed live in interesting times.

Yet what is merely of interest to some—especially scholars and social critics—is of life-and-death significance to others. The floruit of postmodernity in the last decades of this century has affected almost every area of scholarship, including theology and the academic study of religion. We must question, however, the extent to which the learned discussions concerning what the "cultured despisers" call postmodernity have impacted the everyday lives of the vast majority of persons, who today remain shackled by poverty, injustice, and despair. Neither the idyllic, unstructured eschaton foreshadowed by postmodern prophets of ambiguity, "Otherness," and "difference" nor the economic-technological liberation promised by the proponents of "globalization" has seemed to materialize. Indeed, Third World peoples are becoming increasingly restive and defiant in the face of such promises.

In providing us with intellectual and practical instruments for understanding and confronting the anomalies of globalization, and the role of religious forces in that process, no contemporary author is more helpful than Enrique Dussel. Rooted in the histories of the Latin American peoples, his thought nevertheless engages fully contemporary trends in Europe and North America. Not content to remain enclosed within the confines of those histories, however important, he insists on bringing the particularities or "difference" of those histories to bear on the larger, global processes. In other words, Dussel's writings remind us that a truly liberative interpretation of reality will be one that resists both the postmodern absolutization of particularity and the modern negation of particularity (or absolutization of *one* single particularity, the European). Rather, liberative praxis and theory grounds itself in the particular, in the sociohistorical particularity of difference, precisely in order to disclose and affirm the universal implications of difference; the preferential option for the poor generates truth claims valid not only for the poor but for all peoples. "The *Philosophy of Liberation*," insists Dussel, "is a counterdiscourse, it is a critical philosophy born on the periphery (and from the victims, the excluded ones) with a global intent. It has an *express* consciousness of its peripheral character and its exclusion, but at the same time it has a global intent."[4]

GOD, EUCHARIST, AND GLOBALIZATION

Much of the virulent criticism suffered by Dussel and other Latin American liberation theologians over the past thirty years has accused them of reducing faith to political action, thereby eliminating the transcendence of God. Contrary to the opinion of such critics, however, the work of Enrique Dussel and the other principal liberation theologians has been concerned precisely to *safeguard* the transcendence of God over against those theologies which, either implicitly or explicitly, would identify God with the status quo, that is, with the existing social order and the self-interest of those groups benefiting from the status quo. It is this very issue which, in my opinion, must be the starting point for the consideration of Dussel's understanding of religion and, more specifically, Christianity in an age of globalization.

Drawing on the thought of Emmanuel Levinas and Xavier Zubiri (along with that of Martin Heidegger and others), Dussel has elaborated a highly differentiated, sophisticated understanding of "Otherness" and "the Other." In doing so, he has engaged contemporary European and North American conversations on Otherness and difference. The salience and significance of Dussel's discourse on Otherness stem from the fact that, unlike that of most of his interlocutors from the North Atlantic area, that discourse is grounded in a preferential option for the victims of history, the victims of modern conquest. This starting point is precisely what allows Dussel to both preserve the transcendence of God and avoid the tendency of North Atlantic theologies to reduce that transcendence to an ahistorical abstraction. The philosophical analogue of this expressly theological tendency has been the empty, ahistorical notion of Otherness and difference evident in postmodern philosophies.[5] Dussel proposes, instead, a highly concrete, historical Otherness as the mediator of transcendence. "The Other," argues the Argentine philosopher, "will be the other woman or man: a human being, an ethical subject, the face as an epiphany of living, human corporality. . . ."[6] And the word "epiphany" is not incidental to his argument, for the corporeal, historical, human Other is indeed the revelation of the "absolutely absolute Other," namely, God: "'The Other' . . . has an analogous meaning: it can be the anthropological Other . . . or it can be the absolutely absolute Other: other not only than the world but than the very cosmos."[7]

If God is transcendent, that is, if God is not comprehensible within our "world," then God will be found first (not exclusively, but preferentially) in those loci that are themselves incomprehensible within our world, those loci that are anomalous or nonsensical within the world-system. Above all, the transcendent God will be encountered among those persons who, as victims of the world-system, have been excluded from the world-system and thus remain invisible to the "center." Any religious worship that does not *begin* on the periphery, among the excluded victims of the world-system, can only be worship of an idol, a god who legitimates the system of domination either explicitly (e.g., the conquest) or implicitly (e.g., the privatized faith of bourgeois Christianity). True worship originates in "liberative praxis with respect to and for the oppressed in whom one recognizes the epiphany of infinite Exteriority."[8] In Christological terms, the transcendent God will be encountered, first, on the Cross; the Crucified Christ, and all those other persons who continue to be crucified today, must be the starting point of Christian theological reflection.

According to Dussel, the intrinsic connection between the struggle for justice and the worship of a transcendent God is nowhere more evident than in the eucharistic liturgy, which is always at the same time a religious act and an *economic* act. The eucharistic bread is at the same time "the substance of the eucharistic offering" and "the fruit of common human labor, exchanged among those who produce it."[9] Since the bread is "the objectivized life of the worker" whose labor makes possible our liturgical celebration, "those who offer God bread stolen from the poor give God the life of the poor as their offering."[10]

The connection between justice and worship and, conversely, between domination and idolatry is powerfully made manifest in the life of the Spanish missionary Bartolomé de Las Casas. Arriving in the New World as an *encomendero,* Las Casas was eventually ordained a priest, joined the Dominican Order, and committed himself to the evangelization of the Indians. Though known for his charitable treatment of the Indians in his care, Las Casas nevertheless did not initially see a contradiction between his Christian, priestly calling and his role as an *encomendero.* This changed as he was preparing to celebrate the eucharistic liturgy one day. The Spanish Dominican underwent a conversion that would dramatically alter his understanding of his Christian faith, his priestly vocation, his role as a missionary, and, especially, his relationship with the indigenous peoples of America. While studying the Scriptures in preparation for his homily, Las Casas came across a text from the Book of Sirach (34:18–22):

> Tainted his gifts who offers in sacrifice ill-gotten goods!
> Mock presents from the lawless win not God's favor.
> The Most High approves not the gifts of the godless.
> [Nor for their many sacrifices does he forgive their sins.]
> Like the man who slays a son in his father's presence
> is he who offers sacrifice from the possessions of the poor.
> The bread of charity is life itself for the needy,
> he who withholds it is a person of blood.
> He slays his neighbor who deprives him of his living;
> he sheds blood who denies the laborer his wages.[11]

This text opened Las Casas's eyes to the meaning and import of the liturgical action he was about to undertake. As a slave owner, he would be offering to God bread and wine that were the fruit of the labor of the Amerindians in his care, men and women who themselves remained poor and hungry. In the Holy Sacrifice of the Mass, he would be offering to God the "objectivized lives" of his workers; he would be sacrificing *their* lives on God's altar, thereby committing the worst kind of sacrilege and blasphemy. Any God who would countenance and accept such a sacrifice could not be the transcendent, just God of the Scriptures but a mere idol, a "god" who legitimates murder.[12]

This realization led to Las Casas's subsequent decision to release his slaves, himself becoming a tireless defender of the Amerindians. If the Spanish conquistadores and missionaries condemned the Indians for their practice of human sacrifice, he argued, the Spanish Christians themselves were guilty of human sacrifice when, in the Mass, they presented their offerings of bread and wine, which were products of the blood, sweat, and tears extracted from the indigenous peoples of the Americas. If the Amerindians did not accept the message preached by the Spanish missionaries, such recalcitrance was not only understandable but, indeed, justifiable; what the Amerindians rejected was not the God of love preached by the Spanish but the "god" of hatred and violence manifested in their actions. In that context, the Indians had not only a right to reject "Christianity" but a duty to do so, for what they were rejecting was not Christianity but an idolatry more destructive than the "idolatry" practiced by the indigenous peoples themselves.[13]

As Las Casas had so prophetically argued, if at the very heart of the Christian faith is the assertion that "God is love," a genuine respect for and love of the Other is a condition of the possibility for any authentic evangelization. In other words, an authentically intersubjective praxis is the fundamental criterion of the credibility and validity of the Christian faith: "everyone who loves is begotten of God and has knowledge of God. . . . God is love, and he who abides in love abides in God, and God in him" (1 John 4:7, 16).

Thus the possibility of an authentic intercultural dialogue with non-European Christians, or an authentic interreligious dialogue with non-Christians, in no way precludes the possibility of making normative truth claims; such dialogue neither presupposes nor demands a radical relativism which would, like some poststructuralist postmodern philosophies, reject the possibility of making such truth claims altogether. On the contrary, if the central Christian truth is precisely that "God is love" (i.e., God is intersubjective praxis), then that truth is validated when and where one finds true respect for and dialogue with the Other. Conversely, where such intersubjectivity is absent, regardless of any express claims, the truth of Christianity is being denied. Paradoxically, then, a genuine openness to non-Christians and, a fortiori, to non-European Christians is a necessary precondition for Christian evangelization and the development of a truly global Christianity. Truth is constitutively and essentially intersubjective, communitarian.[14]

Here, Dussel points to a fundamental fallacy underlying both modern and postmodern philosophies, namely, the assertion that universality and particularity are incommensurable and dichotomous. Once such an epistemological fallacy is assumed, globalization can only be understood in one of two ways: either globalization involves the dominative imposition of one particular (e.g., culture or religion) on other particulars, or it involves a radical relativism that would deny any particular the ability to make universal truth claims. If the former alternative is characteristic of modernity and the latter characteristic of postmodernity, Dussel posits what he calls a "*trans*modern" alternative:

> Each culture's claim to universality . . . indicates the presence of the universal material principle in all of them, what opposes ethnocentrism. Ethnocentrism or cultural fundamentalism is the attempt to impose on other cultures the universality which *my (our) culture* "claims", before having been intersubjectively and interculturally demonstrated. Each culture's serious claim to universality should prove itself through rational dialogue when there is confrontation with among cultures. And when cultures confront each other historically, dialogue is possible within the universal claims of each . . . The discursive intersubjective moment is precisely the procedural moment that *formally* makes possible such dialogue. . . .[15]

MATERIALITY, RELIGION, AND GLOBALIZATION

Precisely because religious and cultural intersubjectivity is always also material, socioeconomic intersubjectivity, such dialogue presupposes the existence of just material relationships between the participants: genuine dialogue is impossible between master and slave, between a conquistador bearing firearms and an unarmed Aztec woman, between a wealthy person (who refuses to surrender his or her wealth) and a poor person, or between a Christianity backed by economic and political power and Third World religions without access to such resources.

Dussel's emphasis on the socioeconomic mediation of *all* human relationships, including those specifically and explicitly religious in character, remains one of his most significant contributions to contemporary discussions of multiculturalism and globalization. Postmodern discourse on Otherness and difference remains inevitably abstract if it remains inattentive, not only to the cultural, racial, gender, and religious mediations of Otherness but, even more concretely, to its socioeconomic mediations—which are also implied in the Others: "a universal principle of all ethics, especially critical ethics [is] the principle of the obligation to produce, reproduce and develop the concrete human life of every ethical subject in community."[16] If religion and, a fortiori, liberative religion is concerned with human life, it must be concerned with that life in its utter concreteness, namely, in its materiality and corporeality. These, in turn, imply productive and reproductive relationships. This is in no way to suggest that human life can be reduced to production and reproduction. Rather, the spiritual, religious, transcendent character of the person is always mediated by (*not* reduced to or identified with) socioeconomic relationships. These latter necessarily influence (not "determine") the former.

The import of Dussel's argument here is that it guards against an individualistic, ahistorical understanding of globalization. An authentic globalization, which would allow and respect both the particularity of different cultures and their common "claim to universality" (not just the claim to universality of European cultures), means much more than simply an "openness" to other points of views and religious traditions. Such a globalization presupposes a just global economic order, one that would foster the participation of all peoples. In fact, argues Dussel, the contemporary understanding of globalization in the West promotes an affective "openness" while simultaneously fostering and legitimating the active exclusion of billions of human beings from the economic order. Paradoxically, such "globalization" and exclusion go hand in hand. "One should not forget," notes Dussel,

> that the final or macro context of this *Ethics* [of liberation] is the process of *globalization*; but, unfortunately and simultaneously, that process is the *exclusion* of the great majority of humanity: the victims of the world-system. Globalization-Exclusion refers to the double movement in which the global Periphery finds itself caught: on the one hand, the presumed modernization within the formal globalization of capital . . . but, on the other hand, the material exclusion . . . of the victims of that presumed civilizing process.[17]

The starting point for any process of globalization that would pretend to promote a genuine pluralism among world cultures and religions must thus be a particular sociohistorical locus, namely, that of the *excluidos*. "In the victim, dominated or excluded by the system," asserts Dussel, "concrete, empirical, living human subjectivity is revealed, it appears in the last instance as an 'appeal': it is the subject who now can-not-live and cries from pain. It is the appeal of the one who exclaims: 'I am hungry!' 'Feed me, please!'"[18]

In short, an authentic globalization presupposes a praxis of liberation that takes as its starting point the *vida cotidiana,* the everyday suffering and struggles of the victim (of a dominative, false "globalization") and seeks a transformation of those social structures that deny the victim his or her historical agency as a human subject. In other words, the condition of the possibility for creating a "community of communication" wherein a dialogue among equals can effectively take place is the liberation of those peoples who today remain excluded from participation in such dialogue because they are not deemed to be full historical subjects. The precondition for such global *equality* is, paradoxically, a *preferential option* for the victims: "The person who functions critico-ethically *should* (is obliged to) liberate the victim, as a participant (due to the 'situation' or 'position', Gramsci would say) in the same community to which the victim belongs. . . . This obligation has a universal claim; that is, it is true for every act and in every human situation."[19]

TOWARD A TRULY GLOBAL CHRISTIANITY: RETRIEVING THE GALILEAN JESUS

Enrique Dussel's analyses of modernity and postmodernity offer crucial insights into the future of Christianity in an age of globalization. His analyses call for a radical reconceptualization of these categories. More specifically, Dussel calls for a relocation of these categories, a transposition of modernity and postmodernity from their European and North American *theoretical* locus to a Third World *practical* locus. Until now, scholarly analyses of modernity and postmodernity, emerging out of the European and North American academy, have read and interpreted these categories through rationalistic, individualistic lenses, invariably reducing these categories to theoretical constructs which, in turn, "produce" historical consequences.

This process is nowhere more evident than in the Western tendency to identify the origins of modernity with the emergence of the Cartesian *ego cogitans* and, consequently, the practical, material, historical features of modernity with the effects or consequences of Cartesian rationalism. Dussel's recent writings present a thoroughgoing, systematic critique of this profoundly rationalistic interpretation of history. Instead, argues Dussel, the Cartesian ego is the *culmination* of the process initiated by the conquest.[20] This "conversion" is only possible, however, when, like Bartolomé de Las Casas, we view history not from the perspective of the conquistador but from the perspective of the indigenous person. More specifically, it becomes possible only when we enter into practical solidarity with the indigenous person and all victims of domination. Then and only then is modernity revealed, not as merely a worldview or philosophical system but as, much more profoundly, a *way of being, of acting in the world.*

Such a reinterpretation of modernity yields, in turn, a reinterpretation of postmodernity. For, with the possible exception of Emmanuel Levinas, postmodern thought remains beholden to and limited by the very rationalistic, individualistic modern epistemologies that it seeks to subvert; poststructuralist postmodernism presupposes that which it rejects. It presupposes an incommensurability between particularity and universality, between knowledge and reason, between affect and intellect. Indeed, it presupposes them precisely in order to subvert them. If moderns reject the first element in each polarity in order to absolutize the second, postmoderns reject the second in order to absolutize the first. What moderns and postmoderns have in common, then, is their inability to affirm the organic unity of corporeal life *as it is lived*. Both, therefore, silence the cries of the victims: the first by ignoring them and the second by relativizing their universal claims. Modernity suffocates those cries while postmodernity prevents them from making any normative, universal truth claims.

Dussel here effects the same transposition of the theory-praxis relationship that is so central to the thought of all liberation theologians. He, however, has been able to work out this transposition from within contemporary modernity-postmodernity debates in a unique, groundbreaking way, thereby lending his own voice as a Latin American to a conversation that has for too long been limited to North Americans and Europeans. Caught between the Scylla of a modern universalistic univocity and the Charybdis of a postmodern fragmented plurivocity, we are thus offered a way out. Dussel posits a third possibility, the "transmodern," which will avoid both modern universalism and postmodern relativism. While modernity and postmodernity presuppose the same dichotomous, dualistic epistemology, *trans*modernity is characterized by a holistic, organic epistemology rooted in the act of solidarity with the victims of history. Precisely because, as opposed to the operative paradigms (or "myths") of modernity and postmodernity, the notion of transmodernity refers not so much to a new way of thinking as to a new way of living in relation to Others, it rejects the subject-object dichotomy underlying both the modern and postmodern paradigms.

Likewise, the transmodern paradigm proposed by Dussel rejects both the conceptualist rationalism of modernity and the irrationalism of poststructuralist postmodernism. Instead, transmodernity makes possible the retrieval and revaluation of the excluded cultures, the cultures and lives of the victims precisely as *rational*:

> I seek to overcome modernity not through a postmodern attack on reason based on the irrational incommensurability of language-games. Rather, I propose a transmodern opposition to modernity's irrational violence based on the *reason of the Other*. . . . The Other encompasses the peripheral colonial world, the sacrificed Indian, the enslaved black, the oppressed woman, the subjugated child, and the alienated popular culture—all victims of modernity's irrational action in contradiction to its own rational ideal. . . . The discovery of the ethical dignity of the Other purifies Enlightenment rationality beyond any Eurocentric or developmentalist communicative reason and certainly beyond purely strategic, instrumental rationality. . . . Thus I hope to transcend modern reason not by negating reason as such, but by negating violent, Eurocentric, developmentalist,

> hegemonic reason. . . . The transmodern project achieves with modernity what it could not achieve by itself—a corealization of solidarity, which is analectic, analogic, syncretic, hybrid, and mestizo. . . .[21]

Concretely, then, what are the implications of Dussel's argument for religion and, more specifically, for Christianity in an age of globalization? What might a transmodern Christianity look like? What seems clear is that, whatever the answer to those questions, they will not be found primarily in the places and among those groups that have heretofore—or at least in the last five centuries—defined Christianity. No longer can we assume that the "center" of the Christian world is in the North Atlantic region. A transmodern Christianity will privilege one particular social location, that of the victims who, as *excluidos*, most fully reveal the "absolutely absolute Other," thereby safeguarding the transcendence of God against the ever present tendency to identify God with historical success and conquest. The Christianity of the twenty-first century will be defined above all by precisely those excluded peoples who represent the underside of the much vaunted "globalization" currently under way. Whatever the wishes and expectations of ecclesiastical elites and their epigones, the Christianity of the future will increasingly look like the Christianity of Third World peoples (whether these living in their native countries or having emigrated to First World countries). And that Christianity is, as Dussel suggests, "syncretic, hybrid, and mestizo," born out of a solidarity that "bonds center to periphery, woman to man, race to race, ethnic group to ethnic group, class to class, humanity to earth, and occidental to Third World cultures."[22]

Like so much of Third World Christianity historically, the Christianity of the next century will likely be characterized by a "mestizaje," a mixture and confluence of multiple races, cultures, and religions.[23] A Christianity that takes seriously the challenge of an authentic globalization will reject the impenetrable barriers that North Atlantic Christianity has erected between the "saved" and the "damned," between the Same and the Other. If borders between cultures, religions, and nations are necessary to preserve particular identities, those borders will nevertheless allow for *mutual* interaction.[24] A border need not function as a frontier that only expands and excludes; it need not function as a safeguard for the illusory purity of one side. Even if too often denied in practice, an alternative understanding of the border is implicit in the mestizo history of Latin America:

> A border is the place at which two realities, two worldviews, two cultures, meet and interact. . . . at the border growth takes place by encounter, by mutual enrichment. A true border, a true place of encounter, is by nature permeable. It is not like medieval armor, but rather like skin. Our skin does set a limit to where our body begins and where it ends. Our skin also sets certain limits to our give-and-take with our environment, keeping out certain germs, helping us to select that in our environment which we are ready to absorb. But if we ever close up our skin, we die.[25]

Indeed, the emergence of a truly *global* Christianity will represent the retrieval of a long-forgotten element central to the very essence of the Christian faith, namely, the *Galilean* character of God's revelation in the person of Jesus Christ; a truly global Christianity will be a Galilean Christianity, one born on the border between cultures and rooted in the experience of mestizaje.

The multicultural border experience is central to the Christian Gospels. That the Jesus portrayed in the Gospels is repeatedly identified as a "Galilean" is crucial to understanding the Christian kerygma and crucial to understanding the global character (in the genuine sense articulated by Dussel) of the Christian message. In the Synoptic accounts, Jesus comes from Nazareth in Galilee, meets his end in Jerusalem, and, finally, returns to Galilee, where he appears to the apostles after his resurrection (Mark 14:28; Matthew 26:32; 28:7, 10, 16).

The Galilee into which Jesus was born was very much a borderland, a distant part of Palestine bordering on the non-Jewish populations of Syria, Philippi, and the Decapolis. It was thus often viewed by first-century Jews as "a Jewish enclave in the midst of 'unfriendly' gentile seas. . . ."[26] The Roman administrative cities of Sepphoris and Tiberias were centers of Hellenistic–Roman culture. Consequently, Jewish worship in these cities was "dramatically affected by the influences of Hellenistic–Roman culture and political domination."[27] "It is possible, perhaps even likely," argues Richard Horsley, "that some Jews considered themselves faithful even while they utilized what would be classified as pagan or Greco–Roman symbols as a matter of course in their everyday lives."[28]

This Galilean reality is at the very heart of the Christian doctrine of the Incarnation, the belief that God became human in *this particular* person, Jesus of Nazareth. As Virgilio Elizondo observes, "The overwhelming originality of Christianity is the basic belief of our faith that not only did the Son of God become a *human being*, but he became *Jesus of Nazareth*. . . . Jesus was not simply a Jew, he was a Galilean Jew; throughout his life he and his disciples were identified as Galileans."[29]

And precisely as a Galilean, as someone who came from an area of "mixed" races, cultures, and religions, Jesus was scorned and excluded:

> Scripturally speaking, Galilee does not appear important in the unfolding drama of salvation and, culturally speaking, at the time of Jesus, it was rejected and despised by the Judean Jews because of the racial mixture of the area and its distance from the temple in Jerusalem. For the Jews of Jerusalem, Galilean was almost synonymous with fool! . . . The Galilean Jews appear to have been despised by all and, because of the mixture of cultures of the area, they were especially despised by the superiority-complexed Jerusalem Jews. Could anything good come out of such an impure, mixed-up, and rebellious area?[30]

The answer to this question is what Elizondo calls the "Galilee Principle": God chooses "what is low and despised in the world" (1 Corinthians 1:28):

> The apparent nonimportance and rejection of Galilee are the very bases for its all-important role in the historic eruption of God's saving plan for humanity. The human scandal of God's way does not begin with the cross, but with the historico-cultural incarnation of his Son in Galilee. . . . That God has chosen to become a Galilean underscores the great paradox of the incarnation, in which God becomes the despised and lowly of the world. In becoming a Galilean, God becomes the fool of the world for the sake of the world's salvation. What the world rejects, God chooses as his very own.[31]

If the Jewish center of power in Jerusalem could not conceive that God's word could be revealed in such a region ("Search and you will see that no prophet is to rise from Galilee" [John 7:52]), it is precisely in the midst of this multicultural reality that, in the person of Jesus Christ, God's love and power are made manifest.

Thus the universal truth revealed in Jesus Christ is, paradoxically, the truth of the intrinsically intersubjective foundation of all reality. It is in the Galilean *particularity* of *this* person, Jesus of Nazareth, that we encounter the *universal* truth revealed in the person of Jesus Christ: God is love. As Las Casas so courageously insisted, any form of Christianity that allows or legitimates exclusion and domination is, ipso facto, a denial of the very truth it professes and, de facto, an example of idol worship. A truly global Christianity is thus a Christianity that allows for the crossing of borders, thereby affirming in practice the belief that truth is intersubjective, that God is love.

By insisting on the concrete, historical mediation of Otherness in the face of the victim and, hence, in the concrete, historical mediation of the "absolutely absolute Other," Enrique Dussel empowers us to reread history from its underside and thus move beyond the false alternatives posed by (post)modern cultures. Those false alternatives have yielded a "globalization" made possible only by excluding literally billions of human beings from full participation, as equals, in the globalization process. An authentic globalization, one that is truly pluralistic, demands that the process be initiated, not from within the centers of power, but from the margins, from the borderland. And it is precisely there, on the border, that Christians will encounter the liberating God who chose to become human in the person of a Galilean Jew, a mestizo who defies all attempts to turn borders into barriers that separate or into frontiers that expand and exclude. It is in Galilee, then, that a truly global Christianity will be born.

NOTES

1. Enrique Dussel, *Ética de la liberación en la edad de la globalización y de la exclusión* (Madrid: Editorial Trotta, 1998), p. 68 (my translations in this and all subsequent quotations are from this work).

2. Enrique Dussel, *The Invention of the Americas: Eclipse of "the Other" and the Myth of Modernity* (New York: Continuum, 1995), p. 17.

3. Dussel, *Etica de la liberación*, pp. 61–62.

4. Ibid., p. 71.
5. Ibid., p. 63.
6. Ibid., p. 16.
7. Enrique Dussel, *Filosofía ética latinoamericana* (Mexico: Edicol, 1977–1980), 5:51.
8. Ibid., p. 77.
9. Enrique Dussel, "The Bread of the Eucharistic Celebration As a Sign of Justice in the Community," in *Can We Always Celebrate the Eucharist?* ed. Mary Collins and David Power (New York: Seabury, 1982), pp. 56–65.
10. Ibid., pp. 60–62.
11. This text is quoted in the brilliant, inspiring work on the life and thought of Las Casas written by Gustavo Gutierrez, *Las Casas: In Search of the Poor of Jesus Christ* (Maryknoll, N.Y.: Orbis, 1993), p. 47.
12. Ibid., pp. 46–61.
13. Ibid., pp. 154–89.
14. Dussel, *Etica de la liberación*, pp. 202–6.
15. Ibid., p. 164 n. 340.
16. Ibid., p. 91.
17. Ibid., p. 17.
18. Ibid., p. 524.
19. Ibid., p. 559.
20. Dussel, *Invention of the Americas*, pp. 27–48.
21. Ibid., pp. 137–38.
22. Ibid.
23. From its very beginnings on the border between the Jewish and Greco–Roman worlds, Christianity has been a "mestizo" religion, one that incorporates, adapts, and "Christianizes" elements from surrounding cultures and religions. Indeed, the Iberian Catholicism brought to the Americas was itself marked by centuries of intermingling with the Jewish and Muslim cultures and religions.
24. "The quest for human purity," contends Virgilio Elizondo, "defines boundaries and very quickly excludes those who have been the product of territorial transgression. There seems to be an inner fear that the children of territorial transgression pose the deepest threat to the existence of the group and to the survival of its purity." *The Future Is Mestizo: Life Where Cultures Meet* (Bloomington, Ind.: Meyer-Stone, 1988), p. 80.
25. Justo González, *Santa Biblia: The Bible through Hispanic Eyes* (Nashville: Abingdon, 1994), pp. 86–87.
26. Douglas Edwards, "The Socio-Economic and Cultural Ethos of the Lower Galilee in the First Century: Implications for the Nascent Jesus Movement," in *The Galilee in Late Antiquity*, ed. L. Levine (New York: Jewish Theological Seminary of America, 1992), p. 54.
27. Richard A. Horsley, *Archaeology, History, and Society in Galilee: The Social Context of Jesus and the Rabbis* (Valley Forge, Pa.: Trinity Press International, 1996), p. 55.
28. Ibid., p. 63.
29. Virgilio Elizondo, *Galilean Journey: The Mexican-American Promise* (Maryknoll, N.Y.: Orbis, 1983), p. 49.
30. Ibid., p. 53.
31. Ibid.

10

Theory and Alterity: Dussel's Marx and Marion on Idolatry

Michael D. Barber

Alterity questions theory, and yet it takes theory to show how theory has not adequately responded to alterity. Even the philosophical discourse that theorizes about theory and alterity cannot escape this dialectic between theory and alterity. Idolatry, a theological concept that plays a central role in the thought of Karl Marx as reconstructed by Enrique Dussel and in Jean-Luc Marion's philosophy of religion, involves in each case a certain theoretical subsumption of alterity. This chapter presents, compares, and contrasts these two conceptions of idolatry, and traces their implications for the broader philosophical question of the relationship between theory and alterity. Finally, it suggests that neither critique of idolatry can do without the other, if one is to escape new forms of idolatry.

IDOLATRY IN DUSSEL'S READING OF MARX

Enrique Dussel, author of a widely acclaimed three-volume study of Marx based on a careful reading of Marx's manuscripts in Berlin and Amsterdam, admits that his attention to the religious aspects of Marx's thought depends on the practical exigencies of Latin America, Asia, and Africa—all seeking to reconcile their own religious traditions with versions of the Marxist theory that, in Dussel's view, supports the struggle for justice on these continents.[1]

Dussel reads Marx's general theory, which establishes the framework for his more specific account of idolatry, differently from the tradition, which regularly understands Marx as a materialistic reaction to Hegelian idealism. Instead, Dussel begins by pointing out linguistic and conceptual parallels between Marx's *Grundrisse* and the theology of Friedrich Schelling, who opposed G. W. F. Hegel's philosophy of identity. For Schelling, God stands outside of Hegelian being—and hence is Nonbeing—and this Nonbeing by a free act brings into being an independent creation, which contrasts with Hegelian being insofar as it is the necessary unfolding of the divine essence itself. According to Dussel, Marx appropriated this idea of a creative source (*fuente* or *Quelle* as opposed to *fundamento* or *Grund*) for living labor (*trabajo vivo, lebendige Arbeit*) which, while it is nothing with respect to the capitalist system, creates its value. Even though capitalism acts as though it were the Ground, self-founding, like the Hegelian deity, Marx goes behind it to its font, to the laborer who, at the first moment of meeting with capitalist, confronts capital as noncapital, as the nonbeing *(no-ser)* or nothing *(nada)* of capital, who, once subsumed (i.e., hired and thus integrated within the system), creates from out of his or her nothingness the surplus value that makes capitalism possible. Having taken his starting point outside the system, Marx utilizes Hegel's logic as a model for the unfolding of the capitalism system itself, in which the "essence of capital" appears through its various manifestations. While it is true that Marx transforms Hegel's logic into an economics, his novel contribution, in Dussel's view, is not to materialize idealism but to commence with living labor, an analogate of the Schellingian God and to undertake a hermeneutics of capitalism from the perspective of the forgotten alterity that produces capitalist wealth from out of its own poverty and nothingness.[2]

Citing Marx's *Grundrisse,* Dussel starts with living labor, which is the status of the laborer outside of capitalism, "dissociated from all means of work and objects of work," a "total despoliation, a nudity of all objectivity," "absolute poverty," "an objectivity that coincides with [his or her] mere corporeality." But this labor "posits itself as the capacity to work, *deprived of substance, endowed merely with necessities* [e.g., hunger] and faced with its *alienated reality*, which does not pertain to it but to the other person (i.e., the captialist); labor does not posit is own *reality* as *being-for-itself*, but mere *being-for-the-other*." Having contractually exchanged his or her capacity to work in return for a wage that pays for a day's subsistence, the laborer produces a value beyond that which is paid for his or her subsistence—the surplus value—out of which capitalists take their profits, cover other expenses (e.g., rent) and absorb losses, as when supply exceeds demand. On this interpretation of capitalism, Marx's famous quote from *Capital* comes as no surprise: "Capital is dead labor which only reanimates itself, in the manner of a vampire, by sucking on living labor, and it lives the more living labor it sucks on."[3]

This general framework forms the setting for Marx's theory of idolatry, which for Marx essentially involves conceiving an object as a fetish, "apart from any 'relationship-with.'" The following statement by Marx "posits the entire theme frontally," in Dussel's opinion:

> This wise man [Samuel Bailey]—of the Ricardian school—converts value (*Wert*) into something absolute, into a "quality of things" instead of seeing in it something relative, [as pertaining to] the relation between things and social labor, a social labor in which private work is the basis and in which things are not determined as something endowed with autonomy, but rather are the mere expression of social production.[4]

According to the process that Marx calls the "absolutization of value," merchandise to be sold on the market may be considered without regard for the production relationships that brought it into being and, in particular, without regard for the labor time that workers invest in it beyond the time for which they are recompensed for their maintenance and that yields a surplus value for the capitalist. When this process occurs, products seem to possess their value as a mysterious, innate property, as if somehow the capitalist paid for the making of products and then released them on the market, where they gain a profit beyond what was paid to produce them; as if the value "self-valorized" from itself; as if a self-creation of value from nothing were occurring. When the relationship between the production process that endowed products with value as well as the role of labor in that production process, namely, to produce surplus value, is forgotten, merchandise begins to manifest the characteristics of an idol:

> This value, as the ultimate essence of capital, turns into a fetish: made by human hands—like the *baals* or idols that the prophets of Israel denounced—although it is nothing more than human *labor*, objectivated and accumulated [in the thing], yet it has turned into an autonomous power, autonomized, which begins to possess the attributes of a "god": a subject, self-creating from nothing, eternal, infinite. . . .[5]

Marx develops the metaphor of idolatry by presenting capital as Moloch, to whom is offered the blood of its human victims, as the "'foreign god' that was enthroned on the altar next to the old false gods." This god, proclaiming "the production of surplus value as the unique and ultimate end of humanity," demands "asceticism, renunciations, and sacrifices: frugality and prudence, the despising of mundane pleasures."[6]

Dussel rightly observes that this theological language pervades the entirety of Marx's discourse, and he shows how Marx extends the metaphor of idolatry to the different determinations of capital. Merchandise, goods in the marketplace, present themselves as having value of themselves, autonomous, absolute, without relation to the living labor that produced them under the conditions of social labor (as opposed to communitarian conditions). Similarly, money, whose value of exchange is the general equivalent of the exchange values of all other merchandise, appears as detached from the merchandise produced by living labor and so as all the more bearing its value of itself. Hence Marx describes it as the god Mammon and depicts it as bearing the stamp of the beast of the Apocalypse. In a third determination, when living labor is subsumed within the capitalist system as salaried labor, even labor (specifically the force of labor) itself begins to appear as a component of the capitalist system, like machinery, as a piece of merchandise to be purchased in the marketplace. At this point the worker, ignorant of his own surplus-value producing power, believes that the totality of his or her realized labor is equivalent to the salary he receives, as if his or her labor were a thing of value meeting another thing (money) mystically endowed with value in the marketplace, where they are exchanged.

Furthermore, machinery confronts the worker as an animated monster, maintaining an "autonomous figure" over against the worker, as dead labor that "sucks on the force of living labor," even though labor produced the (surplus) value out of which the machinery was purchased. The product becomes another locus of fetishization when the capitalist equates the price of cost (what it costs to produce the product) with the originary value of the product (as it comes from the factory) and when the capitalist makes a profit by selling at a market price above this price of cost or originary value. In this way, the true origins of profit, unpaid surplus labor, are "obscured," "mystified," or "hidden," and it would seem that the product's fetching more value (in the market) than went into it (in the factory) is a kind of creation out of nothing. Likewise, in the circulation of goods (supply and demand), it is not seen how supply and demand do not produce value but rather distribute surplus value (e.g., low demand calls for lower prices that will cut into one's surplus value). Similarly, the circulation of capital, as for instance financial capital (e.g., the gaining of interest), takes place on a plane far removed from the production process and living labor; here, capital appears all the more to generate value of itself. But interest paid (and thus also received) is taken out of the surplus value produced by labor. Marx concludes by noting how the process of fetishization progresses from the production process (close to living labor) to the commercial/financial capital, which seems most able to produce value from itself.[7]

For Dussel, prior economies did not hide the labor of the slave in antiquity or the tribute of the servant in feudalism, but capitalism is adept at hiding the sphere of labor behind the veil of capitalist processes. There is no appearance of idolatry in capitalism, since only capital, merchandise, circulation, interest, and so on, are visible. However, insofar as these mechanisms of capitalism seem both to act autonomously, of themselves, creating value and exacting sacrifices, and to conceal the human productive activity that created their value in the first place, they are idols. Furthermore, just as idolatrous Hegelian being substituted for the true Creator of being, namely, God, who is presented in Schelling's theology and who from outside the system freely creates being out of nothing, so capitalist processes substitute for the true creator of their value, from beyond the system, also creating out of its nothingness: living labor. Thus simply by showing these seemingly secular processes of capitalism as religious, in terms of gods and divine forms, Marx, as understood by Dussel, effectively develops a religious critique of political economy, and thus Marx, for Dussel, is doing far more than exercising the sense of humor for which he was renowned.[8]

Furthermore, in this crossing of discourses, the religious critique of political economy also becomes a critique of religion itself insofar as it is wedded to a false economic god. Thus Marx shows himself preeminently an atheist with respect to capitalism, but in so doing, in Dussel's view, he adopts an antifetishist and anti-idolatrous stance very much akin to that of the prophets of Israel or the founder of Christianity. Dussel contends that this interpretation of Marx as the antifetishist of capital places him within the tradition of a religion of liberation, whose God Marx in no way opposes.[9]

Although Dussel's interpretation presents a Marx open to religion insofar as Marx never embraced indiscriminate atheism or intuitive materialism (such as Ludwig Feuerbach's) or cosmological materialism (such as Joseph Stalin's), Dussel also readily and repeatedly acknowledges that Marx was only an implicit, fragmentary, and negative theologian, who, while not formally pursuing theology, opened a new theological space. In addition, Dussel is cognizant of the limitations of Marx's theology, which constitutes a first negative moment of a dialectic that denies idolatrous gods, as did the prophets. But this negative moment ought to be the propadeutic to the affirmation of an "alterative Absolute" who is revealed in the poor, the widow, or the orphan, who lies on the exteriority of the system and who breaks in, interpellates, calls, and provokes from this exteriority.[10]

The great contribution of Marx, however, is to have delved beneath previous economic discourse, which, for all its pretense to being "scientific," regresses to a "primitive" form of religiosity—idolatry—as Dussel points out in an essay entitled "'Habermasian Theology and Economy."

> Once the "market" or "capital" has been disconnected from "living labor," "economic science" *(Wirtschaftwissenschaft)* occupies itself essentially with fetishized problems within the horizon of the market (or exclusively from the perspective of capital). It becomes concerned with the calculation of the rate of profit (of the valorization of value), without any relation with the person, value (as the objectivation of life), or ethics (as a judgment on "unpaid" labor).[11]

For Dussel, only by beginning with the Other on the exteriority of capital, the one annihilated by the usual economic discourse, can one detect the fetishization of such economic discourse, a fetishization that needs as its condition this annihilation of the Other and effectively promotes it.

> Fetishist autoaffirmation of the totality supposes the negation, the annihilation of the exteriority, of the other or the-other-than-capital.
>
> As a moment practically unrecognized by the previous Marxist tradition, Marx always takes his starting point from the exteriority of living labor, *the other than capital*, whose elimination being supposed, capital is fetishized. This fetishization needs as its condition the annihilation of the other than capital.[12]

IDOLATRY IN MARION'S PHILOSOPHY OF RELIGION

Jean-Luc Marion's philosophy of religion also involves a sustained struggle against idolatry. For Marion, the idol is not so much a false god versus the "true God" of the prophetic discourse, but rather a "manner of being for beings," a mode "of apprehension of the divine in visibility," to be contrasted with its alternative, the icon. The decisive moment in the erection of an idol, according to Marion, has to do not with its fabrication but with the gaze that falls and fixes upon it, making the idol rather than the idol making the gaze. Whatever the idol may be—thing, man, woman, idea, or god—it returns the gaze to itself, acting as a mirror that dazzles the gaze in such a way that its character as a mirror remains invisible, just as in Dussel's view the idols of capitalism are not seen at first as idols. Marion notes how in idolatry the gaze comes to rest, admitting nothing beyond itself and thus separating off from itself for the first time the "invisable," that which cannot be aimed at or taken into view, precisely because it is shut out of view. However much an obscure glimpse of the divine might become visible in the idol, the idolatrous gaze delimits the divine to its own measure.[13]

The idol ultimately becomes understandable by contrast with the icon, in which one looks only to find oneself more radically looked at. Instead of the invisible mirror of the idol that sends the human gaze back to itself alone and cordons off the "invisable," the icon opens in a face that gazes at human gazes in order to summon them to its depth. Thus the icon renders the invisible visible by teaching the gaze to correct itself, to move from visible to visible as far as infinity, to surpass itself by never freezing on a visible. If the idol is constituted through an "aisthesis" that imposes a measure on it, in the case of the icon, an "apocalypse" substitutes for the aisthesis, since the icon recognizes no other measure than its own and its own infinite excessiveness, offering an "abyss that the eyes of men never finish." While the idol dazzles its observers through an invisible mirror, those regarding the icon themselves become visible mirrors of an "invisible gaze that subverts us in the measure of its glory." Whereas the idol is always in the possession of the gaze, which is its solitary master and which runs the risk of seeing no more than its own face without even perceiving itself doing the gazing—like the idolatry of capitalism that is not even recognized as idolatry—another face opens upon one's eyes in an icon.[14]

The idol "can exercise its measure of the divine by concept" insofar as the idolater attempts to comprehend the incomprehensible and refuses to be measured by the excessiveness of the invisible that enters into visibility through infinite depth in the icon, which "obliges the concept to welcome the distance of infinite depth." This conceptual idolatry, by which one presumes to know the divine, define it, and measure it to the dimension of one's grasp, forms the presupposition of the various forms of atheism that often reject the limited concepts of God that idolatries present. Hence, as Marion puts it, every conceptual atheism "is worth only as much as the concept that contains it." Thus Nietzsche's account of the "death of God" is directed against the "moral God," but, like the critique of idolatry by Dussel's Marx, such a critique of an idol does not eliminate the possibility of God but even provokes the coming of a new dawn of the divine beyond the twilight of discredited gods. Marion's extension of the idea of idolatry to conceptual atheism, in which human discourse determines God by equating God with a concept and thus transforms God into "God," one of the infinitely repeatable "gods," nevertheless raises a self-referential question that Marion himself recognizes. If the suspicion of idolatry reaches to every conceptual enterprise concerning God, is the suspicion itself disqualified? That is, one would seemingly have to have at least some nonidolatrous conception of God in order to be able to identify an idolatrous conception. Must one not be somewhere beyond idolatry in order to identify the locale in which idolatry takes place?[15]

To provide just such an overarching perspective, Martin Heidegger makes use of the ontological difference that separates Being from the beings which it transcends even as it reveals itself in them. Onto-theology, insufficiently appreciative of the ontological difference, has reduced Being to an *ens,* the *ens supremum,* which grounds beings from itself as *causa sui.* In Heidegger's view, by conceiving God under the figure of efficiency and foundation, one ends up reducing God to an idol, before whom one is unable to pray, sacrifice, fall to one's knees, play music, or dance—aspects discoverable to anyone attentive to the revelatory power of Being. Although God cannot be equated with Being, like Being, God resists being reduced to a being among other beings and instead needs to be approached with openness to revelation. Heidegger's deployment of the ontological difference to escape onto-theological idolatry raises for Marion the further question as to whether beyond the idolatry proper to metaphysics, there appears another, second idolatry, proper to the Heideggerian thought of Being as such.

> The thought that thinks Being as such cannot and must not apprehend any thing but beings, which offer the path, or rather the field of a meditation, of Being. Any access to something like "God," precisely because of the aim of Being as such, will have to determine him in advance as a being.[16]

Marion aligns Heidegger with Thomas Aquinas, whose preference for *summum ens* over *summum bonum* as the first divine name sets him at odds with St. Denys in a medieval debate that Marion reconstructs. When Denys prefers the goodness of God over God's being, it is not a matter of assigning *summum bonum* as a better name for God, but rather in the apprehending of God's goodness a dimension is cleared "where the very possibility of categorical statement concerning God ceases to be valid, and where the reversal of denomination into praise becomes inevitable." By contrast, for Aquinas the intellect takes precedence and the first thing the intellect conceives is being (the *ens*), since everything is knowable only inasmuch as it is. For Marion, Aquinas's strategy involves a questionable privileging of one *access* to God over another.

> The *ens* appears first, at least on condition that one takes the point of view of human understanding; the primacy of the *ens* depends on the primacy of a conception of the understanding and of the mind of man. The primacy of the *ens* has nothing absolute or unconditional about it; it relies on another primacy, which remains discreetly in the background. But it is this second primacy that one must question, since it alone gives its denomination to the *ens,* to the detriment of the good (and of the Dionysian tradition). . . . From the point of view of the understanding apprehending an object, the *ens* comes first. From the point of view of the Requisite, that gives itself without limit, goodness remains first.[17]

But even if Heidegger succumbs to a second form of conceptual idolatry, how does one think outside of the ontological difference? Would this not condemn one not to be able to think at all? Marion admits that God must be thought only under the figure of the unthinkable. Moreover, since that which I cannot think still remains a concern of my thought and so is thinkable to me, Marion sees the need for an unthinkable that exceeds as much what can be thought as what cannot be thought. The task comes down to one of "working love conceptually."[18]

What seems to be at stake ultimately is the manner of access one adopts toward God, of letting one's language be taken up on the basis of the mystical (rather than epistemological) demands of that to which the language pertains (and to call it an "object" of that language is already to assume a scientific approach). After all, as Marion observes, "A gift . . . does not require first that one explain it, but indeed that one receive it," and, in fact, one's haste to explain may disclose an inability to receive.[19]

In *L'Idole et la distance*, via a linguistic pragmatics, Marion develops more fully this question of access. To begin, Marion examines the language of categorical predication in which one seeks to state the essence of something, to indicate it adequately, to coincide with what it exhausts as an object, to comprehend a subject by the sum of that which is predicated of it, in brief, to produce objects and eliminate the distance between subject and predicate. But the predication, in the sense of the rigor of predicative language, is unacceptable a propos of God and "its impossibility protects us from an idolatry—of supposing that this predication itself is fitting *(convenable)*." By contrast, Denys turns from the *dire* of the language of predication to the word "praise *(louer)*," adopting another model of discourse that would not settle for predicating of God either a category or an inverse category (e.g., "God has no name" instead of "God is this name"), but that rather involves an inverting of the usage of predicative categories at all. Hence, Denys resorts to propositions of the type "*x* praises the Requisite (God) as *y*" and thereby surpasses mere categorical predication by introducing a metalinguistic elaboration that makes explicit the relationship between the praiser and God through the determination *y*. In addition, by employing this type of formulation, the praiser indexes the inadequacy of the attribute being applied to God by the refusing to identify God with the property *y*, which is not being categorically predicated here. This performative language game of praise also clearly incorporates the speaker within its performance because it depends on the play between three terms: the propositional enunciation ("I praise you as *y*"), the praiser, and God. Without the amplified pragmatics that includes these three terms, the discourse of praise would deteriorate into a semantics of predication "as impertinent as it is idolatrous" insofar as it abstracts from and forgets the richer, more reverent matrix from which it emerges. Although this language game of praise requires much further elaboration, Marion manages to enumerate several of its distinctive properties: its significations do not require verification, its prayerful expressions are neither true nor false (as Aristotle also observed), it belongs to a quasi-liturgical form of life, and so on. This game needs to be understood on its own terms.[20]

After such a critique, though, one might ask how theological theory would ever be possible again. And yet there are numerous indications that Marion himself recognizes the need for theological theory, as, for instance, when he insists on the need for apologetics to make it clear that faith has need of speech or listening for its transmission and that one can make use of any means to transmit faith. Perhaps Marion's purpose is not to abolish theological theory but to ensure that it incorporates a concern for alterity—a purpose to which he gives expression when he cautions that "only the Said that lets itself be said by the Father can assure the pertinence of our *logos* concerning him," that the theologian must interpret texts "from the point of view of the Word," and that properly theological language must "let itself be taken up again on the basis of the . . . mystical demands of that to which it pertains." Indeed, the very works by which Marion insists on the rights of the alterity of God within theology, such as *God without Being* or *L'Idole et la distance,* exemplify theological theory at its best, illuminating the insufficient attention to the alterity of God in other theological approaches, the ontotheologists, Heidegger, and Aquinas. And yet certainly Marion's works do not fall under the discourse genre of the Dionysian praiser? Just as Edmund Husserl must occupy a transcendental theoretical plane in order to map out regions of being and the approaches appropriate to them, must not Marion be doing something similar in order to make the case that God differs from other "objects" since one approaches God more appropriately through praise than through theory? Does this theoretical perspective of Marion's suppress the alterity of God in the very endeavor to uncover and preserve it? The dialectic between theory and alterity seems to have just barely begun.[21]

AUSEINANDERSETZUNG: DUSSEL'S MARX AND MARION, THEORY AND ALTERITY

Idolatry in Dussel's reconstruction of Marx is to be located in the theoretical discourse of economics insofar as it detaches its categories from labor, which first produces value out of its nothingness, and attributes to the products of labor (the work of human hands) and the exchange and circulation of these products the power to generate value from nothing and to elicit the sacrificial worship appropriate to a deity. By identifying such theoretical discourse as idolatrous and superstitious, for all its pretense to scientificity, Dussel's Marx illustrates the role of economic theory in the suppression of alterity even as it hides this suppression beneath a theoretical veneer. Thus Marx, according to Dussel, recovers the forgotten exteriority of capitalist totality—through a religious discourse as critical of economic theory as it is of religious discourse uncritical of its own economic presuppositions. For Marion, in the idol the gaze delimits the divine to its measure as opposed to the icon that subverts the gaze, and one can further exercise idolatry by delimiting God through concepts or even by imposing the constraints of the ontological difference on God such that God becomes merely a revelatory locus of Being beyond concepts. For Marion, the alterity of God demands not so much a better theological theory but the forsaking of theory itself in favor of a prayerful/praiseful approach to the Other of theory. Both Dussel's Marx and Marion undertake a critical ethical hermeneutics of economical and/or theological theories. Commencing with alterity, they dismantle those theories that occlude the Other by hiding the Other's production of value or subjecting the Other to epistemic/ontological conditions at odds with the approach the Other requires, interposing an idol between the theoretician and what is God or godlike.

Without gainsaying the achievements of either of these thinkers, one can ask whether these theories, which highlight the deficiencies of other theories with respect to alterity, are themselves sufficiently self-critical. While Dussel's reconstruction of Marx criticizes economic and religious theories that bury the other of capitalism, one wonders whether this reconstruction is sufficiently self-critical of its own potential to marginalize the Other. There is evidence for a lack of self-critique when one compares Dussel and Marion, for while Dussel's interpretation of Marx treats the menace to alterity posed by *capitalist* theory, Marion criticizes theological theory's suppression of alterity *insofar as it is theory*. Hence, Marion, by turning his attention to whether theory itself is suppressive of alterity, at a minimum raises the question of the relationship between theory and alterity to a more self-referential pitch than Dussel does, at least in *Las metáforas teológicas* and "El concepto de fetischismo en el pensamiento de Marx." Given the history of the twentieth century, there is some danger in any version of Marxism that would locate the danger to alterity *only* in capitalist theory without a critical examination of theory itself, including its own theory, in reference to alterity. Moreover, it would not be self-consistent for Dussel to develop Marx's critique of capitalist economic theory on behalf of alterity and never at some point inquire into whether theory in general, including his own, might be detrimental to alterity, although such an inquiry, on a more abstract level than his more concrete examination of capitalist economic theory, need not directly jeopardize his conclusions on the concrete level.

Whereas Dussel's weakness may lie in overlooking the full impact of alterity on theory, Marion tends to favor alterity at the expense of theory. Marion engages in a project of criticizing theological theory that has not dealt adequately with God's alterity, and yet to fulfill just this project Marion in *L'Idole et la distance* must articulate a rather sophisticated linguistic pragmatics theory of language. In addition, in *God without Being*, when he claims that language must be taken up "on the basis of the mystical (rather than epistemological) demands of that to which the language pertains," he inevitably presupposes, without thematizing, a metaphysical/epistemological/linguistic framework that specifies what "approaches" are appropriate or not to what "objects," since God is such that theory is not as appropriate a mode of approach as praise. While the demands of God may well be mystical rather than epistemological, the statements constituting the theory in *God without Being* that coordinates those demands with an appropriate approach, though they can elude self-reflection, plainly seem to have epistemological/metaphysical/linguistic status. Theoretical discourse is required to illustrate the inappropriateness of a theoretical approach to what is approached. Furthermore, none of the clearly theoretical statements of *L'Idole et la distance* or *God without Being* take the form of a Dionysian performative of praise, however much they may seek to preserve the alterity of God that other theological theories slight. Without a self-reflection on the status of the statements in his own works, Marion can fall prey to a similar kind of critique as that which Jacques Derrida proposed to Emmanuel Levinas, namely, that his aspirations to the infinitely Other resulted in an empiricism understood as a philosophical pretension to nonphilosophy—a futile attempt to arrest philosophical discourse without philosophizing.

The criticisms being raised here do not impugn the contributions of Dussel and Marion, but rather suggest that a more generalized problematic arises within their work—the tension between theory and alterity—and that this problematic needs to be considered by a self-reflective, philosophical (transcendental?) approach that makes the problematic explicit at a level above and beyond their concrete analyses of capitalist theory or theology. For how can one consistently criticize other theories for negating alterity without inquiring about the potentiality of one's own theory to negate alterity (Dussel)? Or how can one criticize other theories for not taking account of alterity insofar as they are theories, all the while that one is making use of theory to produce such criticism (Marion)? In other words, how does one incorporate all the critical force of alterity within one's own theory and not abandon theory? Just as Levinas's phenomenology of alterity underlies Dussel's and Marion's concrete analysis of economic and religious theory, perhaps Levinas's own methodological self-reflections on his phenomenology can aid in reconciling this tension between theory and alterity emergent within the works of those for whom he has been a mentor.

Early in *Totality and Infinity*, Levinas undertakes a phenomenology of alterity that does not take for granted the commonsense view of relationships as reversible, where terms are indifferently read from left to right and vice versa, where A goes unto B as B to A. Although such reversibility forms a constitutive strata of meaning within human relationships (to which Levinas builds a bridge by his explanation of the Third), Levinas returns to a forgotten moment of experience, where one faces another person who, radically separate, morally commands one to service from a height and brings a notion of meaning prior to one's *Sinngebung,* independent of one's initiative and power. The Other facing the I introduces an unsettling moment, the permanent possibility of contestation, into a common discourse that will forbid it forever from being merely the unfolding of a prefabricated internal logic. If one were to conceive this relationship as only reversible, as A going unto B as B to A, with A and B equal to each other, one would have to prescind from this moment of facing where the other is given above oneself. One would have to adopt a reflective position (one could call it C) and look upon oneself and the other as interchangeable components "in a system visible from the outside," with the Other no longer accessible as he or she would be to an I facing him or her.[22]

But later in *Totality and Infinity* Levinas undertakes a very interesting self-reflective turn on the entire theoretical perspective of *Totality and Infinity* itself. Although fully aware that the I and the Other cannot enter into a cognition that would encompass them and crystallize them into a system, he yet asks, "Do we not name them together?" *Totality and Infinity* is itself a theoretical work that places the I and the Other on a conceptual map, inevitably viewing them from an outside perspective. Even as it discusses the I facing the Other, given from a height, it itself is not *in* that I-position facing the Other, but rather describes it and locates the I and Other as two loci with varying features characterizing each locus. As if to accentuate the difference between a theoretical perspective that describes the lived experience of the Other and that lived experience itself, Levinas continues by pointing out that the formal synthesis that names the I and the Other is part of a "conjuncture of transcendence, breaking the totality." In other words, subtending the theory that describes the I and the Other, that encompasses them within a totality, that belongs to what is "said," there is a lived, saying relationship in which the Other is experienced as given from a height, as the interlocutor to whom I am responsible, as an unsettling source of ever possible contestation. Later in *Otherwise than Being*, Levinas continues to highlight this difference between theory about the Other and the disruptive, lived experience of the Other by describing how theories function, laying out and synchronizing terms, binding them in syntheses, collecting dispersion into a presence, tying up all loose ends, even including within themselves whatever might threaten to undo a system of thought (e.g., as the pragmatists always incorporate a principle of fallibilism within their theories). But again beneath every "said" that ties everything together, that thematizes the Other, is a saying relationship toward the Other who, "as interlocutor, has quit the theme that encompassed him, and upsurges inevitably behind the said." And even when I thematize this one who upsurges, he or she would upsurge behind that thematization, and so on and so on. Levinas, more aware of his own theoretical approach and less of an empiricist than Jacques Derrida, believes even as early as *Totality and Infinity*, admits in *Otherwise than Being* that all philosophy, everything said, all theory, *including his philosophy*, involve a betrayal of the saying in the said. As a consequence, he would, at least at this point, seem to concur with Marion's critique of theory as theory and thus to engage in a more profound self-critique than Dussel.[23]

But one might object that Dussel's lack of self-critique of his own theory pertains only to his works on Marx and that in these works one ought not expect a more general account of theory, since these works focus specifically on capitalist theory and its suppression of alterity. However, in other works at key moments where such a generalized self-critique after the pattern of Levinas would have been appropriate, Dussel never undertakes such a self-reflection. For instance, in his

Method for a Philosophy of Liberation, subtitled *Analetic Overcoming of the Hegelian Dialectic*, the third edition of which was published in 1991, Dussel examines his own philosophical method, dubbed the "analectical method." But here he falls short of the critique of theory that emerged both from Derrida's critique of Levinas in "Violence and Metaphysics" and from Levinas's response to this critique in *Otherwise Than Being*, published seventeen years earlier than Dussel's *Method.* In a key methodological section, number 26, entitled "El Método Analéctico," Dussel proposes an analectic method that "goes beyond *(más allá)*" a dialectic, "that comes from a higher level (ana-)" than a dialectic, a method that takes its starting point from the other "beyond (*más allá*) the system of the totality." Dussel continues by highlighting the difficulties of thinking the Other from a discursive perspective within the totality. He emphasizes the need for an intrinsically ethical relationship with the Other that is not merely theoretical, that partakes of an ethos of liberation, that involves being silent before the other, listening like a disciple and placing faith in the word of the Other even though it appears confusing to one's own ontological horizon of comprehension. For all the insight fulness of these comments on alterity, which surpass Levinas in several ways, Dussel does not go quite far enough, since he points to the inadequacies of thinking the Other from within the totality without reflecting on the theory by which he portrays the inadequacy of this thinking from within the totality. He fails to reflect upon *this* theory, *these* statements, *his own* theory, which, as theory, still encompasses the other within a totality, like the totalities that Dussel criticizes, however much Dussel's criticisms of these totalities improves upon them.[24]

At another point in this same discussion, linked to the difficulty of understanding the Other from within the totality, Dussel explores whether his discourse about the Other brings the Other within the same. Here Dussel climbs to the same pinnacle from which Levinas asked, "Do we not name them together?" and then proceeded to see the inadequacy of theory to the Other, since it lays out in the mode of "along side of" the direct, full-face welcome of the Other. But at this point, Dussel does not reflect, as Levinas, on the limits of theory, but instead introduces a new distinction. One ought not state that the Other is "different" from the Same, for the word "different" makes reference to Heidegger's ontological difference in which the being that differs from Being still belongs to Being, in which the individual still falls within the totality. Rather, in order to keep the Other from falling under the totality from which he or she is to be distinguished, Dussel recommends that one speak of a metaphysical "distinction," which "indicates better the diversity and does not suppose a previous unity." Precisely where Dussel might have recognized the limitations to theorizing as such, he instead ends up refining further his own theoretical distinctions and protects his own theory from the intrusion of alterity.[25]

This blind spot in Dussel's thinking reappears in *The Invention of the Americas,* where he argues that he is advancing a transmodernity that will not negate reason as such but violent Eurocentric, developmentalist, hegemonic reason, as if his own transmodernist recuperation of the "emancipative tendencies of the Enlightenment and modernity" in dialogue with "alterative reason" will be exempt from the limitations that Levinas uncovers. Furthermore, in his most recent work, *Etica de la liberación en la edad de la globalización y la exclusión*, Dussel presents Levinas as valuing rationality as long as it takes its *origin* from alterity and even acknowledges that Levinas redefines philosophy from the point of view of diachrony,[26] but even here he repeatedly bypasses the self-reflective turn in Levinas's thought. For Levinas, rationality not only takes its start from alterity, but it also betrays the very alterity it struggles to describe, limping after its wrestling match with alterity, like Jacob after the encounter at Peniel—as Levinas himself admits with regard to rationality and specifically the very rationality by which he gives his own account of alterity. In this most recent work, it is instructive that in Dussel's entire fourteen-page discussion of Levinas (with the footnotes), including his explanation of the transition to the second Levinas after *Totality and Infinity,* there is no mention of Derrida's "Violence and Metaphysics," the work that pinpointed the paradoxical connection between theory and alterity in Levinas's own thought. Levinas had already begun to appreciate this paradoxical connection in *Totality and Infinity* but dealt with it much more thoroughly in later works, particularly in *Otherwise Than Being*.[27]

Finally, *Etica de la liberación en la edad de la globalización y la exclusión*, which divides into two parts, each with three principles, articulating positive imperatives in the first part and in the second a negative critique when those imperatives are thwarted, introduces telling modifications in Levinas's phenomenology of alterity. For example, prior to the discursive rationality of the Frankfurt School, Dussel locates an "ethical originary rationality" in which one discourse partner recognizes another as equal, since "to argue seriously one must have already recognized the Other as equal." Later in part 2, when this formal morality of equality is violated, the Other is recognized through an "ethical pre-originary rationality" as a victim of the system, dominated, excluded, not as equal but as Other. While Dussel's legitimate point here seems to be to distinguish an interlocutor integrated within the system from the more deeply suffering victim excluded from it, nevertheless when (in ethical originary rationality) he describes the Other, given prior to discursive rationality (prior to the Third in Levinas's terms), as *equal*, the Levinasian emphasis on inequality, asymmetry, and the height of the Other fades from sight. These features of the Other, belonging to any Other, within or outside of the system, and accessible to the attuned phenomenologist, pose an obstacle to any exhaustive theoretical comprehension of alterity. By eliminating this height of alterity (even in preoriginary rationality, since even the victim is not spoken of as commanding from a height), Dussel eliminates a fulcrum for the critique of every theory, including his own. Moreover, these sections of Dussel's thought leave one with the impression that only that theory that produces the victims that ethical preoriginary rationality affirms is oppressive and that all other theory is free from limitations. Finally, would one not be *more broadly* critical of one's own theory if one recognized one's interlocutor within the system as *also* commanding respect, from a height, even though this interlocutor may not suffer as acutely as does the victim outside the system?[28]

Although Levinas envisions the tremors of alterity rattling throughout theory, it must also be pointed out that this critique of theory is only half of Levinas's picture. A case can be made that when Levinas reflected upon his own philosophical development he came to understand that much more than a betrayal of the saying is going on in theory. For the very theory of *Totality and Infinity,* as good phenomenology, refuses to accept uncritically and delves beneath commonsense thinking and the theories under its sway insofar as they have blanketed over the experience of alterity, the ethical summons, the height, the disturbance to tranquil synthesis that the Other provokes. If common sense and its theories betray alterity, then Levinas's phenomenology reduces that betrayal, however much it might still betray the saying in the said, that is, insofar as it is theory at all. Even the critical showing in a said of how the said betrays the saying involves a reduction of that betrayal, since it improves upon a said that proceeds oblivious to the betrayal of the saying, and thus this reduction of the betrayal represents a positive achievement. The very critique of theory as betraying alterity does not result in a disparagement of reason or philosophy, does not result in skeptical paralysis, but gives birth to a new philosophical vocation, a new model of philosophizing: philosophy is called on henceforth to reduce betrayal of the saying in the said.

> It [God] is non-thematizable, and even here is a theme only because in a said everything is conveyed before us, even the ineffable, at the price of a betrayal which philosophy is called upon to reduce. Philosophy is called upon to conceive ambivalence, to conceive it in several times. Even if it is called to thought by justice, it still synchronizes in the said the diachrony of the difference between the one and the other, and remains the servant of the saying that signifies the difference between the one and the other as the one for the other, as non-indifference to the other. Philosophy is the wisdom of love at the service of love.[29]

One could argue that there are many "saids," the theological or economic or sociological, that betray the saying relationship, that there are many theories that support orders where alterity is denigrated, and Levinas here charges theory with the task of reducing such betrayal and denigration, even as his own theory about theory has done. In this regard, Marion and Dussel in his reconstruction of Marx aim at improving on previous theories that betray the saying in the said to a much greater degree than do their own theories. And so both Marion and Dussel can be seen as continuing the project Levinas began when he allowed alterity to penetrate into the inner sanctum of philosophical theory itself.

Still, one ought not deny that Marion and Dussel have yet to integrate the two poles of theory and alterity as satisfactorily as their mentor has. One wonders if perhaps Marion is reluctant to acknowledge the theoretical character of his own critique of theological theory precisely because such an acknowledgment would seem to coopt alterity. Similarly, Dussel may shy away from allowing alterity to shake his own theory perhaps because he fears that he would undermine the very alterity he strives to defend theoretically.

Perhaps, though, this opposition and reconciliation between theory and alterity can lead to a final, increased appreciation of Dussel's contribution. If Dussel criticizes capitalist theory as idolatry by bringing to light the alterity it obfuscates, then the very alterity he rescues needs to act back upon his own ultimate theoretical perspective. The very alterity he upholds requires the self-critique of his own theory. To be sure, such a critique leaves theory more humble, conscious of its limits and deficiencies, and more aware that it starts with alterity and fails it to an extent like all other theories. But it is from this fragile starting point, chastened by alterity and already responsible to it, that theory commences its vocation of seeking to reduce the betrayal of the saying in the said, wherever such a betrayal may take place, whether in economics or theology. In fact, one can be so concerned about not doing justice to alterity and bemoaning reason's limitations and weaknesses, one could be so beset with legitimate Nietzschean and Levinasian scruples about theory, that one would might never get around to the task of theoretical liberation that Levinas envisions as co-originary with and flowing from his critique of theory—a task that Dussel has already pursued in depth.

In this regard, Dussel's frequent reliance on the spatial metaphor of exteriority can be illuminating, even though the metaphor also appears to move in the realm of reversible relationships where A and B, interior and exterior, are fixed in relationship to each other by a rational view from outside, at the level of what Levinas calls the Third. In the light of Dussel's proclivity to use this metaphor, however, it is no wonder that he has been able to accommodate the rationality-oriented Frankfurt School more than Marion, for instance. But in this rational view from outside, in this reflective removal from what is immediate, one is also able, as both Levinas and Dussel suggest, to take distance from oneself, to see the limited position one occupies, to see from the exteriority but also to see that there is an exteriority. From such a perspective, the meticulous preoccupation with whether one's philosophical theory betrays alterity, as important as it may be, can seem quite narrow in view of the vast suffering that so many others experience at the hands of political and economic forces that easily and constantly cover up their betrayal of the saying in a said. In this context, the very effort to avoid succumbing to theoretical idolatry can itself succumb to a kind of idolatry, in which one fixes one's gaze on an idol that returns one's gaze to one's self without one even seeing it and that confines the mass of human suffering to the *invisable.* If the very alterity Dussel serves requires Dussel to let his theory be shaken, then the very endeavor to allow alterity to shake theory must also, in the name of the very alterity it serves, move beyond the endeavor to shake theory in the name of alterity, toward liberating alterity wherever it is betrayed. In so doing, it will be following the path that Emmanuel Levinas announces and that Enrique Dussel has already extensively traveled.

NOTES

1. Enrique Dussel, *La producción teórica de Marx: Un comentario a los Grundrisse* (Mexico: Siglo XXI Editores, 1985); *Hacia un Marx desconocido: Un Comentario de los "Manuscritos del 61-63"* (Mexico: Siglo XXI Editores, 1988); *El Último Marx (1863-1882) y la liberación latinoamericana* (Mexico: Siglo XXI Editores, 1990); Enrique Dussel, "El concepto de fetischismo en el pensamiento de Marx: Elementos para una teoría general marxista de la religión," *Cristianismo y Sociedad* 85 (1985): 31. Given the debate about the meaning of Marx's own text, it should be kept in mind that this essay focuses on Enrique Dussel's *interpretation* of Marx.

2. *El Último Marx (1863–1882) y la liberación latinoamericana*, 334–87. Some of the texts cited referring to labor as non-being and yet creative in the manner of Schelling's God include the following: Marx, *Grundrisse* (Berlin: Dietz, 1974), 178, 8–14; 183, 6–17; 199, 17–22; 200, 8ff.; 354, 22–35; 357, 45–358, 11; *Manuscripto principal de El capital*, vol. 3, chap. 1.43.

3. *Grundrisse* 235, cited in *La producción teórica de Marx*, 138–39; chap. 1, pt. 3, chap. 7, chap. 3.

4. *Manuscriptos del 1861-1863*, Cuaderno 14, p. 817, cited in "El Concepto de Fetichismo en el Pensamiento de Marx," 36. See also Enrique Dussel, *Las metáforas teológicas de Marx* (Estella: Editorial Verbo Divino, 1993), 277. Dussel explains that the "social relations" to which Max refers here are themselves "negative, perverse, incorrect" relative to communitarian relationships.

5. "El concepto de fetischismo en el pensamiento de Marx: Elementos para una teoría general marxista de la religión," 43; see also 41–43.

6. Ibid., 43-45.

7. Ibid., 31, 37, 45–57; *Las metáforas teológicas de Marx*, 76, 107ff.

8. "El concepto de fetischismo en el pensamiento de Marx: Elementos para una teoría general marxista de la religión," 54-57.

9. Ibid., 57–59.

10. *Las metáforas teológicas de Marx*, 131, 140–41, 153, 237–44, 248–49, 253–55. Dussel believes further that Marx's lack of appreciation for the affirmative moment reduces his revolutionary proposal to a rationalized economico-political project, lacking in a certain symbolic transcendence (p. 254).

11. Ibid., 277.

12. "El concepto de fetischismo en el pensamiento de Marx, Elementos para una teoría general marxista de la religión," 35–36.

13. Jean-Luc Marion, *God without Being: Hors-Texte*, trans. Thomas A. Carlson (Chicago: University of Chicago Press, 1991), 7–9, 10, 12, 27–28, 119, 131, 201.

14. Ibid., 17–22, 24–26.

15. Ibid., 22–23, 29–33. Marion appeals to René Descartes's *idea infiniti* as an example of the icon proceeding conceptually, conceiving concepts that seek to receive the incomprehensible in its own excessiveness.

16. Ibid., 43, 33–41.

17. Ibid., 80; see also 72, 76, 80–81.

18. Ibid., 45–47.

19. Ibid., 97, 101–2, 105, 162, 182, 196.

20. Jean-Luc Marion, *L'idole et la distance: Cinq études* (Paris: Bernard Grasset, 1977), 231–42.

21. *God without Being*, 143–44, 149, 162–63; Jean-Luc Marion, *Proégomènes á la Charité* (Paris: Editions Littéraires et Artistique/La Difference, 1986), 74–79. Indeed, Marion's systematic works can be interpreted as one long struggle against the idolatries by which theory sets the (limiting) conditions for whatever is given to it. Marion's works pursue continually an "enlargement of evidence in donation" understood as a radicalization of phenomenological reduction and the return to the things themselves. Hence he takes Husserl to task for fixating in a Cartesian fashion on consciousness at the expense of the things themselves, the broader field of phenomenology, and limitations in Husserl's understanding of intuition that prescribe limits to phenomenality in the principle of principles. Likewise, he outflanks Heidegger's ontological difference by discovering the donative dimension in the revelations of Being, since whatever shows itself also gives itself. He emphasizes saturated phenomena that exceed the power of concepts to order, and even concludes that since donation is not limited to the consideration of the face of the other and since it does not directly derive from ethics, "the donation of the gift does not depend on ethics, but inversely, ethics supposes without doubt the donation of the gift." One secures a kind of ultimate foundation in donation; how would one think of a nondonation or negative donation, since even to think of them, they would have to be given. Within Marion's work one detects the dialectic mentioned at the outset of this paper. On the one hand, alterity questions theory, yet it is theory that shows how theory is inadequate to alterity; and yet the very recovery of alterity by theory prohibits any triumphalism of theory over alterity. Jean-Luc Marion, *Etant donné*: *Essai d'une phénoménologie de la donation* (Paris: Presses Universitaires de France, 1997), 10–11, 20–21, 32, 59, 79–83, 127–28, 250, 314; Jean-Luc Marion, *Reduction et donation: Recherches sur Husserl, Heidegger, et la phénoménologie* (Paris: Presses Universitaires de France, 1989), 128–29, 237, 239, 245.

22. Emmanuel Levinas, *Totality and Infinity: An Essay on Exteriority*, trans. Alphonso Lingis (The Hague: Martinus Nijhoff, 1979), 35–40, 51, 73.

23. Ibid., 80–81, 195; Levinas, *Otherwise Than Being, or Beyond Essence*, trans. Alphonso Lingis (The Hague: Martinus Nijhoff, 1981), 155–56, 162, 165.

24. Enrique Dussel, *Método para una filosofía de la liberación: Superación analéctica de la dialéctica hegeliana*, 3d ed. (Guadalajara: Editorial Universidad de Guadalajara, 1991), 185–95.

25. Ibid., 189; Enrique Dussel, *Para una ética de la liberación lationamericana* (Buenos Aires: XXI/Argentina Editores, 1973), 1:102–3.

26. It should be noted that in footnote 561, page 407, Dussel misinterprets "diachrony" to be understood as "critical thought," "since the anteriority of sensibility and the victim, *before*, opens, *afterward*, for the responsibility, the ambient of the rational." What is missing here is how reason in exhaustively presenting its discourse finds itself temporally superseded by the other to whom it is addressed. See Enrique Dussel, *Etica de la liberación en la edad de la globalización y de la exclusión* (Madrid: Editorial Trotta, 1998).

27. Enrique Dussel, *The Invention of the Americas, Eclipse of "the Other," and the Myth of Modernity*, trans. Michael D. Barber (New York: Continuum, 1995), 132, 138–39; *Etica de la Liberación*, 359–68, 403–8.

28. *Etica de la liberación*, 210–11; 369–71; 408 n. 572; 420–21; 461–62.

29. *Otherwise Than Being*, 162.

11

Dussel on Marx: Living Labor and the Materiality of Life

Mario Sáenz

> For the reconstruction of a Latin American philosophy it was necessary to "de-struct" the Greek *myth.* For an understanding of the culture of the Latin American people it was necessary to begin from Jerusalem more so than from Athens. Jerusalem spoke of the dignity of work, of the possibility of a revolution of the poor. Athens spoke of the dignity of free noble men, of the impossibility of the emancipation of the slaves.[1]

> It is also clear from these arguments how grossly Feuerbach is deceiving himself when by virtue of the qualification "common man" he declares himself a communist, transforms the latter into a predicate of "Man," and thinks it is possible to change the word "communist," which in the real world means the follower of a definite revolutionary party, into a mere category. . . . He is a *man* or, rather, since F. simply places the essence of man in the community, he is a communal man, a *communist.*[2]

Enrique Dussel's philosophy of liberation strives to be a constitutive element of the "critical community," and it attempts to position itself between the interests of the "(oppressed) victims" and a *legitimation* of the "new world order" under the *last* phase of globalized capitalism.[3] Thus Dussel develops a concept of *transformation* that is moved by the utopian moment implicit in the spatial periphery and the temporal pulsion toward alterity, rather than the developmentalist description of a logic of development that would move inexorably beyond capitalism. Many of the theories of the "center" (the latest phase of critical theory and postmodernism, most notably) have partly resigned themselves to the system by affirming a gray formalism (the so-called praxis of validity in Jürgen Habermas's latest work, for instance), for they originally presented themselves as alternatives to the revolution cum science of the Third and Fourth Internationals. With the moral collapse of "really existing socialism," *Ideologiekritik* and the dialectics of suspicion of the "great narratives" were left with nothing but the formal-theoretic presumable advancements of the Enlightenment: liberal form without liberal content. By contrast to the "self-defeatism" of the privileged, Dussel has developed a systematic theory of human liberation that has assimilated criticisms of his earlier works,[4] while never giving up the "pulsion" to move toward the representation in theory of those who have been oppressed, victimized, and excluded by the system of domination.

Dussel's latest work has been an ongoing debate with some of the theoreticians of the most pertinent ethical theories today (Karl-Otto Apel's discourse theory, Habermas's communicative ethics, and Taylor's communitarian ethics, to mention only a few) and the construction of a material, rather than formalistic, ethics of liberation of significance for the oppressed and exploited of the new world order. But during the 1980s Dussel developed a Marxist interpretation of Marx and effected an appropriation of Marx's economic theory that laid some of the groundwork for the material principle of his current ethics, which is unthinkable, as Dussel has claimed, without an economics (not simply a sociology) of life.

In this chapter, I explore some of the facets of Dussel's appropriation of the "economic" Marx. Dussel develops his analectical interpretation of Marx at three levels: the poiesis/praxis distinction, the living labor/labor power distinction, and the center/periphery distinction.

Here, for reasons of space, I examine only the last two levels. The first level is explored elsewhere. Although the first is more abstract and foundational conceptually than the other two, we need to examine Dussel's conception of living labor in order to understand his conception of poiesis and the materiality of life.

Before touching upon those distinctions, we need a definition of "analectics." By analectics, Dussel means that which lies "outside" or "beyond" the reason of a system of domination; furthermore, it is "the place of affirmation within which the negation of the negation in the system can take place."[5] Every sociopolitical totality is in principle a system of domination, for it excludes exteriority. Only an analectical pulsion can intend that exteriority. The analectical moment is the "positive" moment that remains outside the dialectical negation of the particular, for it points us to the exteriority of systemic person-to-person relations.

LIVING LABOR/LABOR POWER DISTINCTION

This distinction is a key distinction in Dussel's Marxism. It is in fact central to his analectical interpretation of Marx's economic theory. Its guiding thread is the notion that "exteriority," not totality, is the fundamental category in Marx's economic discourse.[6] On it he bases not only his reconstruction of the philosophy of liberation as Marxist, but also his critique of central figures of Western Marxism (notably Georg Lukács, Louis Althusser, and Karel Kosík) as totalizing.

Dussel attempts a synthesis with Marx's thought in several major works of the 1980s. What is characteristic of those books is the following: a close reading of Marx's economic texts, an attempt to bring together Marx's theory with Dussel's own philosophy of liberation and dependency theory, and a rejection of much of commonly accepted Marxist theory not simply for being in disagreement with Dussel's own philosophy of liberation, but also for being in disagreement with the core of Marx's own theory.

In this section of the chapter I concentrate on some aspects of that close reading in order to determine the possibilities opened up by a synthesis of Dusselian ethics and Marxist theory and also to analyze the implicit notion that fundamental concepts of the philosophy of liberation were intuited by Marx. Furthermore, I consider the possibility of synthesizing Dusselian ethics and Marxist theory in a new creative synthesis for the *needs* of the oppressed under what I call postindustrial imperialism.

Dussel claims that Marx's concept of living labor must be interpreted from the standpoint of an exteriority that cannot, qua exterior living labor, be absorbed by the totality of capital. Dussel uses the following passage from Marx's *Manuscripts of 1861–1863* in order to prove his point:

> The dissociation between property and labor is expressed as a necessary law of exchange between capital and labor ["up to now"—says Dussel in a note within the text—"there is only one difference with the *Grundrisse,* but from now there begin important corrections"]. As *not-capital*, not-objectified work, the capacity to labor appears as: 1. *negatively*: not-raw material, not-instrument of work, not-product, not-means of life, not-money; it is work dissociated from all the means of work and subsistence, from all of its objectivity, as pure possibility *(Möglichkeit)*. This total dispossession is *possibility of labor* deprived of all objectivity. It is the capacity of labor as *absolute poverty,* that is, full exclusion from objective wealth. The objectivity that the capacity to labor possesses is the corporeity *(Leiblichkeit)* itself of the worker, his own objectivity. 2. *Positively*: not-objectified work, but as activity, as living source *(lebendige Quelle)* of value. It confronts capital as the reality of universal wealth, as its [capital's?] universal possibility that is found in activity. This work is the one that, as an absolutely contradictory entity with respect to capital, is a presupposition of capital and, on the other hand, presupposes at same time capital.[7]

From the above Dussel concludes the following:

> Thus when the worker has *not* yet been subsumed by capital (or, in its essential and originary principle, by money), he is *not* value, he is *not* money, he is *not* capital. What is he then with respect to the *totality* of capital?—, and do we begin here the debate with Lukács or Kosik? Can it be said that "*living labor*" as reality and category is the same thing as "wage labor" or labor already subsumed within the totality of capital? In so far as it is subsumed, it is a determination internal to capital. But as long as it *has-not-yet-been* totalized, living labor is *reality* (the reality most absolutely real for Marx, and the measure of all unfulfillment in the totality of capital); it is the exterior. We give the name of "exteriority," and the alterity of the other distinct from capital, to this metaphysical position (beyond being or ontological reflection) of the worker in so far as he is *corporeality* (poor and naked body), in so far as he is a *person*, [and] insofar as he is the not-being of capital.[8]

Here we find one of the most novel aspects of Dussel's Marxism. The most well-known interpretations of Marxism (from the Third and Fourth International to the various generations of critical theory, for example) view Marx's conception of the "positivity" or the "negativity" of the worker in a dialectical and yet nonanalectical sense. In this case, the objectification of labor under the rule of capital entails both its poverty once it has been objectified (for the product is alienated from the laborer), as well as its wealth *as* (and not simply *in*) the process of objectification. If that is the case, the reference to wealth is labor power's value *for* capital and not for the laborer who has the capacity to labor. The capacity to labor of living (not yet objectified) labor is not the exteriority of labor (vis-à-vis) the totality of capital that is not absorbed by capital, and yet it is the source of the value of capital. Rather, the capacity to labor is, if you will, the exteriority of labor vis-à-vis the laborer who, under the rule of capital, is alienated from his or her activity. That alienated activity expresses itself as both the activity itself and the capacity to labor.

Metaphysically, it should be said that Dussel's *representation* (although this is clearly not the appropriate term) of living labor as exteriority seems to have a "noumenal" source, although more exactly with a Schellingian flavor to it and, hence, not noumenal! It is beyond what is conceptualizable, and hence it is absolutely positive (see figure 11.2 at the end of this chapter). But its positivity is not the positivity of facts, but rather the positivity of transcendence. It can be pointed to as that which remains unnegated by the system, and—in a Hegelian terminology with an anti-Hegelian focus—as that which is actual but is unconceptualizable. It is thus unrepresentable and yet it can be pointed to. In a sense it is a Kierkegaardian leap into that with which one cannot communicate, for it is not a subject.[9] The difference here is that it is Kierkegaard with a politics. This, it seems to me, is partly the result of the influence of Levinas on Dussel mediated by the radical politicization of the Latin American intellectual during the 1960s and 1970s.

Second, Dussel makes an intimate conceptual connection between living labor and abstract labor. He is aware that it is abstract labor that produces value qua social labor. Also, he defines the exchange value of a commodity as Marx does, namely, as the quantity of labor socially necessary to produce that commodity. Hence, labor power qua commodity has its value determined in the same way, that is, as the quantity of labor socially necessary to (re)produce it. Furthermore, he distinguishes, as Marx does, between social and communitarian work. But then he goes on to say that living labor (qua exterior to capital) is the *producer* of value. By contrast the more traditional interpretation of Marx's critique of political economy is that living labor is the creator of value precisely as abstract (social) labor, and thus as alienated labor, as labor exterior to the humanity of the laborer but *not* "exterior" to capital. It is an externalization or a "parting with" *(Entäusserung)* that takes place not simply at the moment when living labor *creates* surplus value as it works a surplus time beyond the amount socially necessary to reproduce the value of labor power. It has already taken place at the time when living labor *produces* value, that is, when it reproduces its own value laboring the socially necessary time for such reproduction. For *already* living labor is alienated from itself; it has been forced under the aegis of capital to become what it is not, namely, labor power and, thus, a commodity. But Dussel wants to distinguish between living labor *in abstracto* as producer of value, on the one hand, and living labor *in concreto* under, say, the domination of capital *and* beyond necessary labor time for the reproduction of the abstract value of labor power, as the *creator* of (surplus) value, on the other. In this way he distinguishes between the production and the creation of value. He does so, not only to distinguish between the production of value, the production of value as the objectification of life, and the creation of exchange value in the exteriority of living labor from the nothing of capital, but also in order to posit an exterior transcendentality, anterior to the system of domination. This is why in Dussel "living labor" *(el trabajo vivo)* assumes a double dimension as alienated exteriority and, qua labor power, exploited worker.

In the attempt to synthesize Marx's critique of political economy with his own ethics, Dussel overplays, it seems to me, the distinction between labor as producer of values and labor as creator of (surplus) value even under conditions of capitalist domination in which labor as producer of values is already a producer of commodities and itself, qua labor power, a commodity. This is important for Dussel so that the moment of exteriority is preserved even at the heart of capitalist production, namely, the process of production of commodities and the creation of surplus value. He redefines the meaning of the terms "positive," "negative," "exteriority," and "contradiction," as well as "totality." Those terms mean different things in the dialectics of traditional Marxism and the dialectical analectics labored by Dussel.

Dussel's analysis is interesting also in that his criticism of Marxist thought in his early *Ethics* was based on the traditional reading of Marxist theory (whether the one developed by Soviet socialism or the one that developed in Western Europe in reaction to it). For the early Dussel, *that* Marx was totalizing not so much for the reduction of life to production, but rather for the reduction of life to the totality of what-is.[10] Dussel's Levinasian and Schellingian attack of that time was nourished by Levinas's conception of exteriority and Schelling's affirmation of the *positivity* of the Absolute beyond the negativity of the concept. The more recent Dussel has not ceased to be nourished by both of these two fountains of antirationalist (rather than irrationalist) thought. Instead, he has reappropriated Marx by emphasizing the "analectical" and "positive" aspects of Marx's theory of labor.

Intuitively, Dussel's interpretation of Marx's mature anthropology seems accurate. Living labor (LL in fig. 11.1) is exterior to capital (C). In the process of reification (r) of labor by capital within the capitalist system, not only does living labor become a thing, namely, what it is not, and hence what it is becomes *noth-*

Figure 11.1 Schematization of Relationships

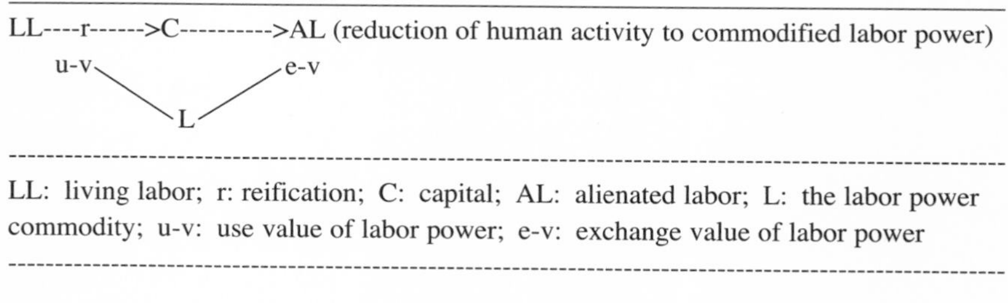

ing to capital, but then it thus becomes alienated labor (AL), and qua labor power, it becomes a commodity valuable for capital insofar as it has an exchange value (e-v) that in its use produces more value than it has (surplus value). It is in the process of reification of living labor, and its consequent transformation into something that *has* exchange value and is, therefore, qua labor power a commodity, that laborers are confronted by the power of the world of commodities as a living power and human relations become mediated and progressively reduced to relations between commodity things (what Marx called the fetishism of commodities). Thus human labor (L) is the source of all value, but itself, qua living labor, it is not a value. Only as alienated labor, as labor power, does it have an exchange value and not simply a use value (u-v). The schematization of these relationships may look like this:

In this schema, living labor is an *exteriority* to the system of capital. In Dussel's philosophy *and* theology, living labor is both *metaphysical* dis-tinctness and, I would add, *metasystemic* dis-tinctness (*lo dis-tinto* rather than *lo diferente*). By "metaphysical" Dussel means to adjectivize those aspects of life that are not reducible to a systemic "totality." This is to be distinguished from "ontological" interpretations of Marxism that, qua ontological, do not according to Dussel move beyond or outside the horizon of the systemic totality. In this case, they are unable to interpret adequately the anthropological dimension of Marx's mature works, says Dussel.

Already in his earlier pre-Marxist *Ethics* Dussel refers to the Other as having an, and being in, exteriority. However, it is not then called living labor but simply the Other, and the system is not called the system of capital but "the Same."

> With the confusion of the Totality with the only dominating pole, the dominated comes to be a dif-ference ("the other") internal to "the Same." If that "other" disrespectfully attempts to arrogate for itself the right and the justice of declaring itself, not dif-ferent ("the other"), but dis-tinct, "outside" then of the Totality, or as "exteriority" (the really *Other*), it would signify a danger to "the Same" as dominating-totality. In this case, "the *Other,*" who defends *its "exteriority,"* would have to be eliminated.[11]

It may be possible to bring together the "ontological" tradition of so-called Western Marxism with Dussel's novel "metaphysical" interpretation through a *metasystemic analectical a posteriori* rereading of Dussel and Marx, as I argue at the end of this chapter. For now, however, I mention a third point regarding Dussel's interpretation of Marx: Dussel brings together in a way that I regard as problematic what Marx has to say on living labor and social labor. Dussel does distinguish between social and communitarian labor, as Marx does. However, when it comes to the question, What creates value? Dussel says that it is living labor, according to Marx. The problem lies in Dussel's interpretation of living labor as "exteriority," that is, as a *metaphysical* category beyond capital. But Marx *does* refer to living labor as *social labor, and social labor is alienated labor to be distinguished from communitarian work.* Either living labor is social labor, in which case living labor is not, *for* Marx, "exteriority," or it is not social labor, in which case it would not be for Marx a creator of values. This is not to say that Marx is right in his views. Rather, it is a statement to the effect that Dussel may here equivocate regarding Marx's views. For Dussel, living labor is "exteriority" but not so unambiguously, it seems, *for* Marx. Furthermore, the equivocation may run deeper, since Dussel does state that, according to Marx, social labor is the creator of value and is alienated labor. If so, living labor is for Marx social and alienated labor.

Nonetheless, we must not lose sight of the fact that Dussel is appropriating Marx's theory and that Marx did have—contrary to Habermas's reading of him[12]–a conception of the human that went beyond instrumentalism and instrumental action, but also beyond the reality constructed by the capitalist system. Dussel seems to claim that that "beyond" is an exteriority to the system, which is nothing *to the* system but is, nonetheless, the *positive* source of the validity of the Marxist critique of capitalism.

Also, running beneath Dussel's interpretation of living labor as exteriority, as the creator of values but itself not value, is the conception of God proper to the Semitic ethical-metaphysical tradition of creation from nothing: For Dussel, nothing is the nothing to the system.

We can see that move more explicitly in a theological work, Dussel's *Ethics and Community*.

> The "value" of the product, then (and we must keep in mind that this value is independent of its function in capitalism), is simply the quantity of objectified human life attaching to that product. It is in complete accord with the Hebreo-Christian concept of "creation" to say that the subject of work, the human person, is the *sole "creative source of value":* human beings produce, *ex nihilo subjecti*—in the absence of any material substrate (and hence, in due course, in the absence of capital as material substrate)—what we call "value" (for the moment, in general, or *in abstracto*).[13]

Dussel, then, thinks that creation out of nothing is the source of value. He goes on to contrast this with nature, which "has no value."[14] That may be true in a

Marxist theory. However, that is not the only "material substrate": social relations are part of the materiality of the human (hence Marx's coinage of the phrase "the materialist conception of history"). Today, cultural Marxists see that material substrate also in the cultures by which we live and have meaning. Ultimately, however, the human creation of value *ex nihilo subjecti* is built on the analogy of God's creation out of nothing. Thus Dussel says that "only God creates from nothing. Out of infinite, unconditioned freedom, God has created the entire universe."[15] Clearly, that is a case, or rather *the* case, of creation *ex nihilo* "in the absence of any material substrate."

Dussel quite rightly uses the Semitic tradition to show how the pretension of capital that *it* creates value is an expression of its own fetishistic nature and idolatry.[16] However, it does not follow that labor power creates value (not even use value, which also requires a "material substrate," and therein lies another equivocation in Dussel, who moves freely from use value to exchange value) independently of the conditions of exploitation under the rule of capital and, more generally, independently of the conditions of life in any social system or, rather, in *some* social system. The abolition of capital and commodity fetishism requires the abolition of labor and exchange value. Marx never gave up this critique of Proudhon and Lasalleanism.

What Dussel is going to try to do can be sensed already. He wants to argue that living labor is, in itself, outside the sphere of capital. To do this successfully in English, we would have to keep in mind that Dussel's *trabajo vivo* is "living *work*," to be distinguished from the usual meaning of "living labor" in the Marxist tradition of the English-speaking world. Living labor in that tradition is already alienated work, to be distinguished from the activity of producing that the human being as such does under any condition of human existence. But Dussel is not trying to create another category. Rather, he is reformulating it on a foundation of exteriority rather than totality. Thus by "living labor" Dussel means an exteriority that is the source of all value but is itself, therefore, without value. We can see this view in a later comment by Dussel on the Marx of 1847 and 1849.

> In this short work [*Wage, Labor and Capital,* 1849] we can see that Marx had not yet developed as a category the concept of surplus value and, furthermore, was not clear about the difference between work (living labor [*trabajo vivo*]), as the source of all value (and because of it without value), and the capacity to work *[capacidad de trabajo]* (or labor power *[fuerza de trabajo]*), which has value. The insistence in the text on the terms "labor power" is perhaps part of the Engelsian correction. [This text was corrected and published by Engels in 1891.][17]

Thus it would make sense to say that on the basis of the relation of domination of capital over labor, "living labor" is forced to sell itself for a wage.[18] For it is one's living labor that *is* also alienated, *besides* one's "labor power."[19] That is, one's living labor is, through wage slavery, alienated from its capacity to labor; furthermore, one's living labor *is* the alienated *subject.* Dussel has introduced here another distinction, namely, one between labor power and the capacity to work. The former is, if you will, practical: it is part of the person-to-person relationship that is intrasystemic. The latter is poietic; it belongs to the human as productive and creative. But it has its metaphysical support in the analectical character of human Otherness and exteriority.

Dussel cites Marx: "By labor power or capacity for labor we understand the aggregate of the physical and spiritual faculties that exist in the corporeality, in the living personality of a human being."[20] This is a telling translation. The English edition translated it thus: "By labour-power or capacity for labour is to be understood the aggregate of those mental and physical capabilities existing in a human being, which he exercises whenever he produces a use-value of any description."[21]

Dussel wants to show that Marx's conception of labor is "analectical." Thus he stresses Marx's indecision in the early section of *Capital*'s first manuscript regarding the worker's *Arbeitsvermögen,* or *Arbeitskraft*.[22] This is a conceptual distinction for Dussel. Unfortunately, Marx was indifferent to either use and he decides in later sections to use the term *Arbeitskraft* (labor power), which ended up "producing significant equivocations in the later Marxist tradition."[23]

> "Capacity" to labor better indicated the "potentiality" *anterior* to the use or consumption of labor (before the contract and the subsumption of living labor in capital). By contrast, labor "power" *[fuerza]* better indicates the "activity" or *actual* use of living labor. Furthermore, since Marx uses the concept of "living labor" only very sporadically, there is not a clear discovery of the difference between the previous "capacity" that has value, the "power" utilized in the labor process, and "living labor" as the subjectivity (i.e., personhood and corporeality of the worker) without value and which has "capacity" and "power" as its own determinations.[24]

Dussel goes on to say that part 2 of volume 11 of *Capital* ("The Transformation of Money into Capital") is the most important subject of *Capital* "because it is here, in the dialectical logic of Marx's scientific discourse in which there takes place the 'passage' *(Übergang)* from non-capital to capital, from 'living labor' to objectified, subsumed, and *'incorporated (einverleibt)'* labor. . . . In this chapter 2 [i.e., part 2 in the English translation] Marx studies the contradiction between the 'owner *[poseedor]* of living labor' and the 'owner of money.' . . ."[25]

But Dussel does not really define yet the meaning of living labor for Marx *from Marx's texts themselves.* Whenever he enters into a description of living labor for Marx, he ends up referring to something as defined by capitalism, for example, the "owner of living labor": living labor as a commodity. However, Dussel seems to be right on a related matter: there must be something "anterior" to labor commodified, something that I take to market, where it is commodified under the conditions of capital. The question is, Is that what living labor means for Marx? The answer depends on the interpretation that we make of Marx, whether as an analectical or a "scientific" (whether "scientific" is interpreted as either dialectical or analytical) thinker.

It seems to me likely that Marx meant by "living labor" that which is reducible to both the capacity for labor and labor power. Thus it has value. It is distinguishable from objectified labor, as variable *capital* is from constant capital. It is labor power for sale (capacity) and capacity in use (labor power). The substance is, if you will, realized in its predicates or determinations.

Nevertheless, I agree with Dussel that there must be something anterior and that this anteriority would represent the "ethical" or the "metaphysical" moment in Marx's critique of capitalism. But Dussel argues that such ethical critique is an integral part of the *categorial* framework of Marx's "mature" writings. Dussel tackles this bull by the horns in his reinterpretation of the philosophical categories implicit in Marx's economic theory.

In "Philosophical Interpretations of Marx's Work" Dussel discusses and criticizes six interpretations prevalent in Western Marxism, namely, those by Lukács, Korsch, Marcuse, Kosík, Althusser, and Habermas.

The common thread in the discussion in this chapter is the failure of these thinkers to realize that Marx's thought grounds itself on that which is exterior and anterior to the totality. Thus he concludes the following on Lukács's interpretation:

> In Lukács there is ontology and nothing else: There is not a superation of ontology. . . . One can see this clearly in the chapter on "The Reproduction of Society as Totality." Thus "social being *[gessellschaftliche Sein]*" is for Lukács the name of the human being. But for Marx "social" is contrasted to "communitarian," and it also has often a negative sense in its most strict sense. . . .
>
> . . . By having overvalued the importance of "totality," he [Lukács] has fetishized it in some sense. One does not see that he discovered the "creative source of value," the "substance" that posits surplus-value *from the nothing* of capital [i.e., from that which is nothing to capital].[26]

Lukács is criticized also for the excessive Hegelianism of his Marxism, as well as for his belittling of Schelling as merely a "reactionary," not realizing, says Dussel, that Schelling was the first post-Hegelian. Of course, Stirner was also a post-Hegelian, but Dussel is interested here in Schelling's "radical critique against Hegel."[27]

Regarding Marcuse's thought, Dussel says that Marcuse passes superficially from Hegel to Marx via Kierkegaard and Feuerbach. It "seems that [Marcuse] ignores the role that Schelling and the 'positive philosophy' played."[28] This latter reference to the "positive philosophy" is significant and fundamental to Dussel's second order reflection on his interpretation of Marx. Dussel speaks about various types of "positive" philosophy, ranging from French positivism to twentieth-century analytic philosophy, but also "'positivisms' such as those of the post-Hegelians (Schelling, Feuerbach, Kierkegaard, etc.) among whom one would have to include Marx himself."[29]

> In this last sense, "positivism" means the recovery of the "reality" or "positivity" of what is beyond the horizon of the world, of thinking, of the system, and not merely as "possibility" or potentiality (the "negative"), but as "reality" (the positive or, that is, that which is revealed for Schelling, what is believed for Kierkegaard, the sensible object for Feuerbach, and "living labor" vis-à-vis capital for Marx.[30]

Regarding Karel Kosík, Dussel argues that Kosík's *Dialectic of the Concrete* is an "excellent expression of 'Marx's ontology.'" Furthermore, he shows the importance of "totality." But Kosík does not go as far as explicitly discovering the "exteriority" and "anteriority" of living labor in Marx as "perhaps the point of departure of all of Marx's thought."[31]

Dussel saves his sharpest criticisms for Althusser and Althusserian Marxism. Dussel states that his major criticism of Althusser's reading of Marx is that Althusser bases it on what Marx says he did and not on an analysis of the development of the texts themselves "line by line."[32] There are, however, more substantial criticisms.

Althusserian structuralism does not allow Althusser to see beyond the "totality." Althusser grounds his analysis on the Engelsian base–superstructure model in which the economic mode of production is the base "in the last instance," or ultimately. On this is based Althusser's anti-Hegelianism and his view of a "Marxist" rupture with Hegel in 1845. For Dussel, however, if there was any rupture, it was in 1857 and it was because of Marx's use of "a strictly philosophical-Hegelian 'problematic.'"[33] Furthermore, Althusser gives too much importance to Marx's 1857 introduction to the *Grundrisse.* But that is a provisional text.

Althusser does not seem to be aware of the distinction between living labor and objectified labor, says Dussel; this is a distinction of "which Marx does not seem to have an explicit consciousness."[34] This point is crucial for Dussel's interpretation. Dussel argues that all the significant later distinctions made by Marx arise from this foundational distinction. Thus in reference to Althusser's privileging of Marx's August 24, 1867 letter and his *Marginal Notes to the Treatise on Political Economy of Adolph Wagner* (1882), Dussel claims that the latter contains obvious Hegelian concepts—such as the notion that exchange value is a "form of appearance" of the value contained in a commodity.[35] Dussel also states that all of Marx's concepts on labor, namely, the double character of labor, abstract labor and concrete labor, use value, and exchange value, are based "on the previous distinction between 'living labor' and 'objectified labor.'"[36]

Althusser's excessive reliance on and misuse of the notion of the mode of production is a "deformation and hypertrophy of a category in Marx." Althusser uses that concept instead of the "'concept of capital in general' (totality of multiple determinations)." This concept is absent in Althusser's interpretation, says Dussel.[37]

Finally, Dussel deals with Habermas's reading of Marx. There are two aspects of Habermas's reading that Dussel "recovers." First, Dussel stresses the connection that Habermas sees between Marx's and Schelling's philosophy of nature (i.e., the naturalization of the human is the humanization of nature) in such a way that in both Schelling and Marx there is what Habermas calls "The Hidden Materialism of the Philosophy of the *Weltalter.*"[38] (The English translation of Habermas's *Theorie und Praxis* does not include this essay.) Second, Dussel points to "the attention that Habermas lends to the western Jewish philosophical tradition."[39]

But Dussel's analysis of Habermas's shortcomings follows immediately. Dussel stresses the fact that Habermas does not have an economic theory of Marx but merely a sociology; also, he questions the lack of analysis of peripheral societies in Habermas's analysis of modernity.[40] An element of the criticism that is fundamental to this work is the issue regarding Marx's conception of activity. For Dussel, as already noted, Marx does not reduce labor to instrumental activity, even if the later Marxist tradition does. For Dussel, the instrumentalization of human activity is part and parcel of the totalization of human activity. It is thus a systemic demand on the human being. This view of Marx's theory of action is going to determine Dussel's criticism of Habermas's Marx. Dussel rejects the view that Marx did not have a "criterion or mediating category that allows him to make the concept of alienation more precise. We have shown, and Habermas ignores this, that 'living labor' is the essential category to allow such precision. . . ."[41]

Dussel thinks, in sum, that Habermas misunderstands Marx when he attributes to Marx a unilateral comprehension of poiesis and a negation of praxis. On this misunderstanding, says Dussel, Habermas bases false conclusions. For in Marx the relations of production have not only an instrumental significance but also a practical one.[42]

Regarding "the configuration of the global process of capital," Dussel argues that Marx is himself arguing at three levels: first, he is trying to show that the "law of value" rules over all the moments of capital, from value to surplus value to prices. Second, that linkage through the law of value of all of those moments is "one permanent and essential 'crisis': . . . a necessary contradiction. This is the question of 'devaluation' that appeared in the *Grundrisse.*"[43] Finally, there is a third "anthropological . . . ethical, metaphysical sense" of the text in question, says Dussel.

> Ultimately, both the "law of value" and the "crisis" of capital attempt to show to the political "everyday consciousness" of the concrete exploited worker that the *totality* of the economic moments of capital (and, because of that, of classical political economy as well: value, price, profit, etc.) are only unpaid *living labor [trabajo vivo]: robbed* human life. The *being* of capital, and the pretended "sources" of income (profit, rent, and wages) are the *not-being* of living labor (the reality of human subjectivity as *exteriority* and anteriority to capital as *totality*). What is least important—even though it has epistemic importance—is the "technical" difficulty of building "scientifically" the categorial mediations from value to prices. What is important for Latin American philosophy, but even more so for the exploited poor, is to discover its metaphysical (more than ontological) *deep intention:* all *dead* or objectified labor (capital) is alienated, subsumed, ethically perverted *living labor.* This not only shows capitalism's necessary or essential collapse (which because of it *can* always be postponed empirically), but also the antihumanity of its own being, the non-ethicity of its radical position, namely, a social relation of exploitation.[44]

Dussel continues ascribing an analectical position to Marx's own mature economic writings. This analectical position requires that living labor be the kind of human activity that is exterior to the capitalist system or any system. It is anterior to the capitalist system of production; this is in part the reason for Dussel's comment that Engels added the restrictive term "capitalist" to Marx's reference to production in its totality.[45] But it also lies underneath it, and it has to be unearthed by a critical investigation. Thus in *El último Marx (1863–1882) y la liberación latinoamericana* Dussel states, regarding the relation of profit to surplus value and, ultimately, to living labor, that there are in Marx four terms of comparison.

> Surplus value and rate of surplus value, profit and rate of profit, surplus value and profit, and rate of surplus value and rate of profit. Surplus value and the rate of surplus value are always the foundation, the invisible, the (ontological) essential with respect to the founded, the visible, what appears (i.e., the ontic phenomenon). The deep level of production and, even more so, the transcendental level of *living labor,* appear under a superficial form in circulation, thus producing the fetishist mirage.[46]

Dussel argues that Marx's critique of the fetishism of capital is a critique "from the subjectivity of living labor" of the inversion of the relationship that places capital as the subject (personifies it) while reifying labor and placing it under the dominion of the thing (i.e., objectified labor). He has support for this in Marx's own writings. The conclusion is Dusselian.

> Marx thinks then from a very clear metaphysical paradigm. Production is the essential, deep, invisible level, where subsumed living labor is exploited and creates surplus value. The essential sphere is not phenomenal. . . .
>
> According to Marx, the relation capital-labor is the first [relation]. It is a metaphysical relation in our sense of the term. It is the relation of the *thing* (i.e., capital as objectified or dead labor) with the *person,* with the subjectivity of the corporeity, that is, the subject (i.e., the exteriority of the poor before the contract with capital). Marx is interested in the person, work, subjectivity, and because of that, he is interested in the umpaid surplus labor that produces surplus value. By contrast, the relation capital-surplus value is secondary, since it confronts objectified labor with objectified labor; neither capital (the totality) nor surplus value (robbed new value) are *living labor* anymore. Furthermore, the relation of capital to labor is concretely variable capital against living labor; while the relation of capital to surplus value is only that of all existing value with the surplus that had just been extracted.[47]

Thus Dussel sides with Marx when he says that "profit is the phenomenal form of surplus value."[48] But what is not "phenomenal" is, according to Dussel, "metaphysical." By the latter term Dussel has meant that which is *beyond the system of domination,* but he has also meant the God of the oppressed expressed in the face of the hungry and suffering *victim.* The metaphysical thirst for oneness with God after the sinful fall expressed in one's acts of injustice toward others seems to be part of many religious practices (e.g., the Jewish Yom Kippur). It is, of course, true that Marx's critique of commodity fetishism is not self-consciously built on metaphysical duality. It is in history and within a social system that one is to find domination and self-diremption or, alternatively, liberation and self-integrity. Yet Marx's thought on this issue is still, as Gramsci once said, encrusted with scientistic positivism. And, in fairness to Dussel, he contrasts metaphysics with ontology,[49] and the totalizing apparent, in Dussel's view, in Western Marxism. That totalizing can be seen in the uncritical and Eurocentered conception of modernity assumed as true by much of Western philosophy and social theory. Through the totalizing of the power of sameness, the cultural other becomes, in Dussel's vivid description of the bestiary created by modern conquest and colonization,

> Oviedo's beast, Hegel's future, O'Gorman's possibility, and Alberto Caturelli's *material in the rough.* The Other is a rustic mass dis-covered in order to be civilized by the European being *[ser]* of Occidental culture. But this Other is in fact covered over *[en-cubierta]* in its alterity.[50]

Here Dussel partly follows on the line of thinking that was also developed, albeit without a class consciousness, a few years before by the Mexican philosophy that arose from the Mexican Revolution. It asserted the *identity* of the Latin American as it was confronted by its negation in Eurocentered thought. Thus the principal philosopher of culture in Mexico's twentieth century, Leopoldo Zea, formulates the legitimacy of *philosophical* reflections on Latin American identity as a critique of the covering up *(encubrimiento)* that began with the so-called discovery *(descubrimiento)* of the Americas. This is a covering up that marks, says Zea, the "first globalization."[51]

> Man *[sic]* tries to manipulate other men, not recognizing in them fellow men but useful or useless objects. . . . Such is the problem, an ancient problem for man and his philosophy—the question of the concrete Being of men occupying a vast region of Earth and subjected to the manipulations of others. They are the victims of a gigantic cover-up over identity begun on October 12, 1492. . . .[52]

Dussel goes beyond Zea's conception of identity precisely in that he formulates the presence of alterity as a repressed latency that is expressed in the exteriority of the present *rostros* of the oppressed of the Americas. The mestizo is only one of them. There are also "the *Indians;* who still remain invisible to modernity"; the enslaved Africans and their descendants; the native *criollo* elites (after the *mestizo*); the peasants; the workers; and the "*marginales*."[53]

Dussel is particularly critical of the myth of modernity that arises to cover up the Other and sacrifice their humanity at the altar of a conception of progress and maturation that is mistaken to be a Western phenomenon.[54] Dussel takes Habermas to task precisely for this prejudgment.

> Habermas . . . suggests an intra-European definition of modernity which commences with the Renaissance and the Reformation and culminates in the *Aufklärung.* Latin America, Africa, or Asia have *no importance* for the philosopher from Frankfurt! In

> this self-centered Eurocentric definition, Habermas identifies European particularity with world universality. . . . Habermas dismisses the relevance of the discovery of Latin America and thereby denies its historical reality, just as Hegel did.[55]

The Euro-centrism of Habermas's view of modernity is disguised by his excessive formalism, which Dussel criticizes for its inability to develop an ethics of content *(material)*, and its consequent inability to develop a critique of late capitalism that is in effect a critique of capitalism.[56]

> [Discourse ethics] does not propose a "*critical* postconventional ethicity," but rather a formal "postconventionality" *within* the hegemony of the cultural ethicity and the system of the North of our planet, without an explicit consciousness of its complicity with that system.[57]

Habermas's formalistic self-image is indeed present in his reconstruction of Kohlberg's theory of ontogenetic development, which—by merely adding to the psychologist's theory a seventh stage in the postconventional level that rather than bring critical theory to bear on a "formalistic ethics"—reduces critique to a formalism[58] that can no longer seize the self-reflective spirit of the masses with "the struggles and wishes of the age."[59] But Habermas's political formalism can also be seen in his latest work, which in its ahistorical and declassed formalism represents the result of the "de-economization" of human material life and, in that way, the very dematerialization of human life. Ultimately, this implies, as Dussel has seen rightly, an uncritical disregard of the place of the periphery in the formation of the economy, the culture, and the society of "the center" of power in today's world.

While there is implicit in Dussel's thought a distinction between the poiesis of life and the praxis of alterity that calls for their reintegration for the sake of the life denied to the marginalized Other, there is, by contrast, in the latest version of Habermas's noncritical theory, particularly in his *Between Facts and Norms* and the earlier *The Theory of Communicative Action*, a sharp diremption of the poiesis of meaning from the praxis of validity.

According to Habermas, the production of meaning is particularizing. But such fragmenting and centrifugal tendencies are countered by the universalizable (and centralizing) tendencies of validity claims implicit in speech acts.[60] Habermas derives the universalizing force of his theory from the latter. On the basis of that ideal, Habermas regards modernity as an unfinished project. Furthermore, he regards the ideals of modernity (i.e, as captured by the European Enlightenment) as still necessary and desirable for the emancipation of humans from unnecessary forms of repression and domination.

It seems to me, however, that the uncoupling of discourse theory from the material conditions of life, to use Dussel's term, throws into question not only the effectiveness of the theory of communication elaborated by Habermas (is it critical?) but also the *validity* of the theory itself (is it true?). It is interesting how for

Habermas the situation is otherwise once the linguistic turn has taken place.[61] In his opinion the "recasting" of practical reason in terms of communicative rationality preserves the issues of precommunicative practical reason without the latter's naive nonreliance on social science. However, Habermas assumes an independent history of ideas that leads presumably to his conclusions thus collapsing issues of meaning and validity.[62]

This presupposition would render Dussel's questions regarding the connection between modernity and its sacrificial myth a purely empirical question to be resolved by retranslating them into the consensus theory of truth proposed by Habermas, and which Dussel *must* accept in order to have a hearing. Ironically, Habermas wants us to simply take for granted the independent and dematerialized history of philosophical ideas that lead eventually to his own linguistic turn.[63]

The transformation of practical reason into what was to become eventually the communicative reason developed first by Apel and then by Habermas himself assumes a philosophical movement independent from social conditions, unless one assumes a progressivist movement in society, as Habermas himself does with the notion of a progressive rationalization of communicative structures and a scientific decoupling of reason from the tradition: "basic psychological and sociological concepts can be interwoven because the perspectives projected in them of an autonomous ego and an emancipated society reciprocally require one another."[64] The reader may find this analogy between social formation and normative levels of maturity peculiarly suspicious, not only because of the very un-Freudian transformation of Freudian psychoanalysis into a transparent ego ideal but also because of the obvious implications regarding relations between different cultures and social classes. Yet we have to keep in mind Habermas's musings regarding "Occidental reason."

> We are implicitly connecting a claim to *universality* with our *Occidental understanding of the world.* In determining the significance of this claim, it would be well to draw a comparison with the mythical understanding of the world. In archaic societies myths fulfill the unifying function of worldviews in an exemplary way—they permeate life practice. . . . The degree of rationality of worldviews evidently does not vary with the stage of cognitive development of the individuals who orient their action within them. Our point of departure has to be that adult members of primitive tribal societies can acquire basically the same formal operations as the members of modern societies, even though the higher-level competences appear less frequently and more selectively in them; that is, they are applied in more restrictive spheres of life.[65]

Habermas then goes on to show, in a lengthy discussion of Weber's theory of rationalization and the "disenchantment of the cultural tradition," how in fact the West has a "high rationalization potential" by contrast to the Orient's "low rationalization potential."[66] In addition to being a good source of raw materials, the Orient must have indeed been a burden calling with the seductive force of all *her* wiles the military representatives of universal reason "back to Mandalay."[67] But this post-Weberian attempt to look at the transition from community ordering to societal ordering in presumably nonbureaucratic ways does end up assuming the philosophical necessity to embrace a noncritical theory (i.e., a theory that refuses to question its own particular interests unless it is done in its own particular terms[68]) because of the philosophical invalidity of critical theory, insofar as this latter embraced the rationality of a content, or what Dussel would call the "materiality of life."

However, questions remain about the generalizability of the theory of a praxis validity claims itself and, to that extent, of the wisdom of a complete linguistic turn as well, unless we maintain open the possibility, as Dussel does, that the production of meaning *affects* the claims to validity of speaking subjects. It may not be justifiable to maintain that the production of meaning represents a historical (horizontal) dimension, while the praxis of validity is presented as solely occupying a metacultural (vertical) dimension. It is precisely the threat of an *imposition* of meaning that accounted for the force of critiques of the (other) subject (i.e., in Stirner, Kierkegaard, and Nietzsche) and the "collective subject" (in Marx).

The decoupling of the praxis of validity claims from the material basis of existence (including, of course, the production of meaning) raises serious questions about discourse theory. It begs the question to claim that discourse theory surpasses the divide between "facticity" and "validity" because of what amounts to its self-referential interest. Self-referential interests can only be tested when the Other as Other interrupts the isolated reference to themselves. Does this mean that the Other has to accept the rules of the game in order to play with validity? Has not the Other as Other brought into question that self-referentiality? What would it mean to include the Other in the language game? It seems to me that the possibility of that dialogue was present in the early works of Habermas in which, paradoxically, the interest of reason in itself was based on the presumed universality of reason expressed in human "quasi-transcendental" interests. But then it was possible to question that reason and its interest in emancipation by an examination of the poiesis that gave rise to its content. Now it is no longer necessary to raise that issue. All roads presumably lead to the North Atlantic, and it is a purely empirical question why it is that now-discursive reason's interest in itself arose first in the West. The strange lack of self-criticism in the latest Habermas reduces itself to an accusation that the Other does not have the cultural resources to criticize discourse theory.

> The development of constitutional democracy along the celebrated "North Atlantic" path has certainly provided us with results worth preserving, but once those who do not have the good fortune to be heirs of the Founding Fathers turn to their own traditions, they cannot find criteria and reasons that would allow them to distinguish what is worth preserving from what should be rejected.[69]

In particular, Habermas's recent assertion that it is possible to channel "the ghetto" to "society's norms" not only expresses the infelicitous representation of the ghetto as the nonsocial, but also it takes away all responsibility from Habermas's own version of the "social" (presumably the ideal speech situation implicit in liberal legal theory) at a time when the issue is not the rechanneling but the transformation of channels, not the validity of discourse theory but its effectiveness.[70]

In fact, the very ineffectiveness of discourse theory may be indicative of a more serious problem: Its interest in the preservation of discourse modes that benefit the real material conditions of existence of small sectors and social classes in societies both at the center and at the periphery of the world-system. If so, then discourse theory functions as a cloak to disguise the preservation of a particularistic poiesis of meaning and privilege. Discourse theory has become the new world order's "*point d'honneur*, its enthusiasm, its moral sanction, its solemn completion, its universal ground for consolation and justification."[71]

In contrast to a linguistic turn that privileges "what-is," Dussel's analectics seeks to show how exclusion and domination are *produced* by the very praxis of modernity, which I develop in the following section.

THE CENTER/PERIPHERY DISTINCTION

This issue occupies a prominent place in Dussel's "philosophy of liberation." Gilberto Pérez Villacampa has stressed how Dussel's move toward the redefinition of the Other as living labor brings the Latin American problematic of dependence into the process of world history. Dussel's "Latin American reading" of Marx, says Pérez Villacampa,

> shows how [Dussel] now brandishes Marx as a critic of the totalitarian culture that has justified the negation of the other, while before [in his earlier writings] he excluded Latin America from the historico-universal process because he considered Marx a representative of eurocentered ontological thought.[72]

Much as the exteriority of Schelling's conception of the positive served as a metaphor for the reconstruction of Marx's economic theory on the basis of the notion of exteriority, Wallerstein's reconstruction of the meaning of historical capitalism is central to Dussel's reconstruction of a *Marxist* dependency theory. According to Wallerstein, we must discard the progressivist model of historical development that has distorted many Marxist theories of development. Addressing both the transition to capitalism and to socialism, Wallerstein argues that

> the image of historical capitalism having arisen via the overthrow of a backward aristocracy by a progressive bourgeoisie is wrong. Instead, the correct basic image is that historical capitalism was brought into existence by a landed aristocracy which transformed itself into a bourgeoisie because the old system was disintegrating. . . . If this new image is correct however, it radically amends our perception of the present tran-

> sition from capitalism to socialism, from a capitalist world-economy to a social world-order. Up to now, the 'proletarian revolution' has been modelled, more or less, on the 'bourgeois revolution'. As the bourgeoisie overthrew the aristocracy, so the proletariat would overthrow the bourgeoisie. This analogy has been the fundamental building block of the strategic action of the world socialist movement.[73]

This model has been influential in Marxist circles, including dependency circles, that, first, saw history as progressing toward socialism on the basis of a model of successively dominant collective class subjects (not much unlike Hegel's conception of the development of the "objective Spirit" along the succession of dominant nation-states),[74] and, second, saw a national subject, a people, assume the role of both the national bourgeoisie and the national proletariat in the poor countries because of the incapacity of both to carry out the tasks of development. Although Dussel has often spoken in terms of the "people," he has done it in the terms of an analectics of exteriority that also attempts to respond against the charges of populism in his theory.[75] It seems to me that Dussel first developed the notion of a popular *exteriority* (under the influence of Levinas and the social tasks and demands of the Argentine situation during the 1960s and 1970s),[76] enriched that conception of exteriority through his Schellingian and Judeo-Christian reading of Marx's conception of living labor, and finally synthesized the two through, in part, Wallerstein's theory of world systems.[77]

Nonetheless, Pérez Villacampa is partially right. Dussel's rereading of Marx links his ethics of the 1970s to a critical theory of dependency that recovers Marxism for Latin America and, ultimately, a new ethics of the Other for capitalist globalization. His search for the origins of dependency theory in Marx's own project is important for the legitimation of dependency theory in Latin American Marxist circles. Apparently, it is one of the two major purposes of Dussel's work on Marx, the other being, as noted above, the reinterpretation of Marx's theory of labor along analectical lines. But it is not a purpose isolated from Dussel's philosophy of liberation. In fact, the conceptualization of dependency theory and that of his ethics share some very profound similarities, which raises an important question: Was Marx's theory implicitly a dependency theory?

Dependency theory may be defined in general *and* simplistic terms as follows: it is an *antidevelopmentalist* theory that describes a system of colonial and, later, neocolonial underdevelopment (and distorted or uneven development) in the countries and regions of what came to be called the Third World. The theory claims that this system of underdevelopment and distorted development was produced and reproduced by the patterns of domination that the countries of the center (or the colonialist and neocolonialist countries) imposed on the Third World to augment the wealth of the capitalist class of the center countries (whether of colonial times or of neocolonial and postcolonial times). The consequence of this, according to the theory, is a development in the peripheral countries that is subordinate to the needs and interests of the capitalist class of the center countries and does not respond to the needs and interests of the people of the periphery (except, often enough, the indigenous bourgeoisie).[78] Instead, what characterizes the social and economic situation of the periphery is high unemployment and low salaries for those employed (including those employed in the new factories producing export products) and generalized poverty.

Thus little changes with every turn of the wheel of international capitalism. In fact, if we add to the description of dependency what is going on today we can discover more of the same, significantly in those countries that have assumed most fully the neoliberal project of development: the concentration of capital in advanced technologies, the collapse of unproductive medium and small capital companies, monetarist policies to reduce income in order to counter inflationary pressures, and a sharper concentration of wealth with a widening gap between rich and poor.

Dependency theory is also a critique of developmentalism, namely, of the belief prevalent then (and now) among bourgeois economic circles that underdeveloped countries only need economic development along the lines of the already developed nations and regions of the world in order to attain social well-being. Dependentists, however, argued that the linear model of development offered by economic planners and advisers erred in two important ways. First, the developmentalist linear model of development assumed a time line of development with the developed countries at one end of the line and the underdeveloped and developing countries at the other end, moving (if moving at all) inexorably toward developed status. But such a characterization of the process conveniently glossed over the marked differences in wealth, consumption of resources, and quality of life—a gap between rich and poor that was growing ever broader. Second, developmentalist theory is blind to the "development of underdevelopment" that is produced by the development imposed by the capitalist countries of the center.[79] In general, dependency theory refers to the internal character of dependence of a socioeconomic system on another. It is important to stress the *internalized* character of the dependence. It is not an external domination of one country or system by another. Instead, the domination and the exploitation of one country by another are intrasystemic: they are part of the system of dependence. In my opinion, the dependence does not have to be coterminous solely with a capitalist system; patterns of internalized dependence may arise in other socioeconomic systems, for instance, in the extinct Soviet bloc. Hence, a critique of dependence and of domination based on the internalization of dependence patterns need not be a critique of capitalism.

But Marx's critique was a critique of capitalism. Does it mean that a dependency theory is not possible as part of that critique? Not at all, but they are not identical. Marx's critique of capitalism includes an implicit critique of imperialism and colonialism, but only within the context of capitalist development. But it is not true that Marx treats colonized and neocolonized countries as countries that could not develop any longer except outside the capitalist sphere. However, the most visible currents of dependency theory in Latin America have asserted, often under the exigency of the revolutionary conditions of the 1960s and 1970s, that if dependency theory has an aspect without which it is not dependency theory any longer, that aspect is the hypothesis that the "peripheral" countries have exhausted their lines of development within the system of dependence to which they belong. In this way, Latin American dependency theory was able to draw as well from the "Latin American Marxism" of the Peruvian José Carlos Mariátegui, who had asserted as early as the 1920s that Latin American development was no longer possible under the sphere of influence of capitalism. Referring to the agrarian situation in Peru during the mid-1920s, Mariátegui wrote in 1926 that bourgeois solutions to the economic problems of the Peruvian countryside were no longer feasible.

> In keeping with my ideological position, I believe that the moment for attempting the liberal, individualist method in Peru has already passed. Aside from reasons of doctrine, I consider that our agrarian problem has a special character due to an indisputable and concrete factor: the survival of the Indian "community" and of elements of practical socialism in indigenous agriculture and life.[80]

That view may complement Marx's view, and that is precisely what most dependentists have tried to do. But Dussel goes further. He develops dependency theory nondevelopmentally from Marx's own *theoretical* project after having transformed Marx's fundamental project as one built *from* and *for* the sake of the exteriority of living labor.

Thus any account of Dussel's development of dependency theory must be prefaced with the awareness that Dussel is critical of "historicist" and "phenomenalist" theories of dependency in Latin America that ultimately became, in distilled form, the mainstream social theory about Latin America in Europe and the United States. Thus Gary W. Wynia's *The Politics of Latin American Development* summarizes a very "un-Marxian" dependency theory when he simply states that it is a theory that holds that "domestic and international structures are inseparable"[81] and that military regimes during the 1960s and 1970s were the result of the requirements of dependent development and for the sake of the stable relations among multinationals, large domestic industry, and the state.[82] Similarly, Francis Fukuyama assumes such a phenomenalist account of dependency in his neocorporativist critique of dependency theory in *The End of History and the Last Man*.[83]

While Dussel provides a sophisticated critique of other currents of dependency theory in Latin America, he simultaneously articulates a conception of dependency theory that brings together Marx's economic works, Wallerstein's hypothesis of the world-system, and Dussel's own dialectical analectics. Regarding dependency theory, Dussel finds historicist works wanting precisely for the underdevelopment of the conceptual categories necessary for understanding dependency, namely, "categories as fundamental as value, price of production, or transference of surplus value."[84] But Dussel criticizes those views that regard dependency theory as merely an application of Marxism; Marx's theory was not a finished project: "to assign us only an 'application' of an unfinished theory—such as Marx's—would be to define ourselves within an unacceptable 'cultural and scientific dependence.'"[85] Yet Dussel argues against the view that a Marxist dependency theory is impossible because dependency theory stresses "national contradictions," whereas Marxism stresses "class contradictions." This position was taken by Latin American social theorists such as Agustín Cueva and was also assumed by Marxist theoreticians in the United States.[86] Thus, for instance, in the same year that Cueva wrote his essay, Elizabeth Dore and John Weeks wrote a critical essay trying to show the categorial incompatibility of Marxist economics and dependency theory. Of course, it is true that while Marx did see possibilities of socialist revolution in some "peripheral" countries, he did not think that they had exhausted the lines of their socioeconomic development within capitalism; that would have been a wrong-headed position, and Marx never took it. But Dore and Weeks did not rest on the historically anecdotal; instead, they tried to show that a dependency theory which assumes such a stand is implicitly stating that "inequality among countries is not the result of capitalism itself, but of a 'country' losing 'its' surplus."[87] If so, Marx's critique of capitalism, as a critique of the "exploitation of labor in the social form of labor power (free wage labor)"[88] by a class of capitalists, rather than a country, becomes de trop. Whether Marx's critique is still adequate or not is another issue. However, a theory of dependency that claims to embrace Marx's own theory would be hard-pressed to show, if Cueva and Weeks and Dore had been right, that dependent capitalism is dependent because of the extraction of its surplus by a country rather than a social class.

Dussel wants to show (against Cueva and, therefore, against theories such as Weeks and Dore's) that class and national contradictions are dialectically connected and, therefore, inclusive of each other. Dussel cites Marx on that issue: "From the fact that profits may be below surplus value it follows that nations can continuously exchange between them . . . without thereby obtaining equal profits . . . except that in this case it does not happen in the same measure as between capitalist and laborer."[89]

Dussel tries to derive dependency theory from the Marxist theory of surplus value. It should be stressed that the Marxist theory of surplus value used by Dussel is the one he develops in his reading of the Marxist concept of living labor. As I stated in the previous section, there are Schellingian and religious metaphors implicit in that reading. However, it is a mistake to carry that metaphor too far. If we did, we would simply transform Dussel's own dependency theory into an undifferentiable affirmation of a metaphysical positivity that is always other than the totality of what-is. Dussel's critique of *developmentalism* is a nuanced recovery of a nondevelopmentalist Marx and a critique of merely sociological and historicist accounts of dependency and exteriority. Thus we must move beyond the Schellingian inspiration and, as I said above, we must keep in mind the influence on his thought of social theorists such as Wallerstein.

Whether in terms of classical theories of imperialism, or more contemporary ones such as dependency theory, social formation, excentric, hybridization models, and so on,[90] all those theories seem to share what Baran and Sweezy called more than thirty years ago the "hunger of the multinational corporations for maximum *Lebensraum*."[91] If I am right regarding my interpretation of Dussel, I think that he would add that multinationals look for "living space" because they need *living labor* for their profits. It is with Dussel's own recovery of the "economic" Marx for dependency theory that I am now concerned.

According to Marx, capital is created from the use of surplus labor. To the extent, however, that more and more capital is converted into constant capital, the rate of profit goes down. It is arguable that the decrease in the rate of profit has been countered by the superprofits obtained by multinational capital through the exploitation of cheap labor in the peripheral countries, although rapid technological changes and the creation of value by new technologies is, oddly enough, not considered by Dussel. However, there is little evidence for thinking that the reason for the superprofits lies in the fact that there is more living labor in peripheral labor than in the labor of the central countries. In fact, there would be less abstract social labor in the labor of the peripheral countries than in that of the central countries precisely because of the relatively low productivity of the labor of the peripheral countries due, in large part, to the use of less productive technologies and, therefore, a lesser organic composition of capital. There is no paradox here. Or it is as much of an apparent paradox as the one exploded by Marx in *Capital:* It is not the quantity of labor power that measures the values of commodities, but rather the quantity of socially necessary labor. The quantity of socially necessary labor in the peripheral countries allows for the making of large profits by multinational corporations even when cutting-edge technology is being used (as is the case with the "maquiladoras" of peripheral countries, such as Mexico). It is not that living labor is producing more value; rather, under conditions of global capital, labor power in peripheral countries has less reproductive value. Couple that with the monetarist policies that effectively keep workers' incomes depressed so that there is less inflationary pressure on prices, and it can be seen that in fact contemporary dependency produces superprofits by reducing what is socially necessary for workers to live and reproduce. That is accompanied by the introduction of cutting-edge technologies in both the central and the peripheral countries.

A passage of great significance for Dussel's own brand of dependency theory is the following by Marx from the *1863–1865 Manuscripts*.

> The fundamental law of capitalist *competition,* which political economy has not yet understood, namely the law that regulates the general rate of profit and the so-called prices of production determined by it, bases itself . . . on this difference between the *value* and the *cost price* of the commodity, as well as on the possibility that arises from that difference to sell the commodity with a profit and below its value.[92]

This is significant for Dussel because it establishes the possibility of a *Marxian* dependency theory that may establish how it is possible for the imperialist countries of the center to exploit the colonized and neocolonized countries of the periphery. Thus Dussel says that the contradiction between price and value of the commodity is merely apparent, for

> in reality, the difference between the "sales price" (there are many types of "prices") and the value of a commodity is equal in global world capitalism as a whole (or in the abstract). Only at this level do they coincide, and that is why the law is fulfilled. In all other cases, whether concrete or abstract, it is a matter of a distribution of surplus value of a capital that is transferred to another [capital]. Global surplus value does not change, but what changes is its presence in the individual capital, in the branch of production, or in the country. Marx is thus able to save the fundamental principle that living labor produces all value and surplus value. Every price is founded on and is derived from some value.[93]

Dussel arrives at this point thus: First, all value and surplus value are objectified living labor. Second, a commodity placed in the market has its "market value" determined by competition (with other commodities); thus competition exerts a leveling function by transferring value and surplus value from some commodities to others.[94] Third, Marx calls "price of production" the process by which competition equalizes profits between branches and countries and distributes surplus value from some capitals to other capitals. Fourth, the "price of production" functions as the center around which "market prices" revolve.[95] Fifth, market value explains oscillations in supply and demand, and not vice versa: ultimately, it is socially necessary labor that determines value and, mediately, market value; market value determines supply and demand; and supply and demand determine market price.[96]

> Work is always the point of departure and arrival. Furthermore, Marx is interested in the ethical question, that is, in the degree of exploitation of labor. . . . If one forgets about commodity value (as some post-Marxisms do, such as is the case with Paul Sweezy), the categorial link between living labor and price is lost, the law of value ceases to fulfill its function, and market mechanisms begin to revolve around and [move] from capital itself; Thus capital is fetishized and living labor is negated.[97]

Dussel argues that Marx had decided to write a treatise on competition explaining more fully the movement of surplus value from one capital to another. For it is by means of competition that surplus value is transferred, distributed, or leveled off; it does not create value.[98]

Dussel argues that this type of analysis is more concrete, and under it falls the issue of foreign commerce and dependency, which would in turn counter the tendency of the rate of profit to fall: "peripheral, underdeveloped, and dependent capital is exploited by central and developed capital; this exploitation is a compensatory mechanism against the law of the fall of the rate of profit."[99]

Dussel stresses that for Marx commercial capital, interest, and credit do not generate value, although the fetishism of capital makes it appear otherwise. Thus Dussel quotes Marx:

> The absurdity of capitalist representation attains here its culminating point, since instead of explaining the valorization of capital by the exploitation of the capacity to work, it goes on inversely by explaining the productivity of the labor force as if the latter were also that mystical thing that is called interest-bearing capital.[100]

So far, then, Dussel has presented two basic points in his reading of Marx's economic theory: living labor is an exteriority to capital, and dependency theory shows how surplus value is transferred from peripheral capital to metropolitan capital. The latter requires a rethinking of capitalism, in particular, a move from unilinear to multilinear conceptions of the history of capitalism. Dussel claims that Marx begins to do precisely that during the 1870s, when he analyzes the peasantry and Russian socioeconomic formations.

> During the 1870s Marx tackled a problematic of great importance for Latin America, which may have something to do with his relatively low theoretical fruitfulness [during that period]. It has to do with the research on less developed capitalist countries, the peasant question, and . . . the issues related to the Russian peasantry. It is possible that Marx finds himself [then] open to a theoretical space that questioned some of the presuppositions of the period preceding 1870, for instance, his use of England as the model for the study of capital *in general,* in such a way that he would have *generalized* as essential to the concept of capital some determinations that were specific to the more developed *central* capital; perhaps, he should have considered it instead as a case of *developed* capitalism.[101]

Thus Dussel attempts to show that there were strains within Marx's theory that should lead us to fruitful developments in dependency theory. Although this does not commit us to say that Marxian theory is a dependency theory, yet the two may be synthesized in a creative and categorially defensible way.

I had mentioned above that Dussel's reconceptualization of Marx's economic theory integrates, in addition to dependency theory and dialectical analectics, aspects of Wallerstein's theory of world systems.[102] Following Wallerstein, Dussel argues that the present world-system arose with the conquest of America. That conquest marked the birth of a new system that led to the eventual collapse of the interregional system in which Europe was only a periphery to the Mediterranean African-Arab center. Also, with the establishment of the world-system, the first *world* peripheries arose—Latin America and then Asia and Africa. According to Dussel this marks the birth of modernity, which includes not only Europe but also what is Other to Europe. Modernity is a global phenomenon, not an intra-European phenomenon. Since its origin, the developmentalist and sacrificial paradigms that legitimated not only the view that Western Europe gave rise to the idea of autonomy but also the legitimation of conquest, colonization, and war against the Other have been attached to it, like a tumor that is knotted to the nerves of an organism.

Dussel argues that the birth of modernity thus gives rise simultaneously to the center and the periphery of the world-system, meaning that modernity is the rise of both the identity of the system (in this case a global system) and the excluded Other qua excluded. It follows, it seems to me, that the Other, while categorially a priori, is historically a posteriori. Thus it is possible to develop a conception of Dusselian critique that is grounded also on the notion of the analectical a posteriori.

The notion of the "analectical a posteriori" may be a non-Dusselian category, for it comes close to the ontological dialectical affirmation that the Other arises from the same. We know that Dussel was critical of ontologizing interpretations of dialectic (at one time, in fact, identifying dialectics with ontology). For Dussel, analectics implies a movement toward an a priori Other. This is so because Otherness, or alterity, is in Dussel a positive actuality that is beyond a totality, and thus it *is*—albeit it is *unconceptualizable within the notions of the totality*—and therefore it is *not for that totality.* What for Hegel would therefore be undialectical dross, Dussel's Shellingianism constructs as the analectical and positive moment of the dialectic. The *a prioricity* of the analectical moment for Dussel is exemplified in his first ethics, in which alterity is typified as an absolute positivity; it is also apparent in his works on Marx in which the other is a metaphysical creator of value from outside capital and capitalism, and in theological works such as *Ethics and Community* in which the metaphysical community is contrasted to the concrete historical society as "alterity" to "sameness." Finally, a similar metaphysical framework is found in his more recent works, such as *Invention of the Americas* and *Etica de la liberación.* Thus, for instance, the references to Aztec and Tupí duality in the first text do point to a notion of analectical a priori as a categorial ground that nourishes Dussel's cultural analysis.[103] In the latter work, there is a similar representation of the analectical moment as a priori when Dussel elaborates on the historical passage from the Neolithic stage 1 to the stage 2 of the early metals as a movement from duality to a masculine unity for which difference and plurality are constructed as sin and the fall.[104]

It seems to follow that for Dussel, alterity can only be portrayed as an a priori positive moment that is denied in all ontologizing. If so, Eduardo Mendieta would seem to be right that Dussel's thought represents the necessary metaphysical complement to the politics of discourse ethics. The implication was that not only did discourse theory stand in need of a metaphysics, but also that Dusselian metaphysics could not be a politics.[105]

However, it is possible to see in the narrative of the rise of modernity a representation of the analectical moment as a posteriori, insofar as it is created in the birth of the new ontology. And yet it is possible to preserve the Dusselian critique of ontologizing (and of any ontological dialectics) insofar as the creation of that analectical moment from the same is not the exhaustion of its reality. In fact, the Other as excluded is one of the integral marks of modernity. In the case of an analectical a priori, the meaning of alterity is metaphysical and protohistorical. In the case of an analectical a posteriori, alterity is historical, but it is not reducible to "the same" of the ontological totality, for the same is not productive of the Other. Instead, both the same and the Other account for the development of the reality that in its inception gave birth to the same as dominator and the Other as excluded and dominated. The positivity of the other—in Dussel's Schellingian sense of positivity—rests also on the fact that it is not reducible to the categories imposed by the same. Finally, that positivity is also apparent in that the Other accounts not only for some of the negative aspects of modernity (its ontologizing and sacrificial features) but also for its liberating "metaphysical" possibilities.

Is the Other "outside" history? Only in the sense that history has a hegemonic quality, but not insofar as that history is or can be contested by the periphery to the hegemonic center. Thus the exteriority of living labor to capital is metasystemic vis-à-vis capital and it is, therefore, a priori to capital. However, it is a posteriori and *intrasystemic* to capital once it has been integrated into the movement of capital production, that is, once it has been through the historical expropriation (e in fig. 11.2) of the instruments of labor by a nonlaboring class (the nascent bourgeoisie), alienated from the laborer as labor power to be bought and used in the production and creation of value (i.e., the reproduction of its value under the socially necessary conditions of capitalist production at a given time and the creation of surplus value "from the nothing of capital," as Dussel says). Furthermore, living labor (LL1 in fig. 11.2) is a posteriori and *extrasystemic* (or *metasystemic*) to capital in the sense that it has a history that precedes the rise of the capitalist system (CS) and incorporates other past systems (PS), that is, other traditions, other social relations, and, as is often the case, other (precapitalist) forms of domination and exploitation of labor.

Thus the historicity of human labor (and need and desire) do not preclude its exteriority to capitalism; on the contrary, it requires it. But it is an exteriority that is only metasystemic (outside the totality of a particular system) and not meta-

Figure 11.2 Historical Antecedents to the Exteriority of Living Labor under Capitalism

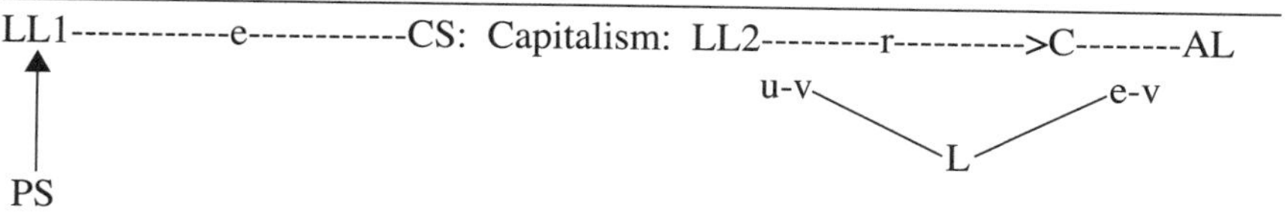

LL1: precapitalist living labor; LL2: living labor under capitalism; L: the labor power commodity; AL: alienated labor; u-v: use value of labor power; e-v: exchange value of labor power; e: expropriation of instruments of labor during rise of capitalism; r: reification of living labor; CS: present capitalist system; PS: past system

physical. This distinction is also methodologically important, for an analectical a posteriori reading of exteriority preserves or keeps open the spirit of critique *on* the analectical moment. The analectical moment's apparent "positivity" disguises its own negativity or self-negation. Therein lies the significance of Hegel's critique of an absolute positivity and his view that all consciousness is "something that goes beyond limits, and since these limits are its own, it is something that goes beyond itself."[106] But this is also, in my view and as I tried to show above, the significance of Marx's own conception of living labor as, to use Dussel's terminology, a "positive exteriority"[107] vis-à-vis capital, Marx's *nicht-Kapital* within the sphere of domination of capital and as itself the negation of precapitalist forms of production. These are the two senses of a posteriori to which I just referred: First, living labor (LL2 in fig. 11.2) is logically dependent on capital (C) insofar as it has become a commodity bought and used in the production process for the production of value and the creation of surplus value; *and*, second, it (LL1) is logically antecedent to capitalism insofar as it has a history of social conditions and precapitalist formations that constitute it.

This effort at a reconstruction of Dusselian critique without an analectical a priori is in part unfair to Dussel, for it should be obvious to anyone that Dussel's thought is profoundly inspired by the phenomenology of religious service to humanity. Schutte's early characterization of Dussel's philosophy of liberation as emphasizing the spatial, in contrast to the more temporalizing philosophy of liberation,[108] as well as Cerutti Guldberg's categorization of Dussel's philosophy of liberation as ahistorical, are true only insofar as Dussel does reject historicist contructions because of their real or imagined tendencies toward hegemony and exclusion. Yet I find it unproductive either to remain bound to the content of Dussel's early work regarding Marxism, feminism, and homosexuality or to be suspicious about the theological and religious aspects apparent in his work. For religious experience and faith do not exclude critique nor does Dussel's conception of the a prioricity of the analectical moment proscribe its construction as an a posteriori and yet irreducible moment of history.

NOTES

1. Enrique Dussel, "Autopercepción intelectual de un proceso histórico," *Anthropos* 180 (September–October 1998): 13–36, 17.

2. Karl Marx and Frederick Engels, *The German Ideology* (Moscow: Progress Publishers, 1976), 65, 639 n. 20.

3. Enrique Dussel, *Etica de la liberación en la edad de la globalización y la exclusión* (Madrid: Editorial Trotta, 1998), 304.

4. See Horacio Cerutti Guldberg, *Filosofía de la liberación latinoamericana,* 2d ed. (Mexico: Fondo de Cultura Económica, [1983] 1992), 32ff. See also Cerutti Guldberg, "Actual Situation and Perspectives of Latin American Philosophy for Liberation," *Philosophical Forum* 20, no. 1–2 (1988–1989): 43–61, 49. See also Ofelia Schutte, *Cultural*

Identity and Social Liberation in Latin American Thought (Albany: SUNY Press, 1993), 203, for criticisms of Dussel's negation of a woman's right to abortion and his judgment of gays and lesbians as "totalizing" because of their homosexuality. But see Dussel, "Filosofía de la liberación desde la praxis de los oprimidos," in *Historia de la filosofía y filosofía de la liberación* (Bogota: Editorial Nueva América, 1994), 172, for a self-correction on those issues criticized by Schutte supra. A similar, albeit less clear, argument is presented by Dussel in defense of the right to homosexuality. It is interesting that in Schutte's mention of this essay (Schutte, *Cultural Identity,* 274 n. 87), Schutte cites Dussel's reference to the person being always an end. I stress instead the reference to the body as one's being because that is precisely the concept toward which Dussel has moved in his recovery of Marx's economic writings, and it seems to be in keeping with some aspects of Dussel's thinking in his latest *Etica* about the materiality and corporeity of human life in community, as I will suggest in this essay. Dussel now refers to himself as a "Marxist" (in a taped interview with the author, Mexico City, 1996). I suspect that Dussel's new Marxism is in part responsible for the critique of homophobia and sexism that he in fact began to develop immediately after his novel reading of Marx. However, does a Levinasian emphasis on gender difference (or, rather, dis-tinctness) constitute an *over*emphasis that retards rather than promotes women's liberation? Can a non-*feminist* theory and praxis effectively move past Simone de Beauvoir's reminder that women have an awareness of their own consciousness, as well as her criticism of Levinas's construction of the *alterité* of the "feminine" as also an expression of "masculine privilege"? (See Simone de Beauvoir, *The Second Sex*, trans. H. M. Parshley [New York: Vintage, 1989], xxii n. 3.) Will the same criticism apply to Levinasian constructions of socioeconomic class? But here, as in constructions of gender and race, we must distinguish, with Göran Therborn, between, on the one hand, "the alter-ideology of the dominating subjects," which seeks "to *mould* the subjectivity of the Other," and, on the other hand, "the alter-ideology of the dominated," which seeks to *resist* the Other, rather than form him or her. In terms of the gendering of the Other, Beauvoir saw Levinas as doing the former. See Göran Therborn, *The Ideology of Power and the Power of Ideology* (London: Verso, 1980), 28.

5. Enrique Dussel, personal communication, e-mail, April 24, 1999.

6. Dussel, *Hacia un Marx desconocido: Un comentario de los "Manuscritos del 61–63"* (Mexico: Siglo XXI Editores, 1988), 57–58.

7. Cited in Dussel, *Hacia un Marx desconocido*, 62–63.

8. Ibid., 63–64.

9. Dussel, *Filosofía ética latinoamericana*, vol. 1, *Presupuestos de una filosofía de la liberación* (Mexico: Editorial Edicol, 1977), 87–88.

10. Marx is "imprisoned within the category of Totality, especially because of the *Gattungswesen* conception of man as humanity" (Dussel, *Filosofía ética latinoamericana*, 1:116).

11. Ibid., 118. Italics mine.

12. Jürgen Habermas, *Knowledge and Human Interests,* trans. Jeremy J. Shapiro (Boston: Beacon, 1971), 281.

13. Dussel, *Ethics and Community*, trans. Robert R. Barr (Maryknoll, N.Y.: Orbis, 1988), 117.

14. Ibid.

15. Ibid., 131.

16. Ibid.

17. Enrique Dussel, *El último Marx (1863–1882) y la liberación latinoamericana* (Mexico: Siglo XXI Editores, 1990), 47.

18. Ibid.

19. In a virtual communication with me the North American economist David Andrews of Cazenovia College made the following clarification: "On my reading of Marx, labor power is alienated. Insofar as workers are paid for a period of time, per hour, per day, per week, it is labor power that is being sold, not labor. A clever or nasty capitalist may get quite a lot of labor out of one hour's worth of labor power by forcing a worker to work very hard, or a worker may successfully shirk and avoid working hard and thereby not give the capitalist very much labor for that hour. The capitalist might like to purchase labor directly but is unable to and therefore must devise means of extracting labor from labor power. Some quantity of labor is alienated, but labor power is also alienated: the worker surrenders its capacity for work for the time in which it is employed in that whatever labor is generated will belong to the capitalist" (David Andrews, e-mail to author, 28 August 1999).

20. In Dussel, *El último Marx,* 135.

21. Karl Marx, *Capital: A Critique of Political Economy,* vol. 1, *The Process of Capitalist Production*, trans. Samuel Moore and Edward Aveling (New York: International Publishers, 1967), 167.

22. Dussel, *El último Marx*, 138.

23. Ibid.

24. Ibid.

25. Ibid., 139.

26. Ibid., 300–301, 302.

27. Ibid., 301–2.

28. Ibid., 306.

29. bid.

30. Ibid.

31. Ibid., 309.

32. Ibid., 316.

33. Ibid., 312, 314–15.

34. Ibid., 317.

35. Ibid., 313 n. 62.

36. Ibid., 317.

37. Ibid., 318.

38. Ibid., 320.

39. Ibid., 321.

40. Ibid., 326–27.

41. Ibid., 330.

42. Ibid., 328–29.

43. Ibid., 51.

44. Ibid.

45. Ibid., 57.

46. Ibid., 63.

47. Ibid., 64.

48. Ibid., 65.

49. Enrique Dussel, *Philosophy of Liberation*, trans. Christine Markovsky and Aquilina Martínez (Maryknoll, N.Y: Orbis, 1985), 19.

50. Enrique Dussel, *The Invention of the Americas*, trans. Michael Barber (New York: Continuum, 1995), 36.

51. See Leopoldo Zea's comments in Vicente Bello Serrano, "A 504 Años, América Busca Democracia," *El Excelsior*, 12 October 1996, electronic edition: www.excelsior.com.mx/9610/961012/nac24.html.

52. Leopoldo Zea, "Identity: A Latin American Philosophical Problem," *Philosophical Forum* 20, no. 1–2 (1988–1989): 33–42, 35.

53. Dussel, *Invention of the Americas*, 120–31.

54. See Lynda Lange's review of Dussel's *Invention of the Americas*, "Burnt Offerings to Rationality: A Feminist Reading of the Construction of Indigenous Peoples in Enrique Dussel's Theory of Modernity," *Hypatia* 13, no. 3 (1998): 132–45, 134.

55. Dussel, *Invention of the Americas*, 35.

56. Dussel, *Etica de la liberación,* 200.

57. Ibid.

58. Jürgen Habermas, *Communication and the Evolution of Society,* trans. Thomas McCarthy (Boston: Beacon, 1979), 89.

59. Karl Marx, *Karl Marx: Early Writings*, trans. Rodney Livingstone and Gregor Benton (New York: Vintage, 1975), 209.

60. Jürgen Habermas, *Theory of Communicative Action*, vol. 1, *Reason and the Rationalization of Society*, trans. Thomas McCarthy (Boston: Beacon, 1984), 130.

61. Jürgen Habermas, *Between Facts and Norms: Contributions to a Discourse Theory of Law and Democracy,* trans. William Rehg (1992; reprint, Cambridge: MIT Press, 1996), 8–9.

62. Jürgen Habermas, introduction to *Theory and Practice*, trans. John Viertel (Boston: Beacon, 1974), 18.

63. Habermas, *Between Facts and Norms*, 10–11, 13–17.

64. Habermas, *Communication and the Evolution of Society*, 71.

65. Habermas, *Theory of Communicative Action,* 1:44–45.

66. Ibid., p. 212.

67. Rudyard Kipling, "Mandalay," in *From Beowulf to Modern British Writers,* ed. John Ball (New York: Odyssey, 1959), 1141. See also Rudyard Kipling, "The White Man's Burden," in *History of the World since 1500,* ed. J. M. Roberts (New York: Knopf, 1976), 736.

68. By contrast, Habermas would call a universal interest reason's interest in itself. He has asserted this view in works as disparate as *Knowledge and Human Interests* and *Between Facts and Norms* (xli). But in the former, there was not a divorce of reason's self-criticality from the material conditions of its existence. See Jürgen Habermas, *Knowledge and Human Interests*, trans. Jeremy J. Shapiro (Boston: Beacon, 1971), 212: *"It is in accomplishing self-reflection that reason grasps itself as interested."*

69. Habermas, *Between Facts and Norms,* 2–3.

70. I am referring to remarks made by Habermas at the 1998 SPEP Conference in Denver, Colorado.

71. Karl Marx, "Toward the Critique of Hegel's *Philosophy of Right*," in Karl Marx and Frederick Engels, *Marx and Engels: Basic Writings on Politics and Philosophy*, ed. Lewis S. Feuer (Garden City, N.Y.: Anchor, 1959), 263. Of course, discourse theory will never assume the role that religion has played in the alienated transcendence of the world. But it has become, in Habermas's latest version, a formalized immanence of the status quo.

72. Gilberto Pérez Villacampa, "¿De la metafísica de la alteridad al humanismo real?" *Islas* 99 (May–August 1991): 160–67, 165.

73. Immanuel Wallerstein, *Historical Capitalism* (London: Verso, 1983), 105–6.

74. G. W. F. Hegel, *The Philosophy of Right,* trans. T. M. Knox (Oxford: Oxford University Press, 1967), 217–18, para. 346–47.

75. See Enrique Dussel, "La 'cuestión popular,'" *Nuestra América* 4, no. 11 (1984): 15–27, 24–26, in which he develops an analectical and Gramscian conception of *pueblo* as an *exterior* social and historical *bloc.*

76. Dussel's work resonates with the work on cultural symbolism and the "being" of the (Latin) American poor by another Argentine philosopher, Rodolfo Kusch, who flourished during the 1960s. Even the anti-Marxism of Kusch, because of Marxism's perceived economic reductionism, shares interesting parallels with the critique of Marxist *ontology* in Dussel's first major ethics. See Dussel, *Filosofía ética latinoamericana,* 1:116: "Karl Marx . . . more Hegelian than the aforementioned [Dussel had just referred in the same paragraph to Feuerbach, Kierkegaard, Comte, Husserl, and Heidegger] stays imprisoned within the category of Totality, especially by the notion of *Gattungswesen* of man as humanity. . . . The category of Totality *[Totalidad]* continues to include all the moments of Marx's thought. All the dialectical oppositions are internal to the All *[Todo]* of nature and history, and, on his [Marx's] part, by man having been reduced to only one praxis, as labor *[trabajo]*, Totality is in the end cultural: *homo faber.*" The Dussel of the 1980s, however, discovers in the same thought Marx's anthropological conception of the human the "dialogical alterity" *[Alteridad dialógica]* not found in the debate with Althusserian Marxism. See Domenico Jervolino, in his "Per una filosofia della liberazione dal punto di vista cosmopolitico," *Anthropos* 180 (September-October 1998): 74–80, 75. Finally, regarding Kusch, see Rodolfo Kusch, *Esbozo de una antropología filosófica americana* (Buenos Aires: Ediciones Castañeda, 1978). In this work, Kusch develops an "ontology of the poor" on the basis of testimonials and an ethnography informed by Heideggerian thinking (p. 37) and the *estar,* rather than *ser*, of the (Latin) American (p. 92).

77. For Wallerstein's influential text on Dussel, see Immanuel Wallerstein, *The Modern World System,* 2 vols. (New York: Academic, 1974).

78. I am grateful to the North American economist David Andrews of Cazenovia College for this essential and important clarification (David Andrews, e-mail to author, 28 August 1999).

79. Horacio Cerutti Guldberg, *Filosofía de la liberación latinoamericana,* 2d ed. (Mexico: Fondo de Cultura Económica, 1992); Gustavo Gutiérrez, *A Theology of Liberation*, trans. Caridad Inca and John Eagleson (Maryknoll, N.Y.: Orbis, 1988) 16ff., 51ff. (15th anniversary edition); and André Gunder Frank, *Lumpenburguesía: Lumpendesarrollo* (Mexico: Series Popular Era, 1974), 13–14, 33.

80. José Carlos Mariátegui, *Seven Interpretive Essays on Peruvian Reality*, trans. Marjory Urquidi (Austin: University of Texas Press, 1971), 33.

81. Gary W. Wynia, *The Politics of Latin American Development,* 2d ed. (Cambridge: Cambridge University Press, 1984), 127.

82. Ibid., 130.

83. Francis Fukuyama, *The End of History and the Last Man* (New York: Avalon, 1992), 99–103. This work by Fukuyama is notable principally for its attempt to ground predatory capitalism (so-called liberal democracy and free-market economics) on what amounts to cultural corporativism or a "community" feeling of solidarity for vertical (i.e., unequal) structures in "posthistorical" societies. See Fukuyama, *End of History,* 237, 318,

326–27, 334–35, 338 for Fukuyama on civil rights, posthistorical adventures of "noble warriors" in "historical" societies, and the legitimation of "megalothymia."

84. Dussel, *Hacia un Marx desconocido*, 324.

85. Ibid., 326.

86. Ibid., 328.

87. John Weeks and Elizabeth Dore, "International Exchange and the Causes of Backwardness," *Latin American Perspectives* 21, no. 2 (1979): 66.

88. Ibid., 65.

89. Marx, *Grundrisse,* cited in Dussel, *Hacia un Marx desconocido,* 328.

90. For a review of the literature, see Patrick Wolfe's review essay "History and Imperialism: A Century of Theory from Marx to Postcolonialism," *American Historical Review,* April 1997, 388–420.

91. Paul A. Baran and Paul. M. Sweezy, "Notes on the Theory of Imperialism," in *Economic Imperialism*, ed. Kenneth E. Boulding and Tapan Mukerjee (Ann Arbor: University of Michigan Press, 1972), 170. This essay appeared originally in *Monthly Review,* March 1966.

92. Cited in Dussel, *El último Marx,* 74.

93. Ibid.

94. Ibid., 75.

95. Ibid., 76.

96. Ibid., 77.

97. Ibid., 77–78.

98. Ibid., 81–82.

99. Ibid., 85.

100. Ibid., 116.

101. Ibid., 133–34. See also 238ff.

102. Immanuel Wallerstein, *The Modern World System: Capitalist Agriculture and the Origin of the European World-Economy in the Sixteenth Century* (New York: Academic, 1974), 1:346ff.

103. Dussel, *Invention of the Americas*, 84–85.

104. Dussel, *Etica de la liberación,* 33.

105. Eduardo Mendieta, "Discourse Ethics and Liberation Ethics: At the Boundaries of Moral Theory," *Philosophy and Social Criticism* 21, no. 4 (1995): 111–26, 121.

106. G. F. W. Hegel, *Phenomenology of Spirit,* trans. A. V. Miller (Oxford: Clarendon, 1977), 51.

107. Dussel, *Hacia un Marx desconocido,* 368.

108. Ofelia Schutte, "Crisis de identidad occidental y reconstrucción latinoamericana," *Nuestra América* 4, no. 11 (1984): 61–68, 63.

REFERENCES

Baran, Paul A., and Martin Sweezy. 1972. "Notes on the Theory of Imperialism." In *Economic Imperialism*. Edited by Kenneth E. Boulding and Tapan Mukerjee. Ann Arbor: University of Michigan Press.

Beauvoir, Simone de. 1989. *The Second Sex.* Translated by H. M. Parshley. New York: Vintage.

Bello Serrano, Vicente. 1996. "A 504 Años, América Busca Democracia." *El Excelsior*, 12 October. Electronic edition: www.excelsior.com.mx/9610/961012/nac24.html.

Cerutti Guldberg, Horacio. 1988–1989. "Actual Situation and Perspectives of Latin American Philosophy for Liberation." *Philosophical Forum* 20, no. 1–2: 43–61.

———. [1983] 1992. *Filosofía de la liberación latinoamericana.* 2d ed. Mexico: Fondo de Cultura Económica.

Dussel, Enrique. 1977. *Filosofía ética latinoamericana.* Vol. 1, *Presupuestos de una filosofía de la liberación.* Mexico: Editoria Edicol.

———. 1984a. "Autopercepción intelectual de un proceso histórico." *Anthropos* 180 (September–October 1998): 13–36.

———. 1984b. "La 'cuestión popular.'" *Nuestra América* 4, no. 11: 15–27.

———. 1985. *Philosophy of Liberation.* Translated by Christine Marlovsky and Aquilina Martínez. Maryknoll, N.Y.: Orbis.

———. 1988a. *Ethics and Community.* Translated by Robert R. Barr. Maryknoll, N.Y.: Orbis.

———. 1988b. *Hacia un Marx Desconocido: Un comentario de los* Manuscritos del 61–63. Mexico: Siglo XXI Editores.

———. 1990. *El último Marx (1863–1882) y la liberación latinoamericana.* Mexico: Siglo XXI Editores.

———. 1995. *The Invention of the Americas.* Translated by Michael Barber. New York: Continuum.

———. 1998. *Etica de la liberación en la edad de la globalización y la exclusión.* Madrid: Editorial Trotta.

Fukuyama, Francis. 1992. *The End of History and the Last Man.* New York: Avon.

Gutiérrez, Gustavo. 1988. *A Theology of Liberation.* Translated by Caridad Inca and John Eagleson. Maryknoll, N.Y.: Orbis. Fifteenth anniversary edition.

Gunder Frank, André. 1974. 2d ed. *Lumpenburguesía: Lumpendesarrollo.* Mexico: Serie Popular Era.

Habermas, Jürgen. 1971. *Knowledge and Human Interests.* Translated by Jeremy J. Shapiro. Boston: Beacon.

———. 1974. *Theory and Practice.* Translated by John Viertel. Boston: Beacon.

———. 1979. *Communication and the Evolution of Society.* Translated by Thomas McCarthy. Boston: Beacon.

———. 1984. *The Theory of Communicative Action.* Vol. 1, *Reason and the Rationalization of Society.* Translated by Thomas McCarthy. Boston: Beacon.

———. [1992] 1996. *Between Facts and Norms: Contributions to a Discourse Theory of Law and Democracy.* Translated by William Rehg. Cambridge: MIT Press.

Hegel, G. W. F. 1967. *Philosophy of Right.* Translated by T. M. Knox. Oxford: Oxford University Press.

———. 1977. *Phenomenology of Spirit.* Translated by A. V. Miller. Oxford: Clarendon.

Jervolino, Domenico. "Per una filosofia della liberazione dal punto di vista cosmopolitico," *Anthropos* 180 (September–October 1998): 74–80.

Kipling, Rudyard. 1976. "The White Man's Burden." Cited in *History of the World since 1500.* Edited by J. M. Roberts. New York: Knopf. Originally published in *McClure's Magazine,* 12 February 1899.

Kusch, Rodolfo. 1978. *Esbozo de una antropología filosófica americana.* Buenos Aires: Ediciones Castañeda.

Lange, Lynda. 1998. "Burnt Offerings to Rationality: A Feminist Reading of the Construction of Indigenous Peoples in Enrique Dussel's Theory of Modernity." *Hypatia* 13, no. 3: 132–45.

Mariátegui, José Carlos. 1971. *Seven Interpretive Essays on Peruvian Reality.* Translated by Marjory Urquidi. Austin: University of Texas Press.

Mark, Karl, and Frederick Engels. 1959. *Marx and Engels: Basic Writings on Politics and Philosophy.* Edited by Lewis S. Feuer. Garden City, N.Y.: Anchor.

———. 1976. *The German Ideology.* Edited and translated by the Institute of Marxism-Leninism of the Central Committee of the CPSU. Moscow: Progress Publishers.

Marx, Karl. 1967. *Capital: A Critique of Political Economy.* Vol. 1, *The Process of Capitalist Production*. Translated by Samuel Moore and Edward Aveling. New York: International Publishers.

———. 1975. *Karl Marx: Early Writings.* Translated by Rodney Livingstone and Gregor Benton. New York: Vintage.

Mendieta, Eduardo. 1995. "Discourse Ethics and Liberation Ethics: At the Boundaries of Moral Theory." *Philosophy and Social Criticism* 21, no. 4: 111–26.

Pérez Villacampa, Gilberto. 1991. "¿De la metafísica de la alteridad al humanismo real?" *Islas* 99 (May–August): 160–67.

Schutte, Ofelia. 1984. "Crisis de identidad occidental y reconstrucción latinoamericana." *Nuestra América* 4, no. 11: 61–68.

———. 1993. *Cultural Identity and Social Liberation in Latin American Thought.* Albany: SUNY Press.

Therborn, Göran. 1980. *The Ideology of Power and the Power of Ideology.* London: Verso.

Wallerstein, Immanuel. 1974. *The Modern World System.* Vol. 1, *Capitalist Agriculture and the Origin of the European World–Economy in the Sixteenth Century.* New York: Academic.

———. 1983. *Historical Capitalism.* London: Verso.

Weeks, John, and Elizabeth Dore. 1979. "International Exchange and the Causes of Backwardness." *Latin American Perspectives* 21, no. 6: 2.

Wolfe, Patrick. 1997. "History and Imperialism: A Century of Theory from Marx to Postcolonialism." *American Historical Review* 102, no. 2: 388–420.

Wynia, Gary W. 1984. *The Politics of Latin American Development.* 2d ed. Cambridge: Cambridge University Press.

Zea, Leopoldo. 1988–1989. "Identity: A Latin American Philosophical Problem." *Philosophical Forum* 20, no. 1–2: 33–42.

12

Power/Knowledges in the Colonial Unconscious: A Dialogue between Dussel and Foucault

Linda Martín Alcoff

Enrique Dussel and Michel Foucault would no doubt have made an odd couple—the global ethicist and the principled localist—but both have brought power and domination center stage to any discussion of ethical norms, discursive rules, and even methods of justification. And there is an audible echo in their respective critiques of the Habermasian style of political theory for its complete inattention to the realm of the concrete, the material, and the embodied. It is also the case, though not as widely known, that Foucault no less than Dussel attempted to contribute directly and actively to revolutionary movements.[1]

Nonetheless, there are significant lines of demarcation. Dussel's patience with postmodernism seems to have come to an end, whereas, although Foucault hated labels, his work resonates with, and in fact has helped to define, the postmodern sensibilities that hold the Enlightenment and its Marxist critics in equal disdain. In contrast, Dussel criticizes postmodernism as being ineffective in its critical goals and as a mere diversion from the fundamental crisis of our times (of which the crisis of reason identified by the postmodernists is only an offshoot)—economic globalization and its resultant global genocide. In Dussel's view, postmodernism's epistemological skepticism excuses the refusal to risk interpreting the needs of the disenfranchised. Foucault, for his part, would no doubt have been horrified at the global sweep in which Dussel casts his universal claims, the absoluteness with which he declares his claims to be valid, and the very project to develop and defend universal ethical norms.

All of this is obvious. Still, I want to ask a question that has a less than obvious answer: Might there be a productive dialogue between the two, even if occasionally volatile? A reason for thinking so is that, despite their significant differences, Dussel and Foucault can be viewed as having complementary projects, the one developing an immanent critique of European discursive regimes, the other developing an external critique from the perspective of the victims of these regimes in the Third World. While Foucault reveals the ways in which subjects are constituted within various modern European institutions, Dussel reveals the myths of modernity through which the colonized Other continues to be construed. One looks inward, whereas the other looks from the outside, so to speak. In a sense, both are transmodern: normatively reflective about the local conditions of all thought.

In this chapter I imagine a dialogue between the two across these different positions. I argue that, in fact, the complementarity of their projects might allow each to offer significant help to the other. The point is not that either Foucault or Dussel should drop his own agenda in favor of the other's, but that certain aporias in each philosopher's work could be resolved without sacrificing their own central theses by making use of certain arguments of the other. I argue that Dussel, in particular, could sidestep some recurrent objections his critics have been making about his homogenized construction of "the oppressed" and its epistemically privileged status by the employment of Foucault's concept of subjugated knowledges.

The following sections of this chapter explore certain difficulties in each philosopher's work that could benefit from and perhaps even be resolved by a cross-pollination. In regard to Foucault, I explore how an attentiveness to colonialism and the formulation of an ethical hermeneutics, such as Dussel employs it, would have (1) allowed him to reconcile the obvious normative undercurrents in his work with his epistemological thesis that knowledge is always connected to power and (2) expanded and deepened his analysis of the deployment of biopower and its regulatory regimes concerning populations. I also use Dussel's work to explore why it is that Foucault's own discourse replicated a colonial unconscious, as critics such as Ann Laura Stoler have demonstrated, despite his sophisticated understanding of theory's relation to power. In regard to Dussel, I consider how Foucault's account of power/knowledge might (1) bolster his justificatory strategies and epistemic claims, thus making them more plausible, and (2) help him avoid the reifications of identity that some critics have alleged. A coverage of these issues in no way exhausts the potentially fruitful topics of conversation between the two but is more than enough for a single chapter. I begin with Foucault.[2]

FOUCAULT'S COLONIAL UNCONSCIOUS

It is useful in this context to begin by considering the debate over Foucault's postmodernism. Some have even wondered whether it makes sense to call Foucault a poststructuralist, much less a postmodernist: his writing up to *The Archaeology of Knowledge* is unquestionably structuralist. Although his focus changed after that work, whether he ever repudiated the earlier approach is dubious.[3] Clearly, Foucault rejected the existence of stable, cross-cultural, deep underlying structures that could be named and grouped and applied to any society, à la Lévi-Strauss, but to the extent that structures can be understood as horizontal and shallow rather than fundamental and deep he was a structuralist about knowledge, power, and experience.

The debate over Foucault's postmodernism, a debate to which he contributed, however obliquely, shortly before his death, has not been as easy to resolve.[4] The normative thrust of Foucault's examinations, as well as the fact that his project was a pursuit of self-awareness, makes his overall oeuvre appear continuous with the modernism one can find in the early Frankfurt School. And he himself strikes a conciliatory note with the critical modernism of Kant when he suggests that the *Aufklärung* aimed toward a "critical ontology of ourselves" and is best conceived as "an attitude, an ethos, a philosophical life in which the critique of what we are is at one and the same time the historical analysis of the limits imposed on us and an experiment with the possibility of going beyond them."[5] Foucault also pointed out that to the extent that modernity is an "attitude" rather than a period of history, an attitude that involves a critical de-reification of the present that entails the attendant project to produce oneself, this attitude must be equally applied to the Enlightenment. In one sense, then, Foucault may be taken as the first (or perhaps second, following Nietzsche) *consistent* modernist, given the fact that his very relationship to modernism was recognizably contingent.

The usual charges that philosophers of the critical theory persuasion, which includes Dussel, make against postmodernism—that it consists of unceasing negativity and relativism, that it disables reason in any form, that it deemphasizes the political and economic in favor of the exclusively cultural—cannot be directed against Foucault. He offered the most important unveiling and internal critique of the methods and effects of modern European domination written in this century, training a generation of theorists to look at the disciplines of the body, the finality of sexual identities, and the slippery decenteredness of power for the ways in which modern Europeanized subjects are yoked to the wheel of political and cultural normativity by new, less easily visible, but no less tyrannical, ropes and tethers. Though his own aporias failed to produce a useful discourse of liberation that might extend globally, Foucault galvanized new developments in feminism, cultural theory, and social science that began to imagine how a different future might be realized.

Thus Dussel's general charges against postmodernism do not apply to Foucault. It is interesting to compare Habermas's criticisms of Foucault in this regard, which are surprisingly weak but typical of the tenor of much of this perspective on Foucault, arguing that because Foucault understands knowledge and power as always *connected,* he therefore *collapses* knowledge to power, evacuating all epistemic criteria from efficacy in judgment.[6] But a necessary connection between power and knowledge does not entail a collapse of knowledge to mere power unless one holds, like the positivists but certainly unlike Habermas in his other work, that knowledge, to count as knowledge, must be made pure of all political concern.[7] Still, Foucault has difficulty in explaining how his own normative interests (however implicit) can be reconciled with an account of power/knowledge. The problem is not that epistemic criteria play no role but that normativity would seem to require a resignation to discipline once again, the reinstatement of a self-policing mechanism by which Western societies divert resistance. For this reason, Foucault never addressed explicitly or reflected on the obvious normative undercurrents in his work. Acknowledging their very existence would threaten the viability of his archaeological and genealogical methods as he understood them.[8]

But once we look at this problem from Dussel's point of view, the solution to this contradiction at the heart of Foucault's work is obvious. Foucault's fundamental mistake is to collapse the sphere of norms into the sphere of normativity. That is, he retreats from norms because he mistakenly thinks they are always involved in normativity: the disciplinary practices of the Confessional, the Panopticon, the self-help manual, all of which produce a self-loathing that can be assuaged only through mastering the techniques of disciplined action. *Moral* norms, his followers continue to mistakenly believe, are always norms of *disciplinary* practice.[9]

However, it is possible to set out a concept of the good, and obligate the individual toward action, but without the normalizing, pathologizing, or disciplining effects of the norms of the modern subject, which are produced and ingenuously enforced in contemporary capitalism. Dussel's material ethical principle, for example, demands that we work to sustain life and work to create social conditions in which such work can be effective, but he does not say how, when, or where. Unlike doctrinal Christianity, liberation theology in Dussel's interpretation outlines no weekly rituals to perform and, unlike modern-day sexual discourses, it implies no types or categories of the nonnormative. "Sin" is not about practices I may perform or fail to perform but about institutionalized domination.[10] Dussel rejects the "social morality" that is focused on individual action and argues instead for the creation of ethical communities, that is, communities without the exploitation of labor, the destruction of the earth, and the systematic production of poverty, malnutrition, and famine.

Dussel condemns not individuals so much as global systems, impossibly large and diffuse, which are more correct targets for moral outrage than the individual acts that modern moral philosophy often condemns out of context, oblivious to social location. Dussel's target is what Foucault might have called the historical a priori of the present, both the material-structural and the narrative-cultural background that makes possible the ongoing global genocide of starvation, deprivation, and war. His ethics resembles the types of strategies that Foucault suggested we pursue which aim toward the disarticulation between power and current truth regimes. Because he is not an individualist, Dussel does not direct his ethics toward prescribing and proscribing individual practice: he recognizes that it is the material-structural background that yields possibilities of action. Moreover, like Levinas, Dussel locates the moral viewpoint in an exteriority, a site of incomprehensibility to the present discourses, a site that thus commands no regulatory regime. Foucault's exposure and critique of disciplined practices and subjectivities similarly aims to uncover what cannot be thought in the present regime in order to produce new subjectivities, new resistances.

Thus neither Foucault nor contemporary Foucauldians need forgo his critique of normativity in order to embrace Dussel's norms. They can maintain the critique of disciplinary normativity as a principle feature of contemporary Western societies while distinguishing normativity from norms, understanding that the disciplinary normativity that Foucault analyzed does not exhaust the realm of the normative or the possibilities for norms.

Moreover, Foucault's account of power/knowledge need not be sacrificed either. Dussel's moral pronouncements have the air of absoluteness about them, but they are not founded in any epistemically transcendental realm by which mortals can grasp the outlines of the infinite. I share to some extent the worry of critics who fear that Dussel's project works to reify the poor and absolutize his epistemic perspective, as I explain in the next section. But this problem does not emerge because he posits the *Ding-an-sich* or denies that power and value permeate all judgment.

Rather, like Marx, Dussel grounds norms not in a value-free science but in, and directed toward, the material, concrete life of the oppressed. And he disallows norms whose application exceeds technical and empirical possibility. This approach provides an immanent and contextual rather than a transcendental basis of justification, even though it then produces global imperatives. Dussel explicitly and forcefully rejects the abstract generalizations about justice one gets from, for example, Rawls, precisely because such generalizations ignore and even deny the material context of their enunciation. He has argued for a philosophy and an ethics of liberation and, in effect, a theory of injustice because *these alone are relevant to a Third World context*. Thus Dussel appeals to grounds that are hardly neutral politically: it is the condition of oppression itself that carries within it the norms conveyed by Dussel's system of ethics. In this sense, the moral knowledge Dussel claims is indissolubly connected to relations of power and is aware of its own historicity.

The second issue I listed above concerned Foucault's analysis of the deployment of biopower, or the realm concerned with the regulation of populations and their sexuality. Although Foucault did address the creation of racialized bodies and the genealogy of racism, he did not approach the theoretical analysis of biopower through any type of connection with colonized subjects or the regulatory regimes of sexuality first instituted in the colonial encounter. He understood correctly that biopower and racism are co-constitutive, that the regulatory control of populations was bound up with the systems of hierarchical classification that worked through the new biological discourses of race. Thus it is even more surprising that he neglected to explore the relation of the regimes of power/knowledge that he located in modernity with colonialism.

It is true that Foucault's conceptual explanation of discursive formations inspired other theorists working in the history of colonialism to develop novel accounts of the role of knowledges in the colonial project and also to explore the ways in which disciplinary practices that became widespread in Western Europe in the eighteenth century were preceded by techniques developed in the colonies.[11] And one might be tempted to say that although his work made possible some such accounts, this was simply not Foucault's project. One cannot fault a philosopher for failing to take up every politically important project, especially not someone like Foucault, who contributed such an extensive, varied, and rich corpus to social theory.

The problem with Foucault's work on biopower, however, is that this omission affects the very core of his claims. Foucault alleges that the modern tactics of power are characterized by the move from premodern forms of power, which were organized toward repression and exclusion, to modern forms of power, which are organized around proliferation and expansion, or the move from the sword, which threatens life, to the norm that takes charge of it.[12] Repression remains an aspect of the modern tactics of power, but it is not its motive force or central organizing principle. Power has moved toward modes of generation and development in which the attempt to prohibit certain actions is replaced by a long list of necessary actions to be performed. However, recent theorists of colonialism have established that the true "laboratories of modernity" existed not in Western Europe but in the colonies, where masses of indigenous peoples were ruled by small minorities of Europeans. There the disciplinary regimes of bourgeois life, the self-discipline and self-control arranged on the basis of various behavioral norms, were first developed quite by necessity. Foucault does not consider this in his account of the modern form of power. Will proliferations and norms continue to be the central concepts necessary for understanding the circulations of power in such a wider context? In particular, where is the analysis of alterity as the formative ground of modernity, the threat whose alarming entry into European cosmographies after the encounter with the New World engendered the very concept of a normative humanity by which the Other might be denied the means to live?

Dussel identifies the defining myth of modernity as the claim that European culture was "superior and more developed" and that the culture of the Other was "inferior, crude, barbaric, and culpably immature."[13] Given this, the normalizing practices governing sexuality as a central feature of biopower might well have emerged not only in relation to the deployment of populations but in the context of establishing and defending Europe's claim to superiority. Establishing the superiority of the elite became suddenly inadequate in the colonial context; the entire *culture* needed to be established as superior, which required a comparative mechanism that could be used across internal divisions of class, race, and gender. Without such a culture-wide comparison, the proper response to the encounter might have been a negotiation between the elites from each culture. A claim of

European superiority could not be maintained if only a small minority of the population possessed the superior attributes. Hence, for example, the "missionary position" became the symbol of Christian and European superiority as a practice that (supposedly) transcended class and other differences. The legacy of this cultural comparison continues today in the form of a birthright attached to whiteness, across all internal difference, to social recognition and economic inclusion.

The discourse of modernity emerged in the first instance in an encounter with a radically different culture. It was this encounter, as Dussel explains, that produced a European subject whose very subjectivity was predicated on the conquest, that is, whose subjectivity was defined in terms of their response to the encounter: the conquest. This was the decisive criterion of demarcation between Europe and its Others, though it required (and requires) a performative repetition to enact this superior status, a repetition apparently without end. Thus the core of the European subject is not a disciplinary regime of normalizing practices but a conquest of alterity, upon which the normalizations are organized toward establishing the justice and justifiability of the conquest. To truly subvert the coherence of this system and its characteristic tactics of power one must not simply repudiate the modern disciplinary regime but develop a rearticulated relation to the Other. I would suggest that we can already see the European subject preserving its defining features despite the growing insecurity of disciplinary identities and the increasing skepticism against norms of all kinds. The new postmodern cynical turn toward political and axiological nihilism has already proven itself quite capable of maintaining a subject that retains the right to conquer and continues to believe in its own global superiority; in fact, its own cynicism is now used to *establish* that superiority against the more "primitive" or "unsophisticated" cultures that retain the capacity for belief in values, religion, and the possibility of political optimism.

Foucault's analysis of modern forms of power is, of course, as necessary to this political critique of modernity as Dussel's reconfigured global teleology. Foucault's conceptual apparatus is necessary to reveal the nature of the laboratories of modernity and the kinds of subjectivity they were able to produce. Still, one is entitled to ask Foucault for an explanation: in his expansive horizontal readings of modern discourses, readings that sought out relations of coherence rather than deep structural causes to provide explanations, why did he forgo attending to the relation between an emerging bourgeois subjectivity and the colonial encounter out of which the very discourses of subjectivity, that is, of subject and object, emerged? The encounter initiated widespread debates over the criteria of humanity, spurred by the question of whether indigenous peoples of the Americas met those criteria. It was out of this debate that the modern social and biological sciences developed, those very discourses that Foucault has illuminated so well.

In her study of Foucault's account of race and racisms, Stoler points out that the primary argument in the *History of Sexuality: Volume One* concerns a shift in the tactics of power prior to the eighteenth century and then beyond it. In the earlier period sex was regulated principally by marital rules governed by the Church; during the eighteenth and nineteenth centuries sex and matrimony separated into distinct regimes of discourse and regulation. Foucault doesn't offer an explanation for this shift, and Stoler suggests that he did not consider such an explanation necessary. She says that

> he only hints at those "economic processes and political structures" in which the decline of absolutism and monarchy and the rise of liberalism undermined the social hierarchies based on lines of descent and called for new ways of naturalizing the inequities on which an emergent bourgeois order was based. Whereas for Foucault, racism has not yet appeared in its modern form, this is precisely that moment when others have sought its emergence.[14]

In other words, Foucault came close enough to the explanation that would have filled in his story to feel the heat, so to speak, and yet remained mystifyingly oblivious.

Clearly, Foucault's myopia was a product of his own historical a priori, which, by his definition, sets out the domain not of the true and the false but of meaning, and thus the domain of that which can even be entertained as possible. By neglecting the importance of colonialism in his explications of what he took to be the key discursive shifts in European modernity, Foucault manifested a healthy dose of Euro-centrism in the form of an implicit but unmistakable denial that anything *external* to Europe could be one of Europe's key constituting elements. The myth of autogenesis has fascinated the masculine unconscious for centuries, according to Irigaray; the myth of being an unmoved mover grounds the European unconscious, according to Dussel. This is the only way that it is possible for Europe to function "as the beginning and end of history."[15]

Dussel argues that such explanations as Foucault's are ultimately "provincial" accounts of modernity:

> While modernity is undoubtedly a European occurrence, it also originates in a dialectial relation with non-Europe. Modernity appears when Europe organizes the initial world-system and places itself at the center of history over against a periphery equally constitutive of modernity.[16]

Thus the effect of Euro-centrism is not merely that it excludes knowledges and experiences outside of Europe, but that it obscures the very nature and history of Europe itself:

> When one conceives of modernity as part of [a] center-periphery system instead of an independent European phenomenon, the meanings of modernity, its origin, development, present crisis, and its postmodern antithesis change.[17]

It could be argued that there is another explanation, an explanation with more ready evidence, for Foucault's neglect of colonialism—his antipathy for causal explanations. It is surprising that Stoler is surprised by Foucault's reluctance to offer an explanation for the transformation in discursive regimes, given his famous antipathy for teleological explanations behind the surface phenomena he studied. Gary Gutting accounts for this as based in Foucault's primary interest in the "'consciousness' (evaluative and cognitive) that *underlies* . . . beliefs and intentions. Consequently, the standard causal approach of historians, while useful as a starting point, cannot of itself answer the questions he is posing." Foucault found the "standard causal approach of historians" incapable of elucidating the historical a priori.[18] Foucault also critiqued the usual sort of causal accounts that refer to *Weltanschauungen* as so amorphous as to be magical. He thought that causal factors, even if they can be established, will only pertain to the subjects of history and thus will be irrelevant to an archaeological focus on discursive formations.[19]

But in Dussel's work colonialism figures as a cause of precisely the historical a priori that Foucault sought out and not in a subject-centered account. Dussel suggests that there are vital connections between Hegel's developmentalist ontology and colonial expansion, as well as Descartes's *ego cogito,* which can stand back and survey the whole of human knowledge and the conquering subject who can name, map, and plunder entire continents. The creation of the myth of modern reason—that imposing "modern Reason" on the vanquished will be to their benefit—can only be fully understood in its material, historical context. Said's *Orientalism*, a text that was Foucauldian only up to a point, provides another example. Said contextualizes his archaeology of orientalist discourses within an overall framework of political economy. Explanations for discursive changes are not to be found merely provincially through horizontal relations of coherence between vastly different textual enunciations, but also vertically through the actual material practices of colonial rule.

Even more importantly, this causal explanation establishes that the fundamental transformation of European discourses will not happen apart from its global context. The postmodernists' belief that their own advancing, internally developing, theoretical and political sophistication will completely transform European knowledges is mistaken. Dussel is very clear on this point: "Modernity will come into its fullness not by passing from its potency to its act [e.g., by a self-development of its own critical agency], but by surpassing itself through a corealization with its once negated alterity and through a process of mutual, creative fecundation."[20]

Thus Foucault's antipathy toward causal explanations cannot free him from the charge of Euro-centrism. Foucault's blindness to his own colonial unconscious is enabled by his refusal to engage with European alterities, which he justifies via a repudiation of causal analyses. Before one follows him in this repudiation, I would suggest, one should consider what colonial desires are invested in this dread of causality.[21]

DUSSEL'S POWER/KNOWLEDGE

Dussel proposes to break through the closed circle of Euro-centric universalism, which is incapable of acknowledging either the alterity of perspective of those on the underside of European modernity or the fact that their suffering is caused by modernity itself. His method for this task involves exposing the universal pretensions of Eurocentric reason as provincial, and he proposes to replace it with the concept of a situated reason that is grounded in the perspective of the poor and oppressed of the earth, particularly of Latin America. It is from this perspective that he proposes to judge the adequacy of existing theories of global economics and of ethics. The perspective of the Other of modernity, then, provides him both the means of critique and the means to construct a more adequate philosophy.

The danger that this approach poses, however, is that any criterion of justification that is bound to a particular perspectival location will tend toward either relativism or absolutism. It will tend toward relativism if it holds that justificatory perspectives are incommensurable and thus that there is no possibility of understanding or judgment between them. It will tend toward absolutism if it holds that justificatory perspectives are not incommensurable and that there is the possibility of understanding and judgment between them, but that one perspective (in Dussel's case, the perspective of the poor and oppressed) is privileged over all others merely by virtue of its location. This makes it indefeasible to objections from the outside and immune from any epistemic or ethical fallibilism, and thus absolutist. No matter which of these alternatives is chosen—relativism or absolutism—such an approach will be fundamentally irrational.

Dussel explicitly rejects relativism and states his intention to use the particular perspective of the oppressed to judge across differences. As a result, he is charged with authoritarianism. Two of the most common criticisms of Dussel's philosophy of liberation are that it must necessarily entail the authoritarianism of the invulnerable perspective and the irrationality of a position that declares itself immune from external critique. Ofelia Schutte raises these criticisms as follows:

> Dussel's approach to a philosophy of liberation has been marked by at least two disturbing characteristics. The first is the postulation of an absolutely untainted source for, or undisputed authority at the origin of, its claims to truth or justice. For Dussel, philosophical truth is a matter of deriving various imperatives from a set of uncontaminated first principles. . . . Second, the ethical and political theory emerging from this approach is marked by a dualistic understanding of good and evil. Ethically, there are two principles: totality (evil) and alterity (good).[22]

On Schutte's reading, rather than enable critique, Dussel's perspectival foundation ultimately obliterates it.

Schutte is especially concerned that this immunity from critique will absolutize the traditional Church teachings that Dussel has defended, especially those that condemn feminism, abortion, and gay rights. Elina Vuola in chapter 8 of this volume takes up these concerns and makes strong arguments about why such positions against feminism, abortion, and gay rights are in contradiction to the basic tenets of liberation theology itself, which seeks to represent the oppressed. But Vuola and others have also pointed out that Dussel's earlier positions on these topics have been revised and, in their view, improved in more recent work in response to his feminist critics. Some, like Schutte, continue to hold that Dussel has not changed his views enough. But however this debate about the substance of Dussel's ethical and political positions comes out, the issue I wish to focus on is the basis upon which he justifies his positions. If this basis is problematic, it will continue to be so no matter how much Dussel revises the substance of his positions.

In his recent book *Ethical Hermeneutics: Rationalism in Enrique Dussel's Philosophy of Liberation* Michael Barber offers a defense of Dussel against Schutte and Horacio Cerutti Guldberg, who has also criticized Dussel for authoritarianism and an embrace of irrationalism. Barber's defense centers on an explanation of Dussel's incorporation of Levinas in his formulation of the philosophy of liberation. Barber is not arguing that Dussel is merely an acolyte of Levinas, and he shows how Dussel develops Levinas's views in novel ways. But he argues that, in regard to this critical issue of the justificatory foundation for Dussel's ethical claims, his use of Levinas is especially important.

Barber suggests that the criticisms made by Schutte and Cerutti Guldberg are based on their lack of knowledge about some of the philosophical traditions upon which Dussel draws, most importantly Levinas. Although Barber does provide some textual evidence to support his claim that Schutte and Cerutti Guldberg are unfamiliar with these traditions, his evidence is circumstantial and relies primarily on the substance of their accusations. From my knowledge of Schutte's work, I would suggest that her critique of Dussel would not be assuaged by a better understanding of Levinas: as a strong Nietzschean, she would, I suspect, make the same criticisms of Levinas![23] Schutte's preference for a creative, transformative approach to ethics, and one that allows for the possibility of total transvaluation, will conflict with the Levinasian project of providing an ultimate foundational bedrock for ethics in the face of the Other. On Schutte's view, critique requires that we be committed to the possibility that *every* norm will undergo a transvaluation; on Levinas's view, critique must be pursued within an *immovable context* of our obligation to the Other and, indeed, that obligation will both limit and structure the process of critique itself.[24] Thus, even if Dussel could be absolved of the charge of irrationalism and authoritarianism, Schutte would be likely to continue to disagree with him unless he were to adopt a Nietzschean approach to ethics.

In my view, Barber ably defends Dussel through his explanation that the Levinasian approach Dussel is drawing from is in fact neither irrational nor authoritarian despite its defense of an absolute ethical principle. In regard to the first charge, Barber points out that, on both of their accounts, one *can* "and ought to turn to principles of consistency, equality, and impartiality . . ." in order to criticize the Other's prescriptions, and that this is required by the very mandate to serve him or her.[25] Blind servility is not in the true interests of the Other. Thus one's absolute obligation to the Other is not obviated when one critiques the Other's claims; critique does not necessitate undermining the absolutism of the ethical injunction to serve the Other. As an assurance against the possibility that such critique will "disguise oppression" or that a critique of the Other will be used to justify maintaining the status quo, Levinas counsels that the process of critiquing and testing norms should be done "against the face-to-face."[26] Also, Levinas characterizes the encounter between self and Other as dialogical, not monological, and as necessarily unfolding in a "struggle between thinkers, with all the risks of freedom."[27] Thus an absolute commitment to the Other does not require one to relinquish one's autonomous critical faculties but to use them both for and with the Other.

Second, in regard to the charge of authoritarianism, Barber argues that, in actuality, taking one's foundation in the Other "affords no consolation or security" and in fact "undermines any pretense to surety."[28] Here a Levinasian position is once again shown to be articulating a new form of rationality instead of embracing irrationality. In fact, Barber quotes Levinas declaring that "the essence of reason consists not in securing for man a foundation and powers, but in calling him in question and in inviting him to justice."[29] This is no foundation in a traditional or classical sense. It provides no bedrock of indubitable propositions or necessary method, but only an ethical dictum that serves as the necessary criterion of validity in all cases of judgment. Still, little is said about how one can know whether one has fulfilled the criterion.

Barber's arguments establish that there is room for both critique and fallibilism within Dussel's philosophy of liberation. But there are other issues that remain concerning his own justificatory strategies and his conceptualization of identity. I will address each of these in turn, suggesting ways that Foucault's work could supplement and strengthen Dussel's in regard to these two topics.

Levinas and Dussel both want to ground philosophy in ethics, but what is ethics grounded in? Dussel rejects the claims of discourse ethics to provide an ultimate foundation for normative claims through principles said to be implicit in the communicative process: Dussel claims that attending to the fact of materiality, that is, to the fact of oppression, must necessarily *precede* the formation of such principles in order to provide the very conditions within which such principles can be judged as adequate. Against this, James Marsh has argued that although materialist principles must necessarily precede the application of discursive principles, it is the discursive principles that are necessary to epistemically justify the materialist principles. Thus they have a logical, if not temporal or practical, primacy.

If Marsh is right but Dussel continues to reject discourse ethics as his foundation, this returns him to the original problem of perspectivalism, at least in part. How does perspectivalism justify itself if all justifications ultimately relate to perspective? What account can Dussel offer for his own foundation that is consistent with the terms of his own philosophy?[30] Moreover, given that Dussel takes the perspective of the Other, it remains to be asked how he locates himself or any theorist in this very process. The answer that discourse ethics gives is that the theorist, like any language user, always already has normative commitments and, in particular, commitments with regard to Others in the dialogical process. Dussel's persuasive criticism here is that such commitments are themselves variant, depending on who is involved in the encounter. The question of who is involved—who can be involved—relies on prior commitments regarding equalizing material conditions. But if this is so, then what grounds or motivates these prior commitments? Here is where Foucault might be useful.

Dussel's project to *descubierto* (uncover) and to *desocultar/escuchar* (heed) the viewpoint of the oppressed resonates with Foucault's project to promote "*an insurrection of subjugated knowledges*" against dominant or hegemonic knowledges.[31] Subjugated knowledges are those that have been disauthorized by the dominant epistemic rules and discourses. They are local and partial as opposed to the knowledges that seek global hegemonic status, not just in the sense that they have not yet achieved dominance but in their refusal to seek dominance. They do not construct competing unitary, formal, totalizing theoretical systems that seek to subsume all local elements within a single umbrella; rather, they are formulated as local in their very structural preconditions or foundations:

> what this essentially local character of criticism indicates in reality is an autonomous, non-centralized kind of theoretical production, one that is to say whose validity is not dependent on the approval of the established regimes of thought.[32]

Foucault makes both political and epistemic arguments to defend this preference for subjugated knowledges. Foucault believed that totalizing theories must by definition impede the development of local critique, and thus they require, in a way subjugated knowledges do not, acts of distortion and omission in order to maintain their own justificatory status. Moreover, the political goal of resistance is abetted by these "naive knowledges" that are located "beneath the required level of cognition or scientificity."[33] It is here in "these local, popular knowledges, these disqualified knowledges, that criticism performs its work."[34] The historical a priori, or unconscious, in place at a given moment will only be subverted by a force from the outside, from beyond what it itself can comprehend or accept; otherwise, its very rules will not be challenged.

Although Foucault's account suggests a political binary, in which subjugated knowledges are clearly and wholly valorized against dominant knowledges, he does not suggest that subjugated knowledges are innocent, or "pure" (i.e., free from the ubiquitous power). All knowledges are "linked in a circular relation with systems of power which produce and sustain [them], and to effects of power which [they] induce . . . and which extend [them]."[35] The difference between subjugated and dominant knowledges is not that one is related to power and the other is not, but the kind of relations they have to power.

How does this help to address the problem of justifying Dussel's claims about justification? Foucault's account offers support for Dussel's charge against both postmodernists and critical theorists that Euro-centrism cannot be overturned entirely from within Europe by his claim that it is in the disqualified knowledges that criticism will do its work. There are no European subjugated knowledges that are as subjugated as those marked non-European, which are often deemed unworthy of any consideration before they have even been heard. This provides a justificatory defense for privileging the perspective of the oppressed that is epistemic and not only moral. But Foucault's account also supports the claim that knowledges cannot be judged purely epistemically in the sense of some value-free process, and that they should not be judged in this way even if it were possible. The location, effects, and particular relation to power must all be considered in assessment. As postcolonial theorist Ania Loomba explains, "innocence and objectivity do not necessarily have to be our enabling fictions. The more we work with an awareness of our embeddedness in historical processes, the more possible it becomes to take carefully reasoned oppositional positions . . ."[36] This helps explain how Foucault's inclusion of epistemic considerations in judging subjugated knowledges ultimately demonstrates that the epistemic and the political cannot be neatly disentangled.

Foucault's understanding that all knowledges exist and are sustained in and through their relations to power softens the Manichean tendencies that the politics of resistance of all types can easily fall into. And it suggests that subjugated knowledges will also require critical genealogies that trace their relations to power and their effects, thus guarding against an absolutist characterization of critical claims.

Foucault's account advises that we should not aim for the totalization of subjugated knowledges, or simply a reversal of the binary. As a consequence, we need not justify a given perspective by showing that it *is* truly universal, capable of expressing the truth for the totality. We need only show that it has disruptive potential or, in other words, that it provides effective critique not just of the surface substance of a discourse but of its underlying logic. The knowledges that Dussel is trying to bring to bear on contemporary Western philosophy are decidedly subjugated ones, existing below the level of cognition, not even subject to debate in the main Anglo-European arenas of knowledge production. Using Foucault, Dussel can justify his privileging of these knowledges over the dominant Western ones on both political and epistemic grounds: they require less violence and distortion than Eurocentric knowledges require just to be maintained, and they provide an effective and expansive critique.

But, one might argue, won't Dussel's claims be weakened by this association? How can he justify the attempt to create a global ethics or to make claims with universal applicability? Foucault's approach would effect a contextualization of Dussel's project and render it more self-conscious about its own location and strategic aims. Neither the call for a global ethics nor the content of Dussel's ethics should be weakened by this: a demand that would range over the whole globe can theoretically come from any location, and given that in this case it is said to come from those around the world suffering the most from the current forms of neocolonialism, this both justifies and explains the global demand. Rather, a contextualization of Dussel's arguments through the use of Foucault's conception of knowledge would strengthen Dussel's claims by rendering them less vulnerable to the sort of skeptical attacks he receives from those who are concerned, understandably, about the dangers of any totalizing philosophy.

Dussel's conceptualization of the perspective of the Other that informs and even defines his subjugated knowledges relies heavily on identity constructions such as "the poor," "the African," "the Amerindian," "the violated woman," and "the oppressed." Commentators have worried about the reifying tendencies of these constructions that might suggest one-dimensional characters who do not have the ability to speak or that homogenize such large groups without seeming to attend to the inevitable differences and conflicts within each category. On the one hand, I sympathize with Dussel's plight of wanting to bring into the center of philosophy a consciousness of suffering and needing to locate that suffering in concrete and particular contexts by what are inevitably clumsy shorthands. How can anyone talk about the oppressed without having to resort to such problematic categories? Can't a writer assume that readers today will be aware of the limits of these identity constructions and the pragmatic context of their use?

On the other hand, it would be helpful to have Dussel's own thoughts about the issue. A few distinctions need to be made here. Dussel's use of identity categories is meant to mark the social locations and collective experiences that yield a critical perspective on the excuses and self-justifications made in the metanarratives of world capitalism. In other words, what he is really after is the epistemic perspective, not the metaphysics of personal identity. Still, assuming that epistemic perspective can be correlated to identity involves one in various commitments about the nature of identity.

Of the identities that Dussel invokes, there is a significant distinction to be made between those that refer to one's social being and social location and those that refer only to one's social location. That is, for categories like "woman," "Amerindian," "African," and so forth, identity refers to a stable and (mostly) unchangeable feature of a person, whereas for categories like "the poor" or "the oppressed," identity refers to where one is located right now on the map of social relations. This is not an identity in quite the same sense in terms of lived experience, though it may be as important or even more important in an individual's life. But it is not quite the same because it is an identity that liberation would remove, whereas the previous sorts of identities may well remain after liberation. Thus the goal in the latter set of identities is to overcome the identity, in a sense, whereas the goal in the former is to liberate the identity. To be sure, in the liberation of "woman," diverse women would have more self-determination in construing their own undoubtedly diverse interpretations of living life as a woman, and some would likely seek ways to opt out altogether. But "woman," unlike "poor," is not an identity that in principle or by definition has to be overcome for liberation. This distinction is then relevant in the epistemic perspective conferred by identity; women may be aiming for a voice *as women*, whereas the poor may also want to be heard but toward the goal of completely eradicating even the future possibility of a life such as they have known. This difference will entail different criteria by which effective resistance is measured.

There are those who argue that any identity constructions—woman, Amerindian, poor and so on—are equally oppressive and equally metaphysical illusions.[37] I do not share that view, nor do I share Foucault's own general skepticism toward identities or identity politics. Nonetheless, some of Foucault's insights about the constitutive relation between power and identity categories could be useful in fashioning an account that would help Dussel elude his critics.

Foucault took an antiessentialist view on at least some identities, notably gay identity. He argued against the claim that gayness signifies something latent within, no matter the outward manifestation or behavior. Still, he did not oppose gayness as an operative term in all cases, and toward the end of his life he actively pursued the experience of being out, or being identified and identifiable, in a gay community. David Halperin says that Foucault portrayed homosexuality as "not a given condition but a horizon of possibility, an opportunity for self-transformation. . . ."[38] Thus he wanted to hold on to the dynamic possibilities for interpreting one's identity without letting it become limiting or stifling.

If lived experience belies the essentialist accounts of identity, how did they come about and why do they persist? This is where Foucault suggests that power, once again, plays the role of not simply labeling preexisting phenomena according to its own ends but of inciting, eliciting, and shaping life in ways that connect with desire as well as the circulations of power. His examples include the notion that we have a sexual identity as heterosexual or homosexual for life and that our sexual identities can be more finely tuned within a typology of perversions reinforced by the pleasures produced for the priest, the doctor, the psychologist, and the host of now legitimated voyeurs who can pry into our practices in the name of salvation or science but, in either case, no doubt enjoying themselves.

These examples may seem far removed from the references to "the poor" in liberation theology or Dussel's philosophy of liberation. But it is instructive in suggesting two points, first, that the concept we have, and promote, of liberation must involve self-determination over the very identity categories that are referred to. All identities are dynamic, though to different degrees. But even those such as gender and sexuality should be approached as "horizons of possibility" rather than names that correspond to inherent characteristics. Second, because identity constructions are not simple correspondences to preexisting natural kinds, and because they are therefore susceptible to the wind currents and directions of modes of power, there needs to be a reflective awareness about the possible (but not inevitable) ways in which given identity categories may feed desire or support dominant power/knowledges. This means that in practice it is important to regularly ask such questions as, What is the source of this identity category? How might it be connected to power and desire? What dominant knowledges will its consolidation help to expand? Today there is excellent work that analyzes, for example, Taino identity, the new pan-Latino identity, and other identity constructions for their political genealogies and ideological effects.

In the United States, categories used to refer to the lower classes have become minefields of connotation. "Welfare mother" connotes black women, even though most mothers receiving assistance are white. "Urban poor" connotes black and brown peoples. By invoking these connotations, politicians can lure rural whites to disidentify with them, as if being a person of color is a prerequisite to being poor and living in a city. "Feminist" connotes overprivileged white women with no children, though most women in the United States support at least a basic feminist agenda. The "oppressed" is not even a category that resonates in mainstream U.S. discourse, and many probably believe that only a marginalized ultraleftist or conspiracy theorist could use such a term. Perhaps it is the case that the invocation of such categories as Dussel's makes progressive theorists in the United States uneasy for entirely local reasons, but identity categories operate in every discourse to signify whole belief systems that may not be made explicit. The transference of liberation theology, which circulates within a primarily Christian context, to a philosophy of liberation that can be effective in a broader domain requires a consciousness of these variable meanings and their possible effects.

I would still maintain, however, that identity categories are entirely legitimate shorthand markers for the kind of epistemic location that Dussel is seeking to marshal against Eurocentric glorifications of globalization. If the only category he ever used was the "the poor," that might indeed suggest that he is unaware of or unconcerned about the conflicts and hierarchies of race, gender, sexuality, nationality, and so on, that problematize the potential solidarity of this group. What exists here is a conglomeration of "subjugated knowledges" rather than a single one, but it seems reasonable to consider the subjugated positionalities en masse sometimes, given their shared disqualified status and critical potential. Thus a more fleshed out account of his use of identity categories, and an account that incorporates Foucault's lessons about their fluidity and potential relation to power and desire, should be all that Dussel's severest critics could ask for.

NOTES

I am grateful to Eduardo Mendieta for his helpful comments on an earlier draft of this paper, which significantly improved the argument. I would also like to thank Mario Sáenz for first introducing me to Dussel's work years ago and Enrique Dussel for his generosity and his hospitality.

1. See, e.g., Didier Eribon, *Michel Foucault*, trans. Betsy Wing (Cambridge: Harvard University Press, 1991); and David M. Halperin, *Saint Foucault: Towards a Gay Hagiography* (New York: Oxford, 1995).

2. For further contrasts and comparisons between Dussel and Foucault, see Dwight N. Hopkins, "Postmodernity, Black Theology of Liberation, and the U.S.A.: Michel Foucault and James H. Cone," in *Liberation Theologies, Postmodernity, and the Americas,* ed. David Batstone et al. (New York: Routledge, 1997), pp. 205–21.

3. Hubert L. Dreyfus and Paul Rabinow, eds., *Michel Foucault: Beyond Structuralism and Hermeneutics,* 2d ed. (Chicago: University of Chicago Press, 1983).

4. Michel Foucault, "What Is Enlightenment?" in *The Essential Works of Foucault,* vol. 1, *Ethics, Subjectivity, and Truth,* trans. Catherine Porter, ed. Paul Rabinow (New York: New Press, 1997), pp. 303–19.

5. Ibid., p. 319.

6. Jürgen Habermas, *Philosophical Discourses of Modernity*, trans. Frederick Lawrence (Cambridge: MIT Press, 1987).

7. *Real Knowing: New Versions of the Coherence Theory* (Ithaca: Cornell University Press, 1996), chap. 5.

8. See, e.g., Nancy Fraser, "Michel Foucault: A 'Young Conservative'?" in *Unruly Practices: Power, Discourse, and Gender in Contemporary Social Theory* (Minneapolis: University of Minnesota Press, 1989), pp. 35–54; and Linda Alcoff, "Feminist Politics and Foucault: The Limits to a Collaboration," in *Crises in Continental Philosophy,* ed. Arleen B. Dallery and Charles Scott (Albany: SUNY Press, 1990), pp. 69–86.

9. In invoking a distinction between norms and normativity, I do not mean to refer to the distinction Dussel, Habermas, Hegel, and others in this tradition make between norms and principles, material ethics and abstract morality, or *Sittlichkeit* and *Moralität*. These terms are used to discriminate between the normative rules that emerge from the life world and thus from particular cultures, and the universal, transhistorical principles that transcend cultural particularity. Foucault would no doubt deny that such a distinction can be made, though he too distinguishes between two levels of moral norms: a more basic (though still contingent) level at the point of discursive regimes that delimit meaningful moral inquiry, and an even more transient and variable level that takes up particular positions made possible within specific regimes. Nevertheless, my argument is that Foucault collapses a *different* distinction, and one that he has much less reason to refute, and this is the distinction between moral norm and disciplinary practice.

10. Enrique Dussel, *Ethics and Community,* trans. Robert R. Barr (Maryknoll, N.Y.: Orbis, 1988), p. 21.

11. See, e.g., Edward Said, *Orientalism* (New York: Random House, 1979). Said explains his debt to Foucault as follows: "I have found it useful here to employ Michel Foucault's notion of a discourse . . . to identify Orientalism. My contention is that without examining Orientalism as a discourse one cannot possibly understand the enormously systematic discipline by which European culture was able to manage—and even produce—

the Orient politically, sociologically, militarily, ideologically, scientifically, and imaginatively during the post-Enlightenment period" (p. 3).

12. Michel Foucault, *The History of Sexuality,* vol. 1, *An Introduction,* trans. Robert Hurley (New York: Random House, 1980), p. 144.

13. Enrique Dussel, *The Invention of the Americas: Eclipse of 'the Other' and the Myth of Modernity*, trans. Michael D. Barber (New York: Continuum, 1995), p. 64.

14. Ann Laura Stoler, *Race and the Education of Desire: Foucault's History of Sexuality and the Colonial Order of Things* (Durham, N.C.: Duke University Press, 1995), p. 37.

15. Dussel, *Invention of the Americas*, p. 23.

16. Ibid., pp. 9–10.

17. Ibid., p. 11.

18. Gary Gutting, *Michel Foucault's Archaeology of Scientific Reason* (New York: Cambridge University Press, 1989), p. 101. Emphasis added.

19. Ibid., p. 249. See also Foucault, "Truth and Power," in *Power/Knowledge: Selected Interviews and Other Writings, 1972–1977*, ed. Colin Gordon, trans. Colin Gordon et al. (New York: Pantheon, 1980), pp. 112–13, p. 117.

20. Dussel, *Invention of the Americas,* p. 138.

21. To be fair, it is not quite true that Foucault never engaged with Europe's Others; see, e.g., his interview on the Iranian revolution: "Iran: The Spirit of a World without Spirit," in *Politics, Philosophy, Culture: Interviews and Other Writings, 1977–1984*, ed. Lawrence D. Kritzman, trans. Alan Sheridan et al. (New York: Routledge, 1988), pp. 211–26. But this is irrelevant to my argument because it is not an attempt on Foucault's part to connect European discourse and its Other, but simply to take note of, and where possible support, the resistance of the Other.

22. Ofelia Schutte, *Cultural Identity and Social Liberation in Latin American Thought* (Albany: SUNY Press, 1993), p. 178.

23. See Ofelia Schutte, *Beyond Nihilism: Nietzsche without Masks* (Chicago: University of Chicago Press, 1984).

24. See especially, e.g., "Ethics As First Philosophy," in *The Levinas Reader,* ed. Sean Hand (Oxford: Blackwell, 1989), pp. 75–87.

25. Michael Barber, *Ethical Hermeneutics: Rationalism in Enrique Dussel's Philosophy of Liberation* (New York: Fordham University Press, 1998), p. 121.

26. Ibid.

27. Ibid.

28. Ibid., p. 118.

29. Ibid.

30. This is meant to question his epistemological, not ethical, foundations, though it includes the epistemic basis of his ethical claims. By "foundation" I do not mean to refer to the doctrine of foundationalism, but simply to the reasons and justification of a claim.

31. Foucault, "Two Lectures," p. 81.

32. Ibid.

33. Ibid., p. 82.

34. Ibid.

35. Foucault, "Truth and Power," p. 133.

36. Ania Loomba, *Colonialism/Postcolonialism* (London: Routledge, 1998), p. 66.

37. See, e.g., Wendy Brown, *States of Injury: Power and Freedom in Late Modernity* (Princeton: Princeton University Press, 1995).

38. Halperin, *Saint Foucault,* p. 79.

13

Epilogue

Enrique Dussel

The editors of this volume, Linda Martín Alcoff and Eduardo Mendieta, who generously conceived and organized this book, initially asked me to comment on the works included in this compilation in a prologue. However, I thought that an epilogue would be better, since it would give the reader time to read through the critiques and expositions of my work presented here. In any event, the task is difficult, since I have to transform myself into a reader of what my colleagues say critically (whether negative or positive) of my work. To fulfill the editors' request, I will put forward some general impressions.

To begin, I would like to make an initial clarification. In Latin America the intellectual has the challenge, in addition to the normal academic duties of the European or American world, of having to establish the bases for the construction of an explanation of the cultural reality from which his or her own reflections emerge. This everyday world is not easily apparent. It is not sufficiently analyzed, and there is a risk in taking the European and North American historical-cultural reality as one's own. The need to deconstruct one's own "ground" demands that the Latin American philosopher have at his or her disposal broader and more precise epistemological instruments than those required by North American or European philosophers. I understood this immediately upon my 1957 arrival in Europe, where I resided for ten years, including two years in Israel. I am, then, a philosopher, but I also have had to learn a vast historical culture and to be trained in the science of religion as indispensable requirements to clarify the prior ontological-hermeneutical question: What does it mean to be a Latin American? What is Latin America as a cultural entity that as my "mother" (as Octavio Paz put it in his *Labyrinth of Solitude*) has a millennial Amerindian history and that as my "father" has a Mediterranean Greco-Latin, Jewish, Muslim, and Christian-Hispanic tradition?

This, however, should not leave the impression that I am conflating epistemological horizons. In fact, even though the title of this work points in the direction of "philosophy of liberation," among the works included there are references to history, theology (in the sense of Kant's philosophical-natural theology or Leibniz's *Theodicy*), and even liberation theology. In addition, some of the contributors have used texts from several of my theological works in philosophical exposition. This gives me cause for concern. In effect, in Latin America, unlike the United States, there is a long-standing secularizing tradition within philosophy of maintaining the distinction between discourses of religion and philosophy. *Being by vocation and profession a philosopher* but also belonging to a Jewish-Christian cultural hemisphere, I have therefore undertaken to obtain, in order to comprehend sufficiently my concrete historical reality, college degrees in history and the sciences of religion.[1] Given the complex historical circumstances in Latin America, I had to be a political activist during the decade of the 1950s, as a student and university political leader, and since the end of the 1960s, as a contributor to the radical renovation of one of the contemporary universal religions (Christianity, which opened the road to a critical moment within the Muslim, Hindu, and Buddhist traditions, namely, liberation theology), which has had profound consequences in popular movements as well as great social and political influence. I helped initiate a tradition called "critical history of the church."[2] I helped formulate the already known and recognized liberation theology as a professor in the IPLA (Latin American Pastoral Institute)—Quito, Ecuador—since 1967. But this did not hinder me *as a philosopher* in initiating, with some colleagues (J. C. Scannone, O. Ardiles, A. Parisí, et al.), the tradition that we named "philosophy of liberation," even while I was a university professor of philosophy (which was my primary task and modus vivendi). I have written works on these three discursive, epistemological fields, but I have always exercised great caution not to confuse them or even treat them in the same work.[3] In the present edited volume, some essays are strictly philosophical (the majority), some are theological (i.e., Roberto Goizueta's and Elina Vuola's), and some move from one discourse to another without explanation or acknowledgment.

The authors of the articles are, in some cases, very knowledgeable about my work, but not in other cases.[4] I would like to thank the latter for having invested the time to get to know my work, although I am concerned that a partial acquaintance with my work can lead to ambiguous or inadequate interpretations. That is why I have given in to the temptation to indicate concepts and ideas in my work that have not been considered here, and other analyses more complimentary of my work. But most importantly I urge the reader to appreciate the circumstances and concrete realities in which philosophers who come from a peripheral world like Latin America, which is by necessity not well known in the "center," must work, and the special circumstances that limit him or her (but also illuminate his or her path), paying special attention to biographical and historical time. A document written during the 1970s, which was created under a military dictatorship and a conservative, fundamentalist (in Argentina, frequently fascist) environment, cannot be compared with a document that was written during the 1990s, created in a context with much more freedom and with a critical awareness of a process already accomplished.

It is thus necessary to keep in mind the biography of the author, and to take into account not only the date of the English version, and not only the date of the Spanish version, but also the actual date of the production of a work. For example, *El humanismo helenico* (Hellenic humanism) was written between 1961 and 1963 (the partial fruit of a doctoral dissertation defended in 1959); it was published in 1976, when I had already been exiled from Argentina. This book remained hidden in the basements of the University of Buenos Aires because it had been banned by the military dictatorship. It was not until 1983, when the first government of the contemporary democratic period was elected, that it was sold in bookstores. So it has remained untranslated, accessible only in Spanish, that is, without having been able to enter into the "discussion" of the philosophy of the "center," until the present.

The contribution by Walter Mignolo, my friend since I first met him in Puebla several years ago while he was delivering a course on postcolonial reason, situates the philosophy of liberation within the horizon of North American debates. I thank him for his constant support and encouragement to continue onward with our work. First of all, I agree with him when he points out that the philosophy of liberation should not "dictate the routes for social transformation of the *victims*" because these victims have already for a long time possessed their culture, their organization, and their political system. Otherwise, the philosophy of liberation would carry out "the dictatorial function of instrumental reason." I agree on this point and thus have always insisted on the attitude of "listening"—of being "all ears" or remaining open to the "interpellation of the other." Such an "interpellation," as a revelation, is an "order" that comes from "above," as Levinas argued, or as the EZLN (Ejércíto Zapatista de Liberación Nacional) proclaims: "Among us, those who lead do not lead by giving orders, but by obeying orders." This would be understood in greater depth if one were not just to think in terms of Marx's "living labor" (which from the exteriority of the totality of capital is subsumed in the essence of capital and thus is not merely a "marginal" moment), but also in terms of the hermeneutical-cultural moment. For example, Nicaragua can be assimilated as a national market, peripheral and dependent to the United States, but its culture, its music, its language, and so on, will always retain a certain *inassimilable* exteriority in which there resides the possibility of affirmation (analytical affirmation of exteriority) as the origin of Nicaraguan liberation (which is now farther away from reality than during the Sandinista government, thanks to the politics of the Pentagon with its ten-year war between the "contras" and the multinationals). This is why I agree that liberation philosophy cannot be taken as the "new sacred project" that is presented to us as "a new, universal, grand theory, a macrohistory." We need to find new ways to confront the "grand narrative" of the colonialist, Western, and North American modernity (as it was deployed recently during the Gulf War and the war against Serbia), and universal rational dogmatism, with a *critical reason* (not a "weak" reason) that takes into consideration the global conditions of oppression in the world without denying to the victims (a Rigoberta Menchú, the EZLN, etc.) *the right to a new vision of global history (always changeable) and of universal principles* that can give some sense to the Di-fference (which I call dis-tinction), to the particularity, to the contingent and always fallible "claim to justice" of those who fight for the recognition of their new rights. I believe that a radical and clear understanding of our "epistemological location" has to learn how to reconcile universality and contingency, globality and difference, critical theory and militancy, under the guidance of the democratic community of the victims themselves—in which the philosopher will never propose the guidelines or the goals but will instead reflect in solidarity and, from the rear guard, justify theoretically (or introduce suspicions into) the decisions of a given community.

It is in this sense that I greatly appreciate and must give special thanks to James Marsh (an authentic philosopher of liberation in the United States) for his comments on my second *Etica de la Liberación* (from 1998). I am in debt for his previous suggestion that I needed to articulate, without either reduction or hierarchy, *material* ethics and *formal* morality. This suggestion, the fruit of years of dialogue that began when I visited New York and that have been continuing for the last ten years, was essential in the project of articulating Karl-Otto Apel's formal ethics of discourse into a more complex ethics, as he explains in his contribution to this volume. Marsh shows in addition that the ruling system about which we have talked concretely, the system in effect, is the capitalist system. It is also necessary to mention that there are other systems of oppression such as the sexist-patriarchal, the racist, the systems of cultural domination over the ethnicities of the South, the system of the nonrecognition of the future generations as it pertains to ecological matters, and so on. I refer to these in my *Ethics of Liberation* because they are at the abstract level of the "different" *fronts of liberation,* for now, and will be analyzed in the future. But here I want to concentrate on Marsh's final critical argument.

This argument could be summarized in the following way: the oppositions "right and good, deontology and teleology, justification and application, duty and happiness, universal and particular" have to be integrated but without giving exclusive "priority" to the material principle, since this would reduce the formal principle to a mere principle of "application." In addition, this is also because all access to the material (the "pre-original ethical recognition of the other as the other," or the fact of misery itself) is "always mediated hermeneutically or communicatively" or finds itself always already within a linguistic, consensual, and formal realm. Finally, "physiological" prediscursive arguments are not convincing and even appear to fall into the naturalistic fallacy that we are trying to overcome. As a way of conclusion, Marsh proposes a "principle of generic consistency."[5] I agree with the way Marsh has formulated the question. Nonetheless, I would have to indicate some levels of complexity that return us to the central intention of my *Ethics of Liberation* (1998).

First, I have insisted that the opposition is not between "right-good, duty-happiness, and so on." This led me to totally reconstruct the "material principle" (which is also universal and not only particular). The material does not have a *direct* reference to the "good" but to "practical truth." I therefore had to distinguish between a "validity claim" and a "truth claim," (following the path opened by Wellmer, although he does not develop it). The "good" in my *Ethics of Liberation* is a synthesis of three "claims": truth (material), validity (formal), and feasibility (instrumental or of possibility). For this reason the "good life," "happiness," values, and so on, are "material" aspects, but in no way are they the last instantiation of the material level. "Human life" is the last instance of the *material,* and it is this life that is the "criterion of truth" (and falsity). The "good" is more complex, for it needs the integration of the formal (the freedom, autonomy, and consensus of subjects), without which it would become a mere vegetable or animal "reproduction of life," but not ethical-human. Because of this complete "reconstruction" of the material principle, now with a universality claim, I had to begin with this principle in the "exposition" of my *Ethics of Liberation*, and for this reason the formal principle would seem to appear there as a mere principle of "application." But I think that if we start the exposition from the formal principle, this will then perform the function of a principle of justification; and in this case, formally, justification will have priority over the material aspect. And even in this case the "good"—as a synthesis of the three "claims"—is opposed to evil, and not to the right, to validity, and so on. It seems to me that the principle of generic consistency gives, in the end, primacy to the formal moment, even though it pays attention to the material considerations, but without noticing that "*what is* argued" or the *content* of practical truth of the argued, presupposes always already a material order that responds to another logic than the merely formal one because in the end it always has a relationship with human life as a criteria of truth. When, under the second rubric, Marsh writes, "As interacting . . . they ought to follow . . . truth" (if one only holds a consensus theory of truth, such as the Habermasian), he uses, in my opinion, another criterion, namely, the material one. In such a case, then, he would not be able to justify the content without reference to the real order under the ruling of the material principle of human life. The phenomenon of dissent is such that she who dissents has access to reality as a practical truth that could differ from what is accepted by the community of communication with intersubjective validity (this is the case of an inventor or a scientist, for example). Consensual validity has to fulfill the formal rules for the acceptance of an argument by the symmetrical participants, but the content of the argument, the discovery of those who are the "affected" and the definition of their "interest" or "needs," presupposes another principle of determination (the material principle of truth, which is always linguistically or hermeneutically mediated, as Apel would require). "To agree" is not to give a *new reason.* New reasons (contents of the arguments) do not only achieve consistency due to intersubjective acceptance but instead through "reference" to reality, as mediation of human life (and in this consists the Greek *pragmata,* what is practical). We ascend to these new truths as living subjects and in order to remain alive (what kills, in the end and in principle, or without considering the circumstances, is false).

Furthermore, the fourth moment of Marsh's argument is found already at another level. This concerns the victims or those who suffer the inevitably unintentional negative effects of acts (norms, institutions, systems, etc.) with a "goodness claim." The three principles are universal conditions (not particular) of the "goodness claim." The serious, honest "goodness claim" is, however, uncertain and contingent by nature (and thus Derrida and Rorty are right, although, contra Rorty, its conditions are universal). A perfect ethical act, or an act with a "goodness claim," is impossible because of the finitude of human existence. With Walter Benjamin, we call those who suffer the negative effects of these acts victims. The correction of the act (norm, institution, etc.) from the perspective of the victims—and because it produces the victim as victim—is the point of departure of critical reason (from Marx, Levinas, Freud, or Horkheimer). This problem is treated in the second part of my ethics. It concerns the critical moment (not any longer formal-material, but positive-negative), from which both Marx and Levinas depart, the *material* recognition of the suffering of the victim in his or her sensible-human corporeality: suffering as an alarm system caused by no longer being able to live humanely (which is the negation of the material principle of ethics, as elaborated in the first part of my ethics). But again, it is possible that a community of communication would consent to attempt, in the first place, to discover the nonethical dimensions of institutions or acts with a "goodness claim" (which in the context of the public or political spheres I will call, in my work in progress, *Crítica de la razón y de la voluntad política,* the "justice claim"), and through a discourse of justification concludes that it is necessary to begin a struggle for the self-recognition of and in accordance with the victims. Theoretically, this is possible; historically, it is from the suffering corporeality of the victims (of hunger, of the injustice of the colonial Creoles, of the humiliations inflicted on women, of the suffering of rape, of the illness brought about by contamination, etc.) that critical movements have been launched. In this case, it would be a concrete material priority and not merely particular.

Now, with respect to the other objection, I have recently written an article on the "naturalist fallacy" in which I study this problem more analytically. My conclusion is that certain empirical judgments (e.g., "Juan eats"), because their subject is a human being who is already responsible and therefore ethical, always necessarily assumes *a concealed, implicit normative content.* The empirical statement "Juan is a human being" includes already implicitly the responsibility for his life, the obligation to protect it and develop it. The question of suicide is central, but it would take too long to develop it here. It is my opinion that, materially, the naturalistic fallacy, in the sense of formal, analytical logic, does not apply to these cases because it is not located at the level of analytical judgments as articulated by Ayer and Carnap. It is not the case that attributes are conflated, as is required by G. Moore. Nor are normative properties derived from natural properties. Instead, and simply, judgments or empirical statements about human beings, which are already implicitly normative, make *explicit* their *normativity* (i.e., a reference to their justification is included and thus they are grounded). These judgments or empirical statements make reference to the reality of the human being as a living being, which are, in the last instance, the *content* of all of his or her acts and the absolute condition of any other act. The dead are not a subject of ethics, nor of a community of communication. In any event, I hope these questions can become points of departure for fertile dialogues in order to develop more effective arguments in favor of the process of the liberation of the victims.

The work of Linda Alcoff is very suggestive because it indicates certain issues that I have to confront in the near future in my dialogues with critical philosophy in the United States. In my last visit to Duke University (in the winter semester of 1998), and with reference to the political philosophy of Ernesto Laclau (who partly incorporates some of Rorty's positions), I came to understand that the North-American critique—which is very different from that which exists in Latin America, and which therefore is new to me—is concerned with the question of the universalism of metaphysical principles that do not sufficiently take into account their "locus enuntiationis," as Walter Mignolo puts it. The issue, then, is frequently articulated from the horizons of Nietzsche as well as of Foucault—two of the philosophers to which the postmodern movement necessarily refers, though we must not forget, among others, Lyotard and Derrida. I have taken into account these two philosophers in my *Ethics of Liberation.* Still, I think that there are two themes developed in the text by Alcoff: (1) the sense of the "universality" of principles (and as a product, in my view, of my debates with Apel) and the purported "immunity from critique" on my part and (2) the theme of diversity of the "difference," which since 1970 I have called "dis-tinction" in order not to locate it on the same level as the issue of "identity."

With respect to (1), I think that Foucault situates himself, validly and creatively, at what I would call the strategic or tactical level. This is a concrete level of reflection which, because it has as a point of departure "strategic reason" (which, in its more noble and positive sense, is a necessary component of the act of good will), requires that we associate constitutively practical reason (which is theoretical-epistemological) with power. In the United States, an interesting "antifoundationalist" movement argues against a theoretical, universalistic reason, whose defense is associated with Apel, for instance. Such a reason must be grounded in a "universal foundation" that has been defended against skeptics and that allows for the deduction or application to particular cases. I have now realized that my position is against such a view, but I must now elaborate my arguments before these new objections, which are posterior to my debate with Apel. The universal "principles" of which I speak in my *Ethics of Liberation* are what Franz Hinkelammert calls frameworks of the delimitation of impossibility. If we remove the antagonism, there is no more struggle for hegemonic control, there is no more politics. The respect for the human life of the other as an antagonist, required by material universal principle, *makes possible politics "as" politics*. The opposite is totalitarianism. If we physically curtail the freedom of movement of the antagonist (e.g., if we lock him or her up in a prison), we foreclose the possibility of politics as the struggle against hegemony, which is to say we contradict the principle of consensual, formal validity, or the democratic principle, that is, the formal, universal principle of the ethics of liberation. This would be authoritarianism, and thus politics would be equally impossible. If a political system affirms itself as being totally perfect, as the best of all possible systems, without acknowledging its victims, the universal and critical principle of responsibility cannot perform its self-corrections, and thus such a system would destroy itself in the long run precisely because of its antipolitical conservatism.

In other words, these principles are not metaphysical principles of self-identity but universal conditions of possibility, or framework conditions, or limits even to the antivalue of any established system as Nietzsche elaborated it in his critique of society. These conditions, or limits, make possible the exercise of power as a "*relational power* that sustains itself of its own accord." Nietzsche as much as Foucault, like many intuitions of the postmodern movement, is assimilated by the philosophy of liberation but in very determined moments of its very complex architectonic, without denying other determining moments. Nietzsche's critique of "values" and his call to create new ones in order to supersede the totality are not all that is necessary. Foucault is necessary in order to situate the discourse of the philosopher within its "cultural location," and especially because of his unique sensibility for the "excluded," the victims of every structure of power and respective epistemology. This is why I do not believe that the *Ethics of Liberation* is immune to critique, if this means to strengthen its development or its conceptual "nucleus." On the contrary, since it only has a *claim to truth* but does not claim to *possess the truth* (dogmatic position), it is by definition open to any critique. Obviously it must remain open to the perspectives of informed, and not merely ideologically motivated, critics. Paradoxically, when I speak of the critique of reason from a position of exteriority, I am criticized for irrationalism, and when I defend, as a responsible, militant intellectual, the universality of the principles of *critical* reason, I am criticized of extreme rationalism. In the end, if I pretend to defend the universality of the material, discursive reason and strategic feasibility, it is *only insofar as I need them to illuminate the universality of the "critical" reason.* It is this critical reason that Nietzsche, Foucault, Levinas, and Marx inevitably exercise in the concrete. And it is this critical reason that is necessary for the liberation of the victims, as Menchú makes explicit. How could I prove to Rorty his complicity with the U.S. cruelty in the Gulf and Serbian wars (without, of course, ignoring the totalitarianism of the Iraqi and Serbian regimes) if I cannot provide a conceptual overview of the rationality of the "world-system" from the standpoint of a *global* critical reason, where the "universal" is a framework of impossibility, within whose globality *[mundialidad]* is included both

Rorty (a white male from the North, etc.), and Rigoberta Menchú (a woman of Mayan descent, a peasant from an oppressed culture, from Guatemala, etc.), and the many "Rigobertas" in Iraq and Serbia, and the other women from the South? There is a dogmatic and dominating universality that has been criticized by the postmoderns, but there is also a "universality" as a condition of possibility of any rational critique whose status is still very obscure, at least as an antifoundationalist position. The question would be, What are we talking about when we are trying to ground, from the perspective of the victims of modernity, a universal, antifoundationalist, critical reason that affirms multiculturality with a certain degree of incommensurability and departs from "difference" (again, which I call dis-tinction), and is to be understood hermeneutically? This rationality has as a project a "globality" *[mundialidad]*, or concrete universality that is not univocal, dogmatic, or totalizing but plural and respectful of differences. It would be post-antifoundationalist.

This leads us to the second objection Alcoff discusses, which is concerned that "the poor" becomes a univocal category of "difference" that is not sufficiently rich to show the pluri-valence of alterity (race, gender, the postcolonial cultures, etc.). On the one hand, it is noted that one may fall into relativism or, on the other, into the absolutism of a self-immunized discourse. In this sense, Alcoff shows us that the Other can be interpreted as a "metaphysical illusion." However, in the *Ethics of Liberation* (1998), I have used the category of "victim" (from Benjamin) and not that of "the poor." In effect, "poverty" is a modality of exteriority, in a strict sense and in our era: paupers are those who, *under conditions of capitalism,* and with reference to the market, "cannot reproduce their life" (as Marx puts it). But in my ethics of 1973, I showed that the "the Other" is diverse: it is the woman in the sexist system, the girl or boy in pedagogy, the poor in the economy, the fetishized totality before any "Other," etc. I showed explicitly that each one of these fields of dis-tinction maintains an exteriority, even epistemological, and, in analyzing the relations between the male and female, this is why the categorical or epistemological horizon of Marx is no longer sufficient and we must turn to Freud, though his horizon is also valid only partially. In 1973, I wrote that "Marx cannot tell us anything on the orgasm" against the standard Marxism of the type espoused by Cerruti Guldberg, who criticized me then from the standpoint of an orthodox "classism." Within pedagogy, or the dialectic between "old and new generations," Paulo Freire is more pertinent, epistemologically, than Marx and Freud, though Marx and Freud can supplement the Freirean reflections to show the economic and ideological conditions of possibility and the ways in which the unconscious conditions the educational processes. I wrote all of this during a period in which dogmatic Marxism reigned, as well as the orthodox psychoanalytical movement (Buenos Aires was one of the capitals of psychoanalysis) and the Piagetian sciences of education in Argentina and Latin America. This diversity of the exteriority, in which there are in addition "degrees" of subsumption and exteriority, where every level of alterity is "distinct," given that, for example, a prisoner in the prison of a "panoptical" society is not the same thing as a mad person in a madhouse of a "normal" or "rational" society in France during the classical age, stands in opposition to the Hegelian contradiction of identity-difference. For Hegel, "being" is what is "different *[Unterschied]*" from the "identity *[Identität]*," which is on the same ontological level. "The Other," on the contrary, is located beyond identity-difference: it is the dis-tinct. In my two *Ethics* (1973, 1998), my reflection locates itself at a more primordial ontological level (1973) or a material level (1998). However, I have always departed from a concrete, strategic level of power, or what I have called the field of practical feasibility—in Latin, *operabilia.* I have always done my reflection at a macropolitical level, historically, economically, and politically, and not, contra Foucault, at the microstructural, since this level constitutes the essence of the philosophy of liberation *as such.* We can see clearly indications of all of this in my *Philosophy of Liberation,* which starts with a chapter entitled "Geopolitics and Philosophy"—a disconcerting title in 1976 to any philosophical work. There I wrote:

> From Heraclitus to Karl von Clausewitz and Henry Kissinger, "war is the origin of everything," if by "everything" one understands the order or system that world dominators control by their power and armies. We are at war. . . . I am trying, then, to take space, *geopolitical space* [I would underscore today] seriously. To be born at the North Pole or in Chiapas is not the same thing as to be born in New York City.[6]

Foucault certainly will be very useful to me in developing the intermediate strategic level, which is that of the micro institutions of power between macro geopolitical, national, international power, and concrete action. It is for this reason that *Ethics of Liberation* could be taken as an introduction to other forthcoming works that will deal with what I have named, as a whole, "fronts of liberation." Taking Michael Walzer's notion of *Spheres of Justice,* I want to talk about "fronts of liberation," which refers to the borderline or borderland, the in-betweenness, the *nepantla* in Nahuatl or Aztec language, of the "sphere," or totality, where there are struggles of emancipation, where there appear the illegal "new social movements." These fronts of liberation point beyond the accepted, legitimate concept of justice, beyond friendship as *fraternité* in Derrida's sense (in *The Politics of Friendship*). They point toward "solidarity" with the victims (or the foe, the dominators of the system). In effect the *Ethics of Liberation* is a "craziness" in defending the victims against the system, in the face of the "wise" and moribund philosophy that dissolves the animosity of the enemy: the victim of the system. Are not the poor Mexican emigrants the enemies of the secure happiness of the white, rich Californians? Oh enemies! (The rich Californians are my enemies.) There are no enemies! (The poor exiled Mexicans are not my enemies.) This theme is not developed by Derrida. He cannot address it because he only expresses a European critical reasoning. He talks about "fraternity" but not about "openness" to the Other who is then no longer an enemy. This is the point of the departure of the *first* front of liberation, the politics and economics of liberation, as an epistemological differential treatment. Thanks to Foucault, I will begin my exposition from the horizon of feasibility, from which I will develop a set of implicit principles (level A), to then delve inside the mediations in general and at a concrete strategic level (B)—where Foucault has a lot to teach us—to finally arrive to the "claim *[pretension]* to justice" (which is fallible, revisable, finite, and necessarily correctable, that is, with the least immunity from criticism). This "claim to justice" is raised with inevitable contingency at the strategic level, toward the structures of political-economic power, of concrete acts that situate differentially the poor and the excluded within this strict level of reference. These structures include the concrete "identity" of capitalism, the "difference" of alienated labor that is subsumed by capital, the poor as the exteriority that cannot live without money in the market (where money is contingent in *having a job*). This is the economic-political "dis-tinction," even in the Foucauldian sense.

I must thank Karl-Otto Apel for having taken with such seriousness and interest the long dialogue we initiated in 1989 in Freiburg (two weeks after the fall of the Berlin Wall). Apel understood the importance of some ethical problems of the South, which gave to his thought a greater globality with respect to North-South relations; but given the rationalist and systematic structure of his discourse, he did not believe it possible to assimilate the challenges of liberation philosophy. Discourse ethics, on the other hand, opened up the whole horizon of the *validity of the formal morality of consensus* for the ethics of liberation (as a fundamental moment of the philosophy of liberation), thus bringing to light the issue of the discursive, free, autonomous, and symmetrical participation of the affected. But in addition to this moment of the ethics of liberation we must articulate a material level (of content or of practical-material reasoning) and another one of feasibility (of instrumental and strategic reason), in addition to the properly critical ones (in the ethical-material sense of an ethical-critical reason). All of these demanded a more complex architectonic to better explain the nature of the "ethical act" itself, particularly from the perspective of the South, the periphery and postcolonial cultures, and from the perspective of the anguishing problems of globalization, postmodernity, and the growing poverty of the majority of humanity.

Prior to writing his chapter for this volume, Apel published two other articles dealing with the philosophy of liberation, to which I responded in other articles that answer his objections.[7] In addition, my "second" *Ethics of Liberation* is a broad architectonic response to Apel's objections, which explains why I cannot clarify in depth my position here. I will only touch on some points.

Thanks to the discussion with Apel, the so-called transcendent economics was transformed into the material universal principle, namely, the deontological demand for the production, reproduction, and development of human life in community, with the claim to include all of humanity as a universal requirement or a "requirement of practical truth." The opponent of the material principle is the cynic who would countenance death or collective suicide. The Apelian principle of consensus is the last one at the moral-formal level, as a "claim of practical validity." For Apel, the ethical "good" is identified as "practical validity." In my case, the "goodness claims" (and not the "good" of the utilitarians or communitarians) has a material component (a claim of practical truth), a formal one (a validity claim), and last, a viability component (or feasibility claim). For Apel, these three principles are located at the level of universality (what he calls *Teil A*). There would be another level *(Teil B),* for the application of the three principles, at the level of institutions. Last, there is the level of singularity *(Einzelheit),* which is an issue that Apel never deals with sufficiently. This is the level of the action itself, of the empirical decision of the norm, and of the concrete organization of the institution or of a real, historical ethical system where the "goodness claim" is brought into action. This would be level C. For Apel, a concrete norm with "practical validity" already fulfills all the requirements of a moral, ethical action. This is a "reductivist fallacy," where the practical validity is practical truth, where the "validity claim" is identified with the "goodness claim," where the "valid *[gültig]*" is the moral, or ethical, and where the material is the anthropological, the ontological, or at the level of values."

Let us take an example. From the proslavery "understanding of being" (the inevitable ontological level, given that it is always historical) and the anthropological acceptance of the slave as a nonhuman, the exclusion and asymmetry of the slave in the community of communication is inevitable. Does discourse ethics as a discourse have the capacity to "discover" the excluded one and to "produce historically" his or her empirical equality as justice? No, because its basic norm presupposes that he or she is a symmetrical participant. Apel himself has recognized that there is always already an empirical exclusion and asymmetry. He thought that a complementary ethics (e.g., the ethics of liberation) could make up for this limitation of discourse ethics. But, in addition, at the concrete level of decisions (the hypothetical *Teil C*), no one will be able to "deliberate" in a *perfect* fashion (for it would be necessary, using Popper's argument, to have an infinite intelligence with an infinite speed). For this reason, the good act or norm, the just institutions, and so on (with a "goodness claim" in order to be more precise) requires in addition to deliberation the intervention of affectivity, of emotions, of solidarity. Pure argumentation that reaches "practical validity" is not the only necessary condition of a good act or a "goodness claim." The participation of those other dimensions ignored by the reductivist fallacy of the rationalism of discourse ethics is required.

This debate has led me to define "the material" (and its correspondent rationality: the practical-material reason), whose last instance is "human life" as a practical criterion of truth (and in the first place as a criterion of practical truth before being a criterion of theoretical truth). Therefore, I accept that before the skeptic, the ultimate *formal* foundation at the consensual level or level of intersubjective validity is the ethical-discursive principle. But the ultimate *material* foundation at the level of truth (and at the level of the motivations, like "satisfaction" of the will, or the level of affectivity) must face the cynic and must show the performative contradiction that is committed when the cynic attempts to ethically justify suicide or death.

Moreover, taking into consideration the exclusion and asymmetry of the many who are affected (from ontology, anthropology, and the empirical convocation in the community of communication of those already recognized as affected), there appears, at a critical level, the whole theme of the "interpellation of the Other." I admit that for the *interpretation* of the empirical and linguistic pronouncement of the other, the horizon of discursivity, is presupposed; but this pronouncement, at a transontological level (at which Levinas is located, beyond Heidegger, and which is incomprehensible to Apel) has as a point of departure the exteriority of the Other in his or her "saying" as the presence of a vulnerable body in the face, a presence prior to the world (the merely "said") and who, from the standpoint of res-ponsibility (which opens up the activity of a preoriginary ethical reason), demands justice. This concerns the question of "proximity" as the "face-to-face" (of the now freed slave), which is not at all merely an ontological experience but is rather the presence of the Other in the world (the ontologically enslaving) as the "in-comprehensible" (for the slave owner, in the Heideggerian sense, and not solely as the "individually ineffable") because it is another freedom, another being that inaugurates another world. This interpellation of the Other does not ground ethics in its first moment (neither formally nor materially) inasmuch as it is a given "goodness claim" (that of the serious, honest slave owner); but instead it "inaugurates" the critical-material moment of the ethics of liberation. This is the issue of the existence of the suffering of the victim (now ethically interpreted) as the nonintentional negative effect of the act with a "goodness claim." To this extent, liberation ethics is not a Weberian ethics of responsibility, which is blind before the victims of the system that Weber justifies. Rather, it establishes a whole critical-material process of ethics that the first Frankfurt School intuited, although without sufficient ethical or philosophical articulation. "Negative materiality" (misery) is the point of departure of critical reason. This is the second moment of the ethics of liberation, and it is totally lacking in a discourse ethics that is purely formal and discursive and that therefore lacks material ethical criteria.

I admit also that Marx did not give sufficient importance to consensual intersubjectivity, which in politics would be a "democratic principle," or to the level of validity. Instead, he placed the "social relation" (as relation of production from the standpoint of a regulative idea of a "community of free men") at an ethical level (as "domination" or "exploitation," and as cause of the creation of surplus value, which is the robbery of objective human life) that discourse ethics ignores as a material determinant of ethics. All of this concerns the question of the material ethical criteria that "orients" the *content* of a discussion, which Habermas explicitly denies is the object of discourse ethics. Discourse ethics does not possess a material ethical criterion that would allow it to judge capitalism, patriarchy, racism, the ecological destruction against future generations, and so on. Everything is left to the moral discussion of the participants departing from their own resources, such as slave owners in Aristotle's Athens, without material criteria for the discussion. This is what I have called "formal moral reductionism" in my *Ethics of Liberation* (1998). In short, I hope to dedicate in my next work (*Critique of Political Reason and Will: Toward a "Justice Claim"*) a central place to the discussion of all the new objections that Apel expresses here.

By writing his chapter, Hans Schelkshorn has increased my debt to him. He made my work the subject of his doctoral dissertation, and later of his Habilitation, and wrote a book in order to present my thought to the German public. Schelkshorn is becoming a recognized Austrian philosopher who will without doubt contribute a great deal. I have to say that his works allowed Apel to read in German a philosophical interpretation of the philosophy of liberation. Meanwhile, Schelkshorn has opened up his own path. I am happy to have served in the process by which he has come to define himself as a thinker self-conscious of his "epistemic location," of someone who thinks from the "center" of the world-system.

In regard to the chapters by Eduardo Mendieta, a young and eminent Hispanic North American philosopher, and by Lynda Lange, I can only hope that they will continue their undertaken paths; I do not have major commentaries to contribute. Michael Barber's contribution takes into account a reading of many of my works. Barber compares my interpretation of the theme of fetishism in the thought of Marx with the theme of idolatry in the thought of the Jean-Luc Marion. This concerns a reflection that moves within the horizon of what Kant called, in *Religion within the Limits of Reason Alone,* natural theology or theodicy (in Leibniz's sense). In this way, Schelling's "theology" is his philosophical theology; the word "theology" should be read in this sense in Barber's contribution.

Marion and Barber touch on the theme of theory, weakening its sense from the standpoint of alterity. Barber objects that I have not put in crisis my own theory. Here, it would be illustrative to review how I approached Marx from the angle of theodicy, or what I called "Latin American archeology (metaphysical antifetishism)." In volume 5, chapter 10, of my *Ethical Philosophy of Liberation*, I began with a "symbolic archeology" (the hermeneutics of Latin American culture), paragraph 67. In paragraph 68 of this work, I expounded on the "ontological fetishization of the system," where my opponents range from Hegel to Heidegger ("totalitarian totalization of the totality," sec. 69). All of this proceeds without making any reference to Marx. I broached the economic question under the heading "The Ethical Status of the Cosmos" (sec. 70). I show, from the "economic" Levinas, that the things of the world have sense as offerings to the Other, as *'avodah* (work service in Hebrew). This discussion concludes with "The Archeological Economics" (sec. 71). This last concerns the theme of the cult. For Hegel, the "cult *(Kultus)*" to the absolute is "the certitude of faith on truth," that is, "the cult is the act that has the end in itself, and this act is faith that is the concrete reality of the divine and consciousness in-itself." At this point Marx enters my discourse for the first time. *The "cult" does not consist in any "intel-*

lectual" (or theoretical) act. The cult, as the essence of religion, puts the cosmos, things, systems, at the "service" (*'avodah*, or *diakonía* in Greek) of the Other. To cite from that early work: "Marx also criticizes the cult of the system: the immolated to the fetish of money, as commodity, this is the worker, the laborer. Marx indicates the correct way of cult to the absolute Other without presupposing it and even without negating it." Here, it is a matter of correctly interpreting a text that a philosopher considered from the perspective of the cultural history of his people: "For mercifulness and not sacrifices I plead!" It is thus that in my first ethics, the theme of "theory" was, even to excess, called into question, following a little the anti-intellectualist *pathos* of Levinas in *Totalité et infini*. "Love of justice," praxis, cult (transforming the product of work into bread for the hungry), became the themes for philosophy, of ethics, of theodicy. The theme of natural theology was not to put theory in question, as is the case for Marion and Barber, but the "economics" of life as enjoyment or suffering, as "service" *(diakonía)* to the Other.

The same could be said with respect to the importance of "weakening" theory, as Vattimo says. It would seem that in the "second" ethics, thanks to the study of the four redactions of *Capital* and the debate with Apel, I began to have a more positive attitude toward "reason." In fact, in *Autrement qu'être* Levinas allows me to "recover" material reason (of life), Apelian discursivity, and critical reason (of the Frankfurt School, for instance), all of which depart from a "suspicion" by Levinas. Almost at the end of *Autrement qu'être*, in chapter 5, section 5, entitled "Scepticisme et Raison," Levinas writes: "Proximity thus means an *anterior* reason to the thematization of the meaning of the subject that thinks . . . a *pre-originary reason* [*raison pré-originelle*] that does not proceed from any initiative of the subject, an *a-anarchical reason*." This is the reason that "recognizes the other *as other*," not the one that recognizes the other as himself within the same community. A recognition of the other as Other lies beyond Hegelian, Apelian, Honnethian "recognition." This is the origin ("preoriginary" reason of the world, of represented signification, of future totalities) of *critical reason*. Indeed, even in *Totalité et infini*, Levinas wrote:

> Ontology, which reduces the other to the same . . . Here theories enter upon a course that renounces metaphysical Desire, renounces the marvel of exteriority from which that Desire derives. But theory understood as a respect for exteriority delineates another structure essential for metaphysics. In its comprehension of being (or ontology) it is concerned with critique. It discovers the dogmatism and naive arbitrariness of its spontaneity. . . . Metaphysics, transcendence, the welcoming of the other by the same, of the Other by me, is concretely produced as the calling into question of the same by the other, that is, as the ethics that accomplishes the critical essence of knowledge. And as critique precedes dogmatism, metaphysics precedes ontology.[8]

Critical reason is prior to the future, postontological world because it is *pre-originary* (preontological: this side of the openness to the world as a sensible corporeality). Having put theory as representation in question in my philosophy, and even as a dialectical-ontological reason with reference to totality, and thus having situated my own theory as responsibility for the Other, I do not, however, cease to attribute to reason a proper function and for this reason I do not fall into skepticism or the postmodern positions that negate en toto reason *as such.* In my "first" *Ethics,* there was only space for reason as the hermeneutical deciphering of the analogical word of the interpellation of the Other. In my "second" *Ethics* there now appeared many types of reason, as the execution of the handling of the world of the logic of language in its different levels. However, reason always remains limited to the finitude of representation and, even within the comprehension of being, as a moment of truth that does not pretend to exhaust either reality or the exteriority of the Other before which there is still room for the expectation of "revelation." The concept of "truth claim" points to the finitude, precariousness, and fallibility of reason. Reality is accessed without absolute certitude, in the midst of doubt, with the need to secure the known through intersubjectivity (as a "validity claim"). This is neither skeptical irrationalism (postmodernism) nor dogmatic or optimistic rationalism. It is a critical affirmation of reason as "the cunning of life": as the management of reality at the service of the responsibility for the Other. This is, in addition, the critical essence of Marx's criticism of capital's fetishism in objective reality, as well as of bourgeois political economy (which exists today as a dogmatic theory with global power), that has absolutized the criterion of the increase of the rate of profit under whose *criterion of truth* humanity, the visibly suffering majority of poor in the periphery and in the center of the world-system, are immolated.

As for Roberto Goizueta, who is a specialist on my thought, I want to thank him for his theological contribution and for having continued to study my latest work, which already signals many changes with respect to the past.

With reference to the contribution by Elina Vuola, who is an admirable Swedish theological feminist whom I had the fortune to meet at a seminar organized for intellectuals of the five Nordic countries in Norway, I would like to situate her criticism in historical space-time. Indeed, to do justice to my "Latin American Erotics," which was written between 1972 and 1973 and was influenced by the discovery of Levinas's ethics of alterity, requires that one first describe the explicit intentions of the author in that work in order to then proceed to its limitations and to its mistakes proper to that period. In this work, I attempted to develop, first, a hermeneutic ("The Erotic Symbolics," para. 42 of my first *Ethics of Liberation*, vol. 3), in order to point out the existence of women in the Amerindian tradition (which is much more important than the posterior Hispanic and Latin American components). Subsequently, I developed a critique of patriarchal, phallocentric ontology (sec. 43). The definition of this ontology was pronounced in accordance with Parmenides: "*Being* sexed is being *masculine*; the I is the phallic subject; *Non-being*, woman, *is not*, that is, it is castration and sexual object, mother and undifferentiated lover because in non-being there is no difference. For this reason and necessarily, every sexual relation is always incestuous and ethically perverse." Patriarchialism conceives, as do the Greeks and Manicheans, ethical perfection as virginity (the Greek *parthenos,* or religious celibacy as virtue). This was the Parmenedian-ontological, or Heideggerian, view concerning gender, sexuality, and eroticism. It is through a phenomenology of eros as the caress that Levinas, following Feuerbach, superseded the ontology of vision and the understanding-of-being. I believe Elina Vuola could have shown the relevance of these pronouncements to the context of Latin American and Euro-North American philosophy in 1972. Nonetheless, there was a significant limit to my account. The metaphysics of erotic exteriority, which had discovered the transontological affirmation of difference of woman as an active subject, as a gender that organizes the emergence of the liberation movement of women against sociohistorical phallocentric machismo, originates from a love or an impulse (Levinasian "metaphysical desire") for the Other as Other (the female Other *[la Otra]* as female Other *[otra],* as I would put it today). Alterity was the essence of erotic love. For the Greeks, on the contrary, erotic love was the love of "the same" as "the same *[tó autó].*" This discovery led me to commit grave mistakes at operative levels, which the feminists from the North immediately noted, although perhaps they did not appreciate the context in which I was in solidarity with "women of the Third World" who were opposed to the feminism from the North, seeing it as ignoring capitalism. For this reason, I mistakenly interpreted as perverse "the love of the Same for the Same," *homo*-sexuality, radical feminism, and abortion as a negation of the Other (filicide). I did not take note that the Other *(la Otra)* is the *alterity of the personhood* of the Other (or *el Otro* [male Other]) in homosexuality, and not only "the same" sex. I did not take note that radical feminist movements, which espoused lesbianism, would also organize in the South and, furthermore, that the radical feminism of the North had virtues that in the South we had yet to discover. In fact, this is what made possible the criticism of the radical feminism from the North, the love of the same by the same, together with the support for the "liberation of women," love of the alterity of the Other. Vuola interprets all of this as a contradiction, but in the context of the South in 1972, it was not contradictory. With respect to abortion, I only saw the elimination of the Other (the child) as an affirmation of the "same" (the couple); I did not see clearly the autonomy, the freedom, and the right of women to their own bodies. Nor did I see clearly that in the dilemma of having to negate one of two lives, only women (and the male in the concrete relation) can have the *last ethical word* because it concerns their bodies (which is the ultimate subject of all rights). I think, however, that it would appear as though Vuola, as well as other critics, does not attempt to see that these mistakes of the moment needed to be superseded from the standpoint of the pronouncements themselves. For instance, that alterity was understood only sexually and not in the personhood of the Other, or *la Otra.* I think that liberation philosophy, in any event, was the first philosophical movement that spoke at the beginning of the 1970s of the "liberation of women" as a critique against patriarchal ontology. For this reason it hurts to be criticized as a patriarchal, taking as a point of reference statements that could be shown to be contrary to the enunciated principles, which are the important ones and which remain even to this day without as radical a formulation; I am referring to the application of Parmenides' ontological formulation to the critique of patriarchal machismo. Even in the case of the theologians of liberation, the first global, theological movement that inaugurated a whole critical discourse of the victims, it was evident that it could not address simultaneous forms of oppression. It was empirically impossible to do so. For this reason, the oppression of women was discovered slowly as the natural unfolding of liberation theology, not against its presuppositions but as a consequence of their development. It is easy to criticize the impossible, that which is found, as the French philosopher would say, "beyond the possible historical critical consciousness." What is interesting is to show how these limits were overcome and what was "impossible" during a period became "possible," or under what conditions and with what arguments, thanks to the irruption of the "*feminine* theological subject," all of which demands a redefinition of masculinity (a task already undertaken that will be developed further in the future).

With respect to the work by Mario Sáenz, which addresses my commentaries on the four redactions of Marx's *Capital*, and other related works, space does not permit me to indicate where we coincide and differ on his interpretations of my work. I am grateful for his wide reading of my works on Marx, but there are some issues that I would like to clarify. The first of these, which is also relevant to Vuola's critique, is that there is a certain lack of knowledge of the Levinasian sense of some of the terms I use, such as totality, exteriority, alterity, metaphysics, ethics, ground, source, and so on. This makes it difficult to follow his reading of my work and obliges me to make a long reference to frequent ambiguities, which sometimes are quite grave, especially if I put myself in the place of Marxist readers, who will see Marx's position distorted (in addition to the distortion that I myself could have committed, of which I do not declare myself innocent). Thus I need to make some clarifications.

Sáenz writes, for instance, "living labor is *an* exteriority to the system of capital." To be in "exteriority" is not to be *an* exteriority ("an" exteriority is without sense). For Marx, "living labor" could be *anterior* to capital; before the contract, *pauper ante festum,* as Marx says. Living labor is "in" exteriority; it can be alienated *in* capital (when it is subsumed) and can be given *after* capital (as unemployed: *pauper post festum,* as Marx also says). "Exteriority" (or internal transcendentality, as Hinkelammert puts it), as a category that refers to "totality," indicates the before and the outside; that is, what is transcendental in and after the "totality" of capital (as system, as an ontological level, as that which is grounded in "being," as value that is valorized in political-economic terms), is "living labor" (a potential worker). The *affirmation* of that living labor is the "analectical moment" that allows for the negation of the negation (the negation of living labor subsumed as alienated labor, which is negated or suppressed in its possible liberation from capital). The issue is simple, and perhaps Sáenz has made it unnecessarily complicated.

Sáenz also writes: "Dussel sides with Marx when he says that 'profit is the phenomenal form of surplus value.' But what is not 'phenomenal' is, according to Dussel, 'metaphysical.'" No. If something is phenomenal it can still be ontological, not metaphysical in the Levinasian sense. For Marx, "surplus" in capital is the ontological *ground* of the *phenomenon* of "profit." What is metaphysical or transontological is the subjectivity itself of the worker (living labor), who, although alienated *in capitalism* as the productive force, can still situate himself or herself as a "source" of a "creation" *[Schöpfung]* of a surplus value beyond the value reproduced in the "necessary time" in order to make up for value of the wage. For this reason, it is creation out of "the nothing of capital," which is to say, it lies beyond the "ground." It is the "source" that is the subjectivity of the alienated worker. Her labor power has been *bought* and her creative subjectivity (living labor) has been *used* without having been paid, and therein lies the ethical injustice. The difference between *labor power,* with value paid for by the wage of capital, and *living labor* as corporeal subjectivity, which possesses a dignity that is greater than exchange value but does not have value because it is the creator of all value, is where resides the possibility of discovering the "creation of surplus value from the nothing of capital." Again, the issue is clearer than Sáenz gives the impression.

In yet another example, in figure 11.2, it is written that "living labor" (LL1) is a moment of a "past system" (PS). Yes and no. Yes, if we consider that living labor was exercised by the feudal servant, but no, when living labor remains vacant, unemployed, in the "poor popular masses" (about which Marx speaks concerning "originary accumulation"). Herein we find the relationship between the poor and the people as the "exteriority" of any concrete mode of production. These are the people who wander Europe, *no longer being* servants and *not being able to become* wage earning workers. In this *no-man's-land*, in their "nothing," in the exteriority of the abandoned servant and of capital (initially and defectively), already present in the medieval city or in the near future, living labor as "absolute poverty" is never in a "past system" (PS).

To conclude, and as I have already indicated, I am presently writing a new work, *The Critique of Political Reason and Will: Toward a Justification of a Justice Claim.* It will concern a "front of liberation," which is looked at from the perspective of a concrete strategic level where the ethics of liberation unfolds and develops. There I will be able to amplify my answers to the objections that have been raised against my *Ethics of Liberation* (1998), departing from a defined *locus enuntiationis* within the structures of power, with epistemological self-awareness, and attempting to continue the construction of the always necessarily incomplete philosophy of liberation.

NOTES

Translated by Eduardo Mendieta.

1. I studied at the Sorbonne, where I attended courses taught by Paul Ricoeur, and at Mainz, where I received a doctorate in history (with a specialization in the history of the church in Latin America under the direction of Joseph Lortz in Germany and Robert Ricard in France), and a doctorate in the sciences of religion in Paris.

2. For twenty years I have been the president of the Commission for Latin American History, CEHILA.

3. The only exceptions are *Dependencia y liberación* (1974), in which I include essays on theological and philosophical topics, and section 5.1 of my *Las metáforas teológicas de Marx* (1993), which includes a theological work in a philosophical-hermeneutical work.

4. Such are, in the first place, Roberto Goizueta, whose doctoral thesis was published as *Liberation, Method, and Dialogue: Enrique Dussel and North American Theological Discourse* (Atlanta: Scholars Press, 1988). In the second place, there is Hans Schelkshorn, whose doctoral thesis in philosophy was entitled "Dialogisches Denken und politische Ethik: Untersuchungen zur Relevanz personal-dialogischen Denkens für eine Gesellschaftsethik bei Friedrich Gogarten, Emil Brunner, und Enrique Dussel" (University of Vienna, 1989), partly published under the title *Ethik der Befreiung: Einführung in die Philosophie Enrique Dussels* (Freiburg: Herder, 1992) and his Habilitation, which has appeared as a book, *Diskurs und Befreiung: Studien zur philosophischen Ethik von Karl-Otto Apel und Enrique Dussel* (Amsterdam: Editions Rodopi, 1997). In the third place we have the philosophical investigation by Michael Barber, *Ethical Hermeneutics: Rationalism in Enrique Dussel´s Philosophy of Liberation* (New York: Fordham University Press, 1999). Other colleagues who have treated my work include Edgar Moros-Ruano, "The Philosophy of Liberation of Enrique Dussel" (Ph.D. diss., Vanderbilt University, 1984); James García Ward, "Comparison of Two Liberation Thinkers: Enrique Dussel from Latin America and Michael Novak from the United States" (Ph.D. diss., De Paul University, 1985); Roque Zimmermann, *América Latina: O nao ser: Uma abordagem filosófica a partir de Enrique Dussel (1962–1976)* (Petropolis: Editorial Vozes, 1987). Theological works that discuss my thought include Anton Peter, *Befreiungstheologie und Transzendentaltheologie: Enrique Dussel und Karl Rahner im Vergleich* (Freiburg: Herder, 1988); Anton Peter, *Enrique Dussel: Offenbarung Gottes im Anderen* (Mainz: Grünewald-Verlag, 1996); Peter Penner, *Die Aussenperspektive des Anderen: Eine formalpragmatische Interpretation zu Enrique Dussel's Befreiungsethik* (Hamburg: Argument-Verlag, 1995); Christofer Ober, "System, Lebenswelt, und Exteriorität: Eine Auseinandersetzung mit den Ethiktheorien von Alfons Auer, Niklas Luhmann, Jürgen Habermas, und Enrique Dussel" (Ph.D. diss., University of Tübingen, 1989). The most complete thesis with respect to bibliographical and biographical aspects is that by Mariano Moreno Villa, "Filosofía personalista de la liberación: Metafísica desde el reverso del ser: A propósito de la filosofía ética de la liberación de Enrique Dussel," 2 vols. (Ph.D. diss., Universidad de Murcia, 1993).

5. James Marsh, *Critique, Action, and Liberation* (New York: SUNY Press, 1995), pp. 133ff.

6. Enrique Dussel, *Philosophy of Liberation*, trans. Aquilina Martinez and Christine Morkovsky (Maryknoll, N.Y.: Orbis, 1985), pp. 1–3.

7. Karl-Otto Apel, "Discourse Ethics before the Challenge of Liberation Philosophy: Second Part," *Philosophy and Social Criticism* 22, no. 2 (1996): 1–26; and Apel, "Discourse Ethics before the Challenge of Liberation Philosophy," in *The Underside of Modernity: Apel, Ricoeur, Rorty, Taylor, and the Philosophy of Liberation*, ed. and trans. Eduardo Mendieta (Atlantic Highlands, N.J.: Humanities Press International, 1996), pp. 163–204.

8. Emmanuel Levinas, *Totality and Infinity*, trans. Alponso Lingis (Pittsburgh: Duquesne University Press, 1969), pp. 42–43.

Name Index

Subject Index

About the Contributors

Linda Martín Alcoff is professor of philosophy at Syracuse University. Her books include *Epistemology: The Big Questions* (Blackwell, 1998), *Real Knowing: New Versions of the Coherence Theory* (Cornell, 1996), and *Feminist Epistemologies* (Routledge, 1993).

Karl-Otto Apel is author of *Auseinandersetzungen* (Suhrkamp, 1998), *Diskurs und Verantwortung* (Suhrkamp, 1988), and *Transformation der Philosophie,* 2 vols. (Suhrkamp, 1973). His work has been translated into English recently as *Selected Essays,* 2 vols. (Humanities Press, 1994–96).

Michael D. Barber is professor of philosophy at Saint Louis University and author of *Social Typifications and the Elusive Other* (Bucknell, 1988), *Guardian of Dialogue* (Bucknell, 1993), and *Ethical Hermeneutics: Rationality in Dussel's Philosophy of Liberation* (Fordham University Press, 1998).

Enrique Dussel is professor of philosophy at Universidad Autónoma Metropolitana-Iztapalapa and the Universidad Nacional Autónoma de México. He has authored more than twenty books on religion, sociology, history, and law, many of which have been translated into English, including *The Underside of Modernity* (1996), *The Invention of the Americas* (1995), *Ethics and Community* (1988), *Philosophy of Liberation* (1985), *Ethics and the Theology of Liberation* (1978).

Roberto S. Goizueta is professor of theology at Boston College and former associate professor of theology at Loyola University. He is a former president of the Academy of Catholic Hispanic Theologians of the United States (ACHTUS) and former associate editor of the Journal of *Hispanic/Latino Theology.* He is author of *Liberation, Method, and Dialogue: Enrique Dussel and North American Theological Discourse* (Scholars Press, 1988) and *Caminemos con Jesús: Toward a Hispanic/Latino Theology of Accompaniment* (Orbis Books, 1995).

Lynda Lange is in the Philosophy Department at the University of Toronto. She has published *The Sexism of Social and Political Thought: Women and Reproduction from Plato to Nietzsche* (1979) and numerous essays on Jean-Jacques Rousseau and feminist theory. She is currently working on a book, *Claiming Democratic Feminism* (Routledge, forthcoming), and is editing *Feminist Interpretations of Rousseau* (Penn State Press, forthcoming).

James L. Marsh is professor of philosophy at Fordham University, and the author of three books on the philosophy of liberation: *Critique, Action, and Liberation* (SUNY Press, 1994), *Post-Cartesian Meditations* (Fordham University Press, 1988), and *Process, Praxis, and Transcendence* (SUNY Press, 1999).

Eduardo Mendieta is assistant professor of philosophy at the University of San Francisco. He is editor and translator of Enrique Dussel's *The Underside of Modernity,* which also contains essays by Karl-Otto Apel and Paul Ricoeur. He co-edited *Liberation Theologies, Postmodernity, and the Americas* (New York: Routledge, 1997). Currently he is writing a book entitled *The Geography of Utopia: Modernity's Spatio-Temporal Regimes.*

Walter D. Mignolo is William H. Wannamaker Professor of Literature and Romance Studies and professor of cultural anthropology at Duke University. His books include *Writing without Words: Alternative Literacies in Mesoamerica and the Andes* (Duke University Press, 1994), and *The Darker Side of the Renaissance: Literacy, Territoriality, and Colonization* (University of Michigan Press, 1995), which was awarded the Katherine Singer Kovacs Prize from the Modern Language Association, and *Local Histories/Global Designs: Coloniality, Subaltern Knowledges, and Border Thinking* (Princeton University Press, 2000).

Mario Sáenz is professor of philosophy at Le Moyne College and author of *The Identity of Liberation in Latin American Thought: Latin American Historicism and the Phenomenology of Leopoldo Zea* (Lexington Books, 2000).

Hans Schelkshorn is assistant professor at the University of Vienna, Austria. He is the author of *Ethik der Befreiung: Einführung in die Philosophie Enrique Dussels* (Herder, 1992) and *Diskurs und Befreiung: Studien zur philosophischen Ethik von Karl-Otto Apel und Enrique Dussel* (Rodopi, 1997).

Elina Vuola has a Ph.D. in theology and wrote her dissertation on Latin American liberation theology and feminist theology. She is currently a postdoctoral research fellow in the Institute of Development Studies at the University of Helsinki. She is the author of *Limits of Liberation: Praxis As Method of Latin American Liberation Theology and Feminist Theology* (Suomalainen Tiedeakatemia [Helsinki], 1997).